Silva, who has worked in graphic design and advertising for most of his professional life, conveys his keen passion for earth mysticism in this probing examination of crop circles. He examines the history of crop circles, human interactions with them, their probable implications, and, in a section that is alone worth the price of the book for supporters, their effects on our current worldview. Silva also delves deeply into the evidence for crop circles' authenticity. In arguing that they are trans-human events, he discusses the role of electromagnetism and its effects, UFO phenomena and their relation to crop circles, the relationship between crop circles and healing, evidence supporting psychic ability, and language's ability to affect information consciously and subconsciously (this section is sure to stimulate those who suspect that crop circles are a hoax). Readers may be inspired to reexamine preconceived ideas, as Silva's explanations are detailed and well researched and avoid technical jargon. Footnotes and an extensive bibliography encourage further exploration. Recommended for psychic phenomena or metaphysical and New Age collections in public libraries, and for collections including contemporary works on controversies in science and mysticism.

—Leroy Hommerding, *Library Journal*

As a long-term croppie it is sometimes difficult to get excited by a new book on crop circles. No such problem here; the book is an easy, yet comprehensive survey of the entire crop circle scene; concise, yet thoroughly satisfying articles on all aspects of the phenomenon. . . .

It has something for everyone interested in the crop circle mystery, light-hearted at times, intensely serious and intricate at others, a book you can cut-and-come-again to. It has an enormous number of illustrations, some in colour, far too many to count, but I reckon in the region of 180!

—George Bishop, *The Circular*

Freddy Silva's *Secrets in the Fields* marks the maturation of crop circle study. It feels almost like a field guide, since it focuses on the visual characteristics of the formations. As a graphic designer, Silva has an appreciation for the "draftsmanship" of crop circles, and he helps the student with his silhouette renderings of the circles. Gathering the most spectacular examples from the last ten "seasons" and presenting them side by side in schematic silhouette fashion, they appear as an uncanny symbolic language.

Silva's day job is to create symbols that easily and unambiguously speak to the broadest range of "consumers"; yet he tackles these highly ambiguous and esoteric symbols with equal skill. A beautiful selection of color and black-and-white aerial photographs give the book a coffee-table splendor, but Silva also includes close-up, ground-level photos that show how the large-scale geometry of the figures is a result of precise architectural arrangements at a much smaller scale.

—Kevin Dann, *Orion*

In *Secrets in the Fields,* researcher Freddy Silva, who's based in Wessex, England, considers why and how the crop circles might have the effects they do on their beholders. Silva has made a fitting selection of b&w and colour photos (many are his own) plus diagrams which he uses with riveting effect. He explores the historical data, scientific evidence, geometries and symbolisms, and talks to fellow researchers and individuals whose lives have been touched by them.

While Silva, like other researchers, can only speculate on the identity of the Circlemakers, he leaves us in no doubt that they exhibit a high degree of intelligence and demonstrate a profound grasp of universal mathematical and geometrical principles. He exposes the hoaxers and debunkers, and enlightens us to the beautiful mathematical proportions embodied in the cereal creations and their relationships with sacred landmarks, ley lines and even the local guardian spirits. Silva taps into the "acoustical alchemy" that is integral to the shapes, and he shows how the designs have resonance with the symbols of ancient cultures and secret societies. He also investigates the theories that music and sound, light and microwave energy are involved in their creation. The humming sounds, light columns, moving light balls and electromagnetic interference reported by many witnesses all add up to important circumstantial evidence. —Ruth Parnell, *NEXUS*

The text is very thorough and provides one of the most extensive analyses of crop circles that I have ever read. Analysis of the history of crop circles is exhaustive as is the analysis of fraudulent crop circles and mathematical relationships within crop circles. . . . A detailed and fascinating read, I would highly recommend it to anyone interested in crop circles.

—James A. Cox, *The Midwest Book Review*

The result of Silva's research is a book that makes bold to grasp the mystery of the crop circles through the competing methods and worldviews of both science and mysticism. *Secrets in the Fields* is possibly the most comprehensive and graphically beautiful book yet written on the circles, providing basic information needed to assess various approaches to understanding this complex phenomenon—and more. Extensively referenced, it has the best bibliography of any book on the subject now in print, a testament to Silva's ability to link seemingly disparate fields of inquiry.

All of the controversial aspects of the phenomenon are covered in depth: reports of flying balls of light and UFOs; pathways of energy reported for centuries by dowsers ("ley-lines"); the relationship of crop circles to underground sources of water; and the remarkable consistency of many circles' geometric patterns with ancient mysticism—the same principles of harmony and proportion used to build the Parthenon, Chartres cathedral and found throughout classical Islamic art.

—Ed Conroy, *Express-News*

A resident of Wessex, England, the author takes us on an exhilarating firsthand field trip into the heart of the mystery. We journey to the scene of the enigma, before, after, and during the appearance of a fresh circle. Silva introduces us to farmers, researchers, scientists, mystics, hoaxers, and debunkers. This deeply informative and copiously illustrated book is the most comprehensive look at crop circles to date. —*Sacred Spaces*

SECRETS
IN THE FIELDS

The Science
and Mysticism
of Crop Circles

FREDDY SILVA

HAMPTON ROADS
PUBLISHING COMPANY, INC.

Cover design by Jane Hagaman
Front cover photo courtesy of Richard Wintle/Calyx Photo Services
Back cover photos (from top to bottom): Andrew King; Freddy Silva;
Freddy Silva; Frank Laumen
Cymatics images from *Cymatics: A Study of Wave Phenomena and Vibration* by
Hans Jenny © 2001 MACROmedia. Used by permission. www.cymaticsource.com

Hampton Roads Publishing Company, Inc.
1125 Stoney Ridge Road
Charlottesville, VA 22902

434-296-2772
fax: 434-296-5096
e-mail: hrpc@hrpub.com
www.hrpub.com

If you are unable to order this book from your local
bookseller, you may order directly from the publisher.
Call 1-800-766-8009, toll-free.
Library of Congress Catalog Card Number: 2002103100
ISBN 978-1-57174-322-0
10 9 8 7 6
Printed on acid-free paper in Canada

To those who persevered to bring us
the truth and the Light.

To those who labored to share
the truth and the Light.

And to those who've yet to see
the truth and the Light.

CONTENTS

ACKNOWLEDGMENTS

My sincere thanks to all those who, in their ways, contributed to the birthing of this work.

In alphabetical order:

Steve Alexander, Marcus Allen, Paul Anderson, Colin and Synthia Andrews, the late Richard Andrews, George Bishop, Kerry Blower, Gregg Braden, the Bretforton Clinic, Paul Broadhurst, Polly Carson, Barbara Hand Clow, Bruce Copen Laboratories, Chad Deetkin, Pat Delgado, Paul Devereux, Collette Dowell, Virginia Essene, Randall and Elizabeth Farrell, Robert Miller Foulkrod, Gerald and Julia Hawkins, Barbara Hero, Michael Hubbard, Frances Hunter, Shelly Keel, Andrew King, Isabelle Kingston, Frank Laumen, Jim Lyons, John Martineau, John Michell, Hamish Miller, Andreas Muller, Ina Nyko, Sharon Pacione, Marigold Pearce, Nick Pope, Lucy Pringle, Jane Ross, John Sayer, Sue Shepherd-Cross, Graham Slater, Ken Spelman, Russell Stannard, Busty Taylor, Reuben Uriarte, Paul Vigay, Dennis Wheatley, George Wingfield, Richard Wintle.

Thanks also to:

The many hundreds of strangers and their kind, supportive e-mails. Your words have sometimes been all I've had to keep going. Bless you.

The librarians of Portsmouth, New Hampshire; Marlborough, Wiltshire; and the British Library, London.

All those laboring souls at Hampton Roads Publishing, particularly my editor Richard Leviton, who recognized my vision.

The music that inspired as the night candle burned: W. A. Mozart and Jonn Serrie.

The invisible souls behind the curtain providing the lines when we think we do it all ourselves; Michael, for the sword in Stonehenge—look what it got me into!

My parents, who still don't know why their son turned out this way.

Signs of Life: An Introduction

Atoms are called vibrations in Occultism.
—H. P. Blavatsky

Five hundred feet above the rolling Wiltshire countryside in southern England, pilot Graham Taylor and his passenger take in an unhindered view of the prehistoric monuments that pepper the landscape below. At precisely 5:30 P.M. on this wondrous July afternoon, the single-engine plane and its occupants glide eastwards above the sarsens and bluestones of Stonehenge, one of the ancient world's greatest feats of engineering.

Below, the conjunction of Sun, summer, and Sunday has brought the tourists out by the hundreds. They mill around the monument, ringed-in by the wide perimeter fencing and several security guards. Some of these guards keep awestruck visitors from wandering off the beaten track; others survey the surrounding fields from their high vantage points for signs of more enterprising, nonpaying attendees. It's a typical working day for tourism, and pilot and passenger soak up the whole spectacle, bird's-eye style.

Minutes later, after a textbook landing at a nearby airfield, the two men part company. The passenger, a doctor, begins the drive home. Coincidentally, the drive entails passing Stonehenge again, this time at ground level. But that will not be happening quickly today: The A303 London-to-Exeter road has come to a complete standstill. Moreover, many drivers have abandoned their cars and are lining up on the edge of a field that borders the road. An accident? People are pointing at something in the field, some are taking photos.

It is now 6:15 P.M. Within a forty-five-minute window some phenomenon has transformed the area into a chaotic sideshow. Something has arrived that had clearly not been there when the two men had first flown over.

When aerial photos of the site make the evening papers they hypnotize the world: embedded in a pristine sea of wheat lies a sprawling impression of 149 circles, varying from one to fifty feet in diameter (see figure 0.1 on page A1 in the color section). The precision and the symmetry of the pattern's curving spine measures a colossal 920 feet long by 500 feet wide.

Most startling of all, the wheat has been swirled and flattened, with the plants' stems bent horizontally just an inch above the soil, and they are undamaged.

These sightseers are gazing at a crop circle—in this case, a stylized representation of a computer-modeled fractal pattern named the "Julia Set."

All this has occurred in broad daylight barely two hundred yards from a well-guarded tourist attraction, and yet nobody was seen creating the cosmic artwork. Further investigation reduced the construction time frame to minutes, the clues coming from a sharp-eyed Stonehenge guard who noticed the formation, fully complete, in between one of his punctual, fifteen-minute rounds, and from a second pilot who had flown overhead a quarter of an hour after Taylor. The local gamekeeper, too, had inspected the field that morning and seen no disturbance. Was it possible that a group of human beings, skilled in both advanced mathematics and environmental art, had mastered the principle of invisibility and flouted the laws of gravity to levitate above the untouched wheat in order to create this masterpiece?

If only the stones of Stonehenge could speak.

Indeed, if only the thousands of other ancient sacred spaces throughout the British Isles could, for they have played silent witness to the thousands of crop circles that relentlessly manifest in their vicinities. What strange attraction exists between these symbols etched on a canvas of plants and the circles of earth and stone, many of them erected eight thousand years ago under the guidance of forgotten Neolithic "gods"?

Whatever the connection, the early Roman Catholic Church recognized the importance of such places of veneration to the degree that it issued orders outlawing their use, only later to superimpose its own houses of the holy upon them. For, as it turned out, these pagan megalithic shrines are not located haphazardly upon the landscape, but strategically, at the crossing points of an invisible—but measurable—electromagnetic energy grid that encircles the Earth—at pressure points where the planet's "data storage" can be accessed.

Or influenced.

At these terrestrial points, the veil between worlds is thin, and the concentration of energy is such that it influences the rhythms of the human body, right down to its state of awareness. Consequently, for many millennia, both the sick and the shamen interacted with these energies, whose properties have recently been recognized by science.

However, around 1600 years ago this contact with the natural world began to take a long turn. With the later assertion of the Inquisition, seventeenth century rationalism, and, finally, materialism, the transcendental purpose of the sacred sites became blurred. They fell into disuse, became shrouded in superstition, and, like batteries drained of energy, they inevitably shut down.

Then in the late twentieth century, the mysterious crop circles began materializing with increasing frequency beside these ancient markers, like signatures from the "gods," returned to awaken a giant, sleeping network at a preappointed time. Crop circles have been shown to possess energetic properties which are not only interacting with the sacred sites, but they are reportedly healing the people passing through their space and facilitating heightened states of awareness.

Figure 0.2

Top: The heart of the mystery. The plants of genuine crop circles are swirled like the spiral of a galaxy, and bent just above the soil, without damage. Bottom: By comparison, man-made crop circles generally create a mess.

And what curious invitation do these crop circles extend? Since the earliest human has walked the Earth, the circle has been the symbol of the meeting place, the temple of gathering and discourse and like lambs seeking guidance in a turbulent Universe, hundreds of thousands of people from all the world's "tribes" have been irresistibly lured to the centers of crop circles.

Inside these temples they are overcome by childlike exuberance and wonder as they meander the latterday labyrinths, each curved path bringing them face-to-face with gracious and unexpected patterns that form the boundary between seen and unseen, touched and emotive. Much rejoicing, prayer, contemplation, and studied inquiry are made inside each of these new sacred spaces. When the pilgrims leave, they disembark into a world that, all of a sudden, seems strangely different to them, for each and every visitor is imbued with a little seed, a seed that is at once invigorating, curative, and enlightening.

And transformational.

Each "seed" opens a gate to endless pastures of knowledge explaining how crop circles are connected with the subtle sciences of

What peculiar force is at work here? How does it create these curious patterns with the plants bent above the soil, their stems lightly scorched as if overcome by a short, but intense burst of heat? Under the microscope, even their cellular structure has been altered—hardly the result of trampling feet! Who has harnessed such technology?

electromagnetism and sound (since discovered to have been used in the construction of stone chambers, pyramids, and Gothic cathedrals); how these frequencies affect the brain wave patterns of people and the behavior of animals; how they are leaving imprints in the water we drink, and possibly encoding new systems of information into our DNA; and how volumes of extraordinary information are encoded into each glyph, including information for new forms of technology.

The crop circle designs are brimming with the Universal language of geometry, a language recognized by the living cells of the human body, facilitating a clearer dialogue between Heaven and Earth and regenerating the transcendental nature latent in every human. Could these twenty-first century mandalas be effecting a subtle change in the consciousness of humanity?

Typically, crop circles appear at the beginning of April and continue until harvest in September. The designs increase in complexity throughout the growing season, compounding each successive year, and over the decades the generic "crop circle" has developed into an array of highly complex geometric forms. The plants flattened by crop circles are neither harmed nor rendered unharvestable.

Given the puzzling nature of this phenomenon, not to mention the startling evidence on the ground, you'd think the subject of crop circles would be at the forefront of media, even of scientific interest. Yet to this day, a myth has been perpetrated that the entire phenomenon is nothing more than a human prank.

There is much bad news for this theory, least of which are the hoaxers' claims to have begun their activities in 1978 in the county of Hampshire, England. Recently published data confirms that crop circles have been manifesting since the seventeenth century, and in the latter part of the twentieth century 10,000 have been reported in twenty-six countries, 90 percent of them appearing in southern England alone.

The hoax angle is apparently not taken seriously within the British government, a fact confirmed by Nick Pope (the former UFO Desk Officer in Secretariat at the British Ministry of Defence) whose duties included the investigation of UFO reports and other anomalous and supernatural phenomena. With access to a substantial volume of information, Pope concludes that, despite some hoaxing, there exists a hard core of genuine crop circles formed in a way that is not yet scientifically understood. Would this explain, for example, the bewilderment of the army officer stationed in the training grounds of Salisbury Plain who, during his nimble negotiation of an active minefield, came across a crop circle? Hardly a site hoaxers would choose.

Indeed it would appear that the British army has attempted to keep abreast of developments. Twenty miles north of Stonehenge another crop formation,[1] this time resembling the spiraling double helix of the DNA strand, was etched upon the undulating fields of Alton Barnes in Wiltshire. With their backs to the hillside that

---

[1]Crop circles are described throughout this book in a manner of styles. For the sake of clarity I refer to "crop circles" as a general term, or when describing events involving simple circles or sets thereof; I refer to "crop formations" or "patterns" when describing shapes incorporating several elements, and to "crop glyphs" where complex designs are involved.

cradles the field, a small group of sightseers stood on the side of the road and watched as a military helicopter hovered above the pattern. Without warning, a second helicopter (bearing an eagle insignia) rose up the slope and flew towards them, hovering for a minute beside the group with its rotors spinning menacingly at head height.

As the blades inched their way closer, Kerry Blower abandoned her video recorder and retreated to avoid potential decapitation. The noise was ear-shattering. As the camera, left on top of Kerry's car, recorded the harassment, the rest of the group, now understandably shaken, hastily retrieved it, bolted for the safety of the car and drove away down the road, the helicopter giving chase.

Upon Kerry's return to the safety of her home, the phone rang. A senior army official had somehow tracked her down and requested the surrender of the taped material, despite the whole incident having occurred on public land.

Why are the authorities afraid of crop circles? What are they protecting?

Perhaps, like me, they are the cats, attracted to the curiosities associated with their manifestation: A world away from Wiltshire, in the never-ending flatness of the Saskatchewan prairies, a Canadian farmer checked the progress of his wheat and stumbled upon a curiosity: an elliptical imprint in his mature crop. Believing it at first to be wind damage, he noticed how the stems were strangely arranged in a concentric manner. From the perimeter, an avenue of dark spines followed the spiral path of flattened plants cursively into the center of the design. At its end lay a perfectly flattened and mummified porcupine, apparently sucked or

dragged into the melée. Whatever caused this crop circle attracted the unfortunate bystander like a pincushion to a magnet.

Curiouser and curiouser.

That's precisely the thought that ran through my mind one bright summer's day as I stood inside a complex seven-sided crop circle, its design reminiscent of a grandmother's embroidered handkerchief. In my hand, a photo I took two afternoons earlier showed two beams of light shining down perpendicularly onto the exact spot where I stood.

Just as I was wondering if my camera inadvertently captured a crop circle in the making, a series of musical notes repeated around me. "Record this. You'll need it later," my colleague said, handing me the tiny tape recorder. No matter how hard I looked, the physical source of the music remained absent.

Those sounds and those two beams of light represented the crumbling of the barrier between science and mysticism for me, and have led me on a journey that resulted in this book, a work containing answers to the questions they raised—answers that might require us to question our perceptions of what we currently term "reality."

Let me put it this way: if you were magically reduced to the size of a grain of salt, you would be able to bounce an atom like a soccer ball on your knee and kick it around for an afternoon. Then again, you couldn't. Because atoms—and for that matter everything in the world that seems physical—are not solid. Science has now established, to its own satisfaction, a fact long recognized by psychics and our ancestors: The atoms in plants, crystals, and the human body are tiny harmonic resonators in a constant state of vibration. In fact, they are governed by the same principles found in music: "Every particle in the physical universe takes its characteristics from the pitch and pattern and overtones of its particular frequencies—it's singing," says author George Leonard (1978).

Atoms, it would seem, are microscopic musical notes.

Just as this barrier between science and mysticism is crumbling in our laboratories, when the accounts of the crop circle phenomenon as imprinted across our landscapes begin to transform the foundations of what we were once taught, our view of the Universe will be shaken.

Perhaps, like me, it will even change your life.

As a British citizen of Portuguese parentage, married to a Canadian but working in Chicago, life for me was already anything but straightforward. Yet I was a levelheaded person, despite the fact that I worked in the high-powered, high-earning, high-caffeine world of advertising.

My first encounter with a crop circle was in the summer of 1990, courtesy of the evening news in Chicago which described a sensational event thousands of miles away in England in the East Field of Alton Barnes. I was enraptured by the image on the TV, oblivious to the commentator's voice and everything else around me. In fact, I cannot remember the time, the day, the location, the TV station, who was in the room, what I was wearing, or if a herd of bison were passing through the house. Yet the effect of that image remains forever branded in my memory.

Why did this image of a crop circle have such an effect, overcoming my normal sense of time and space?

As an art director by trade, this kind of obliviousness was unusual. My analytical brain, permanently switched to sponge-mode, absorbs tremendous amounts of information every day, even trivial stuff such as the style of typeface on restaurant menus, much to the chagrin of my dining companions. From my art student days, I was already conversant with environmental art, when artists armed with combine harvesters selectively furrowed acres of North American prairie to create abstract geometric forms best appreciated from the air.

The "art" in this English wheat field could similarly have been their handiwork, yet none of this crossed my mind as I watched the Alton Barnes pictogram on television.

Nor did that other extreme of options: UFOs and little green men.

No, what I was seeing was a suggestive symbol, and I was transfixed by it as it rambled across to my intuitive right brain, bypassing the left hemisphere of reason, as if a master hypnotist's rhythmic pass of the hand had induced a trance. The symbol made perfect sense to me. It was familiar, like a message I had sent myself a long time ago. Just as under hypnosis a person can be regressed to an earlier age, I felt that crop circles could induce a sense of remembrance, an awakening of subconscious memories—and it was on this day that I began to remember.

I could have easily checked myself into the nearest psychiatric unit, but the pictogram's effect on me seemed so natural. Later I was to hear others confess to the same experience, albeit from different crop circles. I was hooked, and my curiosity begged to know more about this. Books were sought, images were scoured, knowledge was acquired. Eventually I began spending most summers in southern England, ready to visit every crop circle. I was consumed, and in turn, the quest consumed a fourteen-year marriage to my best friend, and I lost both.

Beautiful house, beautiful life, and bountiful finances gone, I returned to complete my "studies" in England.

Now, I hear you say: "This man is a fool; he threw away his perfect life for a few acres of trampled wheat." Yet the incidents I just described are a flavor of some of the things I know. From chapter 1, I will lead you through the phenomenon, including the fraud and misinformation, to the science at the heart of the crop circle mystery. This science is so subtle, so wise, and so awe-inspiring that it has the power to humble you and wake you up to a greater reality.

In putting this work together I have drawn from my personal experiences and those of scores of individuals who have similarly dedicated their time to investigate the nature of this enigma, often at crushing expense—personal, financial, and marital. However, the words presented in this book are not the truth. If they were the "truth," they would only be my truth, which is of no help to you because personal truths can be used to create idols, orthodox beliefs, institutions, power, and, ultimately, control. Instead, what I present here are facts.

Facts can be unwelcome because they have the power to disturb. But if you are open to facts, you are encouraged to seek and to discover the Universal wisdom which, ultimately and ironically, already reigns within you.

I entered this pursuit with an open, objective, and atheistic mind in 1990, only to emerge humbled eleven years later with a newfound belief in and respect for life and its Creator. Perhaps most importantly, in all this time I have consciously tried to keep both my feet on the ground. Believe me, amidst the egos and the misinformation, a grounded attitude is indispensable, and a sense of humor doesn't hurt, either.

As we delve into the heart of the crop circle mystery it will become clear that the circles not only have much knowledge to offer, but they are appearing at this critical moment in our history to remind us of an evolutionary connection that is in our best interests to rekindle—the sooner, the better.

In this book, we shall examine how the appearance of crop circles coincides with ancient predictions, from Egyptian texts to the Bible's book of Revelation. We will see that seeded within the crop circles is a manual offering all citizens of this precious jewel of a planet a unique opportunity to rediscover their potential during these critical days of change. The crop circles offer us mirrors in which to view our present direction and to reflect on this, and the keys to our evolution—a reminder of where we come from and a signpost to where we are headed.

In part 1, we examine the history of the crop circle phenomenon, building a picture of its *modus operandi,* its interaction with people, its effects on our current worldview, and its probable implications.

In part 2, we delve into the evidence in detail, moving from the left brain of science to the right brain of metaphysics. Among the topics covered: the role of electromagnetism, its effects on plants, people, and our concept of matter; "balls of light," UFO phenomena, their correspondence to the nature of the Universe and the relationship of all this to crop circles; the language of symbols and this language's ability to impart information consciously and subconsciously; the thread connecting sacred geometry, temples, consciousness, and crop circles; the part played by sound in the creation of the Universe and in the circle-making process;

the strategic placement of sacred sites, their energetic properties and their effect on living things; Earth energy and the influencing of the Earth's "grid" by crop circles; the memory of water, and the relationship of crop circles and healing; and evidence supporting psychic ability, and the relationships among the levels of reality in the Universe.

As you read the chapters you may become aware of my train of thought transforming from linear logic to thinking "in the round." What may appear at first to be a collection of facts will eventually coalesce into a relevant whole and an overall picture will gradually emerge. Some of these facts are triggers, allowing you to reexamine preconceived ideas. The footnotes and extensive bibliography further support this goal. I encourage you to explore the points I bring up and take what I have written to a new level of personal understanding.

PART ONE

THE HISTORY OF

CROP CIRCLES

1. WEATHER OR NOT

To know all, it is necessary to know very little; but to know that very little, one must first know pretty much.

—Georges I. Gurdjieff

This is a gentle, rolling land, mostly soft with chalk and clay, and the eye is easily seduced by subtly curved lowland hills rich in pastures and crop-bearing fields that sweep

down from tree-peppered skylines. This terrain has borne witness to the activities of Man since time immemorial. But there is mystery here, for amid the sparsely wooded fields, separated by hawthorn hedgerows, hundreds of ancient earthen mounds rise like goosepimples blanketed in green felt. These are the long barrows and tumuli, survivors of ten thousand years of British rain and as many ideologies as Man has cared to invent.

Sharing this ancient landscape are the enchanting stone circles, their needles of stone stoic, determined and proud in the face of change, silent remnants of a gigantic, interconnected network of sites that once covered the Earth during Neolithic times. The same applies to the "hill forts" whose flattened terraces encircled by earthen embankments crown the

Figure 1.1

Mysterious Britain. Top: A cairn or dolmen. Bottom: A series of tumuli, ring barrows, and saucer barrows atop the Neolithic hill fort complex of Windmill Hill.

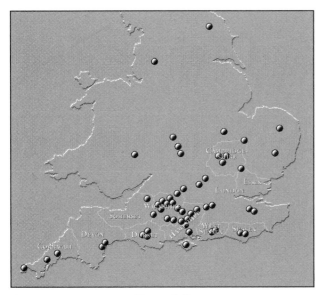

Figure 1.2

Ninety percent of the world's reported crop circles congregate within the old kingdom of Wessex, an area of southern Britain containing the counties of Hampshire, Wiltshire, Somerset, and West Sussex. Significant clusters also exist in Devon, East Sussex, and Cambridgeshire.

summits of sculpted chalk hills and artificially shaped promontories. Yet these "forts," with their curious names such as Barbury Castle and Uffington Castle, have no walled fortifications, nor do they appear to serve any military purpose.

Indeed, there is mystery here, for this is Wessex, an ancient southern English kingdom whose central region comprises the modern-day counties of Hampshire and Wiltshire, and once included parts of Dorset to the south, Somerset to the west, and Sussex to the east.

With an air of nonchalance, Roger Sear walked into the circle of tall swirled grass below the watchful gaze of the ancient Cisbury Rings hill fort. It was the summer of 1927, and young Roger was no stranger to the circles which he affectionately called "witch's rings." This one

was similar to those he'd regularly stumbled upon in previous years throughout Sussex. But of special interest to him were the unusual effects generated by these curious markings: the magnetization of a knife that he had stuck into the soil at the center; a tickling sensation in his feet; the refusal of a dog to enter the circle; and the magnetization of a prized pocket watch which resulted in its demise.

On a previous occasion, Roger had seen the needle of his compass go berserk when he took it into a circle. From then on, it would only point to the circle instead of obeying magnetic north. He had also noticed that a smell akin to "electrical burning" filled the air and that the grass seemed "charged" to the point that the bicycles of Roger and his companion, Sid, were made sufficiently full of static electricity to give them electric shocks. When they returned to the scene later, a second circle had appeared, and despite their exciting adventure, both boys returned home with painful headaches (T. Wilson 1998).

Eight years later, at Helions Bumpstead in Essex, a ten-year-old boy witnessed something even more miraculous: he saw a crop circle manifesting. Although it happened in a matter of seconds, the boy's adult companion brushed off the event as nothing more than the "Devil's twist," a kind of whirlwind blamed for instigating similar disturbances in this area since at least 1830. But what kind of winds were these that rushed about the countryside creating perfectly formed circles and rings with swirled floors, sharply defined edges, and an unaffected central tuft of plants? The swirled plants also appeared to have re-hardened into their new horizontal position, because attempts by both the boy and the farmer to raise them with a pitchfork resulted in the stems springing back down.

Throughout early crop circle history, it is not unusual to hear local farmers and nature enthusiasts reminiscing about walking out around dawn to inspect the fields only to come across these circles and rings, some as large as sixty feet in diameter, of flattened yet undamaged plants. They tell of farm animals behaving erratically, of sheep and cattle acting in a distressed manner prior to a circle's arrival, and superstitious farmhands refusing to touch the odd circles. Some recall sightings of UFOs or bright, colored lights in the vicinity, many of which are substantiated by local police records.

The greatest concentration of these events was in Wessex, as well as the Canadian prairie (T. Wilson 1998). These early sightings were supported by eighty eyewitness accounts from people as far flung as British Columbia and Australia having seen crop circles actually form. It is significant that most of these accounts remain unpublished and yet they corroborate one another. They describe how the morning chorus of birds abruptly stops, replaced by a trilling sound, followed by the agitation of the wheat heads by a tremendous vibration, and the collapse of a section of the field in seconds.[2]

Perhaps the young witness at Helions Bumpstead was not as prone to fantasy as he was led to believe. However, in the 1920s and 1930s, with the wind and even the Devil as prime suspects, nobody bothered to seriously investigate these circular curiosities in the crops, so no answers would be forthcoming for many decades.

In 1965, there was a sudden eruption of simple circles around the Wiltshire town of Warminster, at the snaking Hakpen Hill twenty miles to the northeast, and at St. Catherine's Hill outside Winchester in Hampshire. All three locations are rich in strangely shaped chalk hills crowned with long barrows or tumuli; they are equally steeped in folklore describing apparitions, visitations from nature spirits, and sightings of impossible aerial maneuvers performed by equally improbable luminous craft. Yet it

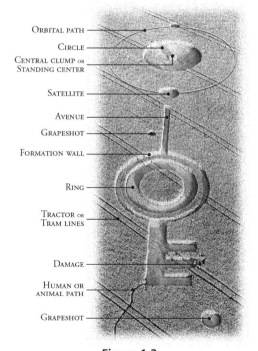

ORBITAL PATH
CIRCLE
CENTRAL CLUMP OR STANDING CENTER
SATELLITE
AVENUE
GRAPESHOT
FORMATION WALL
RING
TRACTOR OR TRAM LINES
DAMAGE
HUMAN OR ANIMAL PATH
GRAPESHOT

Figure 1.3
Terminology of crop circles features.

---

[2] My thanks to Colin Andrews/CPRI, and George Bishop/CCCS for sharing details from their extensive databases.

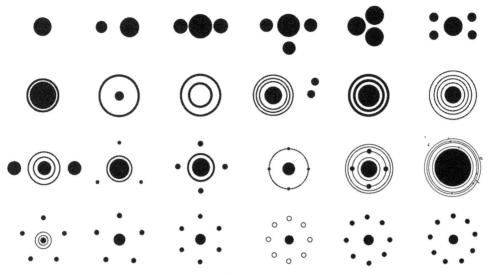

Figure 1.4

Selected crop circles, 1970-1990.

would take another fifteen years before a small report tucked away in the Wiltshire *Times* (August 15, 1980) finally grabbed the attention of science.

The photo of three precise circles of flattened oats beneath the hill fort of Bratton, with the plants spiraled and neatly laid along the ground, attracted the attention of meteorologist Dr. Terence Meaden, who went on to investigate. As founder-member of the Tornado and Storm Research Organization, his interest in weather phenomena led him to postulate that stationary whirlwinds were responsible for the appearance of these circles. Despite the fact that volatile winds generally tend to rip things out of the ground and propel them skywards in chaotic fashion, this was generally considered to be a satisfactory explanation. The farmer involved, a Mr. Cooper, remained unconvinced. He said, "I have never seen anything like it before. It certainly can't be wind or rain damage because I have seen plenty of that, and it is just not that regular."

Mr. Cooper's housekeeper recalled hearing an unusual humming noise coming from the field the night before a second set of circles appeared, a noise that lasted twenty minutes. Mr. Cooper's dogs barked uncharacteristically for most of that night. An investigator named Ian Mrzyglod interviewed Cooper and his neighboring farmer, Mr. Scull, about evidence of human entry into their circles, but the farmers said no suspicious trails were evident, in or out, just circles amid a virgin crop.

The following summer, an electromechanical engineer named Pat Delgado was enjoying the privileges of a quiet retirement in Hampshire when a friend wondered what he would make of the strange markings found in a field a few miles away at Cheesefoot Head. His curiosity aroused, Delgado drove to this horseshoe-shaped amphitheater whereupon he encountered a sight that was to change his life.

Below him lay three imprints: one 51-foot and two 25.5-foot diameter circles, with their centers in perfect linear alignment. With the absence of "tram lines" (the characteristic tractor ruts that nowadays run in parallel lines across most fields), two hundred or so feet of pristine wheat surrounded the formation, its edges perfectly upright, as if traced out with surgical instruments. With the absence of paths running in or out, their positioning surely implied that in order to make these circles, either their creator had levitated from the ground or that these patterns had been imprinted from above.

The impact on Delgado was profound. He took to studying new reports in painstaking detail and began alerting the media to the unusual events dotting the English countryside.

Figure 1.5

Every report brought new discoveries and observations, one of the first being the persistent referencing to nearby Neolithic sites. For example, in 1981 at Litchfield, Hampshire, an invisible magnetic line connecting the centers of two crop circles was identical to the one running through the two prehistoric mounds a few yards to the north; their respective diameters were also identical. By 1983, many crop circles were appearing below hill forts. Quintuplets—large circles surrounded by four small satellite circles, one at each point on the compass like a Celtic cross— appeared below the unusual horseshoe features of Cley Hill, Uffington, and Bratton, and a fourth appeared in Cheesefoot Head.

When yet another quintuplet surfaced later, below Bratton hill fort, the clumsy appearance of the formation's details aroused the suspicion of Mrzyglod, as well as Bob Rickard, editor of *Fortean Times*, a magazine about unexplained

phenomena. Indeed, it seemed as if a non-paranormal explanation was at hand on this occasion. After the *Daily Express* had scooped the story about the real circles, a jealous *Daily Mirror* paid a local family, the Shepherds, to hoax this new pattern close to the original circles. Yet the Shepherds' handiwork showed clear signs of entry, not to mention clear indications of damage to the plants, thanks to their use of heavy chains to flatten the crop.

The hoax aside, Terence Meaden's stationary whirlwind theory had to be expanded to accommodate these new developments. He had proposed that the 1980 three-in-a-line triplets were the result of three whirlwinds (even though the circles' diameters had a mathematical ratio of 2:1, the same relationship that defines the octave in music), and now the quintuplets were a series of whirlwinds in a multi-vortex state, in which, he proposed, the in-flowing vortical motion of the major whirlwind stabilized minor whirlwinds in a symmetrical alignment.

In 1984, the previous year's quintuplets aroused the curiosity of a famous resident in Alfriston when they descended upon the Sussex home of the Labour Party's Foreign Secretary Dennis Healey. Healey admitted he wasn't a believer in UFOs, yet the night the circles appeared below nearby Cradle Hill, his wife had seen a strange bright light in the sky; when he inspected the formation, Healey could find no rational explanation for it. Interestingly, a second Cradle Hill exists opposite Cley Hill in Warminster, home of Britain's most fertile location for UFO sightings.

Meanwhile, Pat Delgado was now joined in his research by another perplexed individual, Colin Andrews, then chief electrical engineer for the Test Valley Borough Council in

Hampshire. Together they began establishing patterns of behavior, including the fact that crop circles were appearing next to, or on top of, areas containing large amounts of water, such as springs, ponds, reservoirs, underground water tanks, even the heart of the watershed itself. In one case, farmer Charles Hall of Corhampton Lane Farm observed how the edge of a crop circle on his property was located within 16 feet of an old pond; he also mentioned that a second pond was still active in the north part of his estate. Weeks later, a second circle appeared within 300 feet of it (Andrews and Delgado 1991).

Contrary to the natural reaction of downed plants responding to sunlight, an untouched crop circle at Gander Down demonstrated how the flattened stems made no attempt to regain their vertical posture, continuing instead to grow horizontally and to ripen. This would be almost impossible had the plants been damaged by force. To add to the mystery, the night before the formation was found, two senior citizens saw a UFO—"A huge yellow-white circular object standing on end, like a funfair wheel"—barely two hundred yards away. Terrified, they reported the sighting to the police who filed a report on this as an "Unidentified Flying Object." Andrews heard the report on his radio and rushed to the location, where he found police officers combing the area with searchlights. Little did they know that this UFO attribution would fit a future sighting elsewhere in crop circle country some years later.

As a logical progression began to develop in the designs from one season to the next, one had to wonder just how intelligent this "wind" had become. At Goodworth Clatford, another quintuplet had three of its satellites connected through their centers by the thinnest of orbital rings, but, in a twist on the design theme, the plants along the ring weren't laid down as usual: they were bent, bowed over so that their heads touched the ground.

When the 1985 season had finished, Delgado organized a meeting with various interested parties to collate evidence and review theories. One party in attendance was Lt. Col. Edgecombe, an officer from the nearby Army Air Base at Boscombe Down, whose pilots were showing increasing interest in the crop formations, monitoring their appearance, and taking photos. Col. Edgecombe argued against the hoax theory, for the most part because hoaxers would have left tracks in the crop, and from his investigation, no such tracks were evident. Intrigued, Col. Edgecombe filed a report with the UFO Investigation Desk at the Ministry of Defence in London.

The researchers began to wonder if someone—or something—was playing a game. Indeed, paranormal events seemed to follow them, as if attempting to demonstrate a supernatural force was masterminding the work. Colin Andrews will never forget how he took home a sample of odd-looking soil from a new crop formation. In hindsight, the design appeared to have been premeditated for him to perform the task in the first place, for this circle and ring contained a novel feature: a straight pathway placed at exactly 120 degrees to magnetic north, running away from the perimeter of the ring. Fifteen feet along, the avenue tapered into an arrowhead shape, at the base of which appeared a small bowl-shaped hole with perfectly smooth sides. Andrews removed a sample from this spot and brought it to his office, which was protected by an extensive alarm system. For the next two weeks, the Andrews' home turned into a supernatural amusement park.

Minutes after the mysterious soil had been tucked away behind locked doors for the night, the infrared sensor in the empty office detected movement and activated one of the alarms. Andrews, a designer of alarm systems and appreciator of their shortcomings, paid little attention to the coincidence—until the following morning.

At 4:15 A.M., the perimeter alarm for the house rang. The electric time clock had failed and would not set, but the next day it came back to life. A few nights later it stopped working again, at 4:15 A.M., this time joined by the separately rigged office alarm, whose microwave detector had been activated at the same time. To add to the chaos, the battery-powered wall clock had also decided to call it a day at 4:15 A.M. This state of affairs carried on for fourteen mornings, a fact corroborated by the Andrews' sleep-deprived neighbors and the unamused local police.

By now, a talented pilot named Busty Taylor had joined Delgado and Andrews. These three, along with Don Tuersley, Paul Fuller, Terence Meaden, and Ian Mrzylglod, created a team which took on crop circle research with great dedication and thoroughness, and to all of whom we are indebted for the vast volume of early data on this subject. Busty was on a routine aerial reconnaissance above Hampshire when he remarked to his passenger: "All we want now is to find all the formations we have seen so far wrapped into one." The next morning, the pair were flying over the exact spot where Busty had spoken these words when the very pattern he had requested appeared in the wheat below; even better, it had a large water reservoir under it (Andrews and Delgado 1991).

As events and strange coincidences gathered momentum, a growing list of possible causes began to be put forward by various individuals and institutions as to what was responsible for disturbing the orderly English landscape with markings more typical of *Star Trek* than John Constable. Predictably, the capricious media adopted the theory of little green men. With crop circle designs now developing into ever more complex configurations, Terence Meaden persisted with his stationary whirlwinds theory, despite the fact that additions to existing designs began to manifest in geometric alignment to (or were superimposed over) existing formations. But how could wind vortices be conscious enough to return to the same location with pinpoint accuracy?

As if to test Meaden's resolve, the Circlemakers (the collective term for the architects of the genuine phenomenon) created a fifty-four-foot diameter circle at Headbourne Worthy. They swirled the plants in standard clockwise motion, but this time laid them toward the center, with a thin band around the perimeter swirled anticlockwise and pointing away from the center. Further, when the stems were lifted, a second layer existed underneath, flattened counter to the top one. Meaden tenaciously stuck to the weather explanation, arguing that the whirlwind had abruptly switched its rotation (T. Wilson 1998). The Circlemakers later replied to this explanation by creating a formation with two annular rings around a circle, each element in contra-rotation to the next.

Weather or not, the bewildered farmers whose lives were becoming affected with increasing frequency by the circle phenomenon decided that the problem should be taken up with Parliament. Despite Delgado and Andrews' findings that a phenomenon of supernatural, possibly extraterrestrial, origin was manifesting, the British government decided, at least outwardly, to stand behind the convenient weather theory. In other words, there was no cause for alarm; everything in the English countryside was normal, according to officialdom.

Anything but normal was the plethora of alternative theories: drunks with string, wild young farmers, disillusioned art students, out-of-work journalists, disinformation people from the military, over-application of fertilizer, interference from mobile phones, flocks of geometrically gifted crows, even sex-mad hedgehogs.

At some point in 1987, hot air balloons were added to the list of probable ways one could drop into the middle of a field without leaving any sign of entry. To maneuver a balloon with its basket at head height and hold it motionless for a few hours whilst the guilty did their work without being spotted would be a supernatural feat in itself. But since the plant media employed so far—primarily wheat and barley—were flexible and relatively easy to imprint by a descending object, some people felt seriously compelled to put this idea into the public domain, so the Circlemakers decided to switch to canola as the next worthy crop canvas.

Given the nature of canola plants it was no surprise that farmer David Steiner agreed to carry out a scientific study on a crop circle discovered in his bright yellow field. Canola stems are very brittle, snapping like celery if bent, and the plants in David's formation were clearly bent at the base, almost steamed into place. As in all crop circles before it, the plants were bent at nearly a right angle, an inch above the soil and just below the first node—the plant's "knuckles." Any damage to canola causes its yellow flowers to die, yet all the delicate flowers were intact.

As if this weren't enough of a puzzle, Andrews and his father were measuring the circle when they saw a bright flash around them, followed by a distinctive noise like crackling. The sound was so loud it was heard seventy feet away by Andrews' mother sitting inside her car at the edge of the field with the windows rolled up (Andrews and Delgado 1991).

Strange noises like this became an increasingly common occurrence, particularly when Andrews visited a new site at Kimpton—an unusual oval ring, approximately thirty feet across.

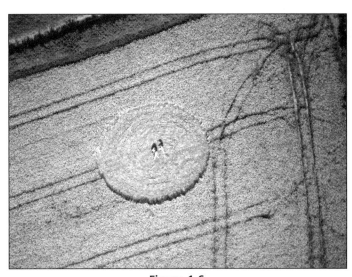

Figure 1.6

Simple circle in canola.

"I've never seen anything like this before," exclaimed the farmer, Mr. Flambert, astounded at the sight of it. Upon their return to the car, two young boys, unaware that Andrews was a researcher, told him they'd seen a glowing, orange object hovering over the area he was examining. Later, unprompted, an elderly couple asked Andrews if he'd come to investigate the "warbling, humming-like" noises they'd heard emanating from the field a few days earlier (Andrews and Delgado 1991).

During further measuring and note-taking, Andrews was spooked by a sudden black shadow which "blotted out the sun for an instant." Later that afternoon, his parents' dog scampered around the field until it froze at a spot adjacent to the ring. Within minutes the dog was vomiting, and only when taken out of the immediate area did the luckless canine recover his vigor. Despite the litany of unnerving events, Andrews felt compelled to return in the evening, whereupon he looked up at the sky in quiet desperation and spoke out loud, "God, if you would only give me a clue as to how these are created." In less than ten seconds he had a reply.

According to Andrews' account, an "electrical cracking noise started to come from a spot about nine feet away. It grew louder, up to a pitch where I expected a bang to follow. Frightened, I looked towards the village to check my quickest route out of the field. I fought to control my panic and remained still. As suddenly as it had started, it stopped. It had lasted about six seconds, although it seemed longer. I saw nothing and nothing moved" (Andrews and Delgado 1991).

It was now the summer of 1987, and reports of crop circles were increasing at a furious rate. In one twenty-four-hour period, fifteen circles appeared around Warminster alone, and with them a rash of new discoveries. Magnetic disturbances played havoc with compasses in some of the formations, and in terms of design, small circles were now superimposed over or overlapped by new formations, while others displayed an ever-increasing complexity of swirl detail.

In one memorable incident, the night after local Wiltshire police were flooded with reports of UFO sightings, a large quintuplet formation appeared at Upton Scudamore bearing a remarkable anticlockwise S-shaped swirl in three of the satellites but reversed in the fourth. Meanwhile, two miles north at Westbury, a circle containing half a revolution swirl was so impressive in its precision that researchers felt walking upon it to be sacrilegious.

The Wingfield family, an interested group from Somerset, also experienced unusual flashes similar to the one described by Andrews. Standing alone on a hill while her family investigated a circle below, Mrs. Wingfield was confronted by a blue flashing light which seemed to be shining on the ground in front of her, pulsating every second or so as if it was reflecting off a spinning, shiny surface somewhere above. Alarmed, she raced down the hill to join her husband who, like Delgado and Andrews, was about to be bitten by the crop circle bug.

The testimonials were piling up. Farmer Geoff Cooper got up one morning to be greeted with his own set of circles: "One night our dog went silly barking, real nasty-like. Usually he would stop on a firm command, but not that night. He went on for ages—he was really upset. I wish now I had looked out, because when I did in the morning I could see five circles had appeared in the corn [wheat] during the night. I don't know what caused them. I don't think they are made by people. We have tried to make them with ropes, poles, and so on, but they just cannot be replicated" (Andrews and Delgado 1991).

One discovery led to another, giving the impression that behind the phenomenon lay an orderly, even premeditated plan. As the end of August 1987 approached, the list of anomalous features multiplied by the week, as did the pace of new reports, by now in the hundreds. But one more episode was brewing that would finish off the year in dramatic fashion.

Just a short distance along the road from Stonehenge, upon the intermittently wooded Wiltshire plain, the small town of Winterbourne Stoke played host to an enormous seventy-five-foot ringed circle with three outlying satellite circles. It had swirl patterns so tight and compressed that from the air it looked as if it was spinning. Despite materializing on a high embankment beside the busy A303 London-to-Exeter road, nothing more out of the ordinary was reported—until two months later.

At 5:06 P.M. on October 22, the Ministry of Defence suddenly found £13.5 million of its hardware missing. Shortly after a pilot radioed in with "nothing unusual" to report, the military air base at Boscombe Down lost radio contact with one of its Harrier jump jets. This "audio disappearance" happened over the precise spot where the crop circle formation had lain a few weeks earlier. Meanwhile, ninety miles southwest from the coast of Ireland, the crew of an American transport plane got the surprise of their lives when they sighted the Harrier casually flying out over the Atlantic, pilotless and minus a roof canopy. The following day, a rescue party discovered the body of the pilot alongside his reserve parachute and life raft a couple of hundred yards from the site of the mysterious circles.

There were seemingly no answers to two questions: Why had the pilot ejected out of a perfectly operational plane? Why had the plane deviated by several degrees from its designated course just at the point where audio contact was lost? The ejector seat was never recovered (ibid.).

With such episodes gnawing away at their cynicism, the media's interest in crop circles began to warm up, and with it the public's curiosity. This increase in inquisitiveness was further fueled throughout the summer of 1988, as

Figure 1.7

The once-flattened stalks have selectively risen in a radial pattern of forty-eight lines and seven concentric rings inside each circle; the damage in the center of two of the circles was caused later by visitors. The formation's triangular alignment would later yield a geometric theorem.

crop circle designs continued to evolve, such as the innovation of appearing in pairs on the same field on separate occasions. Of particular interest was a grouping of three thirty-two-foot circles, all perfectly aligned within an invisible equilateral triangle. Exactly a week later, the tender and previously flattened barley plants inside the circles began to regain their upright posture, and in a most exquisite fashion.

According to the field report, the plants had risen selectively along their nodes in groups of three within an oblong area roughly covering two feet by one foot. The first group of plants raised itself at the node nearest the ground, the second at the mid-node, and the third at the node nearest the seed head. The process was then repeated radially, creating a pattern now consisting of seven concentric rings and forty-eight spokes, as if the plants had been programmed to grow back in selected fashion. Every circle was identical. According to agricultural expert, Dr. Mark Glover, these features are definitely not the result of fertilizers, agrochemical treatment, disease, pest damage, soil type, or even plant behavior (Andrews and Delgado 1991).

With the weather theory in a quandary, Terence Meaden's model of modified vortices now required specific topographical features that enabled crop circles to appear. That is, they could only appear on the leeward sides of hills. Within days, two reports surfaced from the town of Langenburg, in the flat prairie of Saskatchewan, where in 1974 farmer Edwin Fuhr had found five shiny silver discs hovering over his canola, making the plants sway. Fifteen minutes later, he saw the discs bolt into the sky, leaving behind five circles; a similar incident later occurred in the prairies of Manitoba. Back in England, the new crop formations similarly contradicted Meaden's theory by moving to the open, rolling landscape around Europe's largest man-made "pyramid," Silbury Hill in Wiltshire.[3] By July 1988, fifty-one formations lay within a seven-mile arc of this enigmatic prehistoric monument, and from its 430-foot summit, groupings of circles like Celtic crosses gathered together like apostles, as if to collect a message to send out to the world (see figure 1.9).

One such message arrived in the form of a book, *Circular Evidence*. Andrews and Delgado had by now acquired so much data they decided it was time the public be given an alternative to the drunks-with-strings explanations or the weather-based theory still adhered to by officialdom, even though Dr. Meaden fine-tuned his theory by placing the responsibility with superheated columns of air called plasma vortices.[4]

Figure 1.8

[3]Unlike the Egyptian pyramids, Silbury Hill is a conical, truncated mound constructed as a step pyramid of six levels, from layers of chalk, alternating with layers of clay and flint.
[4]Plasma is superheated gas where the neutral atoms are stripped into negatively charged electrons and positively charged ions. It is sometimes referred to as ion plasma. Examples include the aurora borealis, the spiraling column of a whirlwind, and a lit household fluorescent tube.

Figure 1.9

The quintuplets arrive at the base of Silbury Hill. 1989.

With the evidence now available in the bookstands, public interest in crop circles escalated, followed by greater scientific and media scrutiny. *Circular Evidence* and its authors were favorably profiled in such newspapers as *The Wall Street Journal* and *The Times*; one *Daily Mail* reviewer described how the book "took at least this reader's skeptical breath away." But the big question on everyone's mind was this: *Who* is behind these things?

To find out, fifty scientists, engineers, and various other interested parties joined forces in the summer of 1989 for Operation White Crow. This surveillance project amassed truckloads of high-tech equipment, and planned a two-week stakeout of the prolific crop circle location of Cheesefoot Head near Winchester in Hampshire, a site known locally as the Devil's Punchbowl.

The infrared and image-intensifier cameras were primed and poised around the rim of this huge natural amphitheater. A warm breeze rolled off the enclosing fields of gold, flirting around the expectant gathering of researchers.

At three in the morning on the second night of the project, a bright orange ball appeared suddenly over the Punchbowl, and it remained there fairly still for about five minutes until the lights of a passing truck seemingly shooed it away. After that promising start, there was little to write home about, and by the last day it was

His revised theory also suggested that, within such a vortex, columns of contra-rotating air could explain the behavior of plants inside a new crop circle encompassed by a single ring, in which the plants in the circle were laid clockwise but anticlockwise within the outer ring (Meaden 1985).

The Circlemakers obliged him by creating new, single-ringed circles in which the plants were laid in only one direction (see figure 1.8).

obvious that nothing else was going to be recorded on film. As the scientists packed up their equipment, a small group among them was not ready to give up. With clairvoyant Rita Gould, they decided to walk to a neighboring field where an older pair of circles were nested and sit inside one of them in silence, waiting to see what happened next.

It took only ten minutes before the familiar trilling sound surrounded them. Heard by all present, it moved within a few feet of the group in a random, nonlinear path. The noise orbited the circle once, then again. Rita communicated with it: "If you understand our intent, please stop." The noise dutifully complied for a few seconds, then resumed. The surveyors had now become the surveyed. Not feeling threatened, but spooked nevertheless, they decided to leave the site.

However, curiosity nagged at them. George Wingfield grabbed a tape recorder, and five minutes later he and Andrews were back in the circle, and so was the noise which appeared to enjoy the flirt. "Please, will you make us a circle?" requested Wingfield, tape recorder at the ready. But things are never *that* straightforward in crop circle research. As dawn broke, a police car drove by to inform the weary team that a new formation had just appeared in the field to the east of their site. Despite the intense scrutiny, it was obvious the capricious circle-making Puck wished to communicate, but had no desire to be caught at it.

It seemed as if 1989 was going to be the "Year of the Noise." After the recorded hum made its debut on TV, the BBC dispatched a team to Beck-hampton, home to a new 120-foot circle and ring, to interview Andrews and Delgado. In hindsight, the world-renowned broadcasting company would have done well to take out extra insurance on its equipment. The moment the £35,000 high-tech video camera was brought near the circle and its satellite-laden rings, noise bars denoting interference appeared on its screen, followed by an agonizing array of red warning lights. Suddenly, the sound engineer appeared irritated by a loud, penetrating hum, and the camera died. The BBC, though astonished, broadcasted the entire sequence of events to an even more incredulous public.

After the noise had baffled BBC sound engineers and camera repair technicians, it was given a graphic analysis at the University of Sussex. There, it was concluded that the sound contained a harmonic frequency of 5.0–5.2 kHz

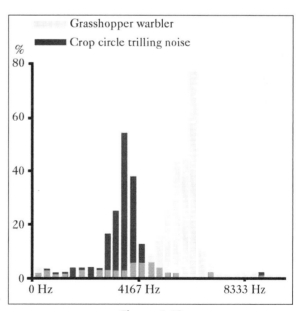

Figure 1.10

Clear discrepancies between the frequency of the crop circle "noise" and the suspected grasshopper warbler, as analyzed by computer expert Paul Vigay.

(kilohertz), identical to the one previously recorded at Operation White Crow at Cheesefoot Head. The idea was put forward that what these "crank investigators" had captured on tape was a bird, the small grasshopper warbler, and yet the skeptics seemed unfazed by the fact that this rare bird frequents commons and marshes rather than rolling fields of grain.

The sounds received a comparative analysis, and not only was the bird's 7 kHz sound proved to oscillate at a frequency 2 kHz above the alien noise, but both sound imprints were audibly dissimilar (as shown by computer expert Paul Vigay's analysis). Cross-checking with all species of available bird and insect sounds, a separate analysis at NASA's Jet Propulsion Laboratory by Dr. Robert Weiss (he analyzed the Nixon Watergate tapes) reached a similar conclusion: It was not an anomaly of magnetic tape or nature, but a noise of *artificial* origin (Andrews and Delgado 1990).

The crop circle debate reached the British Parliament on July 11, 1989, when Teddy Taylor, M.P., asked the Secretary of State for Defence, Mr. Neubert, "What progress has been made in the inquiries initiated by Army helicopters based in the southwest in investigating the origin of flattened circular areas of wheat?" To which Mr. Neubert elusively replied, "The Ministry of Defence is not conducting any inquiries into the origins of flattened circular areas of crops. However, we are satisfied that they are not caused by service helicopter activity."

It is strange that on pages 73 and 82 of *Circular Evidence*, an army helicopter is clearly seen reconnoitering crop circles at Westbury—one of many such incidences. Stranger still, in an article two days previous to the Parliamentary debate, the *Sunday Express* had stated that then Prime Minister Margaret Thatcher was "passing a funding report to the Ministry of Defence."

The focus next returned to the fields around Winterbourne Stoke and a new sixty-foot circle sporting the most complex of floor patterns. It was dubbed the "swastika" because its plants were laid into four quadrants aligned to the four magnetic cardinal points. Overlaid in the center was a nine-foot diameter swirl whose plants abruptly changed direction three times before reaching

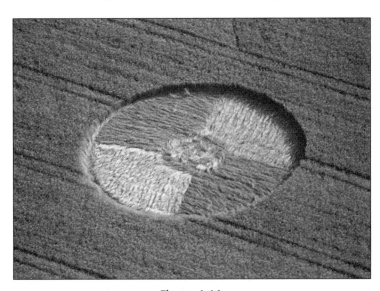

Figure 1.11
With its quartered and interwoven floor pattern, this "swastika" blew down the weather theory. Winterbourne Stoke, 1989.

the quadrants. Around the perimeter, a three-foot wide clockwise band lay partly beneath the quadrants, giving the impression that the plants had been worked backwards and towards the center. Given this woven effect, the circular patch of plants was seemingly synchronized to collapse simultaneously. This effect was unprecedented.

Despite the mountain of evidence that now did not leave much room for weather or human hands as a cause, Dr. Meaden held his ground: "The effect of a descending energetic vortex from the atmosphere, a vortex of air which is ionized to the point of being a species of low-density cool plasma producing an electromagnetic field," was responsible for the simpler, nonhoaxed markings, he said. This mass of electrically charged air would apparently form under certain meteorological conditions, preferably at the base of hills. "Such vortices," he added, "have been seen by numerous witnesses, and in the case of the related summer whirlwind, the electromagnetic fields have been measured by atmospheric scientists working in the USA and North Africa" (Meaden 1989).

But this still could not account for crop circles appearing in all manner of topographical and weather conditions, or for the two circles that appeared in rice paddies on Kyushu Island in Japan. Besides, atmospheric conditions create havoc, not neat circles and rings.

A series of further death blows to the weather theories came early in 1990 with a leap

Figure 1.12
Seven days after appearing, this gigantic circle "grew" a fourth, outer ring. Its previously flattened crop subsequently rose into radials and concentric rings. Bishops Canning Down, 1990.

in the history of crop circle language. A circle at Bishops Canning Down, 300 feet in diameter and orbited by three rings, each six inches wide, developed a fourth ring several days later, essentially making the pattern 1,000 feet wide (see figure 1.12). It was improbable that a descending atmospheric plasma vortex could have *returned* to add a perfectly sited geometric feature to a week-old design.

An even greater repudiation of conventional theories lay at the opposite end of Wessex. At Chilcomb Farm, a circle appeared containing a ruler-straight central pathway of narrower width, leading to a second, detached circle. The design was flanked by four rectangular boxes separated by stands of virgin crop. Freelance writer Ruth Rees subsequently posed the all-important question to the nation's Meteorological Office: "Could any type of atmospheric vortex create crop circles with straight lines and rectangles?"

The reply from a board member of the Royal Meteorological Society stated: "Such patterns cannot be the result of atmospheric vortices, due to the sharp angles that appear to be present in the shapes, and also because of the elaborate, organized nature of the patterns. Real vortices possess rather indistinct edges. . . . Flattening of the crop in a straight line could result from a traveling vortex, but then we would expect the line width to be similar to that of the circle diameter" (Delgado 1992).

Figure 1.13
Chilcomb, 1990.

The late Lord Zuckerman, who had been chief scientific advisor to the British government from 1964 to 1971 and science advisor to the British Royal Family, was also skeptical of Meaden's explanation:

It is inconceivable that a circular downwardly spiraling vortex could create pictograms graced with neatly arranged rectangles of flattened corn. Nor, since Dr. Meaden's hypothesis demands that his presumed downwardly directed vortices generate their effects only in specific topographical and meteorological conditions, can they accept that an elaborate pictogram can be repeated practically to the same dimensions miles from where it was first seen, and in a landscape totally different from the first (Zuckerman 1991).

Surprisingly, Lord Zuckerman's article for the *New York Review* carried none of the sarcastic, dismissive overtones generally associated with remarks by scientists. In fact, the article left one with the distinct impression that Zuckerman saw the mystery as nonhuman and created by a great intelligence.

The weather theory died and the pictogram was born.

Garnished with haloes or semi-circular paths, crop circle pictograms (symbols representing an idea, as in early writing and hieroglyphs) quickly became identifiable with petroglyphs, the rock carvings of the ancient world.

Figure 1.14
Longwood, 1990.

One pictogram at Longwood, near Cheesefoot Head, contained a wilted pathway and four drooping streams, giving the impression of a crying planet, silently protesting humanity's compromising of the delicate balance of nature.

One thing seemed clear: After initial contact through simple designs involving dots and rings, the Circlemakers were now transmitting a message in the form of recognizable symbols.

The public's interest became insatiable. People from all walks of life began streaming into crop circles, and with this tide of visitors came more incidences of crop circle energy interfering with electronic equipment. On one occasion a camera's shutter curtain buckled upwards, something camera repair experts were later unable to explain. This damage was followed moments later by a video camera malfunction such that the camera had to be removed from inside the circle before it regained working order.

News of a more scientific kind surfaced from HSC Laboratory in southern England. This lab had carried out a microscopic analysis of plants taken from crop circles and compared them to

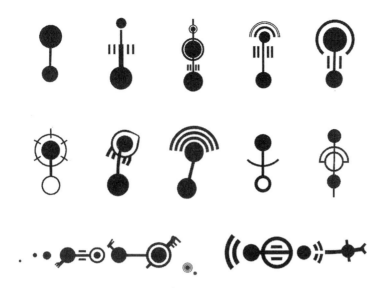

Figure 1.16

Selection of pictogram crop circles from 1990.

control samples taken from elsewhere in the given field. As the two results were displayed side by side, the disparity proved that whatever had made the designs had also altered the composition of the crystalline structure of certain minerals in the affected plants (see chapter 8).

Something else about to be altered was the daily life of the inhabitants of Alton Barnes in the heart of Wessex. During the early hours of July 12, 1990, a loud rumbling like distant thunder could be heard throughout this serene village in the shallow Vale of Pewsey. Dogs barked incessantly and refused to stop. At 2:20 A.M., farm manager Tim Carson decided to check his fields to see if anything was amiss. As he patrolled the perimeter of his east field, an indistinct shape seemed out of place amid the wheat.

When daylight broke, it revealed the imprint of a 606-foot long pictogram—a cyclopean collection of circles, rings, boxes, and tridents, all connected by two straight avenues (see figure 1.17

on page A2 in the color section). To complicate matters, twelve "grapeshot" lay in the middle of the standing crop between tram lines. The formation carried an unusual type of energy, because a power surge of unknown origin had left local car batteries dead.

Significantly, one villager told a local newspaper reporter how he'd tried to walk into the formation at daybreak but had been repelled by an invisible energy field. In fact, when Tim Carson later escorted a television team into the crop formation, he witnessed firsthand how the crew had to keep their equipment outside the circle. Every time they crossed its perimeter electromagnetic interference played havoc with the recording equipment.

At last, a crop circle event made the headlines of the international news, and articles in major newspapers enabled photos to traverse the globe, beckoning tens of thousands of visitors from as far away as Japan to descend in a kind of pilgrimage upon rural Wiltshire. Public and media confidence in official explanations evaporated as crop circle fever broke out.

Inside the Alton Barnes pictogram, even the traditional British reserve melted, as strangers of different classes and backgrounds conversed cheerfully with one another. Some even danced in and around the circles. The place turned into an impromptu carnival. Thousands felt as if a burden had been lifted off their shoulders, yet nobody had the slightest explanation as to why. How many were aware that one interpretation of the oversized "trident" protruding from the head of the crop formation was a representation of Shiva's Trident—a Hindu symbol associated with transformation? This was an apt signature, considering what was now unfolding as the pictogram began to exert a foothold on public awareness. With this one elegant demonstration, were the Circlemakers uniting the tribes of Earth in harmony?

To make sure the authorities would not try to explain away this event, during that same night, the Circlemakers had dropped an almost identical design onto a field a mile away (see figure 1.18 on page A2 in the color section). The farmer who was busy harvesting the ripe crop said that he'd had previous encounters with the phenomenon but never on a scale like this. "It wasn't there when I drove down here last evening, but appeared here during the night. I cannot think of anything that could do this, can you?"

2. WELCOME TO THE MACHINE

One can only wonder what was running through the minds of the authorities as the reserved British public continued to react to the crop circles with zest and as carloads of families swarmed narrow lanes to catch a glimpse of new events. What is certain is that an awakening appears to have taken place, and Wessex, particularly the Silbury Hill area, was again, as it had been thousands of years before, a place of pilgrimage.

At the top of Milk Hill, two of these pilgrims, a young couple, sat together beholding the enchanting landscape. As one of them, Steve Alexander, began videotaping the enormous pictogram below, a small silvery object reflected back the sunlight. Not much larger than a beach ball, it hovered at waist level, brushing the heads of the wheat as it meandered lazily but purposefully towards a tractor working the field. The pulsating disk closed in, gained altitude, and then suddenly disappeared into the sky. When later interviewed, the young tractor driver described how even though a disk-shaped object had flown within shouting distance of him, his subsequent account of his close encounter had been met by ridicule from friends and locals. Alexander's four-minute film would later vindicate him.

That wasn't by any means the only object flying around the Wiltshire countryside. Although Wiltshire has large tracts of army training grounds, principally on Salisbury Plain, and most circlemaking activity takes place some distance from these, camouflaged army helicopters, flying low in and around privately owned fields, became a familiar sight over new crop circles, much to the annoyance of those on the ground. Technically, flying low over private land is not a deviation from standard British army procedure, but it is hard to comprehend how the military machine, reliant on critical timekeeping, allows troops to take a side interest in photographing crop circles—unless, of course, the formations were under scrutiny. But how could they be? After all, the government had already categorically denied the army's involvement. Given evidence to the contrary it would seem the army was suffering from a serious case of joyriding helicopter pilots. Regardless, no serious explanation was

Figures 2.1a and 2.1b

A tube of light was seen descending from the sky, three hours before this four-ring Celtic cross appeared below Morgan's Hill (top). Three weeks later it was overlaid by a second design (bottom). Note how damage to the formations is only evident where visitors have disturbed the plants. Morgan's Hill, 1990.

and Wiltshire alone contributed 500. Now, hardly a day went by without the British press devoting ample column inches to the phenomenon, especially as reports began coming in from all around the British Isles, as well as Bulgaria, Ireland, France, and the Netherlands. The unusual circumstances mounted. For example, the night before the first of forty circles appeared in East Anglia, reports were filed describing orange lights the size of the full moon. At Bickington, Devon, a circle with seven satellites appeared soon after a bullet-shaped object with rows of colored lights was reported flying silently across the area.

forthcoming. Given that highly intelligent whirlwinds were hardly proving a palpable explanation for recent events, the British government also remained suspiciously tight-lipped.

Researchers, on the other hand, now had more reason than ever to speak out. A research group called the Center for Crop Circles Studies (CCCS) was assembled to amass and disseminate reams of information from scores of individuals. Andrews and Delgado followed suit with their Circles Phenomenon Research, which later became Andrews' CPRI (Circles Phenomenon Research International).

The estimated number of crop circles during the 1990 season bordered on a breathtaking 800,

On the morning of July 25, a wildlife photographer camping near Beckhampton saw a column of light shine down from the clouds at around half-past two in the morning. Shortly after dawn, a circle with a curved path was found. A few miles down the road below Morgan's Hill, a farmhand was suddenly wakened by a piercing, trilling noise, just hours before a magnificent Celtic cross crop formation appeared. A few of these circles were accompanied either by balls of light or tubes of light, and in all cases by *that* sound.

In Lincolnshire, two 200-foot formations appeared over the buried location of Durobrivae, once one of the largest towns in Roman Britain. According to the reporter from the Peterborough *Evening Telegraph*, the ground details were far beyond the ability of hoaxers, as the carefully laid strands of wheat "looked more like they had been carefully plaited together" (Michell 1990). This level of precision also applied to the designs: the second formation had dimensions resulting from superimposing the elements of the first formation.

Figure 2.2a

This Sri Yantra mandala is made up of 13.3 miles of etched lines on dry lake bed. The tiny figures in the center are people. Oregon, 1990.

Figure 2.2b

Hindu Sri Yantra mandala. The triangles represent a series of diminishing harmonics.

Reports followed from Canada and Japan, followed by a dramatic event from southern Oregon in the U.S. On August 10, 13.3 miles of the dry lake bed of Alvord Lake was etched with lines ten inches wide and three inches deep, creating a perfect rendition of the Sri Yantra mandala.[5] The "straight" lines that made up the series of triangles were slightly bowed by eight inches, as if the curvature resulted from them being projected from a point high in the sky (see figures 2.2a, b). Eventually, a group of four artists claimed responsibility, even producing a video of themselves supposedly making the furrows of the design with a manually drawn garden cultivator, a job they claim took them from July 31 to August 9 to complete.

However, their efforts to replicate the precise trench with beveled edges in sun-baked earth proved unconvincing, least of all because the video they released showed the cultivator following suspicious dark swaths that looked like pre-existing furrows back-filled with dirt, to convince us that the ruts were being dug for the first time.

The rest of the story seemed equally implausible. First, why would anyone travel several hundred miles armed with a tiller to bake in temperatures exceeding 110° F for ten days? Second, when Air National Guard pilot Bill Miller discovered the original design on an overflight of the Oregon lake bed during a near-daily training exercise, it was already complete. According to his superior officer, Capt. Michael Gollaher of the 124th Tactical Reconnaissance

---

[5]Yantra is a Sanskrit word meaning "geometric power diagram," Sri means "exalted or divine." It is said that contemplation of this symbol brings enlightenment. This crop circle "mandala" was discovered a month after the Alton Barnes pictogram of July 11th, with its trident of Shiva, another symbol of transformation.

Group, there were no signs of a design-in-progress, nor tire tracks leading to or from the formation. Yet when UFOlogists Dan Newman and Alan Decker drove to the site, not only were footprints and tire tracks absent, their own van had left a 1/4-inch-deep imprint on the dry wilderness surface surrounding the mandala.[6] Clearly, human involvement in that "crop" formation can be ruled out.

Back in Wessex, a new surveillance operation began. Between the towns of Westbury and Bratton stands one of the many enigmatic white horse-figures carved into the side of the chalk hills. Above this particular carving lies the Iron Age hill fort at Bratton, with its commanding view of the countryside. Crop circles had already appeared several times here in the past, so it seemed the perfect site from which a three-week monitoring operation could take place. Like Operation White Crow, the idea behind Operation Blackbird, as it was called, was for Andrews, Delgado, and other researchers and scientists to try to catch the Circlemakers at it. A cache of a million pounds'-worth of infrared cameras, video recorders, and image intensifiers were housed in a cabin on the escarpment.

Behind the ancient hill fort lay the edge of the expansive Salisbury Plain with its largely sealed-off military testing grounds, so it came as no surprise when the army announced its intention to join the action. Their participation included officially off-duty soldiers manning the adjacent hill, loaded with night-vision equipment far superior in penetrative ability to that used in the circle researchers' cabin. The fact that these soldiers wore camouflage uniforms was neither consistent with the designation "off-duty" nor with the army's publicized lack of interest in crop circles. (Later, such army patrols would be seen with increasing frequency around the Silbury Hill area, and sometimes in the private farmland that occupied advantageous viewpoints.)

The first night of the Bratton surveillance went by without incident. On the second night, several key researchers decided to retire early. Later, they wished they hadn't.

When first light broke, an imprint in the crop began to reveal itself less than a mile away below the hill fort, although given the oblique angle it was not possible to establish its quality. When Andrews and Delgado, two of the researchers who'd taken the night off, were telephoned, they boyishly raced back to Bratton. Up at the cabin everyone was thrilled. Finally, a real event was caught in front of the world's media! Despite some TV reporters pushing the possibility that perhaps they had been deceived, an understandably excited Colin Andrews announced to the press that a major event had indeed taken place. However, even though a rushed look through the night footage video suggested that something wasn't quite right, the world's press couldn't be kept waiting any longer.

With breakfast television cameras rolling, Andrews and Delgado set out for the formation, but as they approached it, a churning feeling began to form in their stomachs. Something looked abnormal. The characteristic vortices of

---

[6]James Deardorff 1991. Also my thanks to Eric Byler, Assistant State Director of Oregon UFO Research for additional information.

the swirled crop were missing, and the stems of the plants were broken. It was a trampled mess of clumsy circles and haphazard lines. It was a hoax.

Worse was to follow. In the center of each of these ugly circles lay an astrology board game and a wooden cross. Nearby, an incriminating length of red rope had been conveniently discarded for all the cameras to see, the first time that the "tools of the trade" had ever made an appearance. The media lapped it up and fed the deception straight to 50 million viewers at the start of their working day.

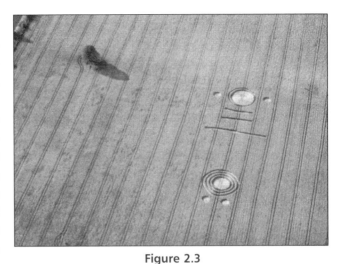

Figure 2.3

A hoax allegedly perpetrated by the British military to fool the world. Bratton, 1990.

Back at the cabin, and after two hours spent analyzing the night-vision and infrared tapes, a subdued Andrews addressed the media again: "I suppose we were already suspicious because of what we'd seen on the video recordings. For a start, it took about twenty minutes for the circles to form, when our research clearly shows that the real circles are there within seconds. . . . The equipment even detected the heat from the bodies of the perpetrators." Despite protestations that they had fallen prey to a crude deception, it was too late: the key figures of crop circles research had been ritually humiliated in front of the nation, by now laughing all the way to the office.

Coincidentally, during the night of the hoax—and only on that night—the soldiers and the two corporals assigned to Operation Blackbird had been conspicuous by their absence (Wingfield 1991b).

Despite this setback, a handful of dedicated, if subdued, researchers stayed back at the cabin on the hill fort to continue the seemingly fruitless project; everyone else bolted from the hilltop stakeout. Once again, they would wish they hadn't been so hasty. Ten days after the hoax, a swirling motion lasting less than fifteen seconds rippled through the wheat— caught by the night-vision camera of Nippon TV, but tantalizingly at the very limit of its vision. It was as if the Circlemakers knew the limitations of the equipment but had wished to reassure those who persevered not to lose faith that here was a *real* phenomenon.

The new crop circle—in shape, a cross between a sperm cell, a question mark, and an equiangular spiral—lay a thousand feet from the

Figure 2.4

Diagram of the crop circle captured on-camera following the Bratton hoax.

infamous hoax, but this time no member of the TV-viewing public was to share in the event. After that last ridicule, crop circles were off the media menu.

It quickly became apparent that a well-planned piece of disinformation had been executed, conveniently in the presence of the world's press. Someone had blatantly gone out of their way to rain on the Circlemakers' parade: perhaps the authorities were concerned that crop circles had become a new religion? After all, enough evidence exists that faith is a wonderful tool for generating states of excellent physical and mental health, even happiness. Fortunately, several individuals rose to the challenge of ferreting out the culprits. A particularly suspicious George Wingfield was quick off the mark:

"Around this time, I received a telephone call from a friend who said he had a reliable contact in a high-ranking position in the military, whose name I'm not allowed to mention for understandable reasons. This man had already supplied sensitive information in the past, which until now always proved extremely valuable. Now he claimed that the Bratton hoax was carried out by a specially trained unit of the army, and that the order came directly from the Ministry of Defence. The operation was carefully planned, prepared in advance and carried out in complete darkness, quickly and precisely. My informant was even able to speak with an officer who was involved in the planning of the operation, which had the highest level of secrecy."

Further corroboration came from the Wiltshire-based German political correspondent, Jürgen Krönig, who was in an excellent position to gather valuable information. His report on the first of three internal conferences held at the Department of the Environment, attended by Members of Parliament, government scientists, and civil servants from the Ministries of Defence, Environment, and Agriculture Fisheries and Food, proved illuminating: "The favourite thesis of the skeptics, that the circles were but a large-scale joke, wasn't even considered. The army was instructed to keep the phenomenon under intensive observation and, if necessary, to take 'appropriate steps.' Finally, it was discussed how the topic should be handled in public; in this discussion, the term 'disinformation' was used" (Hesemann 1995).

There was undoubtedly much interest in crop circles in the upper levels of government, since a number of meetings took place between ministers, the secret services, and the military to discuss the issue. In the end, it was decided to outwardly calm the public while further discreet investigations took place. This is the official approach of Western governments concerning UFOs, which follows an "educational program" adopted in 1953 by the Robertson Panel in the U.S. Project Blue Book, its protocol, officially released in 1977 under the U.S. Freedom of Information Act, describes how governments should have "two major aims: training and debunking."

The plan was to reduce public interest in flying saucers, accomplished chiefly through mass media such as television and motion pictures, where unexplained phenomena were given to the realms of fantasy, allowing them to be easily ridiculed or parodied. Then, a series of editorial articles in the popular press would seek to re-educate the public by presenting case histories where puzzling events were rationally explained away.

However, the problem with explaining away the fantastic is that it sometimes requires unrealistic explanations, and this policy has a history of backfiring. The best example undoubtedly is the explanation offered by the Pentagon over the discovery of "alien bodies" at the famous UFO crash site at Roswell, New Mexico. Press statements issued in 1997 counter-claimed that local eyewitnesses had seen mannequins, dropped from airplanes in 1950 to test a new parachute prototype. These incredible parachutes appear to have had a formidable effect of slowing down their payload, for if we are to believe this official explanation, it took a full three years for these mannequins to reach the ground, as the Roswell crash occurred in 1947.

As for crop circle disinformation, British ex-police-sergeant-turned-UFO-researcher Anthony Dodd did much knocking on doors to amass additional evidence that pointed to some kind of cover-up. He reported: "Local farmers had received instructions from the authorities to harvest the fields in question immediately, whether or not the corn was ripe . . . they [the authorities] wanted to see formations gone from the fields before the public could examine them" (Dodd 1991).

A document from the secret U.S. commission Majestic 12 was leaked to German editor Michael Hesemann, showing how the CIA was seriously concerned about the effect crop circles might have on the population, and that they had gathered substantial information on all aspects of the phenomenon (Hesemann 1995). According to many sources, Majestic 12 was set up to deal with the U.S. military's most guarded secret and biggest headache. Many files claiming an MJ-12 pedigree have been "leaked" to the public, (whether this was done as information or disinformation is still a moot point) and disclose numerous items of allegedly classified information on extraterrestrial life and technologies, information that was classified "higher" than the H-bomb data.

In his *Conclusive Evidence*, Pat Delgado fea-tures one example of an extraordinary effort by the U.S. military to cover up traces of a crop formation in a Kansas cornfield. This included "the influx into a small town of various unmarked government vehicles shortly after the event, the setting up of road blocks, the questioning of residents by men in suits and ties, three large, red hazardous-waste vehicles, animal-disposal vehicles, an electrified fence, the attempted discing and ploughing of the formation, and the spreading of shredded crops on the formation" (Delgado 1992).

In a separate incident, a confidential source contacted me from upstate New York and told me that a neighboring farmer had been approached by a state police officer and handed $500 to immediately cut a crop circle out of his field.

Bizarre behavior, to say the least.

But let's return to Bratton in Wessex. It is certainly feasible that the government had been involved to some degree in masterminding the hoax, because despite intense public and media pressure on the authorities to come up with the real cause behind crop circles, no action had been forthcoming. They simply could not explain what was happening in rational terms. Plants weren't supposed to behave like this, so the easiest way out would be to make the whole phenomenon appear to be a series of fraudulent misdemeanors perpetrated by vandals.

George Wingfield suggested that the superficially convincing hoax would have had to be carried out early on in the surveillance project lest a real event be caught by the cameras, especially as television representatives from as far away as Japan were present. But it seems that a hoaxed circle was not enough for the authorities and so, to move the public mood from debate to ridicule, horoscopes and crosses were added, thus blatantly pointing the finger at New-Agers or occultists, and lending an air of silliness to further discredit proceedings. If suspicion could be cast on the validity of the whole phenomenon, then it would follow that, by implication, surely all circles had been man-made.

"If a hoaxer wished to achieve a masterly deception, he would not then deliberately give the game away with these obvious signs that the circles were man-made," wrote Wingfield. "In reporting the hoax, the BBC said that the objects suggested some kind of ritual . . . no ritualist would conceivably perform under such circumstances, in front of a massive surveillance operation. . . . And who, after all, would happen to have six horoscope game-boards on hand unless all had been well-prepared in advance" (Wingfield 1991b)?

The use of game boards would also have ensured that Delgado and Andrews would not declare the crop formation to be genuine, so this was a shrewd move.

In hindsight, a lax remark to the press by one of the army corporals prior to the hoax at Bratton seemed to sum it all up: "We are here to prove that the circles are caused by people. The scientists are here to prove otherwise."

The military, not surprisingly, had shown a lack of interest in the study and analysis of the Bratton circles, but fifteen miles away, the set of circles that appeared on the same evening received intense scrutiny from an army detachment which included a WISP, a miniature remote-controlled helicopter. Military surveillance of new circles would continue for three weeks.

The formations kept coming. A 600-foot pictogram

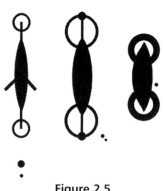

Figure 2.5
"Dolphinograms."

materialized nine miles away from Bratton, beside East Kennett long barrow. In fact, dozens of formations were found just as the crops were being harvested by the combines; when all the grain fields had been cut in Southern England, those in the north were still displaying all manner of markings.

But no matter, the goal of disinformation had been effectively carried out. From now on, barely a pip would be heard from the media or the public about crop circles. No government explanation would be required. Everything was again under control.

The spring of 1991 was accompanied by unusually wet weather in southern England, leaving crops in a relative state of immaturity, and making the new crop circle season splutter and stall until June before finally gathering steam.

The new designs appeared inconsistent with the ordered, fluid progression of the Circlemakers' language up to this point. These took on the shape of "insectograms"—designs based on combinations of circles connected by pathways (dumbbells) from which "antennae" sprouted, as well as legs and ladders, giving the impression of dancers or insects. While some considered that these designs contained a serious message, for others they conveyed a jest, as if to counteract the seriousness of the politics now surrounding the subject. Five insectograms materialized between June and August: three in equidistant, almost linear, field locations across Hampshire; a fourth was placed on the same latitude as Stonehenge; the fifth arrived twenty-one miles to the west, opposite Stonehenge itself in a field that would later host the "Julia Set."

Other impressive crop formations came in the shape of 300-foot long, elongated dumbbells, some with an attachment resembling a key (see figure 2.8 on page A4 in the color section), and still others suggesting whales, turtles, or dolphins. They also came in pairs of virtual carbon copies, which according to accurate ground surveys, showed the discrepancy between copies as a minuscule 0.6–0.9 percent.[7] Such critical measuring by surveyors became crucial to later research: a dumbbell at Beckhampton encoded the Moon's diameter, as well as the mass ratio between Earth and the Moon; a second, this time at Silbury Hill, encoded 19.47°, the latitude at which energy upwells in a "hot spot" on many planets in our solar system (see figure 2.9).[8]

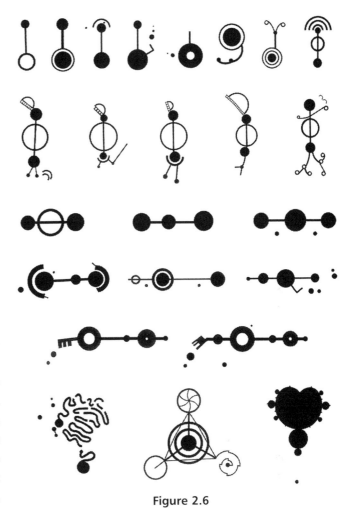

Figure 2.6

Selection of crop circles from 1991. Second row: "insectograms."

In June, a radio operator named Dilling in Bulberry Down, Devon, was listening to Radio Moscow and Voice of America when the broadcast was suddenly drowned out by a series of high-pitched blips and clicks. Dilling knew the origin of such noises because he'd heard them before, at the time when crop circles appeared. The following morning, a new seventy-five-foot circle and ring was visible in a nearby field.

At Lapworth, eighty miles north of the regular circle activity, a farmer was surprised to find that

---

[7]From the meticulous surveys of John Langrish, in the CCCS database.
[8]Interestingly, two thirds of the Earth is covered by water, and any object moving through water generates a wake at an angle of 19.47°. The implications of this number in terms of latitude are discussed at length in Myers and Percy's book *Two-Thirds*.

Figure 2.7
Triple "dumbbell." Froxfield, 1990.

natural tendency to rise. A scientist also found electromagnetic energy lines connecting the crop circle with sixty nearby churches (Delgado 1992).

So, despite the odd hoax, the Circlemakers remained active and innovative, and the continued circle activity spurred yet another surveillance project. At Morgan's Hill, Wiltshire, the new research group set up specialized equipment, including a remote-controlled camera and ultra-sensitive directional microphones. The monitored field suffered a further invasion of its privacy by having its perimeter rigged with an alarm system to detect the presence of any intruder.

By three-thirty in the morning, damp clouds developed into a fine mist that screened the entire field. When dawn broke shortly after, the Sun quickly burned through the drapes of fog to reveal a pristine formation, yet nothing had been caught by the monitoring equipment. By the time the first person reached the formation, his clothes had become heavy from soaking up the dew, his boots caked in mud. But once again, no tracks, no damage, no mud on the plants, said researcher Mike Currie. "It was as if a conjurer had spread a large silk handkerchief over the table, waved his hands,

twenty-five of his sheep had managed to cross the barbed wire fence and were wandering about in an agitated manner. The large oak tree that stood beside the fresh crop circle began to show some unusual behavior as well: the leaves facing the circle had begun to change color abruptly, from summer green to early autumn yellow. The farmer also reported how the stalks were flattened perfectly despite the young age of the plants, which have a

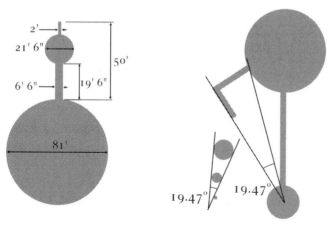

Figure 2.9
Left: Myers and Percy discovered critical measurements relating to the Earth and the moon encoded in this dumbbell. Beckhampton, 1991. Right: In this design they found a reference to 19.47°, the latitude at which energy up-wells on many planets in our solar system. Silbury, 1991.

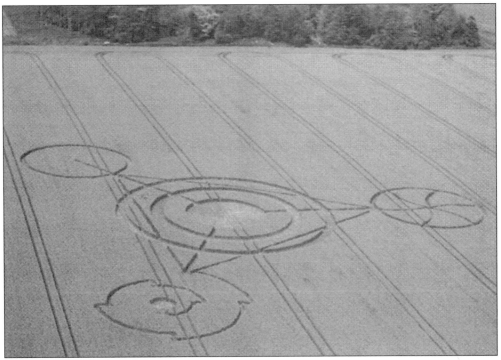

Figure 2.10

"Now Explain This One." The Barbury Castle tetrahedron.

whipped the handkerchief aside and produced, by magic, a white rabbit" (Wingfield 1991b).

Upping the stakes, the Circlemakers decided it was time to pay a visit to the British Prime Minister's residence at Chequers. The stately home stands within a highly secured perimeter of prime Buckinghamshire countryside, guarded by elite security teams and state-of-the-art technology. One can only guess the guard's reaction upon discovering the large Celtic cross-type pattern that lay in full view of the property and barely a hundred yards away from the house. One of its four circles had been replaced by an arrow pointing directly at the residence, then in use by John Major of the Conservative Party. A trident emanated from one of the avenues like a signature. Remember that Hindu symbol, the trident of Shiva?

Putting on a brave face in front of the local press, John Major's PR team brushed off claims that security had been breached in any way and said that the symmetrical markings were nothing more than a meteorological phenomenon. This was a notch up from the previous administration, as the equally Conservative Thatcher had blamed crop circles on poor soil conditions.

Back in Wiltshire, the town of Wroughton had been having its own share of excitement. During the night of July 16, the town suddenly found itself without electricity. The nearby military base also suffered a total blackout and, consequently, scrambled its helicopters. At the same time, residents around the nearby hill fort of Barbury Castle witnessed the by-now common aerial display of small, brightly colored flying objects, followed by what

Figure 2.11

"To create a Mandelbrot Set, one needs a computer."
Until August 1991, that is. Ickledon.

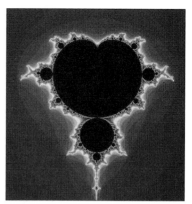

Figure 2.12

A fractal is a computer-generated figure in which an identical motif repeats itself on an ever-diminishing scale. One of the most complex objects in mathematics, the Mandelbrot Set marks the boundary between order and chaos. Ironically, mathematicians say that it also marks the boundary where classical science stops.

many described as a low rumbling noise, akin to that heard at Alton Barnes the previous year. Next morning, having given up interest in crop circles, the British press woke up again: "Now Explain This One," exclaimed the headlines.

Occupying 12,000 square yards lay a labyrinthine design, a collection of circles, rings, and curious circular features connected by paths making the shape of a triangle. What became known as the Barbury Castle tetrahedron (see figure 2.10) marked a quantum leap in crop circle evolution, because here was an unmistakable and identifiable philosophical and alchemical symbol representing the very creation of Universal matter.[9] Not surprisingly, the mesmerizing power of the glyph cajoled the press out of its tired cynicism with a jolt, provoking a knee-jerk reaction from the army which blocked access to local roads, an act that blatantly overstepped their peacetime jurisdiction in Britain.

---

[9]The tetrahedron, a four-sided pyramid, is a fundamental array utilized by energy to transform itself into matter, specifically quartz, which makes up 90 percent of the Earth. It is also a geometric shape underlying the physical Universe.

The symbolism of the formation, reinforced by its strategic location amidst the Neolithic landscape, was not lost on scholars of esotericism who would be busy with analysis for years, or on those examining the connection between geometry and energy, as this crop glyph's design contained yet another coded reference to 19.47°.

That the Circlemakers were also determined to bring orthodox scholars into the ring was evidenced by a matching major event on the opposite side of the country, this time in the heart of the scientific community's territory. Not far from Cambridge University, where French mathematician and fractal theorist Benoit Mandelbrot had taught earlier in the century, another showpiece crop glyph made its mark. Unmistakable to mathematicians, it appeared to be a representation of the Mandelbrot Set, a fractal pattern discovered by the Frenchman as part of a mathematical model explaining chaos theory. The crop formation was mathematically perfect.

In fact, it was unbelievably perfect for some of the University's mathematicians, who were suddenly drawn into the debate. Responses abounded: "Corn circles are either hoaxes or formed by vortex movement of air," claimed prominent scientist Steven Hawking.[10] Other scientists put the whole thing down to a student prank. But *New Scientist*, Britain's respected science weekly, brought some balance and objectivity to the drama and admitted that it was impossible to construct this, the most complicated object in mathematics, without the aid of a computer and a great deal of time.

The precision of this Mandelbrot Set, *New Scientist* wrote, was carefully studied on the ground by a local agronomist and biologist named Wombwell: "It was incredibly precise. Each circle was perfect, the wheat flattened clockwise, and at the base of the heart-shape it tapered down to a single stalk of wheat. Every stalk had been flattened one quarter of an inch above the soil. There were no footmarks, and no sign of machinery" (Davis 1992).

Beth Davis, historian and founder-member of the CCCS, who surveyed the formation just hours before its rapid decapitation at the hands of a defiant farmer, observed a new characteristic feature in the lay of plants: ". . . the stretching or expanding of each band of laid wheat to accommodate to the asymmetry of the form, with several radii from the center node. The two pendant circles have anticlockwise and clockwise floor patterns" (Davis 1992). As with previous formations, this one lay within shouting distance of barrows and numerous other prehistoric features.

On the night the formation appeared, a local woman was driving in the vicinity with her son at 1:15 A.M. The car was followed by a silvery-blue light sphere which flew within thirty feet of the two bewildered occupants before vanishing. The following morning the Mandelbrot Set was discovered by a pilot flying his regular route to work. It hadn't been there the day before.

In an incredible coincidence, the formation itself had appeared exactly a year to the day after an article published in *New Scientist* stated: "With each summer, the crop circle formations become more complex. How long before we will see a complete Mandelbrot diagram" (Hughes 1990)?

---

[10]Cambridgeshire *Evening News,* September 30, 1991.

3. OF CIRCLEMAKERS AND CIRCLE FAKERS

With a portfolio now bolstered by complex mathematical diagrams, 1991 had proved a good year both for crop circles and for the handful of dedicated individuals aiming to make the public aware of them. At least the discussion of crop circles permeated the public forum once again. Even if the Bratton incident had left the impression that "pagan worshippers" were responsible for misusing the nation's grain, or if newspapers such as the *Observer* stated that "Britain's crop circles are caused by squabbling birds," the latest crop formations had left us with a series of events beyond the scope of what human involvement could accomplish.

Circle fever erupted again, and so, on September 9, Britain's *Today* newspaper offered an antidote: "The Men Who Conned the World." At sixty-seven and sixty-two years of age, respectively, Doug Bower and Dave Chorley must have seemed like the world's most active sexagenarians, as the popular daily paper published their remarkable claim to be the makers of *all* crop circles. According to the report

(which ran for three days), the duo described how thirteen years' worth of crop circles had all been done effortlessly by them with a plank of wood, a bit of string, and some help from the moonlight.

More incredible was their home-made adaptation of a baseball cap equipped with a bent wire frame which, they claimed, was used as a sight-line to help construct perfectly straight lines in the dark by referencing distant objects. But researcher George Wingfield wisely pointed out the flaws in this theory: "To really make straight lines one needs a backsight and a foresight attached to the instrument with which one makes the lines. These would both have to be kept in alignment with the remote object. Even with Doug's head set rigidly in cement, the baseball cap method would never allow one to keep straight, even if one could sight on a remote object at night" (Wingfield 1990).

The contraption sounded as absurd as their story. Other claims were equally out of this world: When later quizzed about the technique they had employed to create the four rectangular boxes in standing crop on the first Chilcomb pictogram without signs of entry, Bower and Chorley replied that they jumped or pole-vaulted and the features were a result of their landing. Unfortunately, to jump from a standing position inside a tram line, this technique would require an Olympian leap of more than eleven feet, or an improbable thirty-five feet in the case of grapeshot circles, which the two also claimed to have created with the same novel technique.

Figure 3.1

A crop circle made in front of the world's media by Doug and Dave demonstrating their ability to accurately re-create flattened, spiraled crop. Morestead, 1991.

Apparently they had managed to keep their nocturnal activities secret from their wives for more than a decade (supposedly due to their wives being heavy sleepers). This, in addition to the colossal mileage added to their vehicles, the mud and pollen-stained clothes—supposedly their spouses had missed all these clues of abnormal behavior during the first thirteen years of their activities, only to become extremely suspicious in 1991.

The Bower-Chorley scam had apparently been the product of a boring evening at the pub in 1978; they did it "for a laugh." Their self-confessed motivation to improve the designs from year to year was a defiant reaction to the ever-increasing seriousness of "so-called" crop circle researchers. "It was like being high—we couldn't stop," the two embellished for *Today*.

But now they had gotten too old, and manipulating tens of thousands of square feet of wheat

Figure 3.2

Straight lines are used to mark the initial outline of a hoaxed crop circle. The rest is then filled in, much like a child learning to draw. Overton Hill, 2000.

proved too exhausting. Besides, their consciences got to them and they couldn't lie to their wives any longer: "When we heard the government wanted to make funds available for further research into the phenomenon," said Doug, "we both had the feeling one could use the money better for artificial kidneys and heart transplants."

Their heartfelt concern would have been touching had it not been for the fact that, throughout the 1980s, British government policy had starved healthcare and other essential public services of funds. It seems incredulous that money saved through the elimination of buses and hospital beds be diverted to fund what the government had claimed all along was nothing more than a meteorological phenomenon.

The Doug and Dave diatribe went on and on. For a public unfamiliar with the technicalities behind the phenomenon, their story went down like vintage port. Finally, a human face was produced which seemingly explained the whole fuss. There were no little green men, nor any message of impending doom from God, just two eccentric old jokers.

But the immediate purpose of the scam appears to have been the continuing discrediting of the research community. Following the national embarrassment at Bratton, Andrews decided to move to Connecticut to continue his research in peace, only to have secret agents attempt an infiltration of his home, his family, and the world's largest crop circles database. Meaden and Taylor were tricked on camera into declaring a hoax to be genuine. As a key public member of the CCCS, Wingfield was progressively sidetracked into fighting lies and accusations from all angles, leaving Pat Delgado as the last figure of crop circles research yet to be humiliated.

"Come on, Pat, admit you were had!" the headline screamed. Pat had devoted his time and money unselfishly for over a decade to educate the world about the most incredible event on Earth in living memory. He had taken the matter to Buckingham Palace and kept the British Parliament abreast of the latest research, all in the best interests of humanity. His sacrifice had been total, but now he in turn was being pilloried.

The man who introduced Doug and Dave, reporter Graham Brough of *Today*, invited Delgado to examine a new crop circle in a field in Kent at dusk; it was a repetition of the insectogram designs of that year. The ex-NASA engineer casually told the reporter that it was well-formed and appeared at first sight to be genuine. The reporter duly left the scene and Delgado continued to examine the design in the failing light. But after conducting some tests for electromagnetism, Delgado felt less sure about the pictogram's authenticity.

Brough later presented the two "field artists" at Delgado's home claiming they had made the formation, and all others before it. Aggravated by this transparent media stunt and the barrage of Gestapo-style psychological questioning, Delgado defensively stated, "If this was a hoax then it is another case of some of the people being fooled some of the time. Do not forget that in many different subjects throughout history, experts have been fooled and will probably continue to be so."

But to no avail. The setup worked, despite the serious lack of evidence presented. Incredibly, even the newspaper's photographer hadn't bothered to take photos of either the various stages of construction or of any referencing of the local topography while the pair supposedly "made" the formation; so, for all we know, the crop circle could already have been there. Brough managed to extract enough statements from his victim to make a story for the paper, whose readers fell for the crude deception. *Today* then issued a worldwide press release claiming that Delgado had stated that *all* crop circles were hoaxes—a complete lie. Inexplicably, the story was posted to countries where most people had never heard of a crop circle, much less seen one (Delgado 1992).

A thoroughly dedicated human being was unnecessarily humiliated by the Doug and Dave scam. After that, Pat Delgado hung up his cap and continued his research quietly away from the public eye.

Funny how two insects can damage so much grain.

Yet not everyone appears to have been duped. One saving grace came from the quality British newspaper, the *Independent*: "I find it easier to believe in little green men than in this story by Bower and Chorley," quoted one columnist, and a Swiss newspaper was equally skeptical of the whole episode. These papers may have been referring to the press demonstration later held by *Today* in which Doug and Dave were paraded in front of TV cameras to show the world their prowess at their field art. The results from the first hour of work were one complete circular mess—no swirls, no undamaged plants. So they tried again, this time for two hours.

Again, they achieved the same results: indistinct edges, imprecise alignments, and so forth. Doug and Dave's cosmic artwork resembled the site of a chance encounter between two sexually aroused elephants—with all due respect to elephants.

Some members of the press were non-plussed, but many others felt the pathetic demonstration constituted all the proof they needed, and returned to their desks to subject further newsprint space to poor reporting. The U.S. media accepted the story at face value. *Time* magazine regurgitated the *Today* articles, and ABC's Peter Jennings dished out the same to millions of viewers without any question as to the story's authenticity. Four weeks later, this anchorman also announced that the Soviet Union was to sell Lenin's embalmed body, a statement for which he was subsequently made to apologize. Curiously, no such retraction was ever made for the Doug and Dave story, even though their testimony was quickly breaking apart in Britain.

Despite having had his best friend figuratively shot down, Colin Andrews remained stoically objective throughout the incident. With pieces of hard evidence from his database yet to be released publicly, he quizzed Doug, Dave, and Brough regarding claims that had been made.

Constructed the first crop circles in 1978, had they?

"Yes," they said.

A flick through *Circular Evidence*, the most authoritative public reference source around, proved this to be the date of the first crop circle to be analyzed in the book. "So then who made all these?" Andrews confronted, pulling out a set of photos from 1972. In fact, crop circles were not a modern phenomenon; 298 cases exist prior to 1980, with one dating to 1590. Only recently has this information been published (T. Wilson 1998).

No, they hadn't done those.

Faked all 200 circles since 1978, had they?

"Yes."

Then who made the remaining 2,000 or so? No answer.

Had they been active around the Avebury area? There was an ominous feel to the question.

"No, never have been."

The twosome shuffled their feet. Avebury had been the most active area since 1988.

How had they consistently avoided detection by farmers, campers, researchers, surveillants, guard dogs, night cameras, infrared detectors, and alarm systems? How had they made the unusual ground features on the Celtic cross pattern featured on the cover of *Circular Evidence*? Not surprisingly, they adamantly claimed it was theirs, but in this formation the lay of the crop in the outer ring transformed from a linear flow to an unusual sine wave. And what about the colossal Barbury Castle tetrahedron? How did they do the Alton Barnes pictogram and an identical one a mile away during the same night?

An assortment of replies followed, ranging from "No" to "Not sure" (how can they not be sure of where they were?) with a smattering of "No, we didn't do that one."

During the cross-examination, Peter Renwick, the host farmer of the *Today*-sponsored Doug and Dave PR outing, remarked on the pair's handiwork: "You can see from the corn's lying that something mechanical has actually caused that, it's been caused by people trampling it. The ones I've seen are not like that; they are much flatter, flat as a pancake. This may be some of the answer, but not all of it" (McNish 1991).

However, at the time, there were no real crop circles which the press could use for comparison. Unsurprisingly, the convenient September timing of the *Today* exposé was such that all the fields had been harvested.

The body of the hoaxers' story hemorrhaged as more previously unpublished revelations from Andrews' database tore away at their claims. The pair had supposedly made a formation in the same field at Cheesefoot Head every year for the past fourteen years, yet records indicate this claim to be false; at one point, the struggling duo started attributing previously claimed patterns to other groups of copycat hoaxers. The patient and ever-charitable Andrews gave the cornered pair further benefit of the doubt when they claimed to have made the simple circle at Headbourne Worthy in 1986, even though Andrews swore hand-on-heart that the floor lay was so complex it had to have been genuine. It had taken two days just to draw.

This is Andrews' description of the detail:

The surface swirl was anti-clockwise and towards the center, which in itself is unusual. Most circles start at the center and move outwards towards the periphery, with all the plants lying together. This one had a top and bottom layer of plants, flowing in multiple directions. The surface plants had a brushed effect and consisted of a thin outer band which flowed to the periphery; at the band's inner edge, the plants diverged toward the center and flowed inwards toward a perfect center point. The point where the plants diverged, one towards the center, the other towards the periphery, formed a ten degree angle. When lifting up the surface plants I found two sine waves, 180 degrees out of phase and each emerging from the peak of a single sine wave around the outer band (Andrews and Delgado 1990).

So, did they make this one?

"No."

None of this ever reached the public.

That the two men had made a handful of circles has never been in doubt. As a result of the Bratton incident, hoaxes by copycats, cynics, sociopaths, and general pranksters began appearing, accounting for an estimated fifteen percent of known formations at the time. The significant rise in hoaxing appears to have mushroomed after 1990, ignited by the intense media interest. It therefore seems irrational that Doug and Dave, or anyone else, for that matter, should have persevered with such an endeavor when most of their work not only went unrecognized for nearly two decades, but was often positioned in such obscure locations that only a chance observation by an attentive pilot would have given its existence away. It is worth remembering that the point of being an artist is to have your work seen.

If there was one positive outcome of the hoaxes, they at least provided a standard against which to measure the real article.

But the bigger question here was this: Who had masterminded this highly effective stunt? Andrews detected the fragrance of deception all over the incident. He recalled how a colleague, a CBS reporter, was warned by a French government scientist that the British government would soon be presenting two people to the press as the makers of all crop circles.

During a lecture to the Foreign Press Association, Delgado asked Brough to explain a copyright line that appeared discreetly at the bottom of the original Doug and Dave story: "*Today* has paid no money. © MBF Services." The nervous reporter explained that the words had been added as a joke; if true, this is a violation of journalistic standards.

Wingfield, too, decided it was again time to make serious inquiries. With *Today*'s deputy editor Lloyd Turner on the phone, Wingfield referred him to the odd copyright line. "It is only an agency which had checked the details for us . . . a totally independent press agency, nothing else, a freelance press agency," replied the voice at the other end. "But they brought us in contact with these people, and hence they have the copyright." (Turner later claimed he had invented MBF solely to protect the copyright of the *Today* story. Since this contradicts his earlier statement, it is obvious that in one case he has not told the truth.)[11]

Graham Brough, on the other hand, wasn't so charitable about divulging information. When Wingfield asked for the address and phone number of MBF, Bough hung up.

It looked as if some digging around was going to be necessary.

Two nuggets of information were eventually unearthed concerning these mysterious initials. The first concerned MacFarlane Business Forms, Ltd., of Scotland, a company that supplied rubber stamps for the British government. Was it also rubber-stamping an operation that debunked supernatural phenomena? The second concerned MBF Consultancy, a research and development facility in Somerset; this seemed a more likely candidate.

---

[11]From personal communications with Pat Delgado and George Wingfield. The story is also detailed in Wingfield's article "The Doug and Dave Scam," 1991.

Wingfield recalled a conversation regarding methods of disinformation he'd had with another of his acquaintances, a friend who had worked for MI5 (a department of the British Secret Service). ". . . I was involved in it when MI5 circulated disinformation around the world concerning the Northern Ireland conflict. For this purpose we founded a seemingly private press agency, on whose desks our own people sat . . . [Handing out a telephone number] was to be avoided at all costs. If this proved impossible, a special number was arranged on the end of which one of our men sat."

Wingfield persevered. He followed the trail to Somerset and learned that MBF Consultancy was a scientific research and development company whose co-owner, Dr. Andrew Clifford, is a scientist with a Ph.D. in mechanical engineering and metallurgy. In the ensuing conversation, Dr. Clifford explained to Wingfield that his work was confidential in nature, done principally for the Ministry of Defence, and some of it involving the U.S.'s "Star Wars" military program. But when asked about his relationship to Doug and Dave, *Today* newspaper, or the mythical MBF press agency, Dr. Clifford denied any connection whatsoever.[12]

The trail ends here, and it has not been possible to further establish the connection between the British government and Doug and Dave's debunking tactics. And since we are dealing with an institution which even keeps the number of pens circulating throughout its offices a secret, the situation is unlikely to change.

---

[12]From personal communications with George Wingfield.

4. PHYSICAL FEATURES OF CROP CIRCLES

As we explore the events that have shaped the crop circles phenomenon, let's take a moment to look at the physical features that define genuine crop circles and at how these differ from natural or human-made phenomena.

Bends: One copyright feature of the Circlemakers is the anomalous bend that causes plants to do what they do. It has never been replicated by people. The feature is alien to farmers, and plant biologists cannot account for it. It is a mystery created by a technique mostly unknown to us at present.

The action of plants bending toward the ground contradicts their natural function, so the effect is all the more mysterious in crops such as canola. Canola (oilseed rape in the UK) is fleshy and brittle by nature, the hardest part of its stem being the fibrous segment at the base. Therefore, any attempt at bending it results in the plant snapping like celery. The same applies to a Canadian crop circle in Indian corn (maize in the UK) whose stems are close to 1-1/2 inches thick and require the full weight of a man just to flatten one stalk (T. Wilson 1998). Canadian corn crops are sometimes chemically treated to further increase resistance to the unobstructed prairie wind; their stems are cane-like, and as you'll know if you've ever had one whacked on your head by your kid brother, they are inflexible. Yet large portions of Canadian fields have succumbed to the bending effect as if descended upon by a busload of Uri Gellers.

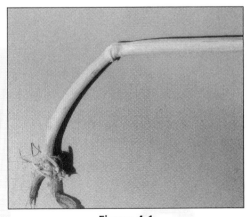

Figure 4.1

Bend in wheat.

Figure 4.2

Young barley rising due to phototropism six days after it was flattened. Sugar Hill, 1999.

The bend often creates another anomaly. Slide your hand under a section of flattened stems and you will find them stiff and resistant to being raised, as if they've been softened like molten glass in a furnace, allowing them to be gently worked and rehardened into their new and very permanent position. But despite this seemingly traumatic experience, the plants remain alive and well.

If they are not crushed, the flattened plants rise two to seven days after being laid down (depending on their maturity), as a result of phototropism, the natural process that allows plants to rise towards the Sun. However, since phototropism generally works on the plant's nodes nearest the Sun, cases where the plants have risen selectively at every node, and in geometric configurations (such as the forty-eight spokes and seven concentric rings at Corhampton) suggest that at some level an outside force has manipulated the natural process and programmed the plants to rise in organized patterns.

Figure 4.3

Despite requiring two different-size radii, the precision in the tip of this crescent is laser-like. Danebury, 1998.

Figure 4.4

A pair of well-defined "grapeshot."

The Circlemakers have created the bend in wheat, canola, barley, rye, and linseed. They've also made liberal use of it in sorghum and prairie grass (in the U.S. Midwest), rice (Japan),

Figure 4.5

How curving walls flute precisely down to one standing stalk. "Scorpion," 1994.

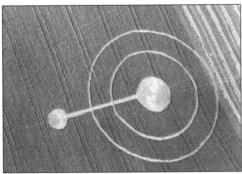

Figure 4.6

Hoaxers have difficulty in re-creating circular precision. Sussex, 1992.

Figure 4.7

Poor definition of hoaxed crop circle. Overton Hill, 2000.

and trees (Wisconsin and Ontario, Canada). Recent research adds grass, tobacco, brussels sprouts, potatoes, sugar beets, and strawberry plants to this list (T. Wilson 1998), but whether some of these are part of the same phenomenon remains unclear. I include them in the interests of reference and open-mindedness. Non-plant substances that seem to have received the same formative energy include snow (Afghanistan),

ice (Russia, U.S., Canada), encrusted sand (Egypt), and dry lake bed earth (Oregon).

Walls: Other than the bend in the stems and the shape in the crop itself, the circle-making force leaves behind no visible imprint. This force is capable of incising pictograms containing over a thousand elements with surgical precision, covering areas up to 150,000 square feet, and with such unerring accuracy

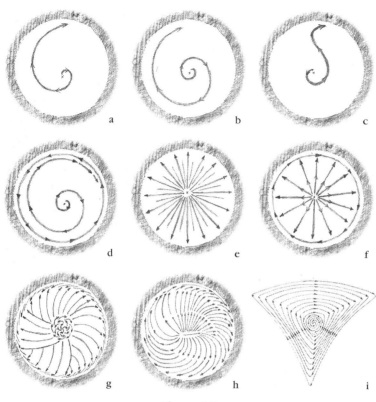

that "curtains" of wheat one stalk wide are sometimes all that separate one circle from another. The perimeter walls resemble the seamless curve of a drum, and where inward-curving walls meet inside a design, the central point can be defined down to a single stalk. (See figure 4.5.)

By comparison, human-made circles tend to leave a series of jerks and undulations along the perimeter wall, the effect becoming more pronounced the greater the length of string or wire employed. This is particularly true if the string is allowed to stretch or drop, or if the central pole wobbles, and where circles touch, an overlapping of areas often occurs due to inaccuracies in measurement.

Figure 4.8

Some of the myriad floor lays: (a) Golden Mean spiral single-turn swirl; (b) Multi-swirl; (c) "S" swirl; (d) Clockwise swirl with contra-rotational outer band; (e) Unusual radial burst, sometimes beginning as a small swirl; (f) Radial pattern with rotational outer band; (g) The Winterbourne Stoke "swastika"; (h) Multi-swirl patterns of 1987, precursors to the design possibilities of the late 1990s; (i) Selective and directional ability of later complex geometric shapes. (Diagrams E to H adapted from Andrews and Delgado's surveys.)

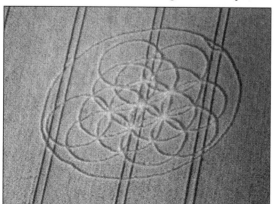

Figure 4.9

How one error in measuring cascades into a total mess. Hoaxed "Flower of Life," Alton Priors, 1997.

Floors: Before the advent of complicated pictograms, the crop circle picture language consisted of simple circles or multiples of them. Although relatively uninspiring by today's standards, their simplicity of design enables us to appreciate the intricacy of their floors. Had all formations been constructed according to one format, probably no investigation would

Figure 4.10

Undamaged crop circle with single revolution clockwise spiral. Note how the center is actually offset to the right. Callington, 1993.

have progressed beyond Meaden's atmospheric vortex theory (Meaden 1991). But the fact that plants in early circles exhibited all manner of organized directional flow confirms that an intelligently guided source was at work.

The most basic example of floor lay (the alignment of plants along the ground after they have been flattened)—and the foundation of nearly every crop circle—is the spiral, a form fundamental to nature. The natural spiral is expressed in the Golden Mean ratio of mathematics (its numerical analog being the Fibonacci Series). In crop circles this spiral requires anything from 9/10 of a rotation to six full rotations of spiral motion before touching the outer wall, the number of spirals depending upon the size of the circle. On close examination of such a spiral, one can see how it is made up of thin strips, not three-foot-wide swaths, the latter typically being evidence of hoaxers' planks or garden rollers. Because it so closely

follows specific natural laws, the spiral shape in crop circles is practically impossible to hoax successfully.

Figure 4.8 shows examples of floor spirals; some were initially noted in the meticulous early surveys of Andrews, Delgado, Meaden, and Mrzyglod (Andrews and Delgado 1991). With the development of the pictograms, the floor lays also developed into a library of designs of evermore complex shapes, but always with the humble spiral as a starting point. As the crop formations further expanded in complexity, so too have the spirals. In the year 2000, an octagonal formation at Silbury Hill had a sixty-foot diameter central spiral overlaid with four smaller double spirals at various points, each effectively creating infinity symbols.

The complexity of floor lays continues beneath the surface. Peel back the first layer, and chances are you will find a second one beneath, placed in counterflow and creating a

Figure 4.12
Man-made swirl. Overton Hill, 2000.

in undeveloped plants. Little did he know that only the previous day such an effect had been witnessed in a beautiful formation at Goodworth Clatford which, according to a report, was "the most breathtaking complex interweaving of stems, as the radially laid wheat burst from the circle, meeting the outside ring, and creating the most elaborate interlacing in the springy, undamaged crop" (Pringle 1993a).

Detailing: As an art director by trade, one of the greatest delights in crop circles for me is in the way the plants are intricately whorled into bundles in their centers. These are deft touches reminiscent of old-world craftsmanship, like ribbons fashioned into handmade bows around a parcel, conveying a sense of personality and care.

unique woven texture. The 1990 Alton Priors pictogram exhibited three layers of counterflow, while a formation at Jaywick, Essex, was five layers deep.

When self-confessed circle hoaxer Jim Schnabel was asked to create a pattern featuring this layered effect in immature crop, he declined, stating that it was impossible to do so

The "Triple Julia Set" formation makes a perfect example, since every possibility of plant arrangement was displayed in each of its 198 circles—a kind of candy store for cerealogists. The "wreath" (see figure 4.17 on page 48.) is exactly what the name implies: a tightly rotated strand of plants, about four inches thick, where the stems are densely interwoven around a central core and raised above the surrounding

Figure 4.13
The rise in complex glyphs requires evermore complex plant lay. Here, a clockwise path has split to the right, the crop gradually combed into a funnel effect, creating a thin passage between two circular standing walls. Liddington hill fort, 1996.

floor lay. The extreme angle of the rotation means the seed heads end up meeting the roots. Any attempt to pry these plants apart will destroy them; the "bird nest" (figure 4.18) is a variation of the above. The "cane hut" (figure 4.19) is simply charming: plants in a circular area roughly one foot wide have collapsed toward the periphery, approximately six inches above the soil, creating an enclosure resembling an African cane hut.

The central standing clump varies in size, from as little as six inches in diameter to thirty feet, but in some cases it consists of seven or eight lonely stems around which an entire circle wraps itself (see figure 4.20). Other unusual features of the circlemaking process include the "dorsal fin" (figure 4.21), in which a bunch of *inflowing* lay (where the floor flows *toward* the center) suddenly rises out of the floor and wraps itself in a very tight whirl motion resembling a logarithmic spiral. The "teardrop" closely follows the "wreath," but is rotated in the shape of two mirror-image Golden Mean spirals (figure 4.22).

The Flattening Process: Another stock-in-trade characteristic of crop circles is the way in which their creation process leaves the plants undamaged, unbruised, and unbuckled. These trademarks can be verified on location to help differentiate hoaxes from the real thing.

Despite the flattening, it is often possible to insert your hand between the layers of plants and the ground, and where the head of the crop touches the ground, you will not find any imprint of pressed plants in the soil. The plants in genuine crop circles also exhibit a springiness to the point where you can walk over freshly laid crop and feel the air getting squeezed out between swirl and soil, and detect

Figure 4.15

In genuine crop circles, the straight line is often an illusion achieved by laying the plants in subtle wave motions. "Pentagrams," Beckhampton, 1998.

Figure 4.16

"Catherine Wheel" effect shows one half of the spiral riding up the circular wall in nine segments. "Koch fractal," Silbury, 1997.

Figure 4.17

Wreath.

Figure 4.18

Bird nest.

Figure 4.19

Cane hut.

Figure 4.21

Dorsal fin.

Figure 4.22

Teardrop.

Figure 4.20

Splayed central clump.

a sharp crunching sound underfoot.[13]

Since the involvement of humans or mechanical equipment would compress the soil beneath the plants, it should be remembered that an interesting feature of the Wessex soil (predominantly composed of chalk) is the prevalence of small chalk balls that even a young child can crumble between his fingers. Yet lift the plant layers and these globules can be seen sitting there uncrushed. Alternatively, when a formation appears on soil containing small, sharp rocks such as flint (a common feature throughout southern England),

Figure 4.23

Intact canola flowers indicate lack of damage. "Eclipse" glyph, Nether Wallop, 1999.

the perpendicular stems rest atop the rocks without leaving crease marks, which again is not the case if weight is involved, as it would be in hoaxed circles.

When left to their own devices, the plants continue to grow and ripen. This is especially important when canola is involved, since any bruising either prevents the delicate, yellow flowers from blooming or causes them to die.

Where formations appear in a mature crop, one often sees single rows of greener plants standing upright, with flattened plants running through and around them like the interlocked fingers of two

Figure 4.24

A row of less mature plants stands unaffected by the flattening process. "Pentagrams," Beckhampton, 1998.

---

[13]Historically, observations such as these have been made with regard to new crop circles when minimal or no sign of entry has been detected.

Figure 4.25

Undamaged poppy lies upright amid flattened crop. The same effect is also seen in tall thistles or weeds that grow sporadically in crop fields. Alton Priors, 2000.

outstretched hands (see figure 4.24). These plants, normally lying at the edges of tram lines, have had their growth impeded by compacted soil, the result of tractors moving up and down the fields during fertilizer applica-

tion. How the flattening process is capable of discriminating between the maturity of plants is a mystery, as is the ability of the Circlemakers to select between plant species, for it is not unusual to find red poppies left standing while flattened barley flows around the upright flowers.

This extraordinary selectivity as to what is flattened and what is not extends to plants of the same type and age, so that odd single stalks are left upright amid a sea of flattened plants (see figure 4.26). This technique proved increasingly useful from 1998 onwards, particularly in crop glyphs involving linear patterns, in which thousands of single upright stalks were randomly interspersed throughout the floors. By implication, such selectivity rules out the use of planks or garden rollers. To further complicate things for hoaxers, after 1999, the Circlemakers sometimes arched the floor lay so that the parts of the plants most likely to have been flattened were those farthest *away* from the soil.

The seed heads are similarly unaffected by the gentle flattening force and remain attached to the stems. When one is fortunate and stumbles upon a fresh formation, it is possible to see how the seed heads are laid down in neat parcels or rows, the heads aligned as if displayed in a museum case.

Figure 4.26

Thousands of single stalks left standing amid the flattened crop. East Kennett "cubes," 2000.

Such features are obviously inconsistent with a "landing," be it by alien craft or planks of wood. Planked plants are either messily laid down, or, in the case of immature plants, laid in haphazard ridges that bounce back like shabby tufts of uncombed, greasy hair. Where force is applied to mature plants, the ripe seeds can be seen all over the circle floor, as the weight causes them to be dislodged from their protective heads.

Figure 4.27

Precision arrangement of plants. Where two or three contra-flowing sections meet, the effect resembles the waters of merging tributaries. Roundway, 1999.

5. Days of No Trust

Omens of impending catastrophe are rarely recognized until the building starts to shake, so nobody could have anticipated the damage yet to reverberate from the Doug and Dave epicenter.

Unable to contain the conclusive evidence favoring a genuine phenomenon, the crudest of political solutions—destruction of personal credibility—was liberally applied to the most public figures of crop circle research like modern-day Inquisition. Perhaps more sinister than the public debunking was the infiltration of research organizations by troublemakers and low-level secret service operatives, who spread rumors and disinformation in a seemingly deliberate effort to destroy working relationships. With the core of their operations destabilized, several research groups imploded.

At one point, two Americans closely connected with members of the CIA (one of whom is associated with intelligence gathering on UFOs),

bluffed their way into Wingfield's home in Somerset. The plan was for the three to leave together to attend one of Wingfield's lectures. Yet minutes before departure, the two "agents" excused themselves, leaving Wingfield to fulfill his appointment alone and the pair with a house brimming with unsecured computer files and confidential papers. A few days later, after his return, Wingfield discovered some of their handwritten notes had slipped inadvertently behind the sofa, and the contents left no doubt as to the pair's involvement in intelligence-gathering activities.

Jim Schnabel, who later admitted that he had hoaxed crop circles, demonstrated the ease with which intelligence eavesdropping had been conducted. At the height of the Doug and Dave disruption, Schnabel carelessly revealed details made by Andrews of conversations the researcher had made privately on his mobile phone.[14] As far as I'm aware, only the military

---

[14]Personal communication from Paul Vigay and Colin Andrews.

have the capacity and the clearance to tap cellphone communications.

Andrews was himself approached to sell his database for a small fortune, in return for publicly renouncing his support of the phenomenon, but he refused it, and still does. The CCCS, at the time headed by Ralph Noyes, a former undersecretary at the Ministry of Defence and member of the Society of Psychic Research, became riddled with infighting. Deception, suspicion, and strategically planted lies forced scant resources to be spent rebutting accusations. In effect, this was the same divide-and-rule approach once employed by despots to control the disparate nationalities of Europe.

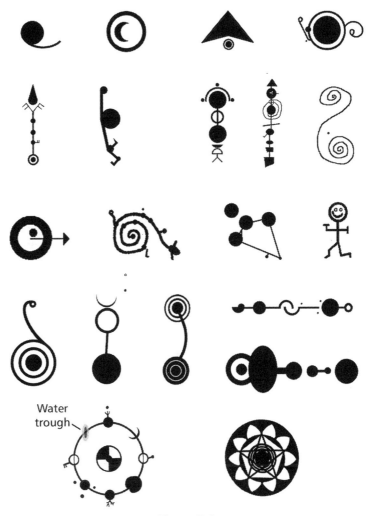

Figure 5.1
Selection of crop circles from 1992–93.

To add to the chaos, the media's about-face created an atmosphere of censorship towards crop circle proponents, giving saboteurs unlimited access to the public ear, and impunity to carpet-bomb the national and international press with articles full of fabrications and skepticism. Books and videos of negative bias were published, influencing even those with a previously sympathetic attitude to become turncoats. Serious research was starved of already scarce funds, while journalists and publishers turned a blind eye to manuscripts saturated with solid evidence of a genuine phenomenon. The climate persists to this day.

With the Doug and Dave debacle now in full operation, those still devoted to the subject faced another obstacle: wide-scale hoaxing. A conservative estimate reveals that as many as 90 percent of formations during the 1992–93 period were seemingly man-made. These years saw pale imitations of existing designs, obscene words, even a penis, together with squiggles, stick figures, and more added to the crop circle canvas, much to the fury of farmers—at least the real phenomenon created works of art without damaging the plants.

Appendages were surreptitiously added to existing designs, fakes laid beside genuine events, and real formations disheveled and sabotaged, all in a coordinated effort to throw researchers off the scent. Plant biologists were particularly hard hit when samples collected from manipulated formations inevitably revealed conflicting data in laboratory tests. Subdued, distrustful, confused— these words sum up the general mood throughout this period.

"If one set out to run a successful campaign to discredit the circles phenomenon, how would one best proceed?" wrote Wingfield. "Governments at war have, in the past, counterfeited large quantities of their enemy's currency in order to devalue and ruin the economy based upon that currency. The same strategy might be used against the circles by whoever is running any disinformation campaign" (Wingfield 1992b).

The growing number of foreign visitors to the circle sites must also have been a primary target of the discreditors. From an authoritarian point of view, it would have made better sense to encourage formations to be faked as precisely as possible, thereby forcing researchers to commit more time and effort to ground analysis. Yet with the fields contaminated with blatantly human-made graffiti, crop circle tourists would take home negative impressions of the phenomenon, wondering what the fuss had been about. This is negative advertising at its most effective.

That the hoaxes were cunningly planned is certain. The more complex fakes were sited away from regular, well-observed haunts, but placed confusingly beside Neolithic sites, just as the real phenomenon would be. The fakes also shared similar signature elements despite being dispersed throughout several southern English counties, suggesting that the same group was at work. A brave colleague of mine who successfully infiltrated one of these bands of criminals discovered they were being paid huge amounts of money to do their dirty work.

The high-profile team of Jim Schnabel and Robert Irving was also infiltrated, this time by UFO researcher Armen Victorian, who posed as a business interest during a phone call to Schnabel. In the taped conversation, later printed in *Magazin 2000*, the surprisingly candid (and in hindsight, careless) Schnabel revealed how the authorities were taking measures to discredit the phenomenon—not just the British authorities, but German, American, and the Vatican (Hesemann 1993). But Schnabel's most disturbing revelation was that he and his partner were being well supported to "feed information" and "take active measures" by a group far above the heads of national governments, by a "supernational organization" (ibid.).[15]

---

[15]Further analysis of Schnabel and Irving's motives are summed up in George Wingfield's article "The Works of the Devil," 1993.

Who or what he was referring to remains to be discovered, but plausible hypotheses point to the Trilateral Commission.[16]

It is interesting to note that the most concerted efforts at discrediting the crop circle phenomenon to date have indeed occurred primarily in the UK, Germany, and the U.S., where even today, well-worn Doug and Dave footage is played repeatedly on TV.[17] A close inspection of their made-for-TV crop circles is rarely shown because in the end, these forgeries bear as much resemblance to the real phenomenon as a box of cereal does to Chartres Cathedral. Instead, beautiful aerial footage of the most astonishing genuine crop circles is grafted to their story. "Implication by association" or "seduction by suggestion" are clever marketing techniques, so a shot of Doug and Dave stacking bricks and a shot of the Empire State Building can be edited so as to infer that they could have built the skyscraper, too.

It may sound ridiculous, but that's exactly the technique by which the ridiculous has become the accepted.

Doug and Dave's devious practices were enough to plant seeds of doubt and suspicion in the public's mind, encouraging them to turn away from the subject since no rational explanation was presented. So when researchers put forward their case, not only were they confronted by an unsympathetic media, their results became harder to accept by a public that had become cautious, skeptical, even condescend-

ing, to those still believing the "fairy tale" of nonhuman-made crop circles.

It is human nature to hoax—for profit, out of jealousy, or for attention—and it is shortsighted to suggest that the crop circle phenomenon has escaped its share of forgeries. The arena of UFO research is similarly rife with manipulated imagery and bandwagoning, just as the medical industry has its share of quacks, and the auto trade its "tin men." Records of crop circles now date back several centuries, so it is likely that hoaxing only began in earnest following serious national attention through the media at the end of the 1980s.

By definition, a hoax is a forgery, and forgeries must borrow from existing sources, so it was not uncommon at the time to see elements of designs already established as genuine to be influencing the human-made attempts, which typically displayed distortions and inaccuracies not found in the originals. However, there was one humorous aspect of the trickery that backfired on the jokers, and it revolved around Busty Taylor. Colleagues at his new job decided it would be fun to send the well-known crop circles hunter on a wild goose-chase by giving him exact coordinates of a field containing "a new event." They knew that Busty could get a plane up in minutes, so they had conspired to send him flying over a field they had checked earlier in the day and that contained no crop formations.

---

[16]The Trilateral Commission is a secretive group of elite financiers and political figures. It was formed around 1973 by David Rockefeller.

[17]Other footage shows people caught making a crop circle at night. This footage featured paid individuals and was filmed with the knowledge of the farmer involved, a point made clear by its originator, John McNish. However, the broadcast networks consistently hide these facts from their audience, claiming the footage shows people caught surreptitiously making a crop circle.

On his return from this field, Busty was greeted by a giggling crowd and was asked whether the new formation had merit. "Yes, very impressive, thank you," replied the experienced pilot, who even secured aerial images of this "new" crop circle. Perplexed at his finding something where they knew there wasn't anything, the coworkers meekly owned up to their intended prank.

Perhaps in resonance with events or in sympathy for researchers, the Circlemakers seemingly reacted to the mood, slowing down the flow of information by drastically reducing the number of genuine events. Perhaps by restraining the momentum, they could allow people to compare the real ones with Man's feeble attempts, promoting the phenomenon without doing anything.

Despite the situation, a new series of incidences were added to the growing list of "happenings." Above a field outside the village of Chilbolton, an ultralight aircraft pilot experienced his engine cutting out abruptly, to his horror. After a miraculous landing, he had several mechanics look at the troubled motor, but no fault was found. It was in perfect condition. The following day, a second pilot, strapped into a similar machine, had his engine also cut out over the same field. Luckily he landed safely, if a little bumpily, in a neighboring barley field.[18]

It appeared as if the air above this particular plot of land was not engine-friendly.

Next morning, the farmer who owned the offending field discovered a double-ringed circle on the same spot over which both pilots had experienced difficulties. At first, this was put down to coincidence, but later in the day a hot air balloonist floating nearby reported suddenly being sucked out of the natural wind current and his craft propelled into a route that led him directly over the newly formed design. The balloon then grounded into the barley next door.

Amid the contrived and primitive patterns, the few genuine examples that did materialize were hidden away in unusual locations so that anyone still interested in chasing the elusive force in the pursuit of truth was pleasantly rewarded. The one thing that could be relied on was the inevitable arrival of a season's "finale"—a design that not only capped the end of a crop circles' season but stood out in contrast and detail, summarizing the year's themes in one masterpiece. The honor for 1992 was bestowed upon a field northwest of Silbury Hill, through which flows one of Britain's most documented geodetic energy currents, the "Michael Line" (Broadhurst and Miller 1992, 2000; see chapter 12 for more information). As with the Barbury Castle "Tetrahedron" and the "Mandelbrot Set" before it, this new pattern was rich in symbolism.

The "Wheel of Dharma" formation—as it became known—looked every bit like a charm bracelet, its 140-foot outer ring anointed with seven logos, each perfectly aligned to their respective magnetic compass points. At first, it looked suspicious, for whoever had laid down this design had apparently not accounted for a water trough standing uncharacteristically in the middle of the field of wheat. Now the metallic object cut across the path of the formation's ring, effectively becoming the eighth symbol on the bracelet.

---

[18]Personal communication from pilot Graham King.

Schnabel wasted no time claiming responsibility for the impressive design, to the degree that he later used a photo of it on the back cover of his crop circles book—a book essentially lampooning the research community as harmless cranks and misguided eccentrics.[19] But the Wheel of Dharma corresponds to an important teaching in Buddhism, each symbol on the wheel corresponding to a path or insight to be mastered by the soul to

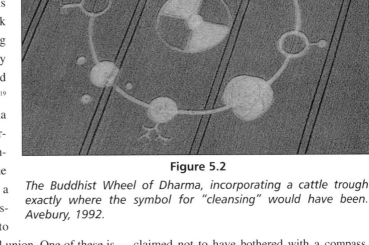

Figure 5.2

The Buddhist Wheel of Dharma, incorporating a cattle trough exactly where the symbol for "cleansing" would have been. Avebury, 1992.

achieve ultimate spiritual union. One of these is the Path of Cleansing, and now in the field it had a physical metaphor—a vessel containing water. Incredibly, the morning the Wheel of Dharma crop glyph appeared, the water level inside the said water trough had dropped over an inch, evidenced by the dark, wet band along the inside perimeter of the metal container.[20]

When prodded about his knowledge of Buddhist philosophy, Schnabel intelligently replied that the meaning behind the symbols was "a load of crap." He apparently made them up on the spur of the moment. Schnabel also

claimed not to have bothered with a compass, yet each symbol was perfectly aligned to the corresponding magnetic points; later analysis would reveal how the symbols were also aligned to the ratio 1:1.618, representing phi or Golden Mean. Schnabel had similarly dispensed with the services of a flashlight since there was enough light coming from the moon, he said.

But how had he managed to incorporate the water trough so precisely into the alignment of the ring? Apparently he'd stumbled upon it by mistake, the moon having suffered a temporary blackout. Further questioning revealed he could

---

[19]One photo shows a diagram of the formation drawn in the dirt on the side of a combine harvester, which Schnabel claims proves his authorship of the pattern. However, a communication by Paul Vigay, who was standing beside the machine along with a group of other researchers, claims there was no such design present, and so the photo must have been shot at another location. A number of statements made in the book about certain situations and individuals, and checked by myself with the individuals in question, have also been shown to be fabrications.

[20]Personal communication from author/researcher Mary Bennett.

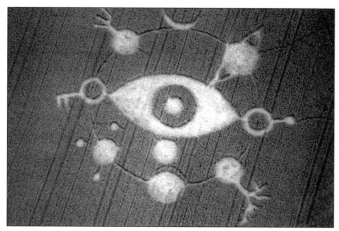

Figure 5.3

Schnabel's second attempt at re-creating the Wheel of Dharma. Lambourne, 1992.

not recall where each symbol belonged in the design. So, as a test of his faith in the matter, he was challenged to produce a replica of the glyph.[21]

In remotest Suffolk, away from the scrutiny of the media, the young American proceeded to indulge his critics. After hours of toil in unfaltering daylight, his replica of the Wheel of Dharma comprised a mish-mash of poorly executed symbols, ranging from the international logo for hazardous nuclear waste to a garden roller and a flying saucer (Pringle 1993a). By the time he'd finished massacring several hundred square feet of harmless plants it was obvious that Schnabel didn't lack a fertile imagination. Unfortunately, it applied to fabricating stories, not his practical ability at constructing philosophical symbols in wheat. A second attempt in Buckinghamshire, this time for the benefit of Colin Andrews' team, proved even less convincing.

If 1992 had been a crop circle year best forgotten in England, the story abroad looked rosier. Reports of activity throughout Europe began to multiply, with the events mimicking the same deliberate pattern of design growth already witnessed throughout England: simple circles, circles with rings, followed by the odd pictogram.

Hungary produced so many reports that a map on which they were plotted looked as if it had been blasted with buckshot. Of particular interest was an unusual triangular design, at which location witnesses had earlier reported a UFO making

Figure 5.4

Encouraged by the media success of Doug and Dave, all kinds of vandals began to use the countryside as a canvas. Devizes, 1993.

---

[21]The geometrical and mathematical aspects of this glyph are dealt with in David Myers and David Percy's book *Two-Thirds*.

strange designs in cornfields. Hungary at that time was a country unfamiliar with crop circles, so its example is useful to study. Interestingly, the Hungarians believed their crop markings possessed a healing energy, and parents took sick children into the designs to be cured. This was an aspect of the crop circles that had already been recorded in England, but the findings had yet to become public knowledge (see chapter 12).

Other reports emerged from Ireland, Belgium, Bulgaria, France, Germany, Italy, Switzerland, Sweden, Australia, New Zealand, Turkey, Brazil, and Puerto Rico. Always it was the same story: bent plants, swirled lays, association with sacred sites, lights in the sky, rumbling sounds, and healings. In one case in Russia, a woman held some affected plants in her hands and felt a pressure or tingling, something that she could not replicate with plants gathered elsewhere in the field.

The phenomenon also showed evidence of interaction with substances other than plants. In the Ukraine, Dr. Vladimir Rubtsov came across a perfect sixty-foot ring imprinted upon the lightly iced Mzha river, shortly after a UFO was sighted hovering above it.[22] Afghanistan reported thirty snow rings "with the detail of crop circles," as observed by an expeditionary group of geologists from Cambridge University in England.

In Egypt, a pictogram discovered in the encrusted sand near Port Safaga was all the more mysterious because of its depiction of a reversed "F"—the symbol of the *Neteru*, the gods of ancient Egypt who brought universal knowledge to humanity and under whose guidance colossal monuments were erected. This intriguing connection will have implications later in our study.

North America, for all its land mass, had remained relatively unburdened by visits from the Circlemakers. The United States reported only fifty-five crop circles up to 1980; Canada fared even poorer with forty-four. But during 1992, no less than thirty-one manifested across the vast, open plains of Alberta and Saskatchewan.

Throughout this sparsely populated region, farmers again reported luminous objects silently buzzing around the night skies prior to the discovery of crop circles. Surprisingly, the Canadians ruled out trickery as a cause because unlike England, Canadian fields were sprayed by airplanes, so the familiar tram lines from tractors were not present—there was *no* access into the formations for hundreds of yards, and signs of entry were definitely absent in these circles. But just like their British counterparts, the plants in the affected Canadian fields were undamaged, cleanly incised, and precisely swirled. Then, thanks to investigative Canadian researcher Chad Deetken, a crop circle in Saskatchewan yielded something unusual.

Farmer Rennick of Milestone checked the condition of his crop as a normal routine. One day, he repeated the exercise only to find a sixty-three- by twenty-two-foot formation in the middle of the field, with no signs of entry. Rennick

[22]Up to a dozen ice rings would later be reported in Canada between the years 2000–2001. Ironically, the Discovery Channel ran a cover story featuring Dr. Terence Meaden, who claimed this new phenomenon, too, was the result of atmospheric vortices. My thanks to Paul Anderson of Canadian Crop Circle Research Network for the information.

had never heard of a crop circle, so at first he assumed the unusual markings had been caused by the wind. Intrigued by the anticlockwise swirls, he scrutinized the unbroken plants with growing curiosity, noting that the soil outside the formation was wet and sticky, yet bone dry and hard as cement within the formation's perimeter. Deetken's report described how "the plants in the field were still green and subtle while in the formation they were dry and brittle, the seeds shriveled like prunes" (Deetken 1993).

Even more interesting was the skid mark made by quills which began at the edge of the formation and followed the swirl rotation towards the center. At the end of the procession of dark spines lay a previously twelve-inch-tall porcupine, now flattened cartoon-fashion into an "X" barely two inches thick.

The flabbergasted farmer examined the condition of the plants inside and outside the formation and established that the incident had occurred some five to six days prior. Surprisingly, the former twenty-five-pound porcupine showed no signs of decomposition, nor did it emit a rotting odor, and examination of the body revealed no wounds or physical damage by wild animals. Since the remaining quills on its body were also aligned with the direction of flow in the circle, it was clear the unfortunate mammal had been dragged into the center, then flattened by a tremendous pressure. But what kind of pressure was capable of doing this to a twenty-five-pound animal while leaving plants of far greater fragility unharmed?

Reports of animal fatalities in crop circles are rare. In fact, animals were known to relocate away from an area about to receive a crop circle. The farmer at Barbury Castle, for example, found his flock of sheep had moved to another part of the area and as far away from the adjacent field and its future crop formation as possible. But as Deetken correctly observed, when threatened with danger, a porcupine doesn't run away; instead, it holds its ground and curls up into a protective ball. So, either the creature happened to be in the wrong place at the wrong time, or had given up its life to provide a major clue to the circle-making process.

Colin Andrews, returning to England for the 1993 season, was quizzed at the airport by his regular taxi driver as to the latest developments in his crop circle studies. As they drove through the formation-free county of Surrey, Andrews related stories of unusual triangular designs that had recently appeared throughout a number of European countries. He had barely finished when a new crop formation in the shape of a triangle came into view beside the busy motorway.

Surrey, a county south of London, was apparently deserving of the Circlemakers' attention during that lean year, for it hosted a second pattern comprising a circle-and-ring with an inscribed equilateral triangle. The deceptively simple design was one of a number of crop circles under scrutiny by a mathematician who, working in Washington, D.C., was discovering that the crop circles contained previously unknown mathematical theorems (see chapter 10). The Circlemakers' intellectual profile was rising by the year.

Only a dusting of notable examples of the Circlemakers' art appeared throughout 1993, and the overall impression of that year appears symbolic of the contrary forces at work. Most patterns were elegant variations on the now-prevalent dumbbell design, even if the telltale signs of man-made attachments were evident. That the dumbbell was such a dominant feature was perhaps the message itself: in Native American lore, for example, the two circles united by a straight line symbolize communication between Heaven and Earth, spirit and flesh. So could it be the Circlemakers were aware of the turmoil and were encouraging us to maintain the line of communication?

The answer may have come in the shape of a pentagonal mandala, the 1993 season finale at Bythorn. Like the Wheel of Dharma the year before, this is a culturally shared

Figure 5.5

A rare appearance by the Circlemakers in 1993. This mandala was claimed to have been man-made, yet the farmer saw it complete nearly eighteen hours before its construction supposedly began. The rough path around the perimeter was made by a visitor. Bythorn, 1993.

symbol of great antiquity, representing for some the integration of Man with cosmos. It is also a symbol of healing, and whether or not the Circlemakers were trying to mend the rift created by the crop circle debate, the interesting coincidence remains that the farmer on whose land the formation appeared cared for sick animals. Further, in Eastern traditions, the ten-petaled lotus pattern in the circle design indicates the third chakra, or subtle energy center, which is associated with the cleansing of emotions. Again, given the current crisis in the world of crop circles, the timing was uncanny.

Despite its seemingly positive message, the Bythorn mandala generated so much acrimo-

nious debate between researchers that to this day even a casual mention of it ignites passions in those who stood on different sides of the fence concerning its authenticity. If there was one example highlighting the degree to which *agents provocateurs* had succeeded in destabilizing the objectivity of the research community, this was it.

Proceedings began after local hoaxer Julian Richardson claimed authorship of the Bythorn mandala. Richardson asserted that he had constructed the complex design during the nights of September 4 and 5. Working alone, the nineteen-year-old supposedly worked the circular paths from nine at night to two in the morning, returning the following night to add the pentagram. How he held the measuring tape and planked the crop simultaneously is a mystery in itself. Needless to say, he must have had a superb dentist.

Like Doug and Dave, subsequent questioning revealed flaws in the claim. Richardson's sequence of construction was inconsistent with the crop lay, which revealed that the pentagram was *overlaid* by the circular paths, not the other way around; the blueprint he supposedly used to create the masterpiece was identical to one drawn up by CCCS president Michael Green, who later admitted to have made an error in his hastily prepared plan—an error that had found its way into Richardson's drawing. And although the young man claimed to have constructed the entire design with one length of rope, careful analysis showed that two separate lengths with a difference of eight-and-a-half feet between them would have been required.[23]

Most damning of all, the farmer and his two employees clearly remember not only seeing the design complete, but seeing it on the morning of September 4, *before* the hoaxer claimed to have employed his rope and tripod (Keen 1994).

Despite their damaging presence, with the benefit of hindsight there is no doubt that hoaxers have provided us a type of litmus test with which to judge the particulars of the real phenomenon. This is especially so in view of the "counterfeit coins" that would inevitably contaminate the crop circle database, both in number and complexity. However, the bubble of objectivity and clarity within which researchers in the Meaden, Delgado, and Andrews era had conducted their business had burst. Now researchers worked in an arena of conflict, especially among egos. The polarized opinions generated by the Bythorn mandala was a reminder that no matter what the final answer to the crop circle riddle would be, it was important to maintain a balanced viewpoint and an open mind.

Writing in the *Cereologist*, Montague Keen pointed this out: "It should serve as a chastening reminder that assumptions about what skillful hoaxers can and cannot do are always dangerous, sometimes arrogant, and occasionally disastrous" (ibid.). Ultimately, the Bythorn mandala seemed to ask for a healing of the rift between factions, a cleansing of hearts and minds. As it happens, after 1993, much of the old guard either disbanded or went solo, making room for others to explore the circles in the fields and discover their secrets.

One of these newcomers was myself.

---

[23]My thanks to computer expert Paul Vigay for this information.

6. PEOPLE CAN'T MAKE THAT

If you could hear a pin drop in the newspaper world, it would have been among articles devoted to crop circles throughout 1994. With the subject now seeming like a huge prank perpetrated by New-Agers and bored pub chums, the media's silence gave the world the impression that the most innovative story exported by Britain since punk music was over. Yet three years after Doug and Dave's "retirement," the crop circle phenomenon showed no signs of abating.

Schnabel himself appeared to succumb to "the work of Satan"—to whom he attributed the origin of crop circles—when he admitted during an interview: "I actually believe there is a genuine phenomenon that is beneath all the hoaxing. I do not see what the nature of it is. Unfortunately, it's probably too rare for people to notice if they just go out in the countryside waiting for something to happen" (McNish 1991).

Yet in 1994, happen it did. A bumper crop of 110 crop circle reports, featuring sixty new designs of a complexity and magnitude that some skeptics found hard to ignore: interlocking crescents generating forms resembling spiders, scorpions, and ancient lunar counting systems. At one point, six pictograms were appearing per night, overwhelming research teams which, ironically, due to the calming effect of the debunking, were allowed to analyze formations relatively free from the interference of armies of curious visitors.

The first of two designs that looked remarkably like maps of constellations demonstrated new techniques in circlemaking, effortlessly laying down large expanses of crop into circular whirls, leaving tiny clumps of rings, dots, and crescent moons standing amid a flattened sea of wheat. Logarithmically spiraling arms unfurled from points whose tips narrowed like pincers down to one standing plant; the curve on one design even required the plotting of 120 reference points when duplicated on paper (see figure 6.3 on page A6 in the color section).

One person not at all impressed by the use of such complex calculus was the farmer, who was allegedly seen receiving a large envelope stuffed

Figure 6.1
Selected crop circles from 1994.

CPRI assistants parked their van in a lay-by overlooking a formation in the near-legendary East Field at Alton Priors. The formation resembled a magic eye. The small group was immediately set upon by two military helicopters that came charging out of the field below and proceeded to harass them by hovering menacingly close to the road. The team climbed back into the van and drove a few yards farther up the hill for a better view. Perhaps they'd stumbled upon a military exercise, although why it was taking place on private farmland was anybody's guess.

with money just prior to running his combine through the formation, despite the crop being too immature to harvest. Regardless, the Circlemakers deemed the information contained in their original creation important enough to merit a practically identical pattern appearing twenty-one days later (see figure 6.6 on page A6 in the color section).

That the army was still keen in all matters circular was proved when Andrews and eight

One chopper fervently chased them all the way to the top of the hill, narrowly missing the side of the road and a resident tumulus by a matter of feet. The situation was tense. Andrews took defensive measures and drove back down the hill. The military doggedly pursued: at all costs, whatever was in that field was not meant for the public eye.

Meanwhile, another group had entered the field on foot from the south and was making its

Figure 6.2

"Spider" consisting entirely of circles and crescents. Barbury Castle, 1994.

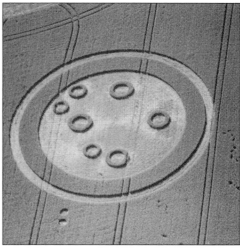

Figure 6.4

One of three ring-type "Galaxies." Froxfield, 1994.

Figure 6.5

The first "Galaxy" formation, destroyed by the farmer immediately after its appearance. Avebury, 1994.

way along the tram lines toward the center of the crop circle. One person could be seen hoisting a fifteen-foot camera pole aloft. Abruptly, one of the helicopters broke away from harassing the Andrews team to seek out the new prey, swooping and low-diving at these "intruders" to such a dangerous degree that the pole had to be lowered to the ground. Apparently, photography was not being encouraged either. Unfortunately for the army, one of Andrews' team videotaped the incident. It then dawned on the unsettled group what the commotion was about. According to Colin Andrews:

> The second helicopter flew away
> across the field, leaving us unattended

for the first time since we arrived. It moved rapidly across the field, to the south of the formation and just north of Woodborough Hill, and stopped as if under command to do so. Presently we saw what looked to be a small flashing light blinking just below and in front of the hovering helicopter. In size and reflective quality it resembled the object seen and filmed by Steve Alexander in an adjacent field back in 1990. As we watched, the helicopter slowly approached the pulsating object. When the aircraft reached a point directly in front of it, the object blinked out and re-appeared behind the helicopter. Within moments the helicopter began to back up until the object was again in front of it, and very close. At this point, the object disappeared. The helicopters then rejoined each other and flew together to the southeast, towards

Upavon Military Base, leaving us alone for the duration of our time at the site" (Andrews 1994).

One incident of a more benevolent nature occurred at Andrews' office back in Connecticut during a visit from Aztec elder Tlakaelel. Although scheduled to arrive at three in the afternoon, the spiritual statesman arrived at exactly 4:15, a time not exactly celebrated around the Andrews home. But then such are the coincidences of this phenomenon.

Tlakaelel was searching Andrews' database for a particular symbol, one he'd been given in meditation in connection with "the place of the last ceremonial dance." As he thumbed through the vast catalog of crop circle diagrams, the humble native leader pointed to a Celtic cross design, one which Andrews had himself premonished back in 1987. But the design was incomplete, and to it, Tlakaelel now added a tail of seven circles and a crescent moon, a design never seen before.

As Tlakaelel departed, Colin's fax machine gurgled with news of a new crop circle just discovered in England, opposite Silbury Hill. It was practically identical to the Aztec man's sketch (ibid.).

Figure 6.7

"The site of last ceremonial dance." West Kennett, 1994.

According to a later report, the farmer's dog began barking uncontrollably at 4 A.M. and continued to do so for the next two hours, presumably during the time when the symbol appeared. When the farmer came across the formation after daybreak, he saw several luminous spheres gliding along its spine. To add to the bizarre set of events, seeds from the formation were later used for a naturopathic remedy experiment. The patient, while suffering no adverse effects from the remedy, developed a temporary rash on her neck identical to the pattern of the unusual crop formation.[24]

Tlakaelel's premonitory crop glyph became the first of three imposing, scorpion-type patterns to appear, the largest more than 600 feet in length and distractingly visible to drivers on the busy Marlborough-to-Devizes road (see figure 6.8 on page A5 in the color section). Together with nine other designs, they formed an amalgamation of crescents and circles, symbolizing lunar principles; they were also strangely reminiscent of 9,000-year-old pictograms based on a lunar counting system found inside a Spanish cave. To prove the point, when this calendar was applied to the May 23 "Scorpion," the formation's shape accounted for the days from the last lunar eclipse to the date of its own appearance.[25]

Such details were somehow lost on science fiction writer Arthur C. Clarke. The respected literary figure chose to back the anti-crop-circle forum by hiring a group of five artists to execute a ten-petaled flower below Hakpen Hill for a documentary debunking the phenomenon (Clarke 1994). To make the small yet pretty flower design took the team two days in bright sunlight, leaving every plant on-site crushed, not to mention the dozens of post

[24]Personal communication from Jane Ross.
[25]Personal communication from astronomer and mathematician Gerald Hawkins, and based on research from his book *Beyond Stonehenge*.

holes pock-marking the clay soil. The construction time alone set a record as the world's longest-developing crop circle.

None of these crucial points were revealed in the biased program: thirty minutes of scant evidence and opinions from supposed "experts," few of whom had any previous connection with the subject.

No comparison was ever made to the genuine article with regard to such anomalous features as alterations to the plant's crystalline structure (as shown in chapter 1). Nor was the fact remarked upon that in this man-made endeavor the comparatively simple pentagonal geometry was inaccurate. These points make one wonder if the Sri Lanka-based Clarke had studied any of the growing body of collected evidence at all—even to wonder why, from so far away, he would bother with a subject that the authorities closer to home were coping with quite adequately. It was ironic that the author of *2001: A Space Odyssey*—in which a mysterious black monolith on the Moon leads to the discovery of a higher intelligence—should choose to discredit a similar phenomenon that manifested every summer on his own planet.

No doubt Clarke's effort fostered more skepticism. But one person he failed to convince was the host farmer. The attentive man had experienced the phenomenon in the past, so when he saw the mess left behind by Clarke's team, his suspicions were aroused. More importantly, he had noticed in the past how animals—particularly birds—stayed away from crop circles, despite the ease of access to seeds which the downed plants offered. Yet in Clarke's creation, the site was immediately teeming with wildlife.

Needless to say, the farmer was converted into a proponent of the phenomenon. But the real mystery was, who or what had possessed Clarke to undertake such a biased exercise?

Meanwhile, other events were taking shape across southern England. A sixfold flower mandala of superior craftsmanship appeared ten miles away in Froxfield, its 350-foot diameter easily dwarfing the Clarke exercise in scale and geometry. Later, Wiltshire's most complex design to date, resembling a spider's web and embedded with geometric ratios, appeared a

Figure 6.9

The Flower of Life, prime symbol of sacred geometry and ancient Egyptian metaphysics. Froxfield, 1994.

stone's throw from the Avebury stone circle (see figure 6.10 on page A7 in the color section).

Forty miles away, hospital patients gazing from their top floor room at the rolling countryside around Cheesefoot Head were treated to the sight of a silver disk hovering casually in the sky, shortly before a new crop circle appeared. A red ball of light also ushered in the first wave of Czech crop circles, three materializing at Klatovy just days after locals witnessed similar strange lights. A dramatic increase of radiation was noticed inside one formation which, as always, appeared in the vicinity of a Neolithic site.[26]

Hoaxers, too, were starting to interact more and more with these flying objects. Having gone home after making a circle, one man returned with friends to show off his creation only to witness a fresh formation yards away and a luminous orange object flying out of it at high speed. That incident was witnessed by the farmer.

In a separate incident at Clatford, two hoaxers were driving past a crop circle they had taken no part in making when a bright orange light flew out of it, spooking the youngsters so much that they decided later to contribute to the research instead. This second incident was witnessed by several other people. Hoaxer Rob Irving was also in for the surprise of his life: While checking out a formation, he noticed two girls approaching, a silver sphere silently gliding behind them along the tram lines.[27]

With farmers' attitudes about public access to their fields becoming more strained by the year (understandably so, due to a frustrating combination of constant trespassing and no forthcoming single solution for the enigma), people requesting permission to access the land often found themselves facing a barrage of heated emotions or even a double-barreled shotgun.

I bore this in mind as I dedicated more time to research in England during the summer of 1995, primarily in the application of infrared photography in an attempt to capture that elusive crop circle energy on specialized film. But as things go in this line of work, I ended up experiencing the energy in an unexpected way.

Ringed by a nimiety of prehistoric sites like a jeweled crown, the ancient English capital of Winchester became the center of the Circlemakers' attention during this season, giving the Silbury Hill/Avebury area time to absorb the previous year's bombardment. One bright June morning, Colin Andrews and I met near this picturesque Hampshire town to begin another arduous day of research.

First on our list was a formation barely four hours old at Whitchurch. My initial reaction to the forty-foot hooked dumbbell was one of disappointment, and I expressed this sentiment to my colleague. Something about it wasn't right with me, least of all because the construction was imprecise. Intuitively the whole thing felt . . . well, normal. After shooting some frames of film, we headed north to another fresh formation.

Perched on a steep bank beside the bustling A34 at Litchfield, the imposing bull's-eye of seven concentric rings lay within a halo of interlocking semicircles, creating a pictogram resembling a torc (a Celtic bracelet). As we

---

[26]Personal communication from Colin Andrews.
[27]CPRI database, Colin Andrews.

Figure 6.11

Selected crop circles of 1995.

parked on a country lane four hundred yards from the pictogram, I instantly felt a pressure on my chest, as if my lungs had filled with water.

When we got out of the car, the energy charge was instantaneous, practically pinning me to the door. I remained motionless in contemplation of the pictogram for a few minutes. "Are you coming in?" Colin shouted, having already negotiated his way into the field. The hypnotic hold on me was broken and I followed, still feeling the pressure of an unseen hand. I could see that, through his years of experience, Colin was familiar with what I was experiencing, so no words of explanation were necessary.

Scarcely younger than the morning dew, the formation stood out as if it had been etched by a

Figure 6.12

A design immortalized in Celtic jewelry, the "Torc" crop circle was later discovered to contain a fifth, previously unknown geometric theorem. In physics, the torc also represents a combination of forces creating motion, just as in optics it is a rotary effect produced by crystals and liquids on the plane of polarization of light passing through them. Litchfield, 1995.

acres of composer Andrew Lloyd Webber's country residence at Kingsclere, now the adopted home of an imposing five-petaled star, despite the property being manned by a twenty-four-hour security team. With the extensive grounds rigged with sensors, and microphones nestled in the hedges, a research team searching for the pictogram was apprehended within minutes of their arrival. But nobody had been caught making the pattern.

The elusive circlemaking force then delivered a series of designs featuring nested crescents which looked remarkably like astrolabes, the navigational instrument used for taking the position of the Sun and stars.

laser, its plants laid tidily in rows on the ground. These were good signs. Around the perimeter, the complex lay was interwoven, the plants abruptly redirected into semicircles; where these converged, the edges of the formation wall fluted down to a single standing plant with lathe-like precision.

"Not quite the same as the other, is it?" I remarked. Colin later confided that the Whitchurch formation had indeed been hoaxed.

I reciprocated by sharing with him the infrared photos which showed a marked difference between the morning's two formations.

The Circlemakers resumed their program on the morning of July 12, undetected, amid the picturesque

Figure 6.13

The precision of the "Torc" is admired by Colin Andrews. Note how the row of immature wheat along the tram lines has not been affected by the bending process.

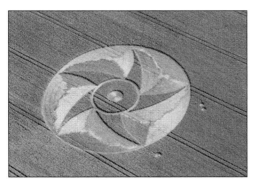

Figure 6.14

Star pentagram, on composer Andrew Lloyd Webber's land. Kingsclere, 1995.

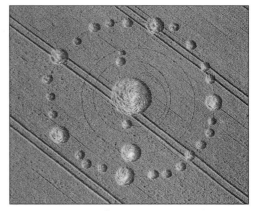

Figure 6.15

One of four "solar system" designs. Note the thinness of the orbital paths. Alresford, 1995.

These were accompanied by five crop formations that took the lion's share of attention throughout 1995, designs that suggested some kind of solar system, hinting of an overall theme based on the mapping of space. The first, consisting of ninety-five circles ranging from one to fifteen feet in diameter, showcased the intricacy now involved in the process. As I viewed it from the air in the morning light, the dew-glistened pictogram resembled a central "sun" encircled by two, fist-wide orbit rings, upon which sat two and three "planets," respectively. Farther out lay a cluster of circles, many lying untouched amid the virgin crop, while the low angle of the sunlight emphasized the tight swirl signatures. According to a meticulous ground survey carried out by my good companion Jonathan Wearn, only one of the circles in the group contradicted the entire clockwise rotation.

What were the Circlemakers pointing to this year? Their home? More pictograms, more teases.

Three days later, a second pattern appeared a few miles east on a large tract of exposed farmland at Longwood Warren, whose owner had shown inhuman patience as the Circlemakers had made this one of their showcase locations year after year. On this occasion the 240-foot pattern turned out to be a precise replica of our inner solar

Figure 6.16

Our inner solar system and asteroid belt, accurate to 99 percent. But why is the Earth missing? Longwood Warren, 1995.

Figure 6.17

Nested crescents. Such designs are reminiscent of astro-labes. Oliver's Castle, 1995.

Ever since that fateful June morning in 1990, Polly and Tim Carson, the farmers of the East Field at Alton Priors had become accepting of crop circles. In turn, the circles continued to make regular visits to their land like vacationing summer guests.

The Carsons have always been one of the handful of farmers who have consistently gone beyond the call of duty to help researchers and scientists pin down, even communicate with, the forces at work in this enigma. In addition to generous public access to their fields, the Carsons took it upon themselves to monitor their land. At one in the morning of June 17, 1996, one of the farmhands completed a thorough scan with an airraid-defying searchlight. Nothing to report.

A similar state of affairs was reached by a group of enthusiasts taking turns surveying the area throughout the night from the prominent location atop Knap Hill, which forms part of the northerly barrier to the East Field. A night of strange rumbling sounds ensued, followed at 5:45 A.M. by a new 600-foot long formation. Lying amid the dew-kissed barley, the 94 circles were arranged like a DNA spiral. The accompanying reports proved just as succulent: a middle-aged couple witnessed several luminous spheres hover above the East Field and project short beams of light into the ground, after which the UFOs flew northwards towards Avebury.

At this time, a Japanese couple living near the Avebury stone circle were disturbed by an

system, down to the planetary orbit ratios around the Sun, here indicated by a majestic sweep of thin, barely eight-inches-wide rings made of standing plants. A necklace of grapeshot represented the asteroid belt. Given that the precision of information depicted by the construction was accurate to 99 percent, whatever had been behind this was indeed proficient at astronomy.

The Circlemakers were also bent on communicating an important piece of information, since one feature of the design would nag astronomers and scientists for years: why were all the planets accounted for except the Earth, which was missing?

Figure 6.18

Selected crop circles of 1996.

unusual buzzing outside their home, accompanied by the frenzied barking of dogs and the bleating of sheep. As the objects shot past Avebury, the bells in the church tower began ringing—in a church that was locked, and whose bells require people to pull the ropes and are not generally rung at midnight.

While this was going on in England, a gathering of native tribes from around the globe was taking place in South Dakota. The purpose was to share with the world the prophesies of the Star Nation people—the off-planet civilizations who are claimed to be the ancestors and teachers of many of our indigenous cultures. At the gathering, Hopi elder Roy Little Sun told of an upcoming solar event and how "the power of the heavens steps down to the Earth. The New Moon is an opening of a gate of Star

Figure 6.19

DNA spiral or sine wave? Alton Priors, 1996.

Knowledge."[28] This reference was to a planetary alignment on June 16, 1996, which would "draw powerful energies to Earth." Is it possible those energies manifested in the East Field that same night?

The number of reported formations by now had reached 8,000 worldwide.[29] Although that year saw declining numbers of circles throughout Britain, the trend towards increasing design complexity continued, creating an unexpected rise in the number of crop circle photographs in the press, even if reporters weren't sure which side of the fence they were supposed to be sitting on.

Historically, a pattern was now developing, with each season contributing what seemed like a core theme, as if a celestial book was being projected to Earth, chapter by tantalizing chapter. The graphic nature of the new designs combined with the field experience of those who took them seriously, meant that progress was made in extricating all manner of mathematical, geometrical, and philosophical information and

just as in the first stages of the phenomenon, it seemed as if with every breakthrough in research, the Circlemakers upped the ante the following year.

But the pupils were learning the lesson, so the stage was set for what became the "year of the fractals." I referred to the first of these, the dramatic 149-circle "Julia Set," at the start of this book. To date it remains one of the most elegant examples of the Circlemakers' art; even discounting the logistics required to carry out such an endeavor—reportedly a 15-minute time window—within sight of one of the busiest monuments in the world, Stonehenge.

The "Julia Set" again demonstrated the ability of the crop circles to passively change people's perceptions. For example, a hostile farmer named Sandell was set on denying access to the formation, claiming it was all the work of drunken pranksters, that someone would pay dearly for this atrocity and other points supported by not entirely passive hand gestures. He was then calmly shown a recent aerial photo of the design in its majesty, Stonehenge looking on in the background. "Bloody hell!" exclaimed the farmer, his heart melting as he studied the picture. "People can't make that!" Hastily, his son was dispatched to the site. The enterprising young man daubed several words across a weathered old board and placed it at the entrance to his field: "See Europe's Best Crop Circle. £2 Entrance."

Which was not a bad thing. It enabled Sandell to receive compensation for the damage

[28]*UFO Reality,* Issue 5, Los Angeles, December 1996.
[29]CPRI database.

Figure 6.20

The elegance of this spiral appears totally at ease beside Stonehenge, itself encoded with many of the geometric laws of the Universe. 1996.

about to be done to his crop, and thousands of individuals were given the opportunity to experience the phenomenon firsthand, a rare example of mutual benefit and one worth emulating.

In spite of the attendant circumstances behind its appearance, hard-core scientists still contended that

Figure 6.21

The clear vantage point of the "Julia Set" as had by Stonehenge security and hundreds of visitors. Yet nobody saw it appear.

the unseen hand behind the "Julia Set" was that of Man. Yet it took a team of eleven people (including myself) five hours just to survey the formation. Over the course of the hot afternoon, our presence attracted the curiosity of dozens of motorists as well as a small

crowd at Stonehenge. How humans making this circle could have avoided detection is beyond me.

A molecular biologist who visited the formation out of curiosity experienced a sensation similar to intense ultraviolet radiation or

Figure 6.22
"Egg of Life." Littlebury, 1996.

Figure 6.23
A large vesica piscis, *symbolic of the Sun, cradles the four phases of the Moon, in the rhythm of the Universal cycle. Liddington, 1996.*

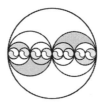

Figure 6.24
The principle of alternation, also known as yin/ yang in Taoist philosophy, is expressed by the equal division of the circle (representing God). As such, an equal division retains equilibrium—only through an asymmetrical division can natural growth occur in any organism. This asymmetry is expressed in the Liddington crop glyph.

gamma radiation exposure, with which he was very familiar. For the rest of the day he experienced nausea, but after sleep he felt an "intense physical well-being and mental clarity" (Pringle 1996).

Of the other forty British formations for the year, a quarter of them were suspicious to me. The rest, however, were stellar. Beneath high voltage wires at Littlebury Green, for example, appeared a 400-foot diameter design demonstrating knowledge of the "Egg of Life," an obscure esoteric symbol whose double tetrahedral geometry symbolizes the first three mitotic cell divisions of the human embryo. Several new formations were also steeped in Buddhist symbolism, such as two representing chakra points, one of which was attached to a snaking, three-quarter-mile-long avenue; another depicted a Mayan Sun glyph.

On the slope of Liddington hill fort, a large yin-yang design represented the solar-lunar rhythm of Universal pulsation, its floor lay resembling flowing water. Practically every head of wheat was precisely aligned in concordant ribbons. A few miles to the north, a perfect *vesica piscis* figure appeared near the Neolithic hill fort at Uffington.

In the U.S., a group of native-looking markings appeared in Laguna Canyon near Los Angeles. The three glyphs appeared on a distinctly unappealing, weed-covered construction embankment adjacent to a toll road. There were two concentric ring formations, and a third of unusual design—two small central rings with fourteen spokes radiating outward in apparently random fashion. Despite the numerous plant species on the steep embankment, only two were affected by bending: English plantain and wild oats.

Since this rayed glyph looked remarkably like local native petroglyphs, researchers Ed and Kris Sherwood discovered that the local tribes, the Tongva and Chumash, both share a similar symbol called the Sun Staff: a steatite stone incised with the Sun's rays, mounted on a stick and used in solstice ceremonies. After careful measuring, some spokes of the crop circle were found to be oriented to the summer and winter solstices.

An ominous message was tied to the event. Tongva tribal stories recount how a spiritual leader, Chingichnish, appeared several hundred years ago to show the people how to live in harmony with the Great Spirit. Desecration of the land would result in three warnings, after which nature would make the people accountable. It was perhaps ironic that there had been much local protest over this toll road which had destroyed the last remaining wilderness in Laguna Canyon.

Was it possible the glyphs had been created as part of the protest? Were the creators aware of the folklore?

At the time of the event, a security guard for the construction company remarked that he and his colleagues had seen strange lights and ghosts, frightening one of them to such a degree that he wouldn't return to work. Samples of the

Figure 6.25

Laguna Canyon glyph. Southern California, 1996.

plants underwent laboratory analysis, revealing abnormally large cell walls and the indication that the cells had experienced sudden internal heating.[30]

Back in England, crop circles continued to out-distance all human-made endeavors, logistically and creatively, and in the caudal days of July they had one more surprise in store. Following an arduous day of measuring, soil sampling, and plant gathering, my field team colleagues and I retired late to base camp. The Sun was beginning its inevitable descent below the hills cradling the serene Vale of Pewsey. We'd barely sat down to a pint of beer when a pilot approached us with word of a new crop circle he'd just seen from the air, on the side of ancient Windmill Hill, placing it on the same northerly magnetic bearing as Stonehenge. That should have been a clue as to what was coming.

"You remember the 'Julia Set'?" said the excited young man. How could we forget. "This is three times larger."

We raced up and down one-track country lanes, but with darkness now blanketing the hill like an ink-black bedspread we returned unfulfilled. An agonizing five hours of sleep lay ahead.

I am genetically indisposed to an early-morning rising, but on this misty morning I made

---

[30]The Sherwoods have done extensive research into crop circles, particularly in the area of "balls of light." Contact them at Millennium Research, Santa Monica, CA.

an exception. Braving the 4:00 A.M. alarm, we drove the ten miles back to Windmill Hill, thinking if this was as important a sighting as we had been led to believe, we needed physical proof of it before the world descended on it. We knew that only two nights before, a group of people had witnessed a display of unusual aerial maneuvers by intensely bright objects over the same area.

The persistent mist held the Sun in check, giving the English countryside that air of perpetual mystery. This formation was not keen to give away its position easily, yet we could sense its presence. We walked past one of the many barrows on this special hill and along a curving field, the bulk of which lay out of view. All of a sudden

we came upon a sight that rendered all vocabulary obsolete. Splayed out before us, the wheat was pockmarked with circles as far as the eye could see, the shape hard to fathom at first due to the relatively flat ground. We would have to walk the logarithmic curves to make sense of the floor plan: a battery of circles, anchored in three lazy arms flowing to a central location, resembling the vortex created by water in a draining bath. It looked like a triple "Julia Set" fractal.

The real challenge was how best to walk upon it. The tightness of the swirls, the pristine lay, not to mention the differences in design applied to each individual circle floor—laying a foot on this work of art would virtually amount

Figure 6.26

"Triple Julia Set." Windmill Hill, 1996.

to sacrilege, like painting the Sistine Chapel ceiling on the floor and then allowing foot traffic.

Our need to examine it was overwhelming, and yet our desire to leave it untouched was nearly as strong, so we compromised by removing our mud-caked boots. Remaining objective at moments like this is a challenge in itself. We stepped forward daintily, feeling the sensation of the air being squeezed out between the laid plants and the ground. No damage was evident. Plants were bent at their bases, but they barely touched the soil and showed no signs of mud or footprints; the soil inside the formation was drier to the touch than that in the surrounding field. Meanwhile, the needle of my compass behaved like a drunk walking the line, indicating a disrupted magnetic field.

Each of the 196 circles in this design was separated by a veil of one to two standing stalks. The formidable central circle was punctuated at the center by a thin circular clump of standing plants eight inches in diameter, with no indication of an incriminating human-deployed tripod or post. The entire formation measured 1000 feet, point to point.

After a moment to check on reality, I began to study the minutia of the formation. The construction detail at the center of each circle was different: a circular standing clump in one gave way to a nest of plants in another; one had had so much torque applied that the plants twisted around each other forming a thick wreath, while the next had the plants bent six inches above the ground, whereupon they fell outward forming a structure resembling a miniature African cane hut. It was as if the Circlemakers had incorporated every facet of their craft into one design for the benefit of anyone who'd spent the past twenty years stranded on a desert island.

Confronted with such details, the "hand of Man" theory was faced with logistical problems. If a group of people had made this, they certainly weren't going to stick around and individually craft 196 circles; they'd be wanting to leave as soon as the first rays of light appeared, and avoid getting caught.

All of this posed some interesting logistics. We'd left the area around eleven that night. At that time of the year, depending on the weather, darkness succumbs to light between three and four in the morning. That leaves five hours of night, maximum; then the farmers make their rounds and the hoaxers' game is up. That would allow 1.53 minutes to lay down each circle, let alone to stake out the computer-precise spirals with circles of varying degrees of diameter. It's too bad the Bratton hoax media people hadn't been at Windmill Hill that morning and showcased this beauty on breakfast television.

It seemed as if 1996 would finish on a positive note. On the afternoon of August 10, a few days prior to wrapping up the season's research, I sat down for a quiet tea in Avebury. I was approached by a man, a stranger to me, who claimed to have met me at the Barge Inn the previous evening—an odd remark since I had not been there last night.

I humored him, and he introduced himself as John Weyleigh.

"Have you come for tea?" I inquired.

"No, just wanted to say hello," he said.

Apparently he planned to do a night watch that evening to capture something related to crop circles on video. He wanted my advice on places where he could most likely see some action, a strange request so late in the season. But I reasoned to myself that he was probably only recently interested in the phenomenon, so I pointed him in the right direction. Besides, he appeared keen to stick it out all night, which not many are thrilled to do, given the damp, cold British nights.

"Adams Grave, Milk Hill, or West Kennett Long Barrow—they afford excellent views," I said, flattered that despite my low-key presence in circles research he should have come to seek my advice. Weyleigh asked where I could be reached, so I recommended the Barge Inn as a reliable message center. The young, timid lad then left me to molest my scones. Through my grandmother I inherited the priceless gift of intuition, and there was something about this apparently benign encounter that smelled closer to week-old halibut than fresh cream tea. I would not have long to wait before my gut feeling was confirmed.

The following evening around ten, I arrived at the Barge Inn with CPRI's U.S. coordinator Jane Ross, to see if any new information had been posted. I entered the near-deserted pub and was immediately pounced on by a very excited

Figure 6.27
The notorious hoax below Oliver's Castle. 1996.

man presenting himself as Lee Winterston: "Are you Freddy Silva?"

I was startled by the approach. I'd never met Lee—a filmmaker and cameraman—yet he scrambled off his chair to meet me like a long-lost cousin.

He claimed that a man named John had been calling for me since lunch time, and Lee had spoken to him on my behalf. John claimed to have captured an important event on video and wanted to show it to me. Lee had John's home and mobile phone numbers, and seemed anxious for me to make contact. Why someone would intercept calls in a pub for a person they'd never met seems strange to me, as the normal procedure is that the barman takes incoming messages.

The whole thing appeared orchestrated. Regardless, I rang John, who sounded nervous for someone who had just "captured an important event" on tape; I for one would be filled with uncontrollable excitement, to the point of calling people I hadn't spoken to since high school. I suggested he come over immediately before the pub closed.

We sat and waited. Ultralight pilot Mike Hubbard and editor Nick Nicholson joined us for a drink. Conversation hovered around a new crop circle at Oliver's Castle which had been found that morning; Mike had flown over it but didn't seem convinced that the crop circle was genuine.

About twenty minutes later Weyleigh arrived, apprehensive and nervous, but with video and roommate. Apparently he'd been camping all night at Oliver's Castle and in the early morning hours, wakened by a sound, he grabbed his camera and began filming.

The footage was incredible. About fifteen seconds long, it showed the panoramic view of a fully formed crop circle, obviously shot from the top of Oliver's Castle. In Jane Ross's words: "Suddenly two pairs of luminous balls of light appeared from the bottom right hand corner of the frame. The first set moved clockwise over the formation, the second set seemed to hover erratically as though inspecting or reconnoitering the circle. At the end of the segment a fifth ball of light shot rapidly through the center of the frame between the two pairs of light balls, from the lower left hand corner to the upper right hand corner of the frame and out of the picture. The final segment contained an overview of the formation from a slightly different perspective."

Figure 6.28

Taken within twenty-four hours, the mess of construction inside the Oliver's Castle formation reveals the hand of man.

Nick and I took turns looking through the viewfinder. We concurred. Five balls of light, of the type similar to those witnessed by hundreds of people, checking out a crop circle like sniffer dogs—all captured on video. Weyleigh was reluctant to play and rewind the supposed original copy over and over for fear of damaging it. Nevertheless, if this turned out to be a genuine piece of footage, it could rekindle the public's passion for the phenomenon. But after the initial excitement the little voice inside me screamed, "remain objective." Rather than rushing to negotiate media rights on the spot, I left a message with Colin Andrews to look at the evidence and see where it needed to go from here. If legiti-

mate, the news would sound twice as convincing coming from someone with his high profile in the subject.

But when Andrews saw Weyleigh two days later the story had changed. Weyleigh said he'd been trying to reach Andrews from day one. During a second meeting on August 17, an even more jittery Weyleigh told a different version of the story. According to Andrews' report: "He said that he went to Oliver's Castle because Freddy had told him that people would be doing a watch there that evening." (I hadn't, since the location was not a routine lookout position for me.) "At five in the morning he was awakened by a buzzing sound and saw a ball of light in the field. His camera wouldn't operate at first, due to moisture, but then did. He trained it on the field where he had seen the single ball of light and was rewarded with its return. He watched through the lens as four balls of light created a crop circle."

When Andrews mentioned this three months later in Connecticut, the penny dropped. Jane Ross and I looked blankly at each other: "What crop circle forming?" At no time did we ever see a crop circle in the act of forming, with or without the aid of balls of light, a fact later corroborated independently by Nicholson and Hubbard (without me prompting them).

There were two versions of the same video!

Nobody had taken the initial bait, so the footage must have been manipulated to make it too sensational for anybody else to refuse it.

The deception continued. When Andrews requested the footage for professional analysis, Weyleigh made himself hard to contact. Messages went unanswered, and eventually a phone contact suggested he did not live at the address given. What was going on here? A money-making scam? A new attempt at entrapment?

Several weeks went by. Weyleigh contacted other researchers, telling them how unsure he was of Andrews' motives, and disappointed that he hadn't called. The truth was, that without the original tape, video analysis would be inconclusive, and since the original was supposedly shot on the inferior commercial VHS tape width (using a camcorder), analysis would prove difficult anyway.

Despite serious doubts over the motives of this cameraman, what later became known as the infamous "Balls of Light" video (with the crop circle forming) entered the lecture circuit full-time, much to the delight (and profit) of a number of not-necessarily "objective" individuals. Their response to the evidence (which was generally swept under the carpet) was that Ross, Nicholson, Hubbard, and I had missed seeing the crop circle forming on-screen—a lame excuse, given the unanimous recall from these witnesses and my fourteen years experience spent in editing studios looking at details on small television screens.

One thing was guaranteed to attest to the truth, and that was the physical evidence at Oliver's Castle. So the morning after the initial meeting with Weyleigh I'd taken the precaution of visiting the site.

Arriving at the hilltop at six in the morning, I found the area shrouded in thick mist, and I feared that even from the steep 250-foot vantage point the exercise might prove fruitless. Then, as if by chance, a puff of wind brushed aside the milky white curtain, and for fifteen minutes I had a clear view of the subject later to cause so much concern. I shot some infrared film, then observed how the simple six-spoked snowflake looked crooked and a little rough, even at a distance.

I returned to the scene later with Jane Ross. The disappointment was immediate: where were the swirls, the unbroken plants, the fluid lay? The whole thing was a mess, irregular in flow and trampled in haphazard directions; the edges were ill-defined and most of the avenues were crudely misaligned. No electromagnetic anomalies were found. In fact, we had seen genuine formations in better shape after three weeks of trampling, yet this one was barely twenty-four hours old.

The ground evidence alone discredited the video. Yet like its predecessors (the Doug and Dave footage and McNish's night-time "exposé") it still ended up being paraded around the media and Internet, this time, ironically as proof that aliens are the ones doing strange things to crops. And while a few researchers continue to milk the situation in light of the evidence, my respect goes to those principled enough not to buy into any more deception, no matter how close to reality the "Balls of Light" video may turn out to be.

A private investigation paid for by Colin Andrews eventually traced Weyleigh to a film editing facility in Bristol, England. Weyleigh— real name Wabe—was a graphic designer and co-partner of the facility, which supplies video post services and animation to professional media productions. Wabe's business partner admitted John's involvement and said that he had urged him to come clean. Three years later, Weyleigh admitted his involvement, even producing footage showing him receiving my initial phone call from The Barge Inn.[31]

---

[31]From personal conversations with Colin Andrews. Full accounts of the private investigation initiated by Andrews is detailed throughout CPRI newsletters, Vols.#5:2, 6:1, 6:2, and on my website, the Crop Circular at www.lovely.clara.net

7. All Come Together

Seventeen years after Pat Delgado found himself at the entrance of a simple circle of plants graciously collapsed at his feet, crop circles had developed into a kind of real-life science fiction. Yet according to orthodox science that was precisely the category into which the whole phenomenon should be relegated. As far as science was concerned, the subject was nothing more than the recreational delusion of kooks, New-Age dropouts, and government conspiracy theorists.

At the start of the 1997 season, one only had to stand on the slopes of Barbury Castle and wonder what it would take for the phenomenon to be given greater acceptance at academic levels. Or would crop circle events overwhelm their present belief system? One thing was certain: Whoever created the six-petaled season-opener in the rape field below knew their trigonometry well, since it incorporated Ptolemy's theorem of chords, not exactly standard curricular fare in mathematics classrooms today.

This auspicious start signaled the beginning of a year seemingly dominated by symbols from esoteric philosophy and sacred geometry. Several crop formations demonstrated knowledge of the Qabbalah.[32] The first, a 150-foot long rendition of the Tree of Life, was greeted with divided opinions, due in part to the overall mechanical appearance and the generous use of tram lines, along which the straight edges of the design had been conveniently constructed.

Whether in reply to or in synchronicity with this unmistakable Qabbalistic symbol, a gigantic snowflake design appeared in the field previously occupied by the "Julia Set," this time witnessed by no one. But the more I looked at the design, the less resemblance it bore to an ice crystal and the more it revealed a coded reference, since each

---

[32]Qabbalah (also spelled Kabbala and Cabala) is a key to the spiritual mysteries of scripture generally associated with the Jewish faith, although its known origins date back to the Chaldeans.

Figure 7.1

Selected crop circles of 1997.

branch of this "snowflake" gave the impression of a tree bearing thirty-two spheres, as in the Thirty-Two Paths of Wisdom contained in the Tree of Life diagram (figure 7.3). Just as ancient doctrines made a practice of shrouding esoteric information in symbols, so it also seemed that the Circlemakers had encoded higher wisdom in living grain.

A mystery of another kind was why did the attendant farmer develop a surprising change of heart this year by denying public access to the crop circle? The normally forthcoming Stonehenge guards were similarly reticent with information, reluctant and uneasy in discussing the issue any further. Had a careful word or two been planted in their ears?

A third Qabbalistic symbol sprouted in Alton Priors, a formation consisting of an outward rotation of twelve equal circles sharing a common

Figure 7.2

"Six Moons." Barbury Castle, 1997.

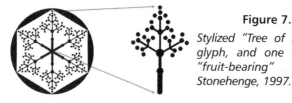

Figure 7.3

Stylized "Tree of Life" crop glyph, and one of its six "fruit-bearing" branches. Stonehenge, 1997.

though none were due for another two weeks. It later transpired that the natural vortex action of the torus is anticlockwise, so we repeated the exercise, this time with marked vigor as we followed the correct energetic rotation of the pattern.

Another characteristic synonymous with the torus is the balance of energy reportedly found in the center, the regenerative power of creation in perfect equilibrium. To demonstrate the existence of this still-point of energy, a number of dowsers located the energy center of the crop circle approximately twenty-eight feet northeast of the physical center. During the exercise, all rotating pendulums became listless within five seconds, as if their natural movement had been forcibly sucked downward by some underlying magnetic force. As it happens, the formation had been perfectly placed along an active line of electromagnetic energy running through the nearby long barrow of Adam's Grave and the adjoining East Field.[33]

circumference—a two-dimensional representation of the tube torus, a diagram of the spiraling, regenerative force underlying all life. A number of people (including myself) initially walked this formation in a clockwise motion, contrary to the lay; in hindsight, this was much like rubbing the cat's fur the wrong way. Consequently, we were met with nausea and disorientation at the other end. Four women who also walked against the natural flow on separate occasions all reported abrupt activation of their menstrual cycles even

Like the torus, fractals are a way of visualizing the creative process, and like the Julia Set, the Koch fractal is a computer-generated geometric figure. Developed by Helge von Koch in 1904 as

---

[33]These lines of electromagnetic energy—geodetic lines—form a type of Earth energy grid, and will be discussed in length in later chapters.

a mathematical study of coastlines (to show where geometric order breaks into chaos), it became the prototype of an extensive family of fractals based on the repetition of a simple geometric transformation. For example, take an equilateral triangle with sides of length 1, to which is added a new triangle one third the size at the middle

Figure 7.4

The twelve rings of the tube torus, quickly overrun by hundreds of admirers. Alton Priors, 1997.

of each side, then repeat the process into infinity. No matter how many times it is magnified, the original pattern remains evident.

Today, this technique is applied to the calculation of uncertain economic principles such as the rise and fall of stock markets, but on the afternoon of July 23, 1997, it was applied to a field beside Silbury Hill.

At two in the afternoon, a group of German visitors reached the summit of the prehistoric mound, and peered around at the patches of light and shadow cast by the broken cloud over the surrounding fields like sunlight through lace. Apart from the commanding view nothing appeared out of the ordinary. Two hours later the Koch fractal appeared, crowned with a perimeter of 126 circles and three outlying grapeshot, all within supervisory gaze of the truncated cone of Silbury.

Once again it was from the air that the visual beauty of the plant lay could best be appreciated.

The 250-foot design grew out of a tightly-spun thirty-foot circular vortex, abruptly conforming to its hexagonal aspect, splitting further out into eighteen smaller half-hexagons and creating the three-pointed stars on each well-defined tip. On the ground, the degree of execution had been so delicate that palm-height poppies remained upright and intact with strands of wheat combed around them.

Like the "Julia Set" before it, the "Koch Fractal" provided one more piece of evidence created under daytime conditions. Esoterically, it was also further proof to some that the hand of Divinity lay behind the crop circles, given how the symbol represented the Seal of Solomon.[34] To dowsers, in particular, it highlighted the part the Earth's geodetic energy lines played in the phenomenon, as once again a major crop circle had appeared upon the unseen Michael Line.

---

[34]The earliest known origin of this design is Asia Minor. To the Hindus it was the Sign of Vishnu, and they used it as a talisman against evil. Today it adorns the flag of Israel.

One week after the breathtaking event at Silbury Hill, this case was reinforced seven miles away on the prominent chalk escarpment of Etchilhampton, where not one, but two crop formations garnished its mile-long wheat field. A geodetic energy line runs through this site, its course meandering through the Vale of Pewsey down to Stonehenge, and marked with tumuli and long barrows left by our distant ancestors, in this case, as a mirror-image of the constellation Draco.

Etchilhampton's two crop formations were poles apart in design. The first was a circle containing a square, gridded with twenty-eight by twenty-five narrow, ruler-straight channels, as if a cosmic surveyor had been out measuring his territory. Some 150 feet away, and in stark contrast to this rigid structure, stood the second formation: a fluid six-petaled flower radiating with Atlantean mystery, the semi-circular lay from its petals creating a spinning motion from the air.

Both formations were contained within the energy line, and a measurement along their axes also revealed a perfect alignment to magnetic north. What's more, both designs could be overlaid on each other to within an inch of tolerance. Who could achieve such precise measurements? Amid the "Grid Square," the air perfectly still, I could hear a crackling noise coming from everywhere yet nowhere, stopping as I stepped beyond the perimeter of the circle.

The undeniable link between crop circles and energy lines came in one Chaplinesque episode, as our carload of people made its way up the road below Adam's Grave. Quite abruptly, all members of our party felt a heavy tension at the base of their skulls, which precipitated an unrehearsed "aargh" from everyone aboard; this was followed by intense chest pressure—we'd just crossed over a geodetic line connecting the Adam's Grave long barrow with various nearby Neolithic mounds, as well as the now-disheveled tube torus formation across the valley.

It felt as if something were brewing, like an electrical charge wound into an over-tightened coil. Was it possible we were sensing another crop circle forming, the pattern already programmed into the

Figure 7.5

The "Flower" and "Grid Square" appeared on the same night. Etchilhampton, 1997.

ground? We arranged a night watch atop nearby Knap Hill, but nothing materialized except the aroma of very damp clothing. The following morning, Jane Ross and I drove across to the opposite side of the valley. Passing through the village of Allington, we experienced the same bodily pressure. When we returned across the same spot in the afternoon, the pressure was still there. We had indeed crossed a second geodetic line from Adam's Grave, this time one that ran along the base of Milk Hill.

We were curious as to what was going to manifest in that location. Never had we experienced such strong energy and discomfort. Before the week was over, our curiosity was satisfied. At six in the morning on August 18, farmer Riley was out checking the condition of his ripe wheat below Milk Hill and discovered a second "Koch fractal" embedded in it, much like its predecessor, except it wore a reverse standing pattern in the center; clinging to its perimeter were a record 204 circles, all in various sizes and each with a thin central clump (see figure 7.6 on page A7 in the color section). The entire formation stood upon the geodetic energy line.

With a construction rate of 1.17 minutes per circle, the logistics were very much against the "hand of man." Besides, the location had been watched for most of the night and nobody had reported intruders;

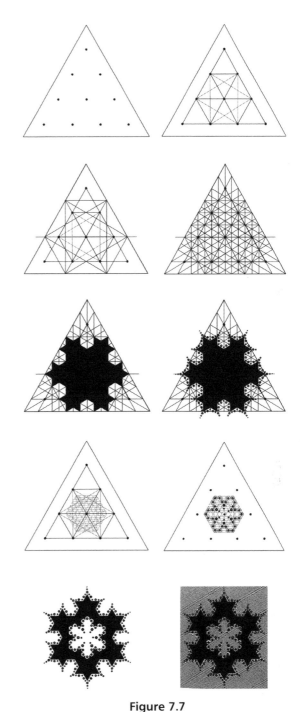

Figure 7.7

The geometric grid that would have been required to make the Milk Hill "Koch fractal."

further, the heavy clay soil was wet and clinging from days of intermittent showers, yet no trace of mud was present upon the horizontal plants, beneath which easily crushed balls of chalk appeared intact.

When I later sat down to analyze the geometry behind the Milk Hill "Koch fractal," I noticed the construction matrix was based on a triangular diagram of profound mysticism containing the Ten Words of God, also known as the Pythagorean Tetractys (see chapter 9). The crop glyph required connecting the ten reference points as a foundation grid, from which sprang the hexagonal framework; then it was a matter of bisecting each angle of the hexagon so that a lattice grid system could reference the various elements of the pattern. This was just for the *outer* part of the design.

To create the central "island," an inverse bisection was required, by which time—had the formation been man-made—the whole field would have resembled a skating rink after three periods of geometric ice hockey. To cap it all off, the halo of circles had to be dropped-in, referenced to each grid line and its corresponding space; finally, the complicated grid required a central reference point, yet the center clearly lay twelve feet into undisturbed crop. Perhaps a hoaxers' tripod had levitated.

I wasn't the only one overwhelmed with the mathematical scope of this art. A world away in Arizona, Rod Bearcloud Berry asked two engineering firms to bid for the job of staking out the 346 reference points that would have been required prior to flattening the wheat: each estimated six-and-a-half to seven-and-a-half days of work. Yet this crop formation had definitely appeared overnight. The statistics were no kinder for a survey conducted under cover of

darkness: that would take eleven days. And there was no way around it, stated the engineers, surveying was the only way this design would ever have been made by humans, and the lucky party would have been billed up to $5340 just for the preliminaries (Berry 1998).

Barely a week following the formation's appearance, Rob Irving was hired to create a crop circle beside the "Koch fractal." Academics were summoned, along with a sprinkling of researchers for the now-standard showdown, this time for the benefit of Sky Television. After trampling a thirty-foot diameter circle with a garden roller, Irving was out of breath and had to take a break before attempting four smaller, irregular circles. Despite the obvious physical and visual discrepancies, a greater effort was spent by the gathered press examining the pale human attempt than its superhuman counterpart. Like all other wonders that fail the test of rationality, the Circlemakers' crop glyph was brushed under the carpet of metaphysics—that comfortable repository under which the unorthodox is hidden from public view by conformists and maintainers of the status quo.

However, it seems the Circlemakers had the last word. As the satisfied TV crew finished filming the hoax, they regrouped at the fractal and arranged to film the farmer driving his combine defiantly through its maze of circles and hexagonal rays. The expensive farm machine, according to its proud owner, had hitherto performed with monotonous reliability. It broke down the moment the formation's perimeter was broken. This TV segment was never broadcast.

"We were asked to design a complex crop formation that could be made at night in under four hours. The formation we designed had over

100 flattened circles and a diameter of 300 feet, putting it on a par with some of the most complex formations to appear in the fields of England over the past few years." So read the statement from Team Satan,[35] a group of three hoaxers who also paraded under the moniker "circlemakers," a name seemingly hand-picked to generate maximum confusion. From now on I shall refer to this group as Team Satan/circlemakers; this will avoid confusion and minimize any comparison with the creators of genuine crop circles, the Circlemakers.

Already well-known as an active hoaxing group throughout the Wessex area since 1994, the three earned a reputation among cereologists for claiming some of the most complex circles. According to the images posted on their website, one would think they created the "Solar System" glyph, the "Triple Julia Set," the "Koch fractal," and according to Irving, the original "Julia Set" which, of course, they would have had to make in broad daylight beside Stonehenge while invisible. But then again it's far more convenient to claim a bank robbery than do the deed yourself, just as it is common practice for multiple terrorist organizations to claim responsibility for the same bomb.

In 1998 though, they found themselves in the enviable position of being flown halfway across the world to New Zealand, to create a crop circle for the benefit of a TV documentary to be shown in the U.S. One presumes Team Satan was well compensated for its time and effort; the farmer alone was paid three times the market rate for his soon-to-be demolished crop.

When images of their handiwork began to surface, it looked as if the crop circle phenomenon was again on the verge of being explained away to the public. The grouping of circles constructed to mimic the "Triple Julia Set" was impressive at first glance, even if a third of the size of the original; it was far messier, and given its basic triangular geometry, skewed and misaligned. At its center lay a circle with a cleft chopped out of the top, a naïve representation of a Mandelbrot Set. But to the team's credit it was a formidable achievement, even if they failed the time limit (it actually took them longer than five hours).

However, accounts by the farmer and a New Zealand newspaper suggested the endeavor was not as innocent as it first appeared: The production crew had employed the services of two forty-ton cranes. Why these should have been used in circle-making was anybody's guess, particularly as equipment of this bulk would have to have been air-lifted into this inaccessible part of the South Island, where even the sheep outnumber the people. The answer came when the documentary premiered in America on NBC in May 1998.

With a running time of one hour, *Unmasked: The Secrets of Deception* devoted just fifteen minutes to the team's endeavor. To establish its credibility as a "serious documentary," the program began with footage from casinos, in which hidden cameras filmed gamblers in the act of cheating. The second segment attempted to demystify séances by demonstrating how, with the aid of hidden wires, candelabras and other objects are made to fly around the room in the dark. This was followed by an exposé discrediting mind readers, who stood accused of deceiving their clients by using black coffee as a

---

[35]John Lundberg and Rod Dickinson, the circlemakers' website (www.circlemakers.org), April 1998.

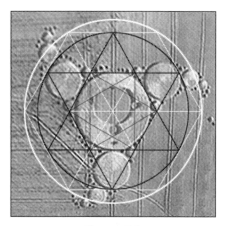

Figure 7.8

Made-for-TV. Elaborate but rough hoax created under artificial lighting by Team Satan/circlemakers. The whole design fails to hit much of the triangular/hexagonal geometry. Dunearn, New Zealand, 1998.

mirror in which they saw designs their clients drew on cards; a stab at psychic surgery practitioners in the Philippines rounded off this seemingly harmless investigation of the mysterious at work.

I say harmless because at first glance all of this seems credible. Gambling cheats caught on hidden camera—what could be more convincing? But flying candelabras and other such parlor trickery were last used during the Victorian era, and coffee and mind readers don't go together, since coffee is a stimulant and hardly useful for inducing psychic activity, which requires the mind to be relaxed.

Clearly, the program was designed to gain the viewer's initial trust, after which it could set up all manner of subjects as frauds simply by association. Thus the stage was finally set for the sharp-dressed presenter to announce "the biggest scam of all—crop circles." After a brief overview and pretty aerial footage, here are some of the claims the writers made, followed

by my clarifications: "Researchers say there's no physical evidence of human construction . . . that there's no disturbance of soil, nor footprints." Actually, researchers say that traces of human involvement, in the shape of footprints, disturbed soil, and damaged plants are signs of foul play.

"Often the ground is hard [inside crop circles]." No, often the ground is muddy in the British Isles. Perhaps the writers had forgotten that it has been known, on occasion, for rain to fall there. In fact, 60 percent of crop circles appear on rainy nights.

Then we are told that the hoaxers "weren't interested in sacred geometry." That was hardly surprising, for despite its carefully designed blueprint, the New Zealand formation was not laid to accurate geometric principles. Such a statement is also an admission of ineptitude, since sacred geometry and obscure mathematical theorems had by now been proven to exist in genuine formations, and fixed mathematical values simply cannot be arrived at by chance (as we'll see in chapter 9).

"No one has ever been caught—until now!" and "made by unknown visitors." Surely if they were caught they *must* be known? The truth is, the whole production was carefully planned on-site over the course of three days, with townspeople turning up to watch as the crew went to work. Even the farmer showed up.

"Another discovery is made as the Sun rises over the crop," the narrator continues, implying that the film crew stumbled upon the hoaxers by accident, in much the same way that Napoleon found himself one morning to be the ruler of Europe by mistake. Joking aside, when the presenter insinuated that the operation had been conducted with the mere help of the moonlight, the penny dropped on those two cranes.

Apparently the New Zealand night turned out to be much darker than its English counterpart, so much so that two powerful lights needed to be suspended over the field to allow the field forgers to do their business. One could argue that video cameras require light to record detail, in which case why was the entire sequence not shot through night-vision equipment? Alternatively they could have waited for that cheaper alternative, the Sun. In any case, neither the crane nor the artificial lighting were seen on air.

The program went on to state how "communication in the dark field was made by a series of silent signals and by holding planks of wood in the air." This may be indisputable, given that even a raised index finger can be seen on the other side of a field when bathed in the glow of ten thousand watts of light. But try it in the dark, when anything twenty feet in front of you has as much luminescence as a lump of coal, and see if you can create a near-perfect geometrical shape, coordinated with your partner standing 300 feet away. Of course, one could paint the planks white, but then why would hoaxers need to wear black camouflage? The height of the plank would also have to be extraordinary, given that some formations in England are found on curved slopes with gradients of more than thirty feet. This means that extraordinary biceps must be standard equipment for hoaxers, too.

Minute by agonizing minute, an elaborate con was perpetrated on an unsuspecting American public, killing the subject of crop circles for good in their hearts and minds by discrediting the phenomenon and its believers through association with seemingly fraudulent subject matter. The episode was laughable if one knew both sides of the story, but sadly, that excluded the majority of the TV-viewing world. Without showing as much as a lintball of research or comparative analysis, nor any counterpoint by anyone from the opposite camp of opinion about the phenomenon, this sixty minutes of televised mischief no doubt succeeded in alienating another segment of potential supporters.

Perched on the other side of the globe, sparsely populated New Zealand was carefully chosen as the venue so as to prevent experienced, pro-crop circle researchers from attending. As an extra precaution, the formation was harvested the moment filming stopped. Yet not all such tracks were covered, for it was later revealed to me that the entire design had been marked out with stakes and string prior to filming—small wonder the three Team Satanists are seen creating a coherent geometric pattern so effortlessly on time-lapse film. They couldn't have gotten away with this back in Wessex. The farmer himself saw the production team filming the set up as he inspected the field out of concern for damage to areas of crop that had not been paid for.[36]

Naturally, such incriminating evidence was never disclosed on air.

To be fair, I was asked by a member of Team Satan/circlemakers to contribute any questions which could be used in discussion on the program, and I did. Not one made it on air. However, one truthful statement by the producers of this

[36]My thanks to Doug Parker and Dr. Jonathan Sherwood for obtaining the initial information. The story was reported by John Cutt, "No UFO Over Dunearn" in *The Southland Times*. References to *Unmasked: The Secrets of Deception* from the U.S. TV documentary aired on NBC TV, May 1998, produced by California-based Tri-Crown Productions.

Figure 7.9

Selected crop circles of 1998.

that spring my intuition told me the year would be dominated by sevenfold geometry for the first time. On a hunch I applied a heptagonal (seven-sided) framework over the Weyhill crop circle. The geometry fitted, and by the end of the 1998 season, three major formations would also demonstrate it.

During a summer when farmers lost the majority of their grain crops to an incessant barrage of gales and rain, hoaxes appeared to account for a proportion of the crop formations, perhaps the worst count of hoaxes since 1992. At least three gangs were hard at work in the Avebury area, evidenced by the general appearance of designs which, by early July, could be categorized by lack of aesthetics alone. The bulk of the shoddy designs were attributed to newcomers, possibly inspired by the fresh wave of TV debunking. A "stingray" formation, for example, had man-made elements grafted on to the original design, its tail in particular.

This appears to have generated a response from the real Circlemakers in the form of a nearby double pentagram, which came with a record of subsequent health incidents. At West Woods, a pattern referred to as "The Queen" (figure 7.12 on page 96) lay across the field from its earlier,

masterpiece of deception was said right at the beginning: "Crop circles are one of the most misunderstood phenomena." With programs like this, it's no wonder.

Thus began the 1998 crop circle season.

Meanwhile back in England, a pilot taking off from the airstrip near Weyhill on April 19 stumbled upon the first formation, a low-key circle overlapped by a circle-and-ring. Having figured out the genuine Circlemakers' capacity to encode the season's geometric message into the first salvo of designs, I labored over the formation's blueprint and uncovered a pentagonal code that would appear in crop circles throughout the season. But

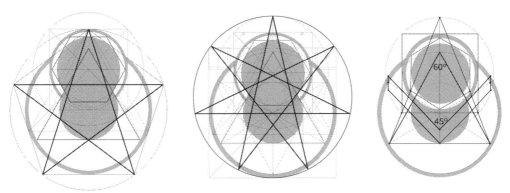

Figure 7.10

Encoded geometry. Left: Triangular and pentagonal; Middle: Heptagonal; Right: The encoded geometry reveals two figures associated with the Freemasons, the set square and compass. Weyhill, 1998.

mostly genuine counterpart; a raggedly executed fractal pattern allegedly commissioned by a leading British newspaper was also attempted behind Silbury Hill.

Undeterred by the hoaxes, the first of the heptagonal patterns showed itself in the East Field in mid-July. Two weeks later on August 8, a group of hoaxers attempted to upstage this by entering the field below Tawsmead Copse under cover of darkness. According to a personal communication to me from a member of the team, they had barely started work when two balls of light chased them. Taking this as a "Do not disturb this field" sign, the group left.

Figure 7.11

"Double Pentagram," with earlier "stingray" in the background. Beckhampton, 1998.

Figure 7.12

"The Queen," one of a number of hoaxes during 1998. West Woods.

Their story appears to have some merit. Orange balls of light *were* seen flying around the copse that night by a group camping across the vale on Knapp Hill and by a second inde-pendent group sitting up on Adam's Grave long barrow. Then, at 5 A.M., a resident walking in the direction of the copse saw the clouds part "as if two glass tubes had descended from the sky." Two hours later, an elaborate seven-pointed fractal glyph appeared. (Incidentally, a separate witness saw the same "glass tube" effect shortly before the appearance of the first West Woods formation.)

Although the formation was hastily cut down, a ground investigation of the new Tawsmead heptagon revealed three mag-netic features—positive, negative, and neu-tral—generated by the three sizes of grapeshot around its perimeter. Barely a hundred feet from the heptagon lay the beginnings of the hoaxers' simple circle-and-ring.

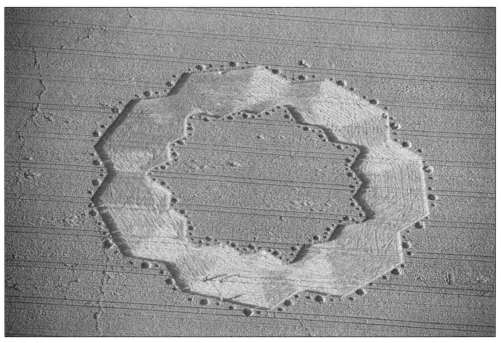

Figure 7.13

One of many predicted crop circles bearing sevenfold geometry. Tawsmead Copse, 1998.

When a third heptagonal formation appeared below Danebury hill fort, I felt as if subconscious communication had indeed been going on, a feeling strengthened when John Sayer, editor of the *Cereologist*, revealed to me that he had dreamt the same design, and whose sketch is similar to the beautiful pinwheel formation.

Someone else enjoying a close relationship with the Circlemakers was a young photographer named Tony Crerar, who on May 3 spent his time photographing the area around Avebury, starting with views from the long barrow at West Kennett. By 3 A.M. the following morning, he had finished his assignment of photographing the setting Moon from the strategic vantage point of the Sanctuary. From this ancient temple, Silbury Hill rose above the undulating landscape and glistened in the pale moonlight; West Kennett Long Barrow lay to the left. Tony packed up his gear and returned to his car for a quick snooze, but with the increasing chill in the air, he took a short drive to warm up instead.

At half past four, he drove west. The rape field lying below the long barrow appeared pristine in the half-light of the creeping dawn. Upon his return to the Sanctuary

half an hour later, he saw that a formidable 250-foot-wide formation had been imprinted on its golden surface (Crerar 1998). The ring of

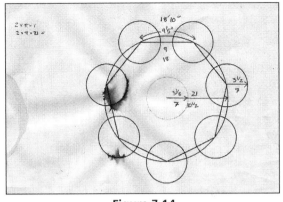

Figure 7.14

Sketch by the editor of the Cereologist *predicting the pattern at Danebury.*

Figure 7.15

Complex heptagonal geometry is elegantly expressed in this curving swastika, symbolic of the Sun and the seven notes of the pure music scale. Danebury hill fort, 1998.

Figure 7.16

The thirty-three-flame "Beltane Wheel" appeared within a two-hour window. The central tracks were made later by people measuring the formation. West Kennett, 1998.

scalloped edges enclosed a radial pattern comprising thirty-three "flames" spread equidistantly around the circumference (requiring a bisection of 10.90909° for each element). Seen from above, as the light reflected back the yellow of the still-intact flowers, the pattern resembled a Roman mosaic, its center lying twenty feet into undisturbed crop.

The date of its appearance—three days after the Celtic solar festival of Beltane—and the thirty-

three "flames" show a definite connection. Traditionally, thirty-three is a solar number and in many religions it is associated with divinity. Dividing the 365-day year by thirty-three gives 11.060606, with eleven years representing the periodic recycling of sunspot activity, and 666 (amidst the zeros), the number attributed to the Sun as well as the "Beast."

The Shilling family, out that morning to appreciate the dawn chorus of birds, had also driven past the same field at four-thirty when it was intact, yet on their return at a quarter to six the crop circle was there. They described the undamaged condition of the plants and the absence of footprints in the heavy dew and moist ground, something they could not prevent altering, even as they gently made their way in.

The following morning, the BBC Wiltshire sound unit was conducting a radio interview inside the crop glyph when havoc was wrought on a tape recorder, the tape speeding up so considerably that it stopped. When the interview was continued fifty yards outside the formation, the equipment resumed normal operation; when the experiment was repeated inside the formation, the technical problems returned.

Later in the day, a cynical crew from ITV Bristol Television also decided to drop by, so the Circlemakers decided to have a field day.

The coverage was shown that evening with no overt signs of disruption, other than the fact that, for those who knew, the segment seemed very short considering the time spent on-site by the crew. The next morning, Francine Blake, who had chaperoned the film crew, received a call from the television technical staff explaining that the televised

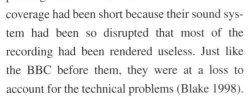

Figure 7.17
Geometry required to generate each of the thirty-three flames.

coverage had been short because their sound system had been so disrupted that most of the recording had been rendered useless. Just like the BBC before them, they were at a loss to account for the technical problems (Blake 1998).

Ironically, the BBC encountered a few problems of their own when they employed Team Satan/circlemakers, plus Doug Bower, to remind their viewing audience that crop circles were nothing more than pretty designs made by a group of skillful artists. Still basking in the glory of their venture on the other side of the globe, Team Satan/circlemakers this time opted for a simple roulette of one hundred circles with a "Y" logo in the center (advertising the website Yell). The result was a geometrically flawed structure, presumably because a forty-ton, floodlight-wielding crane couldn't be so easily disguised in Wiltshire, or the design hadn't been staked out ahead of time.

Instead, trodden circular paths marked the locations of areas to be planked, creating connecting paths between every circle, a feature that certainly had not been evident in the vastly superior "Triple Julia Set" until people began to walk its labyrinth of circles. Team Satan's Rod Dickinson later announced his work to be on a par with the "Triple Julia," but conveniently forgot to mention that his team's artwork was three times smaller, geometrically immature, and unlike its predecessor, recorded no anomalies—electromagnetically, biophysically, or otherwise.

Most embarrassing for the BBC was that the broadcasting station's foray into the undercover world of deception was thwarted within an hour of their work-in-progress, when the group was caught *in flagrante* despite the cloak of darkness. This demonstrated how much harder it is to avoid detection when you try such a venture in a country where, unlike New Zealand, its inhabitants outnumber the sheep.

A few yards away, Doug Bower had been having problems of his own when he *miscalculated* the diameter of his simple thirty-foot circle. So with dawn encroaching, an exhausted Team Satan/circlemakers was drafted to help the veteran complete the project that had now mistakenly doubled in size.

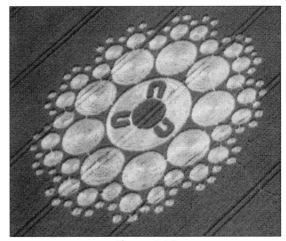

Figure 7.18
More impressive from the air than on the ground. Team Satan/circlemakers' effort. Milk Hill, 1998.

This footage was later aired on the BBC's *Country File*. One of its stated aims was "Could we create a complex crop circle at night without getting caught?" As they *had* been caught—ironically by another group of hoaxers—the answer would seem to be "No."

Such are the coincidences in this phenomenon.

However, a second and subtler aim appears to have been disinformation. The program was strategically aired to preempt credibility or interest in the new crop circle season and to stir up animosity to all things circular in the minds of its principal viewing audience, the farming community. Judging by the dismissiveness and hostility of farmers during subsequent attempts to secure access to their land, the desired effect was achieved.

An air of suspicion had also hung around the steady "disappearing act" by Dave Chorley. Throughout the years of interviews, Bower and Chorley's stories rarely matched, in fact, they became so contradictory that Chorley was increasingly kept out of the limelight. If anything, Chorley gave the impression of being tired of the whole affair. At one point, Paul Vigay (who had on occasion communicated with him) felt that he might be ready to go public with the story. Vigay would never know if his premonition was accurate or if he was being overdramatic, because barely a week later Chorley was dead.[37]

Despite the media's shenanigans, crop circles did not entirely evaporate from the public mind in 1998. On the contrary, with crude formations now advertising cigars, crop circles entered mass culture, even if it meant the sacred and the mysterious became adulterated by marketing. Since hoaxers faced criminal prosecution, these "advertisements" allowed some of their makers to publicly claim their work, and in so doing, exposed their methods.

Writing about Team Satan/circlemakers' "van" crop circle—commissioned by Mitsubishi—Rod Dickinson said: "Uncharacteristically the formation was made during daylight. It took the three of us twelve hours to complete due to the complexity of the design—which had numerous centre-points and compound curves to find and create—and the need for absolute accuracy, the formation wouldn't be much use if it didn't look like the car it was supposed to be representing."[38]

A completion time of twelve hours in daylight? It makes one wonder how he managed those perfect logarithmic curves of the Triple Julia Set (the formation so prominently displayed on his website) in five hours of darkness.

The Mitsubishi commission provided clear evidence of the team's involvement in making a crop circle. However, the following year, they became involved in a more sinister event. On August 7, 1999, a three-page article entitled "The Night Those UFOs Didn't Land" appeared in the British tabloid *The Daily Mail*. The story by Sam Taylor and photographer Nick Holt described how the newspaper had commissioned Team Satan/circlemakers to create an elaborate formation at Avebury, comprising a series of circles arranged within a triangular area, with each circle inscribed with lines to create the illusion of 3-D cubes. The formation appeared on July 28, yet for some reason the up-to-the-minute newspaper printed the story ten days after the event.

---

[37]Personal communication with Paul Vigay.
[38]Rod Dickinson, Team Satan/circlemakers website.

Their team of eight people claims to have slid unnoticed into the field at 11:30 P.M., and for the next six hours Taylor and Holt are supposed to have watched the formation being made. When morning came, visitors were interviewed and their most outrageous theories as to the origins and effects of this circle made the paper for the purpose of ridicule. So far, the story appeared to run true to form, but then the problems started.

At eleven that evening, Chad Deetken, his wife, and three friends were walking along the avenue of stones leading into the Avebury circle, taking advantage of the bright moonlight. After their friends left, the Deetkens stayed there until half-past midnight.

The field in which the hoax was supposedly being perpetrated adjoins this avenue of stones and has a twenty-five-foot incline. By 12:30 A.M. the design should have been well in progress yet the Deetkens, standing in front of where it should be, recall no disturbance in the moonlit field. Two hours later, the sleepless manager of the book shop (700 feet away, overlooking the field) looked out of his window and also saw an undisturbed wheat field. Two other witnesses walked by this site at 3 and 4 A.M., respectively, and still no design was visible.

So where was the group? The newspaper report claims "the light was so bad," and yet the countryside was visible that night thanks to clear skies and a moon so full and bright you could read small print in a newspaper. The account also claims they had climbed an eight-bar gate to access the field, but there are no eight-bar gates in the vicinity, and besides, gates in Wiltshire are generally five- or six-bar. Perhaps they'd stumbled into the wrong county? Or more likely, into the realm of fiction.

Deetken called the newspaper several times to speak to Taylor or Holt for clarification, but got no response. In fact, attempts over the next few months by several researchers (and myself) to speak to them proved fruitless. The paper couldn't even clarify if these people existed. Eventually, calls made to Sam Taylor were transferred to a desk at a rival tabloid, the *Daily Mirror*. Answering the phone call at the other end turned out to be none other than Doug and Dave's mentor, Graham Brough.

Another scam had been fostered upon an unsuspecting British public. Team Satan/

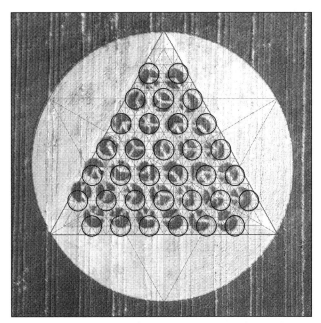

Figure 7.19

Geometric overlay reveals the discrepancies in the design claimed by Team Satan/circlemakers. Avebury, 1999.

circlemakers had laid claim to someone else's formation—an example of "seduction by suggestion."[39] But whose formation was it? From the ground and the air, the evidence did not immediately point to a supernatural source either, as the authenticity of the design was far from convincing.

At the time, I remember being puzzled by two crop circles that seemed to fit neither the normal human involvement pattern nor that of the real phenomenon; these were different. The brittle plants showed that an excessive amount of heat had been used, and the soil, sticky to the touch on the outside, was powdery on the inside—even more so than is normal in a crop circle, and tests for electromagnetism gave no response. The designs also seemed to have sprung from the head of a machine rather than the heart of a sentient being: the first was a set of three interlocking crescents beside Barbury Castle; the second was the Avebury hoax. The words "microwave" and "military" popped into my head, and remained there.

Weeks passed. Then one afternoon I met with a friend, a respected psychic, who was visiting from America. I shared with her various photos of the season's crop circles, pausing over the Barbury and Avebury formations. Without any prodding from me, the same two words came up: microwave and military.

Months later I discussed the Avebury scam with Marcus Allen, UK editor of *Nexus* magazine and a former private investigator. "Look at the field where the Avebury formation was laid," he said. "Look at how little is growing there this season; in fact, how anything growing there looks stunted, even the weeds, as if the area has been microwaved and made sterile." This was indeed the case at Avebury, so I returned to the site at Barbury to see if Marcus's suspicions were founded. All around where the formation had been there was nothing but stunted growth.

What eventually turned 1999 into a positive year was the extraordinary show of strength mounted by the *real* Circlemakers. Since many of the designs are dealt with in greater detail later in this book, I will only touch on a few significant highlights here. The year 1999 heralded ninefold geometry, and a significant number of the formations were predicted, further validating the two-way *exchange* between the circle-making force and its human recipients.

In April, the crop circles demonstrated an affinity for our wonder with the forthcoming solar eclipse by displaying a 640-foot pictogram showing the Moon covering the Sun, in nine stages. At Hakpen Hill, a vortex crop glyph featured nine in-flowing spirals, three of which

Figure 7.20

Was microwave technology involved in the making of these crop circles? All Cannings, Barbury Castle, Devil's Den, 1999.

---

[39]Looking closely at the aerial photos I shot of the Avebury glyph that same morning, one taken on the way out of the area shows a tiny dumbbell pattern on the other side of Woden Hill (which stands between Avebury and Silbury), secluded from the nearby footpath and close to a field gate. Could this be the formation the group actually made?

flattened at their cusps, and took researchers the best part of a year to figure out. On the final day of the ancient Aztec calendar came a nine-coiled "serpent" in the East Field, whose back-combed lay resembled the DNA strand. Was this glyph symbolic of Quetzalcoatl, the Aztec god described as a feathered serpent?

The importance behind this play on nine was later discovered in heliocentric astrological charts for December, which depicted the planets and principal asteroids in three grand trines around the Sun, creating a nine-pointed star in the solar system.

Two geometric "nets" were presented, the first as an unfolded octahedron (an eight-sided Platonic solid) and the second as an unfolded interlocking square that, when folded, resembled an Aztec swastika. It was as if the

Figure 7.21

Selected crop circles of 1999.

Figure 7.22

"Nine Spirals." The flattened curves employ a complex and obscure mathematical method of construction last used in stone circles. Not surprisingly, no one claimed this crop circle. Hakpen Hill, 1999.

Circlemakers were indulging in a game of origami. This latter formation appeared barely two hundred yards from Aztec elder Tlakaelel's "site of the last ceremonial dance."

The suggestion of a thematic move in design from 2-D to 3-D developed as the season progressed, reinforced by an unmistakable cube which appeared near the site of the Mandelbrot crop circle of eight years earlier. Suddenly and dramatically, the designs were acquiring perspective.

This change in dimensional perception developed even more throughout 2000, when the crop circles focused on grid curvature and visual illusion. Some designs pointed to an understanding of Einstein's theory of relativity and quantum physics, in which space and time are interconnected to form a four-dimensional continuum and particles are seen as processes rather than objects.

The first example of the projection of a four-dimensional body in three-dimensional space—a sphere stretching through a net—appeared along the western flank of Windmill Hill (see figure 7.27 on page 108). This was followed by a large grid square at East Kennett, constructed from 1600 flattened and standing portions, subtly graded into four squares, each giving the perception of cubes

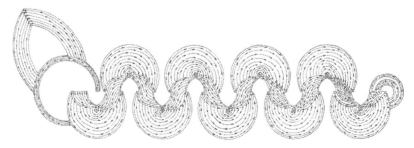

Figure 7.23

A ground survey of the "Coiled Serpent" glyph shows the intricate floor lay. Note the tiny vortices at the tip of each spear. Alton Barnes, 1999.

alternately descending into and rising out of the Earth (see figures 7.28 and 7.29 on page 108). By its very nature, the way the design was seen from above depended on the angle of the light, so according to the time of day, what seemed "up" was also "down," and "concave" became "convex."

What was being conveyed here? That other levels of reality exist beyond our limited senses of perception? Perhaps the Circlemakers were retraining our visual perception, for such a holographic effect presents a challenge for the viewer to question his or her relationship to the image presented, in the same way the visual paradoxes of artists such as M. C. Escher and Monika Bush teach the eye to "see" differently.

These "cross-dimensional" crop circles were supported by a series of flower crop glyphs referencing those invisible wheels of energy, the chakras. Of particular merit was a sixteen-petaled mandala relating to the throat chakra (see figure 7.31 on page 108); a "sunflower" relating to the crown chakra; and a six-petaled lotus flower (with the sixth petal

folded) relating to the sacral chakra.[40] (See figure 7.30 on page A7 in the color section.)

At the southern end of the Windmill Hill complex appeared one such "wheel of energy." For some, the radiating pattern was obviously an idealized representation of Earth's magnetic field; for others, it bore a similarity to a splitting chromosome, even a stylized plan of the hemispheres of the human brain. Regardless of the interpretation, the visual impact was startling, for despite the appearance of radiating bands, not

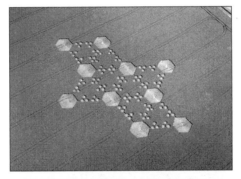

Figure 7.24

"Origami" crop circles. Top: Clatford formation folds into an octahedron. Incidentally, the grapeshot are not circles, but tiny hexagons. Bottom: Silbury formation folds into an Aztec-type swastika.

[40]"Chakra" is Sanskrit for "spinning wheel of energy." The chakras form a collection of vortices that facilitate the entry of energy into major organs, and endocrine or hormonal glands. Six of the seven principal chakras are symbolized by a lotus flower of various petals, each associated with a sound or vibration, and corresponding to the sound of each of the fifty letters of the Sanskrit alphabet. Ironically, there are 50 sounds capable of being vocalized by the human being. This is why Sanskrit is called *Dev Bani*—the language of the gods.

Figure 7.25

3-D crop glyphs. Beckhampton and Wimpole Hall, 1999.

circles and magnetism showed that in 5 percent of crop circles he'd analyzed, the Earth's magnetic grid deviated by 3 to 5 degrees.

The Circlemakers may have been eavesdropping on his thoughts, soon thereafter offering validation in the shape of a ring torus crop glyph. Divided into eleven circular rotations (requiring the division of a circle into 32.72°), each segment had shifted approximately 4 to 5 degrees, giving the torus's doughnut shape a three-dimensional quality (see figure 7.34 on page 110).

Despite the encouraging news, Andrews was besieged by hostility, even death threats, from the crop circle community, particularly from those who had by now staked their reputations on any and every depression in plants being the product of some supernatural force. Understandably, Andrews' next revelation that 80 percent of crop circles he'd investigated during those two seasons had possibly been made by humans was anathema to those with strong opinions on the subject or whose vested interests now stood naked in this controversy.

So, a harmless scientific inquiry cascaded into a mudslinging debate on what was genuine and what was hoaxed, once again demonstrating the degree to which the crop circle community has allowed itself to become polarized. There was no question that many human-made crop circles were being perpetrated during this period. One example was a heart-shaped formation at East Kennett, constructed for a wedding with the farmer's permission. Another was a simple seven-pointed star, the perpetrator of which, Matthew

one curve was used, not even to build the two dipoles. The whole illusion was created by *straight* lines which were the result of plants laid in wave patterns. Where these lines converged at each dipole, the strands of upright wheat were finessed down to four or five standing plants (see figures 7.32 and 7.33 on page 109).

The appearance of the "magnetic grid" crop glyph proved timely. The previous night, a sleepless Colin Andrews had been juggling with the image of a magnetic grid, probably because the subject was foremost on his mind. A few days later, Andrews announced that his research between 1999 and 2000 into the effects of crop

Williams, was arrested and fined.

Yet another appeared not far from Barbury Castle: 400-by 460-foot design incorporating the *Star Trek* logo, an arrow, and Einstein's famous $E = MC^2$ equation. Commissioned by the Science Museum in London for an upcoming exhibition, the project was described by one of the artists involved as "one of the hardest tasks I have ever performed. . . . We were struggling to create straight lines and right angles. There is no way anyone will convince me that these highly complex crop circles are easy to make or that they can be done overnight and in darkness. . . . The *Star Trek* construction was simple and angular, but took two days to complete, and the crop inside was a mess; all of it broke, totally wrecked" (Cochrane 2001).

Regardless of the human hullabaloo, the real phenomenon moved on with its agenda. As the Sun descended over a huge "sunflower" crop

Figure 7.26

Selected crop circles of 2000.

glyph resting between the summits of Picked and Woodborough hills, the season finale of 2000 once again presented a taste of wonders to come. Here, the Circlemakers abandoned the use of circles as a method of construction by presenting a

Figure 7.27

Although quickly damaged by heavy rain and gales, the visual illusion of a sphere popping through a grid can still be seen. Windmill Hill, 2000.

Figure 7.28

"Four cubes." Just one wrong measurement would have ruined the visual illusion. East Kennett, 2000.

Figure 7.29

The maze-like structure of the "four cubes."

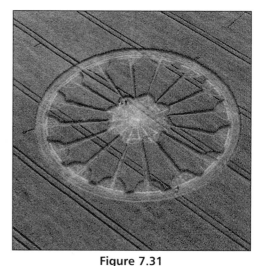

Figure 7.31

Sixteen-petaled mandala. Alton Priors, 2000.

formation created purely from forty-four rotations of nature's own spiral, the Golden Mean (also known as *phi*) each expression requiring a curve in the ratio of 1:1.6180339. Together with its fourteen concentric rings, the design refer-enced 44/14, or 22/7, the convenient ratio for that other mathematical incommensurable, *pi*. (See figures 7.35 and 7.36 on page 111.)

Now explain this one.

Figure 7.32

"Magnetic Grid" crop glyph, complete with two dipoles, each generating positive and negative electromagnetic charges. Avebury Trusloe, 2000.

There is no doubt that the presence of crop circles has become a thorn in the side of orthodox science, creating unease in those engaged in shaping our belief systems, for as fast as crop circles attract new converts, the more effort is applied to discredit them. The Establishment—whether government, medical institution, chemical conglomerate, or Academe—debunks anything "new" to give itself a chance to familiarize itself with so-called unorthodox ideas, own them, and finally make them available to the public once political, military, and/or commercial profit can be made. A good example is the current war on "alternative" medicine. After systematically trashing holistic medicine, the medical industry is increasingly becoming a major shareholder in the supposedly "quack" companies involved in the practice or manufacture of so-called "alternative" cures.

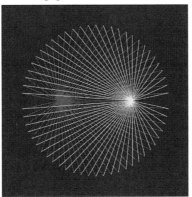

Figure 7.33

The Magnetic Grid's linear geometry creates the 3-D effect of a sphere.

Such centralized control by the few has generally proved an impediment to the advancement of every race, and to understand this

Figure 7.34

Torus ring references a 4° twist in Earth's magnetic grid in each segment. North Down, 1999.

yes, 1,200 years (White 1896). Even as late as the eighteenth century, we find scientists forced to recant their views in publicly humiliating fashion, as Galileo once discovered for himself.

If religious might hasn't been enough of a detriment to the advancement of knowledge (of its rediscovery), the conservative belief system within the scientific community sometimes produces obstacles of its own. Take the case of Johann Beringer, prominent professor of the University of Wurzburg and physician to the Prince-Bishop. During the mid-eighteenth century, Berenger, too, uncovered fossils, yet the news was

is to understand one of the primary functions behind the rise in crop circles, as we shall see in part 2.

Human history has a sad legacy of antagonism towards the "new," and ironically, those who are least qualified to comment on a new subject are also those most actively engaged in denouncing it. For instance, the ancient Greeks were aware of fossils and knew that life on Earth was far older than was accounted for. With the rise of Roman Catholicism, however, there came about a contemptuous attitude towards geology and science, particularly if the findings were at odds with reworked scripture. At one point, theology became so fundamentalist that 4004 B.C. was set as the official date of creation; arguments even raged over which day in October it had occurred. And St. Augustine's personal distaste of astronomy alone held back advances in the study of the heavens for twelve centuries—

received by the church with as much glee as a delivery of pork to a synagogue. His discoveries were also at odds with the scientific viewpoint of the day, and in order to discredit him, two of Berenger's peers—Professor Ignatz Roderique, and Privy Councilor Georg von Eckart—hoaxed a number of look-alike fossils and paid one of Berenger's excavators to reverse the habits of his profession and surreptitiously *bury* the fakes throughout the dig.

Unfortunately for them, the plan backfired, for Berenger took delight in the new finds, considered them authentic, and lectured widely on the subject. Roderique and Eckart, bemused by the apparent failure of their hoax, created ever more elaborate carvings on rocks, at one point inscribing in Arabic the name of Jehovah. Only when Berenger published his findings in 1872 did the two pranksters own up to the world. The ensuing scandal succeeded in not only discrediting

Figure 7.35

"Sunflower," the glory of 2000. Woodborough Hill.

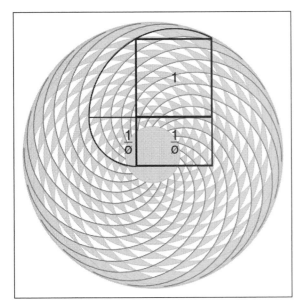

Figure 7.36

Each spiral requires knowledge of ø or phi, that is, the division of an area to the ratio 1:1.6180339, the Golden Mean.

Berenger's original, valid discoveries, but also disgraced Roderique and Eckart (John and Wolf 1963).

That these two men were prepared to risk their reputations demonstrates how seriously the status quo takes the threat to its established views, and the obvious parallel to events throughout research into crop circles requires no further explanation. It also serves as a lesson to researchers and discreditors alike.

The current ridiculing or outright silencing of crop circles investigations throughout the media follows the established trend for subjects that threaten the interests of large groups. One could say television and newspaper company owners are responsible for instigating a cover-up, or that journalists have been lax in "digging up" valuable evidence, even though it has been available to them all along. However, it is important to recognize that the majority of worldwide media companies are not now in control of their own destinies. Many are subsidiaries of multi-national parent companies whose lobbyists have a rich history of directly influencing government policies.

These policies are inevitably fostered upon an unsuspecting public through manipulation of editorial content in media outlets, in which these organizations have either vested financial interests, or control large portions of the advertising budget that makes or breaks a newspaper or television station. Either way, the power of the "system" to sway public opinion should not be underestimated.

Claire Hope Cummings makes a case in point: "Rupert Murdoch's Fox Television, which owns and operates most television stations in the United States, actually shelved a series which documented damaging evidence against the use of hormones in dairy cows and connections between biotechnology giant Monsanto and U.S. government agencies. According to two award-winning reporters commissioned to prepare the story, its removal came just days after Monsanto pressured Fox News Network to drop the series" (1999).

Changing a worldview requires either a major leap in thinking or an event of overwhelming magnitude, such as the crop circle phenomenon. Leaps in mass understanding inevitably undermine the vested interests of the few who stake their reputations, positions, and livelihoods on the "official" perception of the truth. Therefore, the status quo will resist any attempt at anyone else rewriting history.

Back in 1991, the German political correspondent Jürgen Krönig made a succinct, almost prophetic observation about this state of affairs when he wrote:

> Crop circles have initiated a psycho-social mass phenomenon. They have accelerated an already existing process of change in belief systems.

People of all classes, age groups and educational backgrounds are moved by the circles, one could say that the phenomenon helps to break down barriers between people who normally find it difficult to communicate with each other without having been introduced formally.

It's ironic how so many are appearing in England then! To quote Krönig again:

> Paradigm shifts are accompanied by conflicts. The resistance of the old order will become stronger, the more they feel that their position is under threat. The scientific orthodoxy will close ranks and will increase, not least with the help of their media allies, the attack on "dangerous irrationalism." Current events around crop circles have presented us with examples. The activity of the groups of so-called debunkers is an indication of the growing irritation of the representatives of the old worldview. . . . But in the long run, the only people who will have the wool pulled over their eyes are those who don't want to see anything anyway (Krönig 1991).

For all the claims that all crop circles are nothing more than human hoaxes, precious little evidence exists to back up human involvement. In fact, when faced with facts, hoaxers are generally elusive and reluctant to list their claimed designs or to explain their noteworthy features. Recollections of dates and locations prove problematic, details on modes of operation contradictory and often mathematically incorrect.

Researcher Paul Vigay sums up the hoax argument:

> Hoaxers must be able to prove that all formations are hoaxes, for it is they that claim the subject to be a hoax. All the hoaxers have to do is stop hoaxing, that way there would be no more circles. The biggest problem for them is that of the genuine phenomenon. As they have no control over the "real" circles, they cannot force the phenomenon to stop merely because they stop. Therefore, each year, as genuine formations start to appear, the hoaxers have to come forward and say "yes, we did them." They cannot simply give up hoaxing as this will reveal the genuine formations. Hoaxers have effectively given themselves no option but to continue hoaxing for as long as the genuine phenomenon persists (Vigay 1994).

The fallow days between Christmas and the New Year are typically a time when individuals in the public eye, policy-makers, or corporations quietly approach the media to retract statements, make reversals in policy, or pass controversial legislation, the public being distracted by celebrations and hangovers. It was in this spirit that articles appeared in the British press on Sunday, December 27, 1998, bearing a statement by Doug Bower claiming an "unknown force was behind the corn circles," and that it had instructed him to make the elaborate patterns (Brownlee 1998).

Either the phenomenon's most publicized hoaxer believes that behind the scenes lies more than the "hand of man," or preparations were being made for the next Operation Status Quo.

PART TWO

EVIDENCE AND PURPOSE

8. LIVING PROOF

It is perfectly natural to ask if the circles are hoaxes, but very difficult to explain why they cannot be hoaxed satisfactorily.

—Pat Delgado

As we have seen throughout the first part of this book, weather doesn't explain crop circles. So who or what is making them? And how?

The other most plausible answer is that of the hand of man. However, despite the rise in hoaxing, it appears that man has merely aped and appropriated a phenomenon that was not of his doing to begin with.

Hoaxers generally refuse authorship of any particular design, claiming conveniently that doing so ruins the "notion of the artwork" (although the prospect of prison may also be a motivating factor). In which case, should artists such as Van Gogh have refrained from signing their masterpieces, too, leaving themselves to be swallowed by the swamps of anonymity and their artwork to be claimed by every opportunist or failed art school student?

"Art without knowledge is nothing," remarked the enlightened eleventh-century Abbot Suger. So let us examine crop circles in closer detail to get a sense of the mechanics at work, and see what differentiates beauty from the beast.

Time of Creation

"It wasn't there the night before, but I saw it first thing this morning" is the stock-in-trade statement from bewildered farmers making their rounds at the crack of dawn, and it's a sentiment shared by baffled researchers and enthusiasts after damp, all-night vigils. So exactly how long does it take for a crop circle to manifest?

During a dusk watch of the crop-circle-friendly Devil's Punchbowl at Cheesefoot Head in 1986, Don Tuersley and Pat Delgado sat observing the field with night-vision binoculars; below lay a large circle and ring formation. By midnight nothing had stirred, except the fine drizzle that suddenly began to infiltrate the scene. With the first light at 3:45 A.M. came a new circle and ring to the south—yet they saw and heard nothing (Andrews and Delgado 1991).

Figure 8.1

An incoming spiral has entered the circle from the left, split into two (where the person is kneeling), and swirled clockwise towards the center where it is then overlaid by a central fan of plants. The second half of the spiral completes the circle's wall, and where the flows merge, the plants are platted over and under, suggesting an extremely rapid process. Roundway, 1999.

Hundreds of other accounts suggest a brief time window. Less than two hours was the gap between two German tourists reporting nothing unusual from the summit of Silbury Hill to the appearance beside it of the 126-circle "Koch fractal"—in the middle of the afternoon, at the height of tourist season. Fifteen minutes was the time allocated for the "Julia Set" at Stonehenge, again in daylight. The rest of the crop circles seem to materialize quietly between 3 A.M. and shortly before sunrise.

However, an estimated time window is not the same as the actual construction time. From his experience, Pat Delgado believes that twenty seconds is possibly the maximum time of construction: "We conclude this because to achieve a swirled, flattened condition pressed hard to the ground, the stems must have a maximum vertical-to-horizontal transformation time, above which they would be damaged by whiplash" (ibid.). Delgado's thesis is supported by scores of first-hand accounts, all of which claim a whorl motion lasting between five to twenty seconds, regardless of the final size. This is substantiated by the event caught by Nippon TV's camera crew at Bratton (T. Wilson 1998).

Soil and Water

It was an unusually crowd-free morning inside the "yin-yang" crop formation below Liddington hill fort, so much so that the peace allowed me some precious moments to ponder over the circle-making process.

Without spin nothing works, and in nature, spin develops into unfolding vortices in the shape of spirals. Given the spiral nature of crop circles, I reasoned that the Circlemakers could be harnessing some type of natural principle, and since nature is governed by principles that are by-and-large electromagnetic, whatever process lies behind crop circles must be leaving traces. So, just as Colin Andrews once received a dramatic reply to his cry for an answer to the riddle, mine came in the thought "Smell the plants, you idiot!"

I reached down and cut the base of stems in the fresh crop glyph. They exuded a malty fragrance, as if the water within the plants had been heated and cooked them from the inside. The lower parts of the stems were superficially charred, too. I recalled how farmer Joe Rennick in Saskatchewan had noticed the soil within his crop circle had been baked hard as cement, yet throughout the rest of his field it was moist and muddy. Canadian researcher Chad Deetken noticed this as well and said that 60 percent of crop circles appear during *rainy* nights (Deetken 1993). I remembered how during my tour in the Litchfield "torc" formation I found the soil loose and powdery, how at certain points it was even cracked, and how I had found a lump of carbon in the center.

Figure 8.2

Close-up of rock from a crop circle shows the wheat stems have been flash-burned onto its surface.

Figure 8.3

Intense heat has split the interior of this immature barley plant.

I compiled my own data: in 50 percent of crop circles visited, the soil inside new crop circles was noticeably drier compared to the tackier texture farther away from the center. Formations indicating human involvement showed no such discrepancy; rain prior to or during inspection, and patterns older than two days were discounted.

In August 2000, I compared two new formations, across the road from each other at All Cannings, where the plants and soil were identical in type and texture. The first formation was a modest nine-pointed star, with hand-made features that left me unimpressed and which exhibited no electromagnetic anomalies. The soil was as sticky to the touch inside the circle as it was outside. But across the road, the soil inside the rose pattern was not just dry, but was powdered to the point it could be blown away.

A middle-aged couple vacationing nearby told me they had witnessed a large oval craft with a rim of bright lights hovering over the location the previous night, yet because of their low position behind a hedge, they could not confirm that the craft had made the circle. One thing was certain: all the stems in this crop formation were bone dry and brittle, and between the two nodes nearest the ground, they had exploded. Compared to other crop circles I have

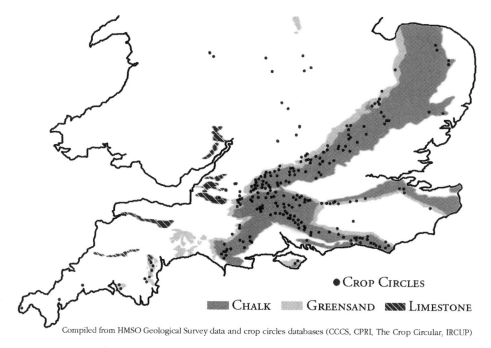

Figure 8.5

Distribution of crop circles in southern England relative to water-bearing strata.

analyzed, this was an extreme example, for generally the plants are just superficially charred.

Historically, crop circles have strategically referenced aquifers, ponds, wells, or underground tanks (Andrews and Delgado 1991). There is also a disproportionately large number of incidences in which circles appear over areas where the groundwater is close to the surface, primarily in southern England where the chalk aquifer, the deepest in the world, provides an excellent moisture trap.

Historian Brian Grist has made a detailed analysis of the positioning of crop circle events and shows how the majority prefer aquiferous ground. This preference for sites bearing a vital relationship with water was further borne out when, in the dry summers of 1989 and 1990, the circles "appeared closer to the edge of the aquifer . . . causing one to wonder whether or not their placements might in some way be influenced by the relative position of subsurface water levels at the moments in time when the events occurred" (Grist 1991).

Similar conclusions were independently reached and reinforced by Steve Page and Glen Broughton ten years later when they found 78.6 percent of recorded crop circles appeared over chalk and greensand (a mixture of sandstone and green earth). When the placement of aquifers is taken into consideration, the figure rises to 87.2 percent (Page and Broughton 1999).

So there appears to be a connection between water and the formative energy of crop circles, and given its effect on the plants and soil, it appears to generate some form of intense heat. With this in mind, I ordered some infrared film.

Kodak Color Infrared film is unique, not least because it renders photographs in false color, giving landscapes a psychedelic quality. It's used prominently in medicine and archaeology for its ability to detect variations in heat; consequently it is applied in aerial photography to uncover buried sites or inspect the health of fields or rivers.

After I examined aerial infrared shots of crop circles, a streak of enhanced discoloration appeared to cross their boundaries, a feature I could not find to the same degree in shots of neighboring fields. In cases involving mature plants, there were streaks of dark red, indicative of a higher chlorophyll content, as if a localized energy source had triggered a sudden burst of growth activity. And the newer the formation, the stronger the result (see figures 8.6–8.10 on page A9 in the color section).

Interestingly, aerial shots of known hoaxes showed no such discrepancies.

Another observation I made again dealt with the Litchfield "torc" formation. This revealed a patch of discoloration running through the center of the immature wheat. These results matched ground observations which showed the soil to be drier, suggesting the surface moisture inside the formation had been depleted.

The tests continued for three years. Photos were also taken at ground level, both one day and then one week after the appearance of each formation. The results indicated a marked *decrease* in the heat-induced variation of the chlorophyll over the period; aerial photographs also showed less of a disruption of surface water. I applied the same protocol to known hoaxes: no discolorations were evident at any time, nor did the heat content vary over the week.

I sent the images to Kodak for further analysis, but the helpful technicians were as puzzled as I. The images included in this book are culled from shots taken under similar weather conditions and time parameters. Since this area of inquiry is still in its infancy, I cannot qualify the results as any kind of proof, but merely as another set of anomalies. However, the groundwater connection persists, particularly in light of a crop circle's appearance in a Japanese rice field which displaced a volume of water comparable to the cubic area of the formation itself.[41]

Pure water in itself is not a conductor of electrical current. To be so, water requires a significant amount of dissolved minerals as part of its chemical makeup, and it just so happens that the water in the southern English aquifer is saturated with alkaline chalk. Chalk is a piezoelectric substance (it builds a static charge under pressure) composed of small prehistoric sea creatures, all containing tiny amounts of magnetite that once enabled them to orient to the Earth's magnetic field. The net effect of billions of pieces of magnetite locked together and pressurized, together with the energized groundwater, is the creation of a low magnetic field. This is especially so if the chalk is spread over a substantial geographic area, which the southern English chalk beds are. That combination makes this part of the world one of the largest natural conductors of electrical energy.

John Burke, one of the three members of the Massachusetts-based research group Burke

---

[41]The calculation was made by Paul Vigay.

Levengood Talbot (BLT), has been studying the relationship between the underground aquifer, water table, and crop circle occurrence since 1992. According to his research, the Wiltshire aquifer has had some of the highest seasonal fluctuations, which coincide with a process called adsorption, an electrical charge created by water percolating through porous rock. Burke comments:

When you've got a lot of water in an underground aquifer or water table fluctuating through the porous chalk, a lot of electric ground current is created. We were able to measure that in numerous ways in 1993. Such currents are taking place in the ground and creating signature magnetic fields. We measured the actual electric current with electrodes in the fields and sites that are getting the most and the largest crop circle activity. Around Silbury Hill, in the two days following a thunderstorm, as the water settled into this surface chalk aquifer, it created these electric ground currents. We did a magnetic survey in the field and detected wide variations in the magnetic fields there. Four days later it received a major formation. Four days after that we re-surveyed that field and the variations had evened out (Burke 1998).

Burke found similar correspondences between crop circles in North America and the limestone aquifer which underlies the Great Plains. Limestone is the chemical twin of chalk and the next most porous rock.[42]

Confirmation of other unusual behavior in the ground under crop circles came from a number of separate sources. In 1990, crop and soil samples from a formation at Culhampton (Devon) were sent to Delawarr Laboratories in Oxford for radionics analysis. A comparative test revealed the affected plants' vitality had been reduced by 20 percent; the soil showed a depletion of nitrates by 40 percent, and phosphates and sulfates by 30 percent; and elevations of cobalt, carbon, molybdenum, titanium, plutonium, and zinc were noted, elevations not evident in control samples. The report concluded that a "fierce and quick heat . . . has denatured the soil and destroyed natural elements" (Delgado 1992).

Two years later, American physicist Michael Chorost announced that preliminary tests on crop formations had unearthed four unusual radioactive isotopes (vanadium, europium, tellurium, and ytterbium) with a short half-life (the decay rate of radioactive nuclides). None were naturally occurring (Chorost and Dudley 1992a).

A survey with a Geiger counter revealed how one of the 1994 "scorpions" had a background radiation level 50 percent below normal at the edges, yet 150 percent above at the center. Below Oldbury hill fort a military team sealed off the field while checking for background radiation inside a large pictogram that registered radiation 300 percent above normal—or so they claimed—the only known case of its type.

During Project Argus, an endeavor by the Center for Crop Circles Studies which used

---

[42]Incidentally, the Pyramids of Gizeh were constructed using a colossal volume of limestone blocks. The properties of these pyramids are known to generate electromagnetic and acoustic anomalies, so a connection may yet exist between pyramid makers and Circlemakers.

gamma-ray spectroscopy and DNA analysis to track anomalies in formations, the most compelling set of results came from the magnetic surveys of soil samples in and around crop circles. The tests were performed by an investigator with no knowledge that some of the formations had been deliberately manufactured for the project. He detected a high percentage of anomalies demonstrating a relationship to the visible boundaries of the crop circles, the implication being that the ferrites (iron compounds) in the soil inside genuine crop circles had been magnetized (Chorost and Dudley 1992b).

Further soil samples were tested in the U.S. by Chorost's partner, nuclear physicist Marshall Dudley, and showed dramatic discrepancies in alpha radiation, varying from 27 percent below to 198 percent above average (ibid.). Alpha radiation consists of tiny electrically charged, high-speed particles and is one of the three types of radiation emitted by radioactive substances. Dudley added that since the radiation is short-lived, it is unlikely that health risks are involved in people exposed to crop circles, although he suggested that people avoid visiting one within an hour of its appearance until normal radiation levels are regained. This could explain why the Circlemakers go about their work predominantly during the night when most normal people are sleeping and away from the fields.

The tests continued. The CCCS then commissioned ADAS research laboratory in Cambridge to analyze soil samples from fifteen formations. The results indicated some cases of unusually high levels of nitrates in the soil following the appearance of a crop circle.[43] Although the results were not conclusive, it is important to note there are only two ways to raise the nitrate level in soil: through over-application of fertilizer or by administering an extremely high electrical charge (Green 1996).

Dudley independently confirmed the presence of chemical alterations in other English soil samples and showed how they were able to absorb more water after being exposed to this unusual energy source. A possible explanation lies in the excitement of the local magnetic field, whereby oxygen atoms behave differently because magnetism affects the way they bond with other compounds. During a dehydration process, oxygen atoms are less abundant. Dudley's data also showed how soil composition and radiation readings fluctuate

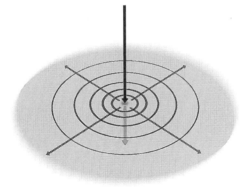

Figure 8.11

Magnetic field strength around wire carrying a current. (See also figure 8.14.)

---

[43]The department in this government-run laboratory responsible for the tests was shut down immediately after the test results were announced, under the excuse of "waste of government resources," even though the project was entirely funded by the CCCS. For complete details, see Thomas 1992.

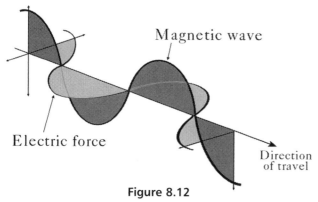

Magnetic wave

Electric force

Direction
of travel

Figure 8.12
Electromagnetic transverse wave.

depending on their location in the crop circle. Why the inconsistency?

Since energy is composed of vibrations or waveforms with peaks and troughs (also known as nodes and antinodes), it is feasible that when the crop circle energy source interacts with the ground a shockwave spreads outwards like ripples in a pond. There is a principle in physics that highlights this. A wire carrying an electric current has an associated magnetic field whose field lines are detected as a series of concentric rings; however, the field strength is reduced the farther it is from the wire. This "ripple-type" energy has been detected in crop circles (see chapter 12), and such a rippling effect is often seen in ground swells (as captured on slow motion film) following the detonation of underground nuclear tests.

Did Dudley's results reveal an electromagnetic fingerprint of concentric rings left behind like the

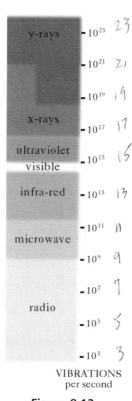

γ-rays -10^{23} 23

-10^{21} 21

-10^{19} 19

x-rays -10^{17} 17

ultraviolet -10^{15} 15
visible

infra-red -10^{13} 13

-10^{11} 11
microwave

-10^{9} 9

-10^{7} 7

radio -10^{5} 5

-10^{3} 3

VIBRATIONS
per second

Figure 8.13

The known electro-magnetic spectrum.

peaks and troughs of a frozen shockwave?

One thing is certain. People trampling plants do not affect the watershed or the molecular structure of plants and soil. Given such observations, let us now look at the role played by electromagnetic radiation.

Electromagnetics and the Energy Grid

The Universe is an expression of visible and invisible frequencies of light. When this light energy interacts with gravity the rate of spin of its molecules slows down, the myriad frequencies express themselves as matter, and the form and the color of every organism and every object is thereby determined. Light is both particle and wave, and it transfers its energy by means of a rapidly alternating electromagnetic field in the form of two waves: one electrical, the other magnetic which lags a step behind. Electromagnetic waves are *transverse*; that is, their two components move in tandem, perpendicular to the direction of travel. The transverse wave carries information vital to the cells of every organism, particularly the DNA in the human body.

The number of times a wave occurs in one second along a given length (the wavelength) determines its frequency, which is also called vibration or oscillation; this frequency is measured in hertz (Hz). Consequently, one wave equals one vibration per second, or 1 Hz (1000 Hz = 1 kHz; 1 million Hz or 10^6 Hz = 1 MHz; 1 billion Hz or 10^9 Hz = 1 GHz).

The relevance of this to crop circles is that electromagnetic waves can cause both interference and heating effects. While Andrews and Delgado were measuring a pair of circles at Bratton in 1987, they noticed the needle of their compass spinning anticlockwise. Since the compass lay untouched on the ground at the center of the circle, they could not account for this erratic behavior; it hadn't been knocked and no metal objects were near it. In fact, when the needle finally became stationary they attempted to reproduce the effect by placing a steel tape near it, with negative results (Andrews and Delgado 1991).

Years later, Professor Charles Thomas visited crop circles in Wiltshire and Cornwall, armed with a sturdy, brass-cased P11 aircraft compass, the kind that once accurately guided bombers during World War II. His objective was to see how a magnetically sensitive instrument would react inside a crop circle.

Inside the Alton Priors "Key" formation of 1991, Thomas was surprised to see a deflection in the predicted compass bearing by as much as 15° east. This acute difference was strongest in the center of both circular areas of the pictogram and especially when the P11 was placed three feet above the ground; further, the new bearing moved in the same direction as the lay in the flattened plants. When the P11 was placed on the ground, the needle performed just as erratically, this time flickering 5–10° west before finding north again.

In the company of CCCS' Vice President George Bishop, Thomas visited a grouping of new circles in Callington, Cornwall, where he was again surprised by compass deviations. Thomas stated, "The process of crop circle formation in these cases appears to have produced a local magnetic anomaly detectable with a reliable instrument. One could add the comment that the anomaly appears to be linked to the direction in which stalks are flattened and that the strength of the anomaly appears to vary with distance from ground level. There may be a suspicion that the magnetic field is created at the time of formation and decreases through time" (Thomas 1991/92).

I, too, have encountered compass anomalies with varying degrees of deviation, depending on the age of the crop formation. Within the "Triple Julia Set" my compass needle had trouble locating north, and it wobbled as if confused for at least ten minutes before settling down.

Since 1927, clues have hinted at the involvement of magnetism in crop circles, in the form of the magnetization of watches, pocket knives, and bicycles. In recent times, a Japanese researcher found that a battery pack with fourteen hours of available power drained instantaneously the moment it touched the floor of a new crop circle. I have loaded fresh batteries into cameras and photographed successfully outside formations, yet the moment I cross a circle perimeter, the batteries are drained. As the BBC well knows, video equipment suffers from interference and performance failure. Photographic cameras fare no better: reports of buckled shutters, failed drives, and loss-of-power abound. Such reports can be multiplied by the hundreds.

The year 2000, in particular, turned out to be an expensive one for camera equipment. The ominous signs of trouble began inside the "lotus flower" formation below Golden Ball Hill. Any equipment with an LCD (liquid crystal display) began to polarize; Paul Vigay's monitoring devices were registering extraordinarily high frequency readings; then my camera failed.

A few days later, I went to the lab to find out if my prized Nikon had made a recovery, but the technical diagnosis was not good: "Fried circuit board, very unusual. Interesting. We have had a record number of identical problems with cameras this summer, and the strange thing is, their owners all claim the problems happened when they took them into crop circles. I really don't believe in crop circles." Somehow he didn't seem so adamant after I'd finished telling him where my camera had been.

In Devon, George Bishop's camera played a sort of photographic hopscotch when it refused to work every time he stepped into a crop circle, yet operated perfectly every time he stepped out; a visitor to the "Tube Torus" formation had an identical experience. They should consider themselves lucky: a professional photographer shooting the Littlebury 1996 formation from the air had all three cameras fail simultaneously.

Mobile phones, which rely on electromagnetic frequencies to communicate with local towers, are also prone to crop circle energy interference. Paul Vigay found a conversation with his father abruptly curtailed the moment he crossed the perimeter of the Alton Priors "Key" formation. The meter on the phone indicated that no signal was present wherever he walked in the crop circle, yet it shot up to full signal whenever he held the phone outside its perimeter. To prove this was not a coincidence, he proceeded to walk around the entire field, up and down tram lines and across a local road. Again, only the area inside the crop circle prevented a signal from reaching the phone. Not surprisingly,

this was the moment the admitted skeptic dove head-first into crop circles research. It is worth pointing out that the formation was not a regular circular area but a complex dumbbell with a chiseled appendage.

The size of the equipment affected seems inconsequential. When the defiant combine harvester short-circuited as it crossed the Milk Hill "Koch fractal" little did it know what rich history it shared with other farm machinery entering crop circles. At Warminster, a tractor harvesting a field lumbered through a circle and had its entire electrical system fail the moment it crossed its perimeter. Farm hands were asked to push-start the machine, eventually towing it across the circle. Yet as the tractor emerged out the other side, its systems jumped to life. A separate incident at Everleigh involved a tractor seized by what the farmer described as "static discharges which shone like sparks over the body of the vehicle." The next day, a single circle appeared at the same spot in the field.

At the weirder end of the scale, farmers also report the deflating of perfectly sound, heavy-duty tires inside crop circles, tires designed to outlast the life of the machinery. In all incidents, no sharp objects or puncture marks were ever found, nor defective valves. In Surrey, three tires belonging to two separate vehicles, using the field at different time intervals, suffered a collapse of their metal structures (Pringle 1999). Remember, these are no-nonsense people with their hands too full running their farms to waste time on "supernatural flim-flam."

The electromagnetic energy that may be causing these problems appears to be present some distance above the ground, exerting a temporary debilitating effect on aircraft engines. In the early 1980s, a helicopter pilot flew regularly over crop circles and got so fed up with the equipment in his cockpit going haywire that he has refused to fly over their airspace ever since.

If these incidents sound expensive, they are. But a shot of retail therapy won't make you happier: one man had the magnetic strips on his credit cards completely wiped clean after visiting the "Nine Crescents" at Hakpen Hill (1999), while the ones left "cooking" in the hot interior of his car were unaffected.

One of the most unusual field tests I've come across in connection with charting distorted energy fields occurred in the "Triple Julia Set." There I met two men using digital clocks to look for discrepancies in missing time. Leaving one clock miles away at their accommodation, they kept the second one inside the formation for twenty minutes. When they later compared both time pieces, a discrepancy of five minutes had occurred.

Several accounts exist in which time appears to have been altered, three of them associated with the "Triple Julia Set" alone. The effect can be physically experienced, and

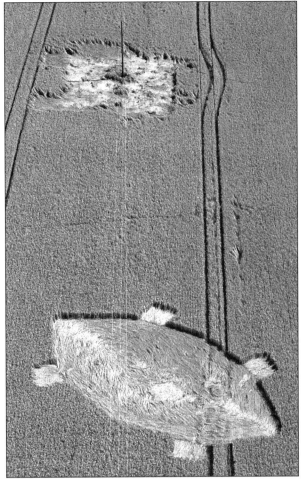

Figure 8.14

The electromagnetic energy that created the crop circle appears to have carried along the overhead electricity cables to the nearby pole and discharged itself as a rough version of the original design. Froxfield, 1994.

many are the times when I have walked into crop circles to perform simple tasks requiring a few minutes, only to rendezvous with my colleagues nearby and find myself arriving *hours* late. Mine is not an isolated case, as many other researchers' furious wives will gladly tell you.

Six investigators at Operation White Crow also experienced problems with time when, dur-

ing the brief encounter with the trilling noise, an hour and a half elapsed. In a separate incident, a crop circles watcher reported how he had been on regular reconnaissance of a field when he realized that the shadows cast by a particular group of trees a few yards away was at odds with the rest of those surrounding the field. As he walked over to check this out he discovered he had lost half an

Figure 8.15

This formation, made entirely of ellipses, seemingly demonstrates knowledge of the dynamic theory of the wave-field of a magnet. Cisbury Rings hill fort, 1995.

be taking place inside crop circles? The effects on compasses and all manner of electronic equipment would suggest so; in fact, the association between magnetism and crop circles is one of the longest threads running through the phenomenon's history. In recent years the hints have appeared in the crop circle patterns themselves: In 1995 "solar system" crop circles appeared along the A272 near Winchester, and below Cisbury Rings, a crop formation made entirely of ellipses seemingly demonstrated our knowledge of the dynamic theory of the wave-field of a magnet. (See figures 8.15 and 8.16.) But the most enlightening for me was the "Beltane Wheel" crop glyph with its thirty-three flames.

hour. Even more puzzling was that upon walking back to his original spot he gained back the time he lost. The following morning he returned to continue his surveillance and discovered a new crop circle there with three satellites.

The missing time scenario was highlighted at Westbury in 1982 when Ray Barnes witnessed a crop circle forming yards away, "which took no less than four seconds," and noticed how the shadows around him happened to fall at the wrong angle. Meanwhile, the farmer, farther away in the field, had performed twenty minutes' worth of labor in the time it took Barnes to turn around.

Missing time in crop circles might stretch credulity, or perhaps not. The slowing down of clocks in motion is already a well-tested process in particle physics (Capra 1986). These strange effects of time in relation to crop circles may prove to be a significant indicator of the process involved in their creation, since time, to a large degree, is governed by gravity and its ability to *slow down* the speeds of light. Consequently, if time is affected, the circlemaking process could be interacting with the local electromagnetic, even gravitational, field.

Could a subtle alteration of the magnetic field

Figure 8.16
Other magnetic-type crop circle designs. Avebury Trusloe, 2000; East Meon, 1995.

Beltane is the Celtic spring festival for honoring the Sun. Consequently, the flames of the Beltane Wheel often garnished Celtic and Lusitanian sundials, just as its crop circle counterpart garnished the field beside West Kennett Long Barrow three days after the Celtic festival.

This is where the implications get interesting. As we know, the Sun is our biggest local supplier of electromagnetism, and its gravitational pull on all planets in the solar system is formidable. Dividing the Earth's 365-day circuit around the Sun by those thirty-three flames gives 11.060606, the convenient number of years in the sunspot cycle.

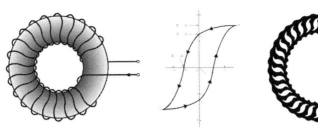

Figure 8.17

Left: The process of magnetization of a ring; center: a typical hysteresis curve; right: are these processes suggested by the "Beltane Wheel" crop glyph?

Could the crop circle's flame motif be telling us something? Maybe. The shape they make is known in physics as a hysteresis loop—a curve on a graph describing how an object of nonmagnetic material is given magnetic field strength by increasing or decreasing the local magnetic field. Applying this principle to plants (a nonmagnetic material), is it possible that an altered or reversed magnetic field strength has been applied to induce them to fall? The interference to compasses and electronic equipment suggests so.

What's more, such a defined change in the local magnetic field can be used to either repel or contain energy, acting like an invisible electric fence, and as such can conceivably be used as a shielding device. This would explain why electrical equipment is interfered with only upon crossing the crop circle's perimeter.

There's another element that would contribute to changes in the local magnetic field—

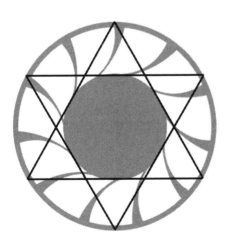

Figure 8.18

"Torus Ring" crop glyph and its encoded hexagonal geometry. Esoterically, the hexagon is associated with the Sun. North Down, 2000.

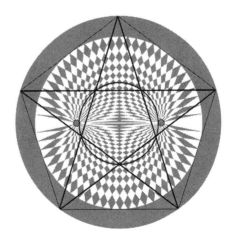

Figure 8.19

The hidden pentagonal geometry in the "magnetic grid," which appeared a few miles away. The pentagon is representational of living organisms, which are, of course, affected by magnetic fields. Avebury Trusloe, 2000.

spin. Earlier I mentioned that everything in the Universe comes about through spin, and judging by the way the plants are laid, so do crop circles. A spinning vortex is capable of generating a magnetic field, particularly so in water, itself a conductor of electromagnetic energy. As we already know, water plays a key role in the location of crop circles, and perhaps more importantly, it is found inside the plants' stems.

Two years after the "Beltane Wheel," more clues surfaced as to the role played by magnetism in crop circles. The most obvious was the "Magnetic Grid" glyph at Avebury Trusloe. At this point, Colin Andrews discovered the Earth's magnetic field to have shifted locally between 3° and 5° within crop circles, a claim that was supported within weeks by Japanese scientists.[44] By way of validation, shortly after Andrews' public

announcement, the Circlemakers dropped a ring torus crop glyph two miles away, its eleven arcs twisted by 4°, giving the design a three-dimensional feel.

By now, two other crop glyphs had appeared nearby with a similar 3-D effect. Perplexed, I located all four crop circles on my map, sipped my coffee, and looked blankly at the dots. When a flattened tetrahedron revealed itself across the Avebury landscape, I followed the trail.

The tetrahedron is the primary geometric structure of matter, and I recalled how in the Barbury Castle tetrahedron crop glyph each "step" of the ratchet section had deviated from magnetic north—by 4 degrees.

With the "magnetic grid" glyph at the center, I began to connect the dots, measuring everything relative to magnetic north (which that year lay

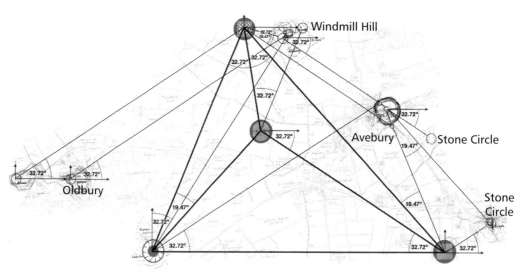

Figure 8.20
*Relationship between selected crop circles of 2000, local sacred sites, and the angles 32.72°
and 19.47°.*

---

[44]Personal communication with Colin Andrews.

Figure 8.21

Four-degree shift from magnetic North. Barbury Castle tetrahedron.

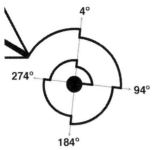

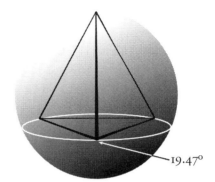

approximately 4.5 degrees west of grid north), and discovered that the four formations referenced each other by either 32.72 degrees or 19.47 degrees. Historically, crop circles have appeared near sacred sites, so I extended this process and found that these angular relationships also exist between the crop circles and the sacred sites, as well as between the sites themselves.

Let us look at the significance of these numbers: 32.7272 degrees, a circle's 360° divided by 11. Now, if you take a tetrahedron (a four-sided pyramid) and circumscribe it within a sphere, such as the Earth, its points touch the sphere at 19.47°, and on planets in the solar system such as Venus, Earth, Mars, and Jupiter there exists a magnetic anomaly, a point where energy up-wells, and every one of these points is located between 19° and 20° latitude—19.47° to be precise.[45]

Figure 8.22

A circumscribed tetrahedron touches the surface of the sphere at a latitude of 19.47 degrees. On Earth this energy "hotspot" is marked by the Hawaiian volcanoes.

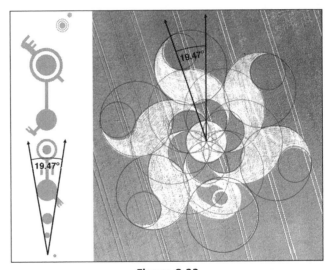

Figure 8.23

Crop circles referencing 19.47: left, Alton Barnes 1990, and right, Golden Ball Hill, 2000.

---

[45]Whenever a tetrahedron is circumscribed by a sphere, the ratio between the surfaces of these geometric solids is 2.72, a transdimensional constant. 2.72 is the convenient number for the Megalithic Yard, the unit of measure used by the architects of stone circles and other sacred sites, including the temples of ancient Egypt. 2.72 is also the number of transformation.

The number 32.72 is associated with the Grand Gallery of the Great Pyramid of Gizeh, 32.7 inches being one of the critical measurements found in this corbelled chamber. Converted to frequency it becomes 415 Hz, the note A-flat. Coincidentally, 32 Hz is also the fundamental frequency of the harmonic music scale (see Hero 1992).

Are these angles and numerical relationships clues, exchange mechanisms between gravity and mass, perhaps between dimensions?

More to the point, is this exchange mechanism reliant on the 3–5 degree out-of-phase rotation of the magnetic grid, as suggested in these crop circles?

Clearly, the energy behind crop circles is capable of distorting the local electromagnetic field, and interacting in strange ways with objects and people. But it's also leaving "fingerprints" on the plants.

I found this out for myself in 1997 while sitting inside the Etchilhampton "Flower" crop glyph, quietly absorbed in sketching its exquisite lay. Nearby, three other enthusiasts admired the artistry (the Circlemakers', not mine). Abruptly, a crackling noise like static rose all around us; the others heard it too because they stopped to see where the sound was coming from. They stared at me, I stared at them. It was reminiscent of the discharge from high voltage wires, so my first reaction was to look for electricity pylons. There were none. I held my ear to the ground but it wasn't coming from the flattened crop either, nor from the standing crop at the perimeter.

It was just "there," maintaining a steady level, and surrounding us for a good ten minutes before my colleagues and I had to leave. As I crossed the perimeter of the formation, silence returned. Two years later at Roundway, I experienced the same crackling noise, this time in late-afternoon in a field already infiltrated by the crackling from nearby high-voltage wires, enabling me to establish that both sounds were audibly dissimilar.

Hissing sounds are not uncommon in crops, for it is the natural reaction of the damp wheat heads expanding in the heat of the rising Sun. However, none of my experiences have occurred early in the day. A similar incident ten years earlier at Dog-leg field, near Winchester, occurred at seven in the evening. Despite the calm evening, a loud hissing and crackling sound was accompanied by a pulsating beat within the circle's perimeter.

Is it possible that a type of electrical "coating" has attached itself to the plants?

While studying electronics, Paul Vigay invented a small electrostatic detector for identifying hidden electric cables. Because it was exceptionally sensitive, the device could detect minute electrical current flows in plants and people. One day his mother came home with a batch of wheat stalks for her flower arrangements and asked Paul to test his device on the drying stalks. Intriguingly, the probe sensed a charge in some, but registered no reaction in others. Ushered out of the kitchen while his mother moved the stalks around, he came back into the room to retest the batch and the results were consistent with the first run. The test was repeated several times until his mother revealed that those not reacting had been taken from a crop circle.

Vigay decided to repeat the test in a living crop circle at Cheesefoot Head. Walking down the tram line with the device, the LED display flashed to show the plants were discharging as they should. But as Vigay crossed the perimeter of the formation, no readings were registered within the entire crop circle; and as he made his exit at the opposite end of the formation the readings rose. He repeated the test several times from different entry points and achieved identical results. Was the lack of electric charge in the circle due to the crop having been flattened? Apparently not. Tests inside a section of the field that had suffered wind damage revealed readings consistent with normal plants.

Questions arose when analysis of another crop circle showed no deviation from normal plants. To Vigay's credit, this formation had been deliberately man-made as part of Project Argus protocol, a fact that had been kept from him at the time. Vigay concluded that the circlemaking force appears to ground the current within the perimeter of the design (Vigay 1995).

Growing grain carries a neutral charge during the night, changing to positive by the day. If the plants are being manipulated electromagnetically, it is necessary to first apply a negative charge to allow the plants to repel the normal magnetic field so that they point away from the center—and negative charges have indeed been measured in plants which were inside or adjacent to crop circles.[46] Such an alteration should manifest itself in the way the plants' roots are aligned. Roots are geotropic by nature, and therefore grow downward and toward the center of gravity. Since they are sensitive to changes in the magnetic field, any change in their alignment is a strong indication that the Earth's magnetic—possibly gravitational—field has been altered. This is the case in crop circles, where the roots are known to realign opposite the bend in the stalk, like an S-shape, contrary to their normal habit (Audus 1960).

In 1993, tests using a standard electrostatic voltmeter also revealed that the standing crop inside a formation was "coated" with a charge ranging from 10–20 volts per inch. By 1999, this charge had risen, some crop circles registering 30 volts, and in one case in excess of 100 volts (Hein 2000).

There is no doubt that electromagnetic energy occurs in crop circles, and in certain cases it can pack a punch. In the village of Spaldwick, Cambridgeshire, alarms went off at 2 A.M. due to a sudden power surge shortly before the discovery nearby of a large "Celtic cross" crop circle. But these villagers had nothing to complain about, after all, the 1991 Barbury Castle tetrahedron took out an entire town's electricity, plus that of twenty square miles of surrounding countryside, and the "Beltane Wheel" formation even silenced local radio. These power surges remain unexplained by utility companies, and the indication is that not only are we dealing with a considerable generation of power, but the higher the design complexity involved in the crop circle—the square footage affected—the stronger the discharge.

Biophysical Changes

If an artificial or electromagnetic energy source is interacting with the natural cycle of plants, it is natural to assume that the effect is verifiable at the microscopic level.

In 1988, Andrews and Delgado sent plant samples from crop circles, together with controls, to Signalysis Laboratory in Stroud, England. The samples were processed by Kenneth and Rosemary Spelman in accordance with a procedure approved in the German government's "Pharmacopoeia for Homeopathy" for spagyric preparations. This process is

---

[46]From tests carried out by John Burke of BLT Research, Cambridge, MA.

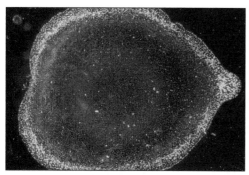

Figure 8.24

Crystalline energy patterns: control sample.

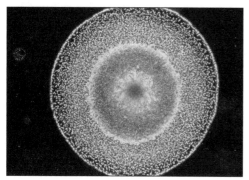

Figure 8.25

Center of crop circle.

normally used in the diagnosis of human blood samples, since it allows for the crystalline structure of minerals dissolved in fluids to be examined under a microscope.

Their results revealed how the irregular pattern in control samples had taken on a structured pattern inside crop circles and that energy of some type had changed the plants' crystalline structure (Andrews and Delgado 1990). A separate barrage of tests on samples, this time taken from a crop circle in Argonne, Illinois, by

molecular biologist Kevin Folta, even showed that the DNA was considerably different from the controls (Chorost and Dudley 1992a).

After the Spelmans' tantalizing report was published, Delgado was contacted by another interested party, Dr. W. C. Levengood from Michigan, who hoped to follow up on the UK experiments. A respected biophysicist, over the course of his multi-disciplinary career Dr. Levengood has conducted investigations into such areas as the effects of solar and cosmic rays on the reproduction of living organisms and the relationship between ion transport and vigor selection in seeds. He holds six patents and has written fifty peer-reviewed papers.

Levengood's curiosity led him to investigate the possibility of molecular changes in crop circle plants. After performing thousands of hours of field work and laboratory studies on hundreds of crop circles, as well as controlled, man-made scientific experiments and tests on control samples, he detected a series of statistically significant anomalies.

One of the first puzzles Levengood came across concerned the seeds. Seed heads collected from crop circles contained seeds that were often severely stunted, malformed, and lower in weight and/or reduced in size. Levengood attributed this to a premature dehydration of the seeds, their development arrested at the time the crop circle was created.[47] The critical time for such alterations appears to occur early on in the seed's development, the effect becoming less visible relative to the seeds' maturity; when mature, an increase in seed growth occurs.

---

[47]Speeded germination of seeds is associated with a plant's orientation to a magnetic pole or the introduction of an artificial magnetic field during germination. In fact, planting seeds aligned to the north is a centuries-old ritual in rural folklore.

To see how the seeds reacted when germinated, Levengood conducted closely monitored fourteen-day laboratory trials to compare their growth cycle with controls. He noted that the crop circle seeds reacted variably, depending upon the presumed intensity of the circle-making energy as well as the age of the plants when affected.

The results show an inconsistency with natural plant development. In some of the immature plants, the seeds failed to germinate; in young plants, they did germinate but with grossly depressed development in roots and shoots. Plants affected in the late life cycle by crop circle energy developed in a manner inconsistent with seeds of that species, revealing accelerated germination and increased vigor in the more mature plants; the latter exhibited a growth rate 40 percent faster than normal and had a healthier root structure.

What kind of energy is capable of altering a plant's natural life and growth cycles? To find out, Levengood tested a sample of plants in a commercial microwave oven. The results revealed that the closest similarities to crop circle samples—even at the microscopic level—occurred when the plants were subjected to thirty seconds of microwave exposure, not too far off from the range of circle-making time described by eyewitnesses. Evidence of this rapid heating was corroborated by a superficial charring of the plant tissue which left deeper layers unaffected, thereby indicating the brevity of the action.

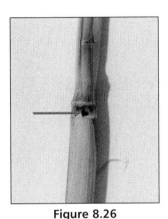

Figure 8.26

A blown node. The small hole has been created by pressurized, superheated water forcing its way out of the stem. Note the charring effect.

In his first peer-reviewed paper on crop circles, Dr. Levengood stated that "the affected plants have components which suggest the involvement of rapid air movement, ionization, electric fields, and transient high temperatures combined with an oxidizing atmosphere. One naturally occurring and organized force incorporating each of these features is an ion plasma vortex, one very high energy example being a lightning charge" (Levengood 1994).

Another conundrum concerned the plant's nodes. These fibrous protuberances are the hardest portions of the stem, allowing a plant to support its weight and maintain its upright posture. Levengood found the nodes in crop circle plants to be grossly enlarged and expanded, much more than could be accounted for by trauma, exposure to chemicals, or pest infestation. Phototropism and gravitropism both play a role in the bending of nodes, yet these natural processes take time to develop and cannot account for the massive node-bending observed in new crop circles. The slight node length extensions observed in man-made formations proved statistically insignificant.

By far the most important discovery in Levengood's research pertained to the nodes' bract tissue, the thin membrane supporting the seed head that enables nutrients to be supplied to the developing embryos. Levengood found an abnormal enlargement of the tissues' cell-wall pits; these are the minuscule holes that allow the movement of nutrients. Here, he discovered a series of expulsion cavities or "blow holes," as if internal liquid had been forced out from inside the plants. Again, this is not found in normal crops under any known circumstances.

In striking contrast to the control samples, the elongated scars show how a rapid expansion took place inside crop circle plants, the result of the water in the cell walls being *suddenly* heated. With nowhere to escape, the water forces its way outwards by exploiting the weaker sections of the tissue, thereby creating the scars.

Levengood concluded that "the energy mechanism producing quantitative alterations in the plant stem nodes falls within the framework of a straight-forward and widely applied principal of physics [Beer's Law] dealing with the absorption of electromagnetic energy by matter," strongly suggesting that an energy source "originating in the microwave region" had boiled the water inside the plants' nodes, effectively transforming it into steam (ibid.).

Michael Chorost reached similar conclusions in his published report for Project Argus. He found the circle-making phenomenon induces radiation anomalies, heats plants rapidly and briefly through a rapid pulse of unknown energy, sometimes scorching them; and that it swells their cell wall pits, interacts with the development of the seeds, and leaves radioactive traces in the soil (Chorost and Dudley 1992a).

But if microwaves are the answer, certain things need to be taken into consideration. Microwaves are an electromagnetic energy wave with a frequency above 1 GHz (10^9 Hz). Microwave energy quickly dissipates after initial contact with an object, yet sensors capable of detecting electromagnetic frequencies show that an energy residue remains in the crop circles long after its appearance, sometimes for years.

Moreover, the side effects of microwaves are generally inconsistent with the particulars of crop circles. Recent studies into microwaves and cellular phones show how detrimental these frequencies can be to the human body (Whitlock 1999), just as Marconi once discovered in his early experiments, much to his horror, how these frequencies killed animals close to the source. Such detrimental, even fatal, side effects on humans or animals is unheard of with crop circles. Microwaves are also capable of rendering both soil and plants sterile, and in crop circles this is a rare exception.[48] So, it is likely that the energy behind crop circles lies elsewhere in the electromagnetic spectrum, and it may not be the only type of energy involved.

If you cast your mind back to the early history of crop circles, Terence Meaden proposed that stationary whirlwinds and plasma vortices were somehow responsible for making crop circles. While the weather-based theory has proved to be implausible, Japanese scientists have demonstrated in laboratory conditions how plasma (essentially a superheated, ionized gas) is capable of organizing itself into simple concentric shapes, with alternating layers of positive/negative charge, reminiscent of the shapes and directional plant lay of early crop circles and rings.

One could argue, then, that the energy behind crop circles is natural, and that an intelligent source is able to control it to a very fine degree. How else can we explain a "natural phe-

---

[48]If you will recall, this has only been observed twice (by Marcus Allen and myself), once at Avebury, once at Barbury Castle crop glyphs (1999). With regard to dead animals, the flattened Canadian porcupine incident is perhaps the exception. However, in chapter 11 the same effect is attributed to sound.

nomenon" that selectively avoids houses, towns, gardens, and parks? That produces hundreds of geometrical and philosophically significant shapes of great complexity? That interacts with, even reads the minds of, its human observers?

Over the past few decades, Japanese scientists have been investigating how physical manifestation is based on energy spun from the vacuum energy field of space. In his book *Paradigm of New Science—Principia for the Twenty-First Century*, the Japanese scientist Dr. Shiuji Inomata proposes that the vacuum state is an energy field in which consciousness is integrated with electromagnetic and gravitational forces to create matter. His theoretical model illustrates how energy transmutations, such as the manifestation and demanifestation of matter, might be capable of taking place according to such principles.[49]

Spinning this energy from one state into another appears to be correlated to the Golden Mean spiral, the spiral of nature; hydrogen, too, seems to be involved in this process, a particularly important point since it is fundamental to water, and both water and spirals are fundamental to crop circles.

This energy's residual effects also appear to support Delgado's early speculation: That crop circles are created in two stages, the first priming each stem so it is programmed to move in a predetermined direction, the second activating it to fall to its intended position (Andrews and Delgado 1991).

In which case we shouldn't just be looking down at the ground, but also up at the sky.

The Aerial Component

Jack Spooncer spent thirty successful years in the aerospace industry designing engines for Rolls Royce and Westland, during which time he developed an enquiring mind and a working knowledge of polymers. He is also trusted enough to hold NATO security clearance.

One night during the hot summer of 1997 he was driving back to his farmhouse, sited above an aquifer of unusually high pressure and in a part of Dorset rich in Neolithic sites. As he turned the corner towards his property he came upon an incredible sight: "A large dome of light, about two hundred feet in diameter, was touching the corn field. There were thousands of points of light, like diamonds, all aligned and geometric. It was glistening, shimmering like a hologram." He heard a high-pitched sound permeating the surrounding area, but just as the headlights from his car shone through the translucent bubble, it disappeared.[50]

Early next morning, two well-defined half rings of flattened crop appeared, their "stems perfectly brushed, crunching underfoot." Jack reasoned that had his car not interrupted the work-in-progress, a more complex pattern may have manifested; Jack also speculated that a high degree of magnetic flux may have accounted for suspending the droplets of water in regular patterns.[51] Natural forces at work? Or did Jack catch the Circlemakers at work?

[49]Published in 1987 in Japanese, and referenced in John Davidson's *The Secret of the Creative Vacuum: Man and the Energy Dance*.
[50]Spooncer's "glistening bubble" is remarkably similar to eyewitness reports during the second appearance at Fatima by the Virgin Mary in September 1917.
[51]Personal conversation with Jack Spooncer.

Catching the Circlemakers at it was the last thing on my mind as I sat one afternoon on top of a hill while having a picnic with friends. I was compelled to pick up my camera and photograph what seemed an ordinary shot across the Vale of Pewsey. The sky was overcast and shadows faint—hardly a captivating image. Two days later a heptagonal crop formation appeared beside Tawsmead Copse at the same general location as my photo.

Later I received accounts from two people who had independently seen a "tube of light" descend into that field, one at 5 A.M. prior to the appearance of the formation, the other two days earlier in mid-afternoon, around the time of my picnic. When I took a look at the photograph it showed two rays of sunlight beaming through the clouds (see figure 8.27 on page A8 in the color section). As a seasoned photographer, it occurred to me that rays of sunlight can only be shot when one is facing the Sun, and at the time the photo was taken, facing east, the Sun was already in the west. Further, shafts of sunlight tend to expand in width the closer they come to the horizon, but the edges of mine were perpendicular.

Laboratory analysis confirmed that light had not fogged the film, for the rays did not run the width of the entire negative, but started inside the exposed image of the vale and stopped at the horizon. What is even more remarkable is that I don't recall seeing these beams at the time I took the photo. This is by no means the first time these tubes of light have been photographed. A couple visiting a formation at Alton Priors in 1991 took five photographs of what looked like a column of white cloud accompanied by small white lights directly above the dumbbell crop circle (Pringle 1999).

Evidence suggests that not only do these tubes precede crop circles, but that on some occasions they are directly involved with the process. Over the course of our conversations, Nancy Talbott had often expressed to me her frustration at not being able to see a direct manifestation of a crop circle and the agency behind it. Given that Nancy is a grounded, matter-of-fact individual, this wasn't surprising. In August 2001, she traveled to Holland to help parapsychologist Dr. William Roll gather geomagnetic and electromagnetic data. Roll was himself interested as to whether an element of human consciousness was involved in the crop circles. Their hosts, the van der Broekes, had had crop circles appear outside their home, and their son Robbert had not only had premonitions of some of these, he'd also photographed unusually bright lights and orbs inside them.

Around 3 A.M. on August 21, when Robbert and Nancy were looking out across the bean field to the rear of the house from separate rooms, they heard the local cattle "bawling raucously," accompanied by the neighbor's dog. Then fifteen minutes later "a brilliant, intense white column, or tube, of light—about 8 inches to 1 foot in diameter, from my vantage point—flashed down from the sky to the ground, illuminating my bedroom and the sky as brilliantly as if from helicopter searchlights. My room was so bright I can't, in retrospect, understand how I could so very clearly see the 'tube' of light outside—its distinct edges—but I could, for about a full second, and there seemed to be a slight bluish tinge along the sides of the tube."

Two more tubes of light would be seen in a space of six seconds before the two ran out to the field and found an elliptical crop circle with an appendage resembling the letter "T." A veil of steam rose faintly out of the ground. Robbert described the tubes as spiraling, and maintaining the same width from the sky all the way down to the ground.[52]

Talbott and van der Broeke's recent eyewitness account is one of many such close encounters. In 1966, not far from the majestic white chalk cliffs of Dover, a man walking in the rain saw what he described as "a translucent glass tube" descend from the sky. With the rain visibly deflecting off its surface and the nearby livestock "seemingly transfixed" by loud hissing sounds, the tube sealed off an area of grass and created a crop circle (T. Wilson 1998).

On the afternoon of August 24, 1990, a farmer tending his field of winter barley behind Golden Ball Hill suddenly found himself in a similar situation, standing ten feet away from a three-foot-thick rotating, perpendicular tube whose earth-bound end stopped short of the ground, while the other end rose stratospherically to a point out of view. The tube remained stationary as a swirling motion manifested in his crop.

The idea of a controlled energy employed within a tube—something like a laser—to create a crop circle is supported by Ray Barnes. He once witnessed a "line" descending into the crop, then moving across the field to become stationary, whereupon it sank down and rotated, generating a flattened swirl in four seconds (ibid.). These tubes appear to retain some form of residual energy. An eyewitness in Westbury describes seeing smoke from nearby fires blow across a field and reach a crop circle only to hit an "invisible wall" and

skirt the design; above the crop circle, a vapor trail from an airplane at 25,000 feet was seen breaking apart as it crossed this tube (Pringle 1999).

Apparently, a mass of energy is projected in a self-contained stream from a point high above the Earth. For energy or liquid to travel inside a tube, a spiraling, rotating motion is required for effective movement to take place; the closest examples of this method are the way blood circulates through veins or water goes down a plug hole.[53] The Russian metaphysician P. D. Ouspensky describes this process in terms of light: "The electron is transformed into quanta; it becomes a ray of light. The point is transformed into a line, into a spiral, into a hollow cylinder" (Ouspensky 1931). The philosopher describes this model of a ray of light consisting of particles lying close to one another lengthwise "with two kinds of thread." Perhaps this is the electromagnetic transverse wave, the combination of electric and magnetic waves, one lagging slightly behind the other.

Regardless of what we call the energy inside these tubes, it seems to send a "code" which tells the plants what to do and when. However, the process leaves a unique fingerprint in the design. Normally, when you shine a flashlight against a surface at a distance, the result isn't a circle of light, but an ellipse, particularly if the flashlight is not perpendicular to the surface. In the case of a light beam projected from high above the Earth, the initially circular projection has to contend with the Earth's curvature, the

---

[52]From an interview with Jeff Rense, on the *Jeff Rense Radio Show,* November 19, 2001.
[53]*Daily Telegraph,* 1998, op. cit.; and Dr. A. J. Scott-Morley, cited in David Elkington's *In the Name of the Gods,* p. 171.

progressively denser atmospheric layers which act as lenses, and the gradient of the ground. Consequently, crop circles appear slightly elliptical. The "distortion" varies from the circular from as little as eight inches to as much as fifteen feet, the effect being more pronounced when the circles appear on the sides of hills.[54]

The elliptical shape of crop circles may support the possibility that they are either created or activated by a beam. Such a beam must be capable of passing through clouds and rain with little attenuation or loss of energy, and within the confines of our present technology, an electromagnetic frequency around the microwave spectrum would achieve just that.

As the evidence shows, the tubes of light originate from a point beyond the range of our vision. But, on occasion, they have been known to be attached to something.

On the night of July 13, 1988, around 11:30 P.M., Mary Freeman was driving south next to the Avebury stone avenue. She noticed how the underside of a cloud near Silbury Hill had a golden white glow and was a great deal brighter than the glow from the Moon, which was not full. The hazy shape of an oval object seemed to protrude from inside the cloud. Suddenly, a tubular beam, as wide as a football field, plunged out of the cloud towards the ground to the south of Silbury. Freeman changed her direction of travel and raced towards the beam, which remained in place for some three minutes.

She remembered this incident clearly because all the objects in her car suddenly levitated around her as if the vehicle had been caught up in an energy field. Within thirty-six hours, farmer Roger Hues discovered the first of the five "Celtic Cross" formations at the base of Silbury Hill.

Three years later, a young man out riding his bike in Butleigh, Somerset, heard a high-pitched humming sound. As he looked up he saw a stationary, silver, bell-shaped craft project a spiraling vortex of "aura-like" light into a field and make a twenty-nine-foot crop circle in the early wheat, which in April was barely a foot high. The event was over in a few seconds and occurred in broad daylight (Wingfield 1991b).

A similar experience occurred above the East Field, this time at midnight. Intrigued by a similar buzzing sound, a couple living nearby walked outside their house to find a set of colored lights swirling in the pitch-black sky. Twenty minutes later the lights congealed into one object from which a beam of white light descended onto the field. Five hours later the "DNA" crop glyph was discovered.

Given such clear incidences involving aerial phenomena popularly know as unidentified flying objects, we are faced with postulating that an outside source is the agency responsible for interrupting the seasonal flow of cereal crops. But, too, isn't it ridiculous to make "space brothers" the likely culprits?

Enough material has been written on UFOs to stock a generous-sized aircraft hangar, and I shall provide an overview of this equally misunderstood area of knowledge. If you are inclined to pursue it further, T. J. Constable's *The Cosmic*

---

[54]This "defect" is employed in the design of columns in Greek temples, giving them the illusion of appearing rectangular from a distance when in fact they are rounded.

Pulse of Life provides an excellent grounding in the subject, as does Johannes von Buttlar's seminal work *The UFO Phenomenon*, featuring scores of reliable and close-up reports from civil and air force pilots. There are accounts of daylight encounters, planes crashing, pilots killed in pursuit of UFOs, and statements from air traffic controllers, statesmen, and even astronauts.

As with crop circles, human contact with UFOs predates the twentieth century; in fact, it is recorded in the *Ramayana*, one of the sacred Indian sagas, dating to 6000 B.C. Here you will find written accounts of "two-storied celestial chariots with many windows, roaring like lions and blazing with red flames as they ascend into the sky to fly like comets"; the *Mahabharata* and other Vedic and Sanskrit texts describe similar events. In shamanic cultures throughout southern Africa, UFOs are referred to as *abahambi abavutayo*, the "fiery chariots" (Dutt 1961; Gordon 1962).

A papyrus stored in the Vatican tells of a UFO sighting in Egypt during the reign of Tuthmosis III in 1500 B.C. The object is described as emitting a "foul odour," an observation often reported by latter-day victims of close encounters. In the *Chronicle of William of Newburgh*, 1290, it is written that the abbot of Byland Abbey in Yorkshire was about to say grace when, "John, one of the brethren came in and said there was a great portent outside. Then they all ran out and Lo! a large round silver object, not dissimilar to a disc, flew slowly over them and excited the greatest terror"; a similar report of the period exists in Matthew of Paris' *Historia Anglorum*.

Despite persistent and often contradictory denials by members of today's military, the subject of UFOs has been active within the ranks of air forces around the world since the 1940s. As General Benjamin Chidlaw, USAF Commander of Continental Air Defense, once remarked: "We have stacks of reports of flying saucers. We take them very seriously when you consider we have lost many men and planes trying to intercept them" (Stringfield 1957, Good 1987).

This would explain why a sizable document on public safety such as the U.S. Fire Officer's Guide to Disaster Control Manual, Second Edition, devotes thirteen pages to UFOs, and preparedness in the event of a crash or attack. On the other hand, the existence of a U.S. government agency researching UFOs is purportedly classified "above top secret," denying access even to the president, and federal law empowers NASA's administrator to impound, without a hearing, anyone who touches a UFO or its occupants. Sobering advice indeed.

Once in a blue moon, however, the authorities give the public a taste of what they must surely know. During an American television documentary in 1960, the Pentagon accepted UFOs as intelligently guided machines whose technology could not be accounted for on Earth. Lord Dowding, England's Air Chief Marshall, stated: "The existence of these machines is proved." There exists a substantial list of UFO sightings made by NASA astronauts: One account from the crew of Apollo XII states that a UFO followed them all the way from Earth orbit to within 130,000 miles of the moon (Hynek and Vallée 1975). Would this perhaps explain why IBM sold the U.S. Air Force's Space Surveillance Team a supercomputer in 2000 "to better detect and identify unidentified flying objects in Earth's orbit" (Reuters 2000)?

According to David Ash and Peter Hewitt, "The real problem with UFOs is not a shortage of evidence, but rather the absence of any scientific explanation for their existence and behavior. It is difficult if not impossible to accommodate UFOs in existing scientific thinking" (Ash and Hewitt 1990). The astrophysicist Dr. Jacques Valleé also concludes that just because UFOs violate the laws of motion, as we presently know them, does not nullify their existence (Valleé 1975).

Senior citizens, children, policemen, even military personnel have reported large structured craft six to thirty-six hours before the appearance of crop circles. Farmers around the Barbury Castle area have witnessed military jets and helicopters scramble to intercept balls of light or silent flying objects which then proceed to toy with their chasers, sometimes blinking out and re-appearing behind the craft giving chase. Busty Taylor has witnessed so many rotating objects with blinking lights that during his time as a driving instructor he's used these sightings as a reliable test of his students' alertness at the wheel. That these objects are not the lurid imagination of quirky British country-folk is confirmed by identical reports from around the world, including eyewitnesses from rural areas of Romania, Hungary, and Russia, countries where the words "crop" and "circle" had, up to that point, never been associated.

Former Yorkshire police sergeant Anthony Dodd has written extensively about the connection between the increase in UFO activity prior to crop circle activity. In 1991, members of his UFO organization investigated an incident on June 29 in Bristol, England, when dozens of witnesses called the police shortly before midnight to report a large red object crossing the night sky above the city. After it descended into nearby fields, a helicopter appeared and began to give chase. When the craft shot away at high speed, the helicopter returned to the field, combing it with its powerful searchlight. The next morning, residents discovered a large dumbbell pictogram at the site (Dodd 1991).

The presumed circle-making craft are not necessarily large. With the increase in the number of visitors to crop circle sites since the 1990s, the number of eyewitnesses reporting small silver-colored spheres has steadily grown, one of the best examples being Steven Alexander's daytime footage of the blinking sphere below Milk Hill, the event witnessed at close quarters on the ground by a farm laborer (see chapter 1).

The objects appear capable of traveling at high speed; they are noiseless in flight, but emit a loud hum when hovering in position above a field. They vary in size from tennis to beach ball, and are capable of maneuvering at sharp angles with dexterity and as the British military has experienced over Alton Priors, they can toy with helicopters at will. They are most often seen at night between the hours of 11 P.M. and 3 A.M., as colored balls of either exceptional luminescence or translucence.

One morning, as she poured my first cup of coffee, my bed-and-breakfast host, Marigold Pearce, told me of an experience that "may or may not be relevant to your research." Returning home at 2 A.M. from her night shift as a nurse, she was driving along the dark Vale of Pewsey when she saw "an exceptionally bright orange headlight" following her car at high speed. Believing it to be a motorcycle in a hurry, Mrs. Pearce gave the speeder passing room. But as it shot past her car, she was amazed to find it was a small, incandescent, unmanned sphere. It hovered along the road for a short distance before making a lazy curve over the hedge and across the fields. Apparently the local people are so used to these balls of light they do not pay them much attention any more, and Pearce was no different.

Paul Vigay had a similar experience shortly before the appearance of the "DNA" crop circle. As he neared a bend in the road above the East Field, a bright light raced around the corner at approximately sixty mph. Believing it to be the light from an approaching motorcycle (although it was far too close to the ground for that), and worried about the dangerous speed for such a narrow road, Paul stopped his car. He expected the oncoming vehicle to drive by, but instead, it changed direction and flew *over* his car. Vigay's car engine cut out immediately. Behind the ball, a van was bombing downhill in hot pursuit, but having trouble keeping up with the sphere. The object then left the road and was tracked for five minutes by four separate surveillance groups interspersed along the ridges above the Vale of Pewsey.

Jane Ross had witnessed some of these balls of light prior to the summer of 1997, so she made a request for them to "manifest" to a group of people by way of validation that she wasn't losing her marbles. Following a healing ceremony inside the "Bourton Star" crop formation in July, seven of these objects obliged, and were seen dancing silently above the neighboring field at Easton Hill and its resident long barrow. They flickered in a nonlinear fashion; they were too low for stars, too silent for aircraft, too tall for flashlights or tractor headlights, and too abrupt for weather balloons or military flares. They glowed with light of unusual brightness in green, orange, red, and purple shades. They were observed (and videotaped) to move around casually for fifteen minutes before switching off, leaving the kind of afterglow one sees with halogen bulbs. Two other witnesses were present; I was one of them.

Balls of light like these have been filmed by Japanese film crews stationed at Adam's Grave long barrow in Wiltshire, some just a couple of hours prior to a crop circle forming in the fields (figure 8.29 on page A8 in the color section). Much daylight footage has also been shot by the public. One notable incident, this time from a camera mounted on the earthen rim of Barbury Castle, showed a number of these small incandescent guests wandering in and out of the "Dolphins" crop circle below. And on one of my many ultra-light flights, my pilot and I were overtaken by a silver sphere, which changed to red as it glided past us 200 feet away. The incident took place near Golden Ball Hill which was perhaps named due to its association with such phenomena.

Putting together all these reports of flying objects, a pattern begins to emerge, and a confusing one at that. Large structured craft; small, silver, and seemingly physical spheres; small, *luminous*, and seemingly physical spheres; balls of light that run the gamut of the visible color spectrum—how can they be all these things?

This following example provides a clue to the nature of these so-called UFOs. While investigating a series of crop circles in Cornwall, CCCS' chairman George Bishop took photographs which later revealed a green globe and a strange red object; other images were pockmarked with translucent white globes. Bishop was adamant that these "balls of light" had not been visible at the time the images were shot. It was believed that a defect in the film processing had taken place (later proved not to be the case), until identical light phenomena appeared in other visitors' photos, nine in all, some even shot at night.[55]

Hundreds of examples of light phenomena have since been captured on film, and not just inside crop circles, but in stone circles, too (see figure 8.28 on page A8 in color section).[56] With the exception of people of psychic ability, the "balls of light" are never visible to the naked eye at the time the photos are taken, suggesting they are forms of energy at various stages of manifestation.

Science has established that the physical world is made up of atoms spinning at very high rates. In questioning the nature of the Universe, many physicists and metaphysicians have developed an understanding that different rates of spin govern different states of matter, even consciousness. As such, UFOs, balls of light, and other "paranormal" phenomena are inhabitants of a reality governed by rates of spin (some call it vibration) that differ from ours. Hence they are as real on their plane of existence as we are on ours. To illustrate this point, our visual cortex is capable of seeing a tree as long as the atoms that make up the tree vibrate at the same frequency as the human eye and its information processing mechanism. If the tree's atoms were to vibrate at a rate 2 Hz below the frequency of the eye, the tree would either "disappear" or the eye would register the tree as a "ghost."

When objects from other levels of reality alter their rate of spin they are observed as increasingly physical phenomena in our dimension.

Additionally, as their frequency moves along the electromagnetic spectrum we see these objects in different colors, as author and UFO researcher John Keel observed: "When the objects begin to move into our spatial and time coordinates, they gear down from higher frequencies, passing progressively from ultraviolet to bluish green. When they stabilize within our dimension, they radiate energy on all frequencies and become a glaring white" (Keel 1975).

This ability to transubstantiate matter would require, among other things, an understanding of the illusion of time, the function of gravity, knowledge of the proposed three speeds of light, and the spinning vortex action of molecules (Myers and Percy 1999), techniques attributed in the past to mortals such as Jesus Christ, the prophet Mohammed, and the Greek philosopher Apollonius of Tyana (Ash and Hewitt 1990; Yogananda 1996).

Studies into bioplasmic energy fields and orgone energy by such notables as Rudolf Steiner, Wilhelm Reich, and Semison and Valentina Kirlian clearly show that we are surrounded by a life-force energy which is interactive, yet seemingly invisible to the limited human range of vision. Mechanistic thought has brainwashed us into believing this energy source does not exist but, on occasion, the etheric world does show itself. An aura, several inches thick, was witnessed around the Tibetan Grand Lama by Dr. Alexander Cannon, a distinguished scientist and celebrated psychiatrist of his day (Hall 1937). This same aura is graphically represent-

---

[55]Personal communication with George Bishop.
[56]Many incidences of otherwise invisible balls of light have been photographed during controlled experiments by the Santa Barbara-based researchers Ed and Kris Sherwood of Millennium Research.

ed by the halo framing the heads of Jesus Christ and the Christian saints.[57]

That this force is associated with consciousness was hinted by the Nobel Prize-winning father of quantum theory, Max Planck: "There is no matter as such! All matter originates and exists only by virtue of a force. We must assume behind this force the existence of a conscious and intelligent Mind. This Mind is the matrix of all matter."

It appears that a number of sources contribute to the creation of crop circles. Given that these forms can react to the thoughts of people in their vicinity, these forms are either conscious, or at the very least, intelligently directed. Regardless, the increasing sighting and filming of "structured" craft, balls of light, even tubes of light that seem to originate from beyond Earth's atmosphere, all support the hypothesis that an aerial-borne outside agency is involved.

Even so, we can rule out crop circles as landings by alien craft. Classic UFO accounts, such as the Australian "UFO nests," are generally associated with squashed plants, indentations, electronic disruption, paralysis, burns, and harmful radioactivity. For example, in 1954, a number of people saw a craft flatten a field of corn in Mexico; that circular area yielded no further plant growth after the incident (Randles and Fuller 1990). A Uruguayan farmer witnessed a rotating, glowing orange ball flatten grass into a circle, scorching it in the process; this incident caused electrical failure and the subsequent death of his dog.

Given the ground evidence of crop circles, such reports suggest that circlemaking and landing UFOs are two separate phenomena, albeit sharing some attributes (electronic disruption, for example). Whatever your stance on UFOs, the cumulative evidence that someone not entirely of terrestrial origin is associated with a significant number of crop circle events is beyond doubt, even if less than 20 percent of crop circles are preceded by a UFO or other intelligently behaving light phenomena.

In which case, who or what makes up the remainder of this intelligence?

---

[57]As with the halo around Christ, we see energy or light emanating from the fingers of many Indian Gods. This energy field or aura is referenced in at least ninety-seven different cultures.

9. THE LANGUAGE OF LIGHT

The man who speaks with primordial images speaks
with a thousand tongues.

—Carl Jung

It is said that one mark of an advanced civilization lies in its ability to communicate vast amounts of information by encoding it in the shortest possible space, such as in an abstract symbol. Small wonder, then, that a symbol can stimulate us consciously, interact with us subconsciously, and affect our emotions with greater speed and at a much deeper level than language. For example, a mandala can create inner peace just as the reversed swastika, as last employed by Hitler, can mobilize people for war.

Recognizing the function of symbol, its importance, and its use by advanced civilizations is fundamental to understanding why the Circlemakers choose to communicate with designs that not only seem cross-cultural, but reference knowledge which today is considered esoteric. It also allows us to interpret their rich

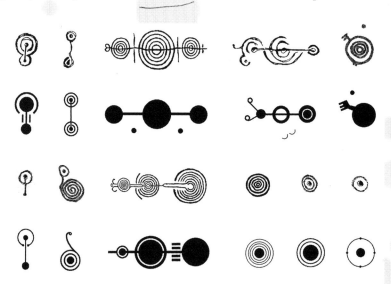

Figure 9.1
Early crop circles can be identified with petroglyphs from around the world.

vocabulary and extract whatever information is encoded within it. This deciphering exercise may seem intellectual at first, yet since the ultimate effect of a symbol is to awaken the senses, the language of crop circles ultimately speaks to the heart.

Early civilizations chose to communicate by using an iconography based on natural and Universal principles. Much of their symbolic language survives throughout the world in the form of rock carvings, pottery design, and sometimes, whole temples of veneration. Perhaps our most famous symbols are the Egyptian hieroglyphs, created by a culture that understood the connection between material life and etheric nature. Combining literal meaning and pun, their hieroglyphs communicate much more than a pharaoh's exploits. As metaphors of the world above and the world below, they were also used to raise the level of a person's awareness. This was achieved by encoding the glyphs with a code that unlocked information buried in the subconscious, where the "owner's manual" lies permanently stored yet remains largely inaccessible to the left-brain personality.

Symbol is related to that other primordial vehicle, myth. Myth stems from *mutus*, meaning mute, silent, signifying those things which are inexplicable to the physical world unless explained through a "verbal" symbol. As such, myth relates a sacred and truthful story from outside the boundaries of temporal space, revealing a cosmological reality in a way no other method

can (Benoist 1975). As such, myths are stories explaining phenomena of nature, the origins of humans, and the exploits of gods. They provide a Universal work of literature that serves as a foundation for correct conduct in life, and whose shared commonalties herald from a common source: a fountain of knowledge whose archetypes were, and continue to be, accessible to all.[58]

Therefore, symbols preserve information for thousands of years, unadulterated by the tides of time or whimsical changes in custom, religion, and politics. And because their fundamental message remains unadulterated, symbols serve as mnemonic devices that help us remember.

Like our distant ancestors, indigenous cultures that share similar symbols and myths recognize crop circles as receptacles of Divine truth. They see crop circles as the vessels of communication between two worlds. An account by Credo Mutwa, a traditional healer who saw thirty crop circles during his travels throughout South Africa, illustrates this point:

> Over the centuries, people had discovered that the star gods sometimes communicated with human beings through these sacred fields. Time and again, strange circular depressions were seen in the centre of these fields. These depressions were called *izishoze zamatongo*, the great circles of the gods. . . . The stalks of corn or millet are never cut by the gods when they form these

---

[58]In Greek, *symballein* is depicted as a boat, a receptacle of the sacred that acts as a mediatory vehicle between intuition—that is inner tuition—and physical reality, waking the individual and transporting it to its roots in the spiritual realm where everything is order, measure, and proportion. A church or cathedral served a similar purpose, and it's not by accident that their vaulted ceilings symbolize the inverted hull of a ship, or why the passageway to the altar is called a nave, giving us navis, or boat.

Symballein

depressions. It appears as though a great circular disk-shaped force has descended on the field. It presses the corn firmly into the ground, without breaking the stalks or damaging the plants. Then the force appears to spin, resulting in the strange spiral appearance of the fallen stalks (Mutwa 1996).

Like Egypt's hieroglyphs, today's crop glyphs are cryptic and generally require an understanding of the meaning concealed beneath the first outward layer of expression. They are multilayered, ambiguous, metaphorical, instructional, even inspirational, containing myths not so much to be read but absorbed subconsciously.

Figure 9.2

The trident motif of four crop glyphs of 1990 (Allington Down shown above) is often carved on Neolithic stone chambers and other sacred spaces associated with transformation.

And because they are abstract, they present a challenge not just to our linear style of thinking but to our desire for immediate gratification.

The evolution of crop glyphs unveils like the plot in a mystery play, and we participate not as spectators but as players, offered clues that build from scene to scene. Subtly the story emerges, inevitably gelling into a mystical whole. This smooth unfolding of the storyline is disrupted by hoaxes, yet for those in tune with the plot, the fakes become evermore obvious, like glitches in the logic of the script.

The appearance in 1990 of the Alton Barnes pictogram was the point in the mystery at which my participation was engaged, and something in my subconscious memory was triggered as I entered the stage. What enlightening power lay behind this alien-looking glyph?

The "circle and trident" at the head of the Alton Barnes pictogram is essentially a reversed "E" attached to an "O," or eye; these are clues to the nonphysical nature of its creators. Interesting here is that the word "alien" loosely breaks up into two old Hebrew words: *El Ayin*. *El* means "god"; *Ayin*, the sixteenth letter of the Hebrew alphabet, has the value "0" and represents "eye." *El Ayin* could therefore mean "The Eye of God" or God's omnipresence; in ancient Egypt this was the Eye of Horus, the ultimate source of Light or enlightenment: an expression of such being the cobra or uraeus upon Pharaoh's brow (Elkington 2001).

The Eye of Shiva, too, is associated with the third eye, and Shiva's symbol is the trident; this appears as the twenty-third letter of the Greek alphabet, *psi*. This, of course, suggests psyche, in essence, a collection of wave forms otherwise known as brainwaves. Since Shiva is associated with transformation, one can begin to understand what a powerful tool for transformation this crop glyph was. For at the sight of that formation thousands of people across the world began to awaken and remember.

In India's sacred text, Bhagavad-Gita, Krishna says to Arjuna: "Whenever evil appears to be conquering, I emerge." It appears the "gods" are returning through the crop circles.

Over the years I have noticed how a specific crop circle suddenly awakens a group of people, as though we are cued onto the stage to play our choreographed parts. Crop circles appear to trigger some distant memory that has lain dormant in our genes. I always hear the remark: "It was something I recognized but could not place." This seems particularly true for those individuals closely involved with decoding the crop circle enigma.

The Spiral: This re-membering, this bringing back to the mind, begins with the one element we all share in common with crop circles: the spiral.

Nature manifests in spiraling motion, first as living light, swirling and thickening into energetic lines of force. From these lines descend the four phases of matter: light, gas, liquid, and solid. This creative process was described in somewhat cosmic terms long ago by Dionysius the Areopagite: "God is light. . . . The Universe, born of an irradiance, was a downward-spiraling burst of luminosity, and the light emanating from the Primal Being established every created being

Figure 9.3
Spiral-type crop circles.

in its immutable place" (Duby 1966). According to the Hermetic Law of Vibration, spirit descends into matter, and by the same law, matter inevitably ascends to spirit, and clairvoyants are known to see energy leaving a person at the point of death in the form of spirals.

That essence of spirit, indeed, of life itself, is represented by that most evocative of spirals, the galaxy. Down here on Earth, that living energy is seen inside Neolithic stone chambers, such as Newgrange in Ireland. When sound frequencies were administered to its smoke-filled chambers, the acoustic vibrations were captured in the smoke as rising spirals (Jahn, Devereux, and Ibitson 1996).[59] Interestingly, at the points where the spirals appeared, the mound's builders had etched similar designs in the stone walls.

One of the functions of such sites as Newgrange was for the practice of chanting or "toning." Such use of resonance was intended to alter one's state of awareness, a tradition carried into churches, and why you find such things as *altars* and *en-trances* in these latter-day sites of worship. The spiral's life-giving properties are also applied in the manufacture of biodynamic

---

[59]The experimenters were struck by the similarities of other rock art inside Newgrange to the resonant sound patterns characterizing its chambers. For example, a number of these petroglyphs feature concentric circles and ellipses that are not unlike the plan views of the acoustical mappings. In others, sinusoidal or zigzag patterns resemble the alternative nodes and antinodes. To the modern viewer, the rock etchings are a form of art, yet to the ancient pilgrim they were instructional diagrams.

farming treatments. Such preparations have been proven to imbue and amplify health-giving properties in plants and once-sterile soil (Tompkins and Bird 1992). In terms of design, the spiral form is evident in the shape of the pine cone, sunflower, or head of wheat, and reflected in a number of crop circles.

The product of spiral motion is the humble crop circle. Because it lacks visual impact, people snub the simple crop circle in favor of today's more complex pictograms and glyphs, yet since the beginning of time the circle has been the symbol of the Prime Creator, the Godforce from whose creative spirit the Universe was created. Paradoxically, all that emanates from it is also contained within it. (By the same token, it is not unusual to find that a single small crop circle can sometimes pack more electromagnetic energy than a 200-foot pictogram.) It's remarkable how this life-giving force—whose explanation has forever eluded scholars and philosophers—should be so neatly and simply embodied.[60]

As we have seen in the history of crop cir-

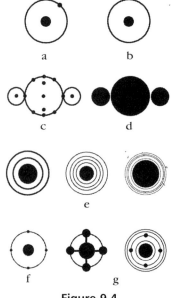

Figure 9.4

(a) and (b) Hydrogen molecule and crop circle; (c) and (d) Water molecule and crop circle; (e) Crop circles suggestive of the orbits of electrons around an atom; (f) "Celtic Cross" crop circle suggests the carbon molecule; (g) Other "Celtic Cross" crop circles.

cles, the single circle has evolved into all kinds of symbols, the simplest of all being the splitting of the circle into two, symbolic of the eternal opposites: light and dark, matter and anti-matter. These evolved into the triplets (Father, Son, and Holy Spirit). With the appearance of rings, the crop circles brought an unmistakable association with the chemical elements of life, particularly oxygen, water, and hydrogen molecules.[61]

The central crop circle encircled by four satellites (the quintuplet) became the first recognizable logo due to its resemblance to the Celtic cross. This is the central life-force or God holding the four elements of earth, wind, water, and fire in equilibrium, a fundamental principle of models of Creation throughout ancient cultures from the Indo-Aryan to the Native American. This symbol is known in chemistry as the carbon atom, the very symbol of the human being.

One important difference with the "Celtic Cross" crop circles is where one of the elements is asymmetrical. This illustrates a fundamental

---

[60]In gematria, the Greek word for "oneness," *monas,* adds up to 360, the number of degrees around a circumference. (Gematria is a Qabbalistic method of interpretation based upon the numerical value of the letters in the words in both Greek and Hebrew alphabets.)

[61]Hydrogen is the most plentiful element in the Universe and a basic ingredient of life. One of its signs, a ring around a nucleus, is not dissimilar to the Egyptian hieroglyph of the creator god Atum; they referred to the nucleus as the point of creation and the ring as the path where creation flows.

Figure 9.5

Early pictogram crop circles.

principle in physics in which chaos achieves order, yet at the point of equilibrium, order begins transforming into chaos. In other words, it is the process of creation, in which any living system cannot remain static (much like our need to inhale and exhale). An example of this appeared at Silbury Hill in 1988, where one of the satellites in the "Celtic Cross" crop circle spiraled in the opposite direction.

Straight Line: The first phase of communication from the Circlemakers, in our time, was based on a foundation of cosmological principles common to humanity. The Circlemakers began the 1990s with a new phase of language development. The straight line was without question the most important evolution in crop circle parlance because it is a culturally shared symbol.

For example, in petroglyphs of the American Southwest, two circles connected by an avenue—the dumbbell—implies speaking. Two circles of differing sizes represent commu-

nication between Spirit and the physical world. Four boxes flanking the avenue of a crop circle suggest we are in communication with the four earthly elements. When the connection between humanity and nature is broken, as it is today, the two circles at either end of the avenue are not connected. The straight line is also representative of the Western way of "ruler-straight" logic (as opposed to the circular Oneness of nature).

Many prehistoric symbols also attribute a solid circle to the male principle, and a ring or circle with ring to the female. Joined by an avenue, these become symbols of the sacred marriage.

Half-Rings: This growing communication link was augmented by the appearance of half-rings crowning crop circles, effectively giving them the appearance of haloes or solar deities. Thanks to surviving examples of the petroglyphs of deities from around the world, these crop circle designs can be correlated with an expression of divinity. The blending of haloes, half-rings, boxes, and dumbbell, for example, creates the symbol of Inti, the Peruvian Sun god, whose descent to Earth is shown by a line moving down to touch the circle. Since the Sun was associated with deity in antiquity, the symbol we draw today to symbolize the Sun—the rayed circle—became also the sign of the Solar Logos. A perfect example of this appeared at

Figure 9.6

Crop circles representing solar deities.

Figure 9.7

Solar Logos. Etchilhampton, 1990.

Figure 9.8
Earth Goddess symbol from 2000 B.C. and pictogram at Chilcomb, 1990.

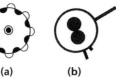

Figure 9.9
Ceres. Fordham Place, 1990.

Etchilhampton, its radiating Sun connecting to the ring of Mother Earth and blessing Her with its eternal light.

The Earth Mother: Perhaps one of the most enduring cross-cultural symbols around the world is the Earth Mother with her arms outspread in a nurturing pose. Since crop glyphs appear primarily in wheat—the basis of bread and the staff of life—it was only a matter of time before the symbol of Ceres (another Earth Mother expression) appeared in the fields. She is the goddess of harvest and the fertile unification of opposites, and was depicted in an elegant but simple crop design.

Incidentally, the origin of cultivated wheat is as alien as the designs imprinting upon it, for there appears to be no native plant on Earth from which it has descended. Its origin is associated with ancient gods who introduced it as a gift to aid the development of civilization. These gods, Triptolomos and Quetzalcoatl, in particular, are said to always travel in "serpent rafts" or "fiery chariots."

The concept of fertility has also made its mark in the crop circles. One dramatic pattern at Cheesefoot Head (see figure

9.10) is also found in Rosicrucian imagery as the symbol of the fertile union between male and female. A similar principle lies behind the split ovum design at Rough Down (see figure 9.10), where the crop circle design shares an affinity with the design of nearby Avebury stone circle. The spurs on the Rough Down formation show knowledge of the paths taken by the Michael and Mary geodetic lines as they flow through the sacred site (more on this in chapter 12).

The Tetrahedron: One of the most important alchemical and Hermetic symbols of all time is the tetrahedron (the four-sided pyramid), principally because of its function as the prime bonding pattern of matter. The figure was well known to Qabbalists and Rosicrucians (who stem from the Egyptian Mystery schools), and it survives in Gnostic manuscripts of the Middle Ages, even in a rare work from 1735 by the German Gnostic Georgius von Welling (von Welling 1735; Petraeus 1578).

Although it is sometimes veiled in the obscure alchemical language common to the period, the tetrahedron describes the process of creation (see figure 9.12). The balls on the tips of the triangle represent the three prime alchemical elements: salt, sulfur, and mercury. These are spun together and held in equilibrium, as the breath from the Creator (the central circle with outwardly radiating rings) activates the process. Sometimes the elements are described more fundamentally as water, fire, and air (also veiled in Western religion as the three sources of Light: Father, Son, and

(a)   (b)   (c)   (d)

Figure 9.10
(a) Cheesefoot Head, 1995; (b) Rough Down, 1991; (c) sperm fertilizing egg; (d) Avebury circle with path of male and female energy lines.

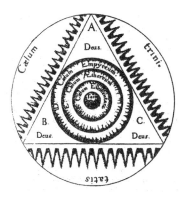

Figure 9.11

Qabbalistic diagrams from the seventeenth century works of Robert Fludd: (a) The "Divine Triangle"; (b) The emblematic manifestation of the trinitarian nature of the Universe.

Figure 9.12

Alchemical tetrahedron from Michespacher's Qabbalah in Alchymia, 1616.

Holy Spirit) which are contained within the triangle of equality.

The tetrahedron is also said to be a formula "for changing base metals into gold," a promise which sent many ardent alchemists on a futile, centuries-long quest to be the first to amass riches. Unfortunately, the allegorical meaning of this transformation was often overlooked, for the process has little to do with changing metals and more to do with the inner transformation of the individual. The tetrahedron is a guide to understanding the Universal mechanics of light, sound, and magnetism, and how an understanding of

such transforms the base metal (physical human) into gold (spiritually enlightened human).

Early one morning in 1991, this process of material manifestation reappeared at the foot of Barbury Castle. As scholar John Michell discovered, the structure of the tetrahedron crop glyph represents a collection of numerical, musical, and geometrical harmonies which founded the prevailing order in every old civilization. Michell explains:

Figure 9.13

It demonstrates the principle of Three in One by means of a central circle which exactly contains the combined areas of the three circles around it. Moreover, the sum of all the four circular areas in the [crop glyph] is 31680 square feet. . . . In traditional cosmology, 31680 was taken to be the measure around the sub-lunary world, and the early Christian scholars calculated the number 3168 as emblematic of Lord Jesus Christ. The same number was previously applied to the name of a leading principle in the pagan religion (Michell 1991).

Michell, a brilliant and insightful scholar of the antiquities, particularly of gematria and the works of Plato, said of this number 316.8 that it is the number of feet in the circumference of the lintel ring at Stonehenge and the perimeter square of St. Mary's Chapel in Glastonbury; it is a ratio of the 31,680 miles of a perimeter square around the Earth, or the number of furlongs of its mean radius. "The number 3168 is superabundant, the Pythagorean term for a number which is exceeded by the sum of its factors. The sum of all the numbers which divide into 3168 is 6660, connecting the number of the Lord Jesus Christ with that of the Beast of Revelation" (Michell 1988b). To Michell, the Barbury Castle crop glyph represented nothing less than a divine revelation.

The Moon: Shifting from the cosmic to the astral were the crop glyphs of 1994, taking on the

Figure 9.14

Top: lunar crop glyphs; bottom, left to right: Scorpion, Oroboros, spider, and web.

form of "thought bubbles," then mutating from them through the incorporation of crescents into glyphs resembling spiders and scorpions. Several of these crescent glyphs bear a striking similarity to astrolabes, instruments formerly used to measure the angle of the Sun and stars and to mark the stereographic projection of spheres. Circles and crescents were a particular feature of lunar counting systems in use around 7000 B.C. throughout Iberia (Hawkins 1973); the calendrical explanation is reinforced by the fact that in 1994 there were thirteen crop glyphs of this type—the number of months in the lunar year.

With this key in hand, one meaning behind the 600-foot "Scorpion" formation was unlocked. As it appeared at the point when the Sun's eleven-year sunspot cycle was at its ebb, the formation's eleven-circle tail seemed to reference the appearance of a forthcoming solar eclipse at a time when the Sun itself was in the zodiacal sign of Scorpio. Another conundrum revolved around the three grapeshot near the base of the glyph's "tail." Later that year three planets—Venus, Jupiter, and Pluto—would appear close to Scorpio during the new moon of November 3, with Scorpio lying 11° south of Earth's equator. Since the "head" of the formation consisted of two concentric rings, with a third offset, it was postulated that these marked the orbits of the three planets, with the offset ring symbolizing the erratic nature of Pluto's orbit.[62]

The predictive and symbolic nature of this glyph is one example of the multilayered communication aspect inherent to crop circles. It also illustrates how important it is for academics of different backgrounds to remain open to the

---

[62]Based on information compiled by Doug Rogers/CCCS Connecticut.

cross-pollination of information, seeing as it took the insights of archaeology, astronomy, and astrology to decipher this crop glyph alone.

The last lunar-based glyph of 1994 outwardly looks like the Oroboros, the dragon eating its own tail, Greek symbol of the infinite cycle of the cosmos. Its thirteen circles again reference the lunar cycle, with the Moon reflected as a crescent at the head of the design. Esoterically, the destiny of the Moon is to reabsorb forms and re-create them—purify them, if you like—so the appearance of lunar references in 1994 seems apt. Given the acrimony and the hoaxing that had unfolded in the wake of Doug and Dave, 1994 marked a resurgence of communication from the Circlemakers.

In certain African cultures, the spider is also symbolic of such two-way communication, so it is not by accident that we saw that season bookended by "Spider" and "Spider Web" crop glyphs, the latter symbolically placed beside the lunar temple of Avebury.[63]

The rebirth of the female Moon is often symbolized by a goddess emerging from a flower. Such a "flower" appeared in 1995 at Kingsclere, its five petals partitioned into a pentagram (geometric symbol of the Moon) and shaped like boar's teeth, a cross-cultural symbol of the virile power of the life force.

The Planets: Heavenly is certainly a fitting description of the formations of 1995, the year when crop glyphs generally appeared to take on the form of planetary trajectories,

even galaxies. Of the four "planet" patterns, the most studied was the "Solar System" formation at Longwood Warren, not just because it showed the orbits of our inner planets with 99 percent accuracy,[64] but because the Earth was missing from the layout. Much speculation surrounded this omission, the majority of which was not entirely optimistic. However, astronomer Gerald Hawkins (noted author of *Stonehenge Decoded*) provided a logical and positive decipherment.

Figure 9.15
Kingsclere, 1995.

Hawkins took the exact alignment of planets indicated in this crop glyph and calculated the two occasions during the twentieth century when their positions appeared as such in the solar system. The first, November 6, 1903, is remembered as the day the Wright brothers proved at Kitty Hawk, North Carolina, that, given wings, man could fly. The second, July 11, 1971, marked another milestone in flight: the spacecraft Mariner 9, the first craft ever to orbit Mars, was making its way to our red neighbor.

So it would seem the Circlemakers left out the Earth to point out they were dealing with *our* preoccupation with *non-earthbound* activities.

Figure 9.16
Longwood Warren crop glyph (left), and other solar-system formations.

---

[63] Ancient sacred sites were created so as to invoke specific energies. Consequently, the gender is indicative of the type of energy flowing at the site. Avebury was built as a lunar temple (female, receptive energy); by comparison, Stonehenge is a solar temple. When the Roman Catholics superimposed their churches over pagan sites, they continued this principle when attributing them to a particular saint (for example, St. Michael churches rest upon positive/male energy lines).

[64] Personal communication from Gerald Hawkins.

Figure 9.17

Relationship between crop circle and the X-ray pattern in beryllium.

And in case anyone feels like stamping coincidence on this explanation, the events took place sixty-seven years apart, a fact precisely referenced by the number of "asteroids" and grapeshot encircling this crop glyph.

Just as crop glyphs incorporate such macroscopic concepts, so can they demonstrate microscopic ones. Located within shouting distance of Harwell Laboratory, where the science of atoms is researched, a crop design appeared whose construction showed the same geometric pattern found in the X-ray fractal array of beryllium, which in turn bears a striking similarity to the construction patterns prevalent in sacred geometry and mandalas (see figure 9.17).

The Grid Square: One of the primary concerns of ancient philosophies such as Qabbalah, Hermeticism, or that of the Freemasons, was the effort to measure or estimate philosophically the parts and proportions of the microcosm, and through this to create on Earth a mirror image of the order of the Universe.

The blueprint they used was the circle, symbol of the realm of God or the macrocosm, inside which was inscribed the square representing the physical world.[65] To undertake the measuring of the physical world, the

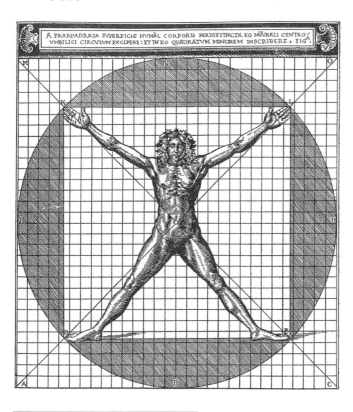

Figure 9.18

Vitruvius' checkerboard blueprint was used by the Egyptian Freemasons for transposing the archetypal world of God onto the physical plane.

---

[65]Fundamental to the order of the Egyptian Freemasons were the Three Tables which represented the mathematical laws of the Universe: The circle as the ethereal, the square as the transformation of the ethereal into matter, and the rectangle containing the proportions of the Golden Mean, and said to govern the principles of sound and light.

square contained a grid; an illustration of this exists in Cesariano's *Edition of Vetruvius* and Cornelius Agrippa's *De Occulta Philosophia*, in which we see the outstretched limbs of Man contained within the square as the foundation of the world, with the man's navel as the center (this diagonal division of the grid square will have deeper implications explained in chapter 13). In addition to its use by the Freemasons, this checkerboard emblem was the tracing board of the Dionysiac architects, whose function and origins can also be traced back to the Egyptian Mystery schools, and whose influence on architecture and the arts pervaded India, Asia Minor, and the Mediterranean countries, eventually finding its way to England.

"One of the most illustrious of their number was Vitruvius," wrote philosopher Manly P. Hall, ". . . in the various sections of his book, Vitruvius gives several hints as to the philosophy underlying the Dionysiac concept of the principle of symmetry applied to the science of architecture, as derived from a consideration of the proportions established by Nature between the parts and members of the human body" (Hall 1932).

These enlightened beings also referred to themselves as the Sons of Solomon, whose hexagonal symbol (Solomon's Seal) is prevalent throughout sacred geometry and crop glyphs. This connection with architecture reaffirms the importance of sacred geometry and its encoding into sermons of stone throughout the world. As Hall elegantly phrases it:

The supreme ambition of the Dionysiac Architects was the con-struction of buildings which would create distinct impressions consistent with the purpose for which the structure itself was designed. . . . They labored, therefore, to the end of producing a building perfectly harmonious with the structure of the universe itself. . . . As a logical deduction from their philosophic trend of thought, such a building—*en rapport* with the Cosmos—would also have become an oracle (Hall 1937, 1928).

Such is the philosophical importance behind the grid square. If you had an inclination to be immersed in these thoughts, 1997 was a particularly good year to do so. Approximately 100 feet south of the stylized six-petaled Seal of Solomon at Etchilhampton lay a second glyph—a large circle enclosing an unusual grid square, consisting of twenty-eight parallel lines by twenty-five (creating twenty-nine by twenty-six rectangles). From the air, the 120-foot-wide design resembled God's morning waffle, although it also

Figure 9.19
"Grid Square" crop glyph. Etchilhampton, 1997.

brought to mind Plato's description of Atlantis in *Critias*, a rectangular plain defined by channels of water.

As mentioned earlier, the grid square was used as a blueprint. Upon it were placed geometric, geodetic, and mathematical calculations—information based on the accurate study of nature that provided the foundation of great civilizations, particularly that of Egypt. The "Grid Square" crop circle not only makes reference to that information, but shares tantalizing associations with Egypt, beginning with its most famous building. Located at latitude 51° 20' 05", the "Grid Square" references the slope angle of the Great Pyramid of Gizeh with an infinitesimal deviation of 0° 00' 51". And where the base of the pyramid is deviated from north by 0° 0', 0° 3', 0° 3', and 0° 0' respectively, the "Grid Square's" base shows practically identical compass deviations of 0° 0', 0° 5', 0° 3', and 0° 0'.[66]

Comprised of twenty-eight by twenty-five lines, the design of the "Grid Square" appears to deliberately reference other natural processes: twenty-eight represents the days in the traditional lunar month, the number of days required for cells of the outer layer of skin to regenerate, and the pound-weight of carbon in the average human body. The lunar cycle once provided the foundation for the number of characters in the Arabic alphabet, itself created according to the lunar mansions; the prophet Muhammad is himself compared to the Full Moon, as is the Egyptian god, Osiris (Schimmel 1993; Schneider 1994). The number twenty-eight also references the

Royal Cubit (measured by the width of four fingers multiplied seven times). As a distillation of precise calculations of the Earth, it was the favored unit of measure used in the building of Egyptian temples and in the calculation of geographic distances.

The number twenty-five contains important references of its own. It is the square of the sacred number five (the pentagram, symbol of living things). As such, it was regarded by Christian Gnostics as the perfection of the five senses, and consequently, a measure of the enlightened being. And so the number twenty-five marked the spiritual resurrection of the individual. In relation to the Great Pyramid, twenty-five pyramid inches mark the length of another precise system of measure, the sacred cubit, an exact ten-millionth of the Earth's polar radius.[67] This unit was used in the construction of the Pyramid's antechamber, which encodes the number of days in the solar year. The chamber is 5 cubits squared (Mück 1958; Rutherford 1945).

The "Grid Square" glyph's choice of 28:25 therefore seems hardly by "accident," referencing as it does such an array of universal relationships. The same can be said when we look at the design not as lines, but as a series of rectangles—twenty-nine by twenty-six in all.

The number twenty-nine is symbolic of the leap lunar month and the number of bones in the human skull. The number twenty-six represents the number of vertebrae in the human spine, the numerical value of "Jehovah" in gematria, and the days of rotation of the Sun relative to the

---

[66]My thanks to Andreas Müller for his meticulous survey.
[67]The British inch and the Imperial measuring system is largely derived from the Egyptian cubit system. Livio Stecchini explores the Egyptian system of measures and its influence on subsequent civilizations in Peter Tompkins' *The Secrets of the Great Pyramid*.

Earth (Gaunt 1995). Most important of all, 26.943 is the square root of the slant height of the Great Pyramid. Interestingly, 2694 is the unified harmonic of the structure of the hydrogen atom (Cathie 1995), the primary element of life.

The level to which this information exists in this crop circle shows that its makers are working with the same principles of wisdom once employed by the founder gods of Egypt. Given that both the Egyptians and the Circlemakers have rarely used measure and metaphor by accident, let's take the associations further. Aside from 28:25 and 29:26, other numerical coincidences abound between the "Grid Square" and Egypt.

To begin with, the total number of rectangles of the "Grid Square," to which is added the complete crop glyph itself, is identical to the foot-length of the Great Pyramid, which is 755.

Then we have 55:30, the number of rectangles along two edges of the "Grid Square," and it's average meter length. When calculating the middle latitude of their kingdoms the Egyptians took 55° 30', and halved it. The reason for using this northern latitude was that it measured the same length as one degree of longitude at the Equator. Coincidentally, 55° 30' marks the location of sacred sites on the Scottish isle of Arran, a sister power point to Avebury, which itself lay seven miles from the "Grid Square."

One degree of latitude consists of sixty minutes, and in the northern kingdom of ancient Egypt the length of minute measured 900 Egyptian *khe*; 900 is also the area of the "Grid Square." Also, the length of a minute for the southern kingdom was 3600 *khe*—the area of the "Grid Square" multiplied by four, the number of its edges.

The only numerical connection that shows any wild discrepancy is 29:53 (the 29 rectangles along one edge of the "Grid Square" plus the 53 total lines). The geodetic reference point for the mapping of Egypt was marked by the siting of the village of Saqqara—named after the god of orientation—at 29° 51' north (Tompkins 1988; Rutherford 1945).

These connections would imply that the "Grid Square" crop circle has a strategic mapping purpose. In fact, it would seem that someone is out to measure something in relationship to the Earth, if not the Earth itself (this will be examined in chapter 13). Yet the connections do not end here. Ironically, there stands at Saqqara a six-step limestone pyramid containing a blue tile chamber whose walls are decorated in rectangular segments which, at first glance, one could easily mistake for an aerial photo of this crop circle.

Clearly, a relationship exists between the creators of ancient Egypt and this group of Circlemakers. No doubt other numerical relationships await our discovery. However, without making matters too complicated, I'd like to return to the two most obvious pairs of numbers given by the "Grid Square"—28:25 and 29:26. Conspicuous by its absence in that sequence is the number 27. Perhaps this was an invitation to investigate, particularly as this number is full of associations with energy and its movement in space.

Constructing a circle and a square of equal areas ("squaring the circle") has been one of the greatest challenges to geometers. One way of achieving an accurate result is to use a ratio of 27.32. Such a "squared circle" is geometrically encoded in the positioning of the stones at Stonehenge, just as 27.32° forms the angle between Stonehenge and its attendant tumulus to the east, the same one that generates its geodetic power. Interestingly, 27.32 is also the relative percentage in the diameters of spinning disks used in magnetic levitation (Myers and Percy 1999).

If we view the "Grid Square" from the air as a three-dimensional object, it resembles a set of densely packed cubes. Mathematically, twenty-seven is three cubed, just as twenty-seven points are required to geometrically define a hypersphere (a 4-D sphere) in our three dimensional space (ibid.). And speaking of spheres, the period of revolution of the Moon around the Earth is 27.2 days.

In Old Testament gematria, twenty-seven is the number of light, just as in Hebrew it is the number of *illumination* (Gaunt 1995), something this particular crop glyph has not been short of. The number twenty-seven is also the difference in frequency between the notes F and G. Arithmetically this is split into two parts, the lesser of thirteen units and the greater of fourteen units. The minuscule region between these parts is called the "Pythagorean comma," and it is marked by the note F-sharp (Levin 1994).

F-sharp is regarded with great respect by the ancient Chinese as Hu, the tone of the Earth. Native American flute makers to this day tune their instruments to serenade Mother Earth to this note. It also appears to have had significant influence among the pyramid builders of ancient Egypt. After he conducted a series of experiments inside the Kings' Chamber of the Great Pyramid, acoustic engineer Tom Danley identified four resonant frequencies, or notes, that are enhanced by the dimensions and materials used in its construction. The notes form an F-sharp chord which, according to ancient Egyptian texts, was the harmonic of our planet. Moreover, Danley's tests show that these frequencies are present in the Kings' Chamber even when no sounds are being produced.[68] So we see yet more connections with our Egyptian ancestors. (However, the full implications of F-sharp relative to the "Grid Square" crop circle will be revealed in chapter 13.)

By virtue of its design—unique at the time—the "Grid Square" gives the impression of a metaphysical surveyor at work, perhaps more so in view that the design resembles the net of geodetic energy that clings to the Earth. This has not been described yet in this book, but it was rediscovered in modern times by Ernst Hartmann. The "Hartmann Grid" is spaced out in lines 8.25 inches thick, each line spaced in intervals of 6.5 feet (north to south) and 8 feet (east to west), creating an invisible rectangular net closely akin to the mathematical roots of the Great Pyramid (Merz 1987). As it turns out, the average rectangle in the "Grid Square" crop circle is in ratio to Hartmann's grid, including its spacing, with a discrepancy of the thickness of an ear of wheat.

Figure 9.20
"Sunflower" glyph, symbolic of the crown chakra.

---

[68]From an interview by Boris Said on the *Laura Lee Radio Show,* Seattle, October 1997; www.lauralee.com; also Christopher Dunn's *The Giza Power Plant: Technologies of Ancient Egypt.* Much of what was discovered remains secret under a nondisclosure agreement with the Schor Foundation.

Images of Eastern Faiths: The association between crop glyphs and elements of Eastern faith have been particularly strong over the years, the most dramatic example undoubtedly being the revered Sri Yantra design, its thirteen miles of lines and triangles etched into a dry lake bed in Oregon. This was matched in

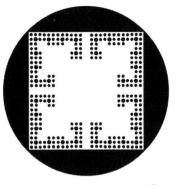
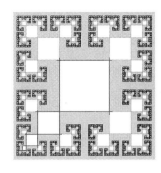

Figure 9.21
Relationship of Windmill Hill crop glyph to a square fractal. 1999.

England by the "Sunflower," the crowning point of the 2000 season and a fitting title considering the design is reminiscent of the thousand-petaled lotus of the crown chakra as represented in Hindu iconography.

Residing in each of the seven main chakras are seeds of sound, the activation of which is traditionally done through the chanting of mantras. One of the most powerful of these is the *bija* mantra ("secret name"), which Hindu texts describe as a relationship between life energy and sacred sound belonging to no language. When directed at the crown chakra, this mantra is said to evoke the image of a sunflower unfolding. This same image can be created by singing a prolonged, high-pitched note and directing its vibration onto powder.

The first of two Windmill Hill crop glyphs also carries Eastern overtones, and its design is based on the foundation geometry for temples dedicated to the Hindu god Vishnu, the Preserver. It also bears a striking resemblance to

the square star branch of the Koch series of computer fractals.

This overlapping of Western fractals and Eastern imagery applies to the "Triple Julia Set," whose interlocking spiral motif is found throughout Buddhist faiths. This motif is said to represent the threefold nature of the soul, as well as the fundamental structure of creation.

In Dzogchen (said to be the highest form of Tibetan Buddhism), this threefold spiral is representative of the stages to enlightenment: using compassion and knowledge to overcome the limitations of the physical world; contemplating the mechanics of duality and freeing the spirit from rationality; and finally, the liberation from conditioned existence and the achievement of wisdom.[69]

Chakras and Teardrops: The Eastern connection was particularly strong throughout 1996's crop circle season. Two strange glyphs, believed at first to be, on one level, a form of Sanskrit, turned out to be symbols for the root

---

[69]A similar process exists in the Egyptian Merkaba (light-spirit-body) which describes the geometric energy array around every cell as well as the human body. The energy field is composed of a spinning star tetrahedron. It is said that by influencing the rate of spin, a person is able to overcome the gravitational field of the physical world.

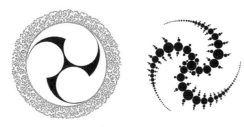

Figure 9.22

The Tibetan Wheel of Joy and its crop circle counterpart.

chakra and the solar plexus chakra in a more ornamental form than usual. The glyphs at Roundway and Etchilhampton were each marked with a teardrop, the Hindu symbol for a chakra (see figure 9.23).[70]

Yet these glyphs conceal a second layer of meaning. The Etchilhampton formation, if placed with the tear at the top, makes a hieroglyph resembling a sphinx. The Sphinx is associated with the attainment of knowledge, and in Egypt this enigmatic figure rests atop a reputed Hall of Records containing a library of information about the Atlantean civilization and the Universe. In Western symbology, however, the Sphinx is represented by the horse (depicted in this crop glyph with its tail in the air) and is associated with transformation (as a result of enlightenment through knowledge); in Islamic art, the winged horse bearing the Archangel Gabriel (the bringer of annunciation and truth) wears a teardrop upon his breast. This is the tear of Isis, who sheds her tear for the transformation of the world.

The Roundway crop glyph (see figure 9.23) with the tear pointing towards the front paws reveals Anubis, guardian of souls in the Egyptian Underworld. Looming over Anubis is a hatchet, ceremonial symbol of the Pharaoh asserting

Figure 9.23

Top: Solar plexus chakra/horse crop glyph, Etchilhampton. Bottom: Root chakra/Anubis with axe, Roundway, 1996.

---

[70]Channelers around the world at the time shared the sentiment that Earth was in the process of opening Her heart chakra. Since this would first require an activation of the lower chakras, these two crop glyphs appear to be a form of validation.

his power; both are nestled within the laid crop shaped like a pyramid. Since the circle represents God, the tear emanating from God is symbolic of the Son descending to the physical plane. It would seem, therefore, that we are presented with a parable describing consciousness descending from Heaven, bringing with it Universal knowledge and that through such wisdom, the Light will reassert its power on Earth. Some might term this the Second Coming.

The Lotus: I picked up this spiritual thread in the year 2000, thanks to an

Figure 9.24
"Lotus." Golden Ball Hill, 2000.

unfolding five petal "lotus" crop glyph at the foot of Golden Ball Hill. Flowing towards a folded sixth petal was what appeared to be a ball with a flame or a seed.

In Hindu philosophy, the lotus is the "flower of Light," a symbol of matter and spirit, cause and effect. Its leaves, flowers, and fruit are said to form the figure of a circle, so it is considered a symbol of perfection. Its petals represent spiritual unfolding, and the seedpod the fecundity of creation—the "superhuman" rising out of and above the mud of the physical world. Consequently, the "flame" in this lotus glyph represents unfolding wisdom and spiritual revelation.

The lotus is an indispensable attribute of every creative god and one finds its image engraved on all the monuments built along the Nile as well as on the headdresses of the divine kings who built them. Buddha, too, is said to have manifested as a flame from a lotus. Its association with creation is beautifully described in an Eastern myth: During the Nights of Brahma, Vishnu floats asleep on the primordial waters, stretched out on the blossom of a lotus which grows out of Brahma's navel. His goddess consort, Lakshmi, arises before him from the lotus beneath her feet. At the churning of the Ocean of Milk, Lakshmi is re-formed of the froth of the foaming waves and appears before an assembly of astonished gods, borne on a lotus and with another lotus held in her hands.

In essence, the myth is analogous to an individual stepping out of ignorance, and through knowledge one's true nature opens like

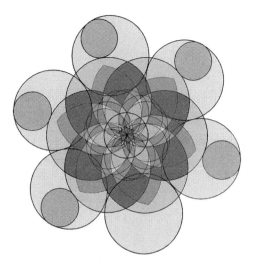

Figure 9.25

With the outer petals shifted 19.47 degrees relative to the inner petals, the circular geometry of the "lotus" gives the impression of spin.

petals to reveal the inner, enlightened being. On another level, the myth serves to illustrate the constant unfolding process of manifestation. As with the sphinx and the horse, the lotus has its Western counterpart in the rose, the symbol of truth (see figure 9.26 on page A10 in the color section). This appeared later in the summer of 2000 at the base of Dragon Hill and Uffington hill fort, where an enigmatic figure carved out of the chalk sits in the shape of a white horse.

Connecting the Thread: The Eight-Spoked Wheel: Crop glyphs that reaffirm the regenerative aspect of life have on occasion encoded predictions or processes with far-reaching implications, particularly when connected like a string of words that over time reveal a bigger picture. We begin with that controversial "Wheel of Dharma" (1992), a reference to the Buddhist path of initiation. It has counterparts in the Egyptian mysteries and Celtic shamanic

culture, while Islamic culture portrays this by the octagon, representing the Breath of Allah.

Based upon the octave, the eightfold spiritual path is undertaken by a soul to achieve its highest level of Self. Every soul reincarnates to experience a specific path in life in accordance with its evolutionary need, attaching itself to a physical being a day before it is birthed by the mother; subsequently, it chooses to experience being blind, bullied, poor, wealthy, faithful, charitable, and so on, but always in accordance with a specific path. When every path has been mastered, the soul achieves total understanding of its Self and the laws of Universal being. To put it another way, it finds God within. Should the soul not achieve its purpose in one lifetime, it may repeat the process. Think of it as a kind of Divine driving test.

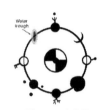

Figure 9.27

"Wheel of Dharma." Silbury, 1992.

Each of the symbols representing the eightfold path adorns a compass point on this crop glyph: occupying the north slot is the short trident of the Sun, the central fire and source of wisdom; in the northeast is the crescent Moon, the path of inspiration, regeneration, and rebirth; in the east, the keyhole symbolizes the gaining of insight; in the southeast, the heart of Bos, the bull, the path of ascent through truth and strength; in the south, the horns of Cernunnos, symbol of our animal nature and the path of the regenerated soul coming forth; in the southwest, the cosmos, marked by the triad of body, ego, and soul, harmonized through insight; and in the west, the key of Mercury, representing illumination and the emergence of spirituality which unlocks the Mysteries within the individual.[71]

This leaves us with one final symbol. Or it doesn't, since in the crop glyph a physical water trough stands in its place. Did the Circlemakers miscalculate or was this apparent error trying to point something out?

The remaining symbol pertains to the Path of Cleansing. On one level, to bathe in water is to immerse oneself in knowledge; knowledge leads to enlightenment, and enlightenment inevitably brings social change. Is the "Wheel of Dharma" crop glyph prophesying coming changes?

If we look at ancient timekeeping traditions, they point to our present time as the end of a grand evolutionary cycle and the birth of a new age, the Age of Aquarius—the sign of the water bearer and an apt description of a water trough. Hopi, Lakota, and Cherokee traditions refer to our present time as the Fifth World, and they too maintain that it is coming to a close. But it is the Mayan calendar of the Great Cycles that provides another clue. According to this 18,000-year-old timekeeper, the present cycle is completed in 2012 A.D.; its remaining 20 year sub-cycle was set in motion in 1992 (Arguelles 1985), precisely the year this crop glyph appeared. Is it possible then, that the missing symbol is pointing to a final phase in our present evolutionary chain?

The Serpent: This train of thought continues in 1999 with the "Coiled Serpent" crop glyph which, as it happens, appeared on the very day marking the end of the Aztec calendar. Outwardly, its nine coils are symbolic of utmost expression (the Trinity times three), of perfection itself, while its head tilts in anticipation of the next stage of expression (see figure 9.28 on page A10 in the color section). The serpent represents the creative Universal energy, and for this reason the Aztec/Mayan/Toltec god Quetzalcoatl is depicted as such (*Coatl* represents energy moving in waves or spirals, a precursor to the electromagnetic wave of science); the coiled serpent is also known as *kundalini*, the life force that rises from the base of the spine, stimulating the chakra system as it spirals toward the crown chakra in the top of the head.

Which brings us to the head of the crop glyph itself, a *vesica piscis* emerging from a circle. This can be viewed symbolically either as the Egyptian spear point or the Catholic bishop's mitre, symbols of Ultimate Light and Sun respectively (Elkington 2001). As the seed of the ultimate Light, Jesus Christ is often depicted sitting within such a motif. So again, in one respect, this glyph is representative of the ultimate creative principle.[72]

However, the coils of the serpent are also symbolic of positive and negative polarities, the forces of disorganization and transformation. So what exactly was this crop glyph transforming?

---

[71]The Eightfold Path is synonymous with the 8x8 trigrams (64 hexagrams) of the *I Ching* of the Chinese Taoists. These are combinations of yin and yang energy patterns thought to represent all possible cosmic and human situations (McKenna and McKenna 1975).

[72]Both the "Coiled Serpent" and "Lotus" crop glyphs share the same "seed" symbology, and ironically they appeared in adjacent fields during 1999. The "Coiled Serpent" was preceded by two similar designs three and nine years earlier, this time in the very same field (the "DNA" and the Alton Barnes pictogram). The head of the "Coiled Serpent" may also be representative of the Moon eclipsing the Sun, and this glyph preceded the solar eclipse of August 1999.

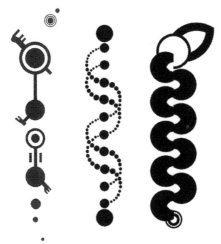

Figure 9.29

Is someone trying to say something? East Field pictograms from 1990, 1996, and 1999.

Traditionally, gods attributed with a serpent cure, physically or spiritually, were regarded as resonances or wave patterns (Elkington 2001). If you view the "Coiled Serpent" crop glyph horizontally it resembles a standing wave pattern, just as shown on an oscilloscope (see figure 9.30). Its "mitre" or Sun now appears to creep above a horizon. In reality, as the Sun rises over the horizon, living organisms (particularly wheat and barley) become more receptive to light, given that DNA is reliant on this electromagnetic force for information. As the frequency of solar

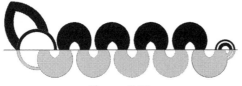

Figure 9.30

"Coiled Serpent" glyph depicting the sunrise.

energy rises above the horizon it imprints itself in all living organisms.

Given that the barley of the "Coiled Serpent" was uniquely laid down like a DNA spiral (which had appeared as a crop circle three years earlier and in the same field), one can speculate that this crop glyph was encoding energy into the living Earth. If so, what is this energy doing?

DNA: One possible explanation lies in a bizarre-looking crop circle from 1991 which produced a myriad of explanations concerning genetics, not least because it resembles a splitting chromosome (see figure 9.31).[73] It was named the "Froxfield Serpent" (after its location). At first it was postulated that the Circlemakers were making a statement about our DNA's state of health due to the weakening of the ozone layer, but when author Gregg Braden looked at this glyph, something made him explore it in a different direction.

He found that out of the sixty-four codons in our genetic code, forty-four are unused (Rothwell 1988; Braden 1993). Since nature rarely designs things superfluously, such apparent redundancies along the DNA strand may be structures waiting to be activated. Braden took the segments of the formation, none of which were identical in length, and calculated them as a percentage of the whole design. Then he took a map of the human DNA containing the significant locations of amino acids and superimposed the relative percentages from the mapped crop circle. He concluded:

Of the nine break sites, one is an area known as ribosomal RNA [ribonucleic

---

[73]Other views are expressed in *Cyphers in the Crops,* edited by Beth Davis.

acid], one plots into an area known as Cytochrome Oxidase II, one is in ATPase subunit 6, and the remaining plot onto URF (unassigned reading frames) 3, 4 and 5. While all of these locations are significant, the six URF locations are particularly interesting. URF sites mark zones within the DNA molecule that appear to be "unused," at this time,

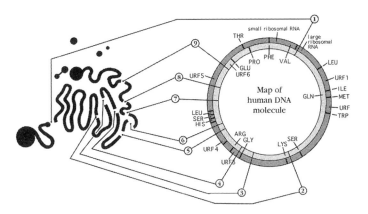

Figure 9.31

One-of-a-kind ribbon crop circle at Froxfield 1991 (left) references strategic breaks in the human DNA.

in the coding of the amino acids. If, for some reason, these sites are shut down (breaks), coding will not occur. If new proteins, resulting from new amino acids are to occur, these sites provide the staging area for the building of these structures (Braden 1993).

The data from the "Froxfield Serpent" makes us wonder if we are looking at a coding sequence taking place via crop glyphs. RNA can be likened to data in a computer disk, part of which lies unused, as if allowing for further instructions. A predictive reference supporting this train of thought exists in Tablet 8 of *The Emerald Tablets of Thoth,* an ancient Egyptian text: "Man is in the process of changing to forms that are not of this world. Grows he in time to the formless, a plane on the cycle above. Know ye, ye must become formless before ye are one with the Light" (Doreal 1925).

It is too soon to prove that changes in human DNA can be directly linked to the sudden build-up of crop circles—even if a DNA glyph did appear once in the same field as the "Serpent"—primarily because no funds or protocols exist to carry out such testing. However, support for the theory that electromagnetism in crop circles is capable of altering DNA comes from the pioneering work of Dr. Chiang Kanzhen (a formerly imprisoned Chinese scientist who escaped to Russia), who researches bioenergetic communication. Dr. Kanzhen's work demonstrates how

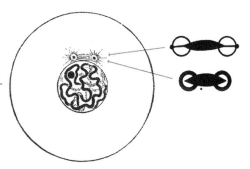

Figure 9.32

Division of the cell. Note the similarity of two crop glyphs from 1991 to the centrosomes (arrowed).

DNA is a passive data storage device comprising active material carriers in the form of bioelectromagnetic signals. These are photons possessing corpuscular and wave properties capable of transmitting energy and information.[74]

These photons operate at the extreme ends of the electromagnetic spectrum, namely, at very low frequencies (which excite the photons) and very high frequencies (the bandwidth capable of transmitting large amounts of information). Any excitation of the bioelectromagnetic field is therefore transmitted to the DNA, and in laboratory experiments genetic information has already been successfully transmitted from one organism to another (Kanzhen 1993).

For more than a decade, Irish molecular biologist and immunologist Colm Kelleher has also researched the structure and properties of the 97 percent of our genetic material that does not code for protein, and discovered that more than a million sequences in human DNA have the property of being able to "jump" from chromosome to chromosome. When activated to jump, these sequences, or "transposons," are capable of large-scale genetic change in a very short time.

Kelleher proposes that the activation of the transposons is done through the intense spiritual energy experienced in altered states such as shamanic initiations, near-death experiences, and UFO close encounters. Anecdotal reports of spontaneous healings of cancer, auto-immune diseases, and a variety of chronic illnesses during these heightened states are increasing.[75] As we shall see in the following chapters, healings and heightened states of awareness are also associated with crop circle contact.

The third piece of supporting evidence for the crop-circle/DNA link comes from a report by Dr. Berenda Fox, a holistic practitioner in the U.S. who researches immunological testing and therapy. Her analysis of blood samples collected since the early 1980s shows that people have developed what *appears* to be a third strand of DNA. People seem to be changing at a molecular level, says Dr. Fox.[76]

Some of the reported symptoms associated with this change include a feeling of not "being here," exhaustion, the need for extra rest, mental confusion, lack of concentration on routine tasks, and aches and pains which appear to have no specific cause. Women go through hormonal changes, experiencing earlier (or later) menopause, and men experience frustration through the exhaustion caused by the process. Many of these same symptoms have been associated with exposure to crop circles (see chapter 12).

If such hypotheses are correct and molecular changes in the human body are underway, the evolutionary consequences are on cue with ancient predictions that have foreseen changes in humanity's spiritual and physical structure as

---

[74]The bioelectromagnetic field is a material carrier of biogenetic information that can be transmitted from one organism to another.

[75]*Journal of Scientific Exploration,* National Institute for Discovery Science, vol. 13:1, Spring 1999, 9–24.

[76]Shortly after these announcements, Dr. Fox's office was raided by the U.S. Food and Drug Administration. Dr. Fox, a former consultant to the Fox TV Network (no known connection) is believed to have gone into hiding. I leave it to the reader to read between the lines. At the time of writing, my research into Dr. Fox's work could not be taken any further.

it nears the close of cycles. Moreover, indigenous cultures mention that signs would appear on Earth as the changes accelerate.

Are crop glyphs the "Language of Light" described in *The Keys of Enoch*, as revealed to J. J. Hurtak in 1973, "to prepare mankind for the activation of events that are to come to pass in the next thirty years of earth time"? The "Keys" were revealed to Hurtak shortly before the unfolding of recent crop circle activity, yet he described them as "geometrical light structures used to transcribe knowledge from Father Universe to Son Universe" (Hurtak 1977).

The link between these proposed light structures and crop circle designs has some validity, and in later chapters I discuss how geometry, sound, and light work synchronistically in the crop circle process. Enoch's teachings also stipulate that these symbols would help propel humanity from one state to another, aid its spiritual development, and assist science in understanding the Universe. The Light language, Hurtak said, would be given to help us cope with this change: the "spiritual gifts of the Holy Spirit given so spiritual man can work with the Light Beings."

"Since these teachings are applicable to the various sciences," wrote Dr. Hurtak, "not everyone will comprehend all of the Keys equally, nor will the full complexity of each Key be fully meaningful at the present time of our participation. . . . Therefore, not all the Keys will appeal to the same type of scientific and consciousness evolution because they work on various levels of understanding and are connected with the totality of knowing 'the Light'—the primary frequency of the Infinite Mind" (ibid.).

At this point the skeptic might well ask: "If these beings—the Circlemakers—are so advanced, why don't they communicate in plain, ordinary English? Why put people through such an agonizing obstacle course, cloaking their messages behind the veil of symbol and obscure philosophical iconography?" Well, would we be bothered to get out of the car to investigate a field emblazoned with "Good Morning, Earthlings. We Come From Mars." Would we care to analyze the plants, the soil? Look for hidden geometry or math, or build an intellectual profile? Probably not.

As the sinologist Sukie Colgrave points out, based on analysis of the works of Confucius, the trouble is that "while words contain genuine meanings which reflect certain absolute truths in the universe, most people have lost contact with these truths and so use language to suit their own convenience. This led, Confucius felt, to lax thinking, erroneous judgments, confused actions and finally to the wrong people acquiring access to political power" (Colgrave 1979).

Thus, words do not possess the same ability to carry a message as do symbols, and any book on etymology shows how the meanings of hundreds of everyday words used in our most basic transactions have been corrupted during the course of even a hundred years. Not only are words dependent on the abilities of those who come into contact with them, they are vulnerable to poor translations from one language to another. Besides, written and spoken word is only an approximation of reality, whereas the form of a symbol is generally a direct expression of its function (see chapter 11).

The Circlemakers are using symbols based on Universal principles, all of which are bound within the human body. As such, their symbols in the fields are capable of bypassing the brain's

Figure 9.33

Communication by the Circlemakers in Latin. Milk Hill, 1991.

left hemisphere of reason, enabling the exchange of information to take place at a cellular level. In turn, this enables individuals, if they so choose, to raise their vibratory rates, preparing them to receive this language of light through the heart. The Circlemakers' approach shows great understanding of the human psyche because symbols are mysterious, and the mysterious arouses our curiosity, pushing us to examine our knowledge, thereby gaining insight.[77] As Thomas Carlyle once said, "In a symbol lies concealment of revelation."

These symbols remain timeless and intact despite thousands of years of passing through the revolving doors of religion, politics, and ideology. They seem to have been carefully screened so as not to antagonize any particular segment of the population. And because no crop glyph means only one thing or offers a single solution, they are difficult and elusive for the rational-minded to accept.

Having said this, on the Celtic harvest festival of Lammas (August 2) in 1991, events prompted the Circlemakers to send a message in a different format. By this time, hoaxing and contamination of evidence was underway to debunk the phe-

nomenon and undermine public confidence in all matters circular. Against this background of deception, the Circlemakers dropped a series of markings upon the formation-fertile field below Milk Hill. So out of character was the scripted pattern that at first it was dismissed as a hoax, yet closer inspection proved otherwise.

The Milk Hill script, as it became known, appeared to be some type of language. It was comprised of two words separated by three line breaks, with a ring at each end suggesting beginning and end. Was this Morse code from the Circlemakers? Gerald Hawkins felt it was important enough to gather a team of twelve scholars and decipher it. Several months, 18,000 common phrases, and 42 languages later, they arrived at an acceptable solution.

They agreed that the circles at each end marked the message breaks; the tram line marked the bottom of the characters, and the twin upright lines formed word breaks. The message, therefore, contained two words or numbers with no abbreviations. To make sense, the message had to be an exact character-by-character substitution code, and it had to be cognizable.

Hawkins and his colleagues finally figured the message was in the guise of post-Augustan Latin: the first word, *OPPONO*, translated as "I oppose." The second word provided an object for the verb as *ASTOS*—"acts of craft and cunning." "I oppose acts of craft and cunning."

In context of the Doug and Dave deception,

---

[77]The word mystery stems from the Greek *muo*, "to close one's mouth, to be silent."

this interpretation of the message was timely and direct in its distaste of events shortly to take place. On the other hand, the use of post-Augustan Latin, plus the fact that six out of seven letters used for the script are traced to an obscure Knights Templar-based alphabet, once again raised the Circlemakers' intellectual profile.[78]

Of course, they could have communicated in English, but would anyone have believed them?

"No further messages were written in this Knights Templar-based script after 1991. Nor did anyone come forward to claim that he or she made the inscription," Hawkins said. "Actually if any hoaxers do come forward, then we have a short Latin quiz we would like them to take."

---

[78]The Milk Hill script decoding is from a personal communication with Gerald Hawkins. References to Templar and Runic alphabets are from Nigel Pennick's *The Secret Lore of Runes and Other Ancient Alphabets.*

10. The Geometry of Crop Circles

Know, oh, brother . . . that the study of sensible geometry
leads to skill in all practical arts, while the study of intelligible
geometry leads to skill in the intellectual arts because
this science is one of the gates through which we move to
the knowledge of the essence of the soul, and that is the
root of all knowledge.

—Ikhnân al-Safâ

There is a great misconception as to why
sacred geometry is "sacred." Some believe that
ancient peoples lacked sophistication and intelligence,
so watching a bisection of lines create
orderly geometric patterns constituted "magic."
Others argue that it was because of its association
with buildings in which gods were worshipped
and blood sacrifices made to appease
their wrath.

"Sacred or canonical geometry is not some
obscure invention of the human mind," wrote
Paul Devereux, one of the world's leading writers
on Earth mysteries, "but an extrapolation by
it of the implied patterns in nature that frame the
entry of energy into our
space-time dimension. The
formation of matter and the
natural motions of the Universe,
from molecular vibration
through the growth of
organic forms to the spin
and motion of the planets,
stars and galaxies, are all
governed by geometrical
configurations of force. One

Figure 10.1
Stonehenge.

can dissect a plant or a planet and not find the Maker's blueprint anywhere in sight, of course: it is inherent" (Devereux 1992).

Sacred geometry is a mirror of the Universe, and as such, it is timeless. It is also a form of communication that can be accessed at ancient places. As Devereux says, "It is the ultimate systems language." As we are about to see in this chapter, we are rediscovering this language in crop circles. However, to establish the presence of sacred geometry in crop circles without first understanding its purpose and impact on society—the state of human consciousness even—is to miss a vital function of the glyphs. Let us then briefly examine sacred geometry and its place in the greater scheme of things.

Our experience of and reaction to all things beautiful is made possible by our ability to distinguish order from chaos. When we recognize the perfection inherent in a Greek temple or a painting by da Vinci, we are subconsciously responding to proportions bound by the universal laws of geometry. To quote the geometer Robert Lawlor: "The practice of geometry was an approach to the way in which the Universe is ordered and sustained. Geometric diagrams can be contemplated as still moments revealing a continuous, timeless, universal action generally hidden from our sensory perception. Thus a seemingly common mathematical activity can become a discipline for intellectual and spiritual insight" (Lawlor 1982). A substantial body of evidence for this is found in the unlikeliest of sources, Religion.

As stated in Islam (particularly Sufi, its mystical half)—and echoed in the Jewish and Hindu religions—sacred geometry enables humanity to see the archetypal world of God. At its heart, the Arabic faith still contains an unadulterated snapshot of this primordial truth, in the geometric figures adorning its mosques and art forms. Consequently, Islam has served as curator and preserver, maintaining the purity of the philosophy of geometry, "akin to the Pythagorean-Platonic tradition of antiquity but in a totally sacred universe free of the nationalism and rationalism which finally stifled and destroyed the esoteric traditions of Greek intellectuality," to quote the eminent Arabic historian S. H. Nasr (Critchlow 1976).

It's not certain from where the terrestrial origin of this knowledge stems, since the forms of sacred geometry are just as evident in Celtic, Tibetan, and Buddhist art—even in native North American sand paintings. In other words, sacred geometry is a universal principle shared by cultures that seemingly had little or no contact with one another.

One of the earliest known practitioners of sacred geometry were the Egyptians. Its proportions were embedded in the ground plans of their temples, their frescoes, and in the Great Pyramid at Gizeh, whose structure contains many mathematical laws since attributed to Pythagoras. But although the enlightened Egyptians used geometry for all manner of terrestrial applications—hence *geo-metry*, "measure of the earth"—their aim was metaphysical. Egyptologist John Anthony West postulates: "The whole of Egyptian civilization was based upon a complete and precise understanding of Universal laws. And this profound understanding manifested itself in a consistent, coherent and inter-related system that fused science, art and religion into a single organic Unity" (West 1993).

The symbolic language of Egypt, together with its texts on medicine, mathematics, and

science, demonstrates the Egyptians knew how the world works, and they did so without the advantages of computers or electron microscopes, proving that one does not need advanced technology to access or understand the finer realms of life. And because the Egyptians recognized sacred geometry as the mechanism of the heavens, they applied it liberally across the landscape for millennia as a way to bestow Universal order on Earth, a concept encapsulated in the Hermetic maxim, "As Above, So Below."[79]

Figure 10.2

Many ancient temples were designed to encode the figures of sacred geometry. The plan of Stonehenge is unique in that it features many of these figures (squared circle, pentagram, hexagram, and heptagram shown here for simplicity).

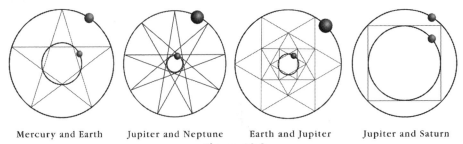

Mercury and Earth   Jupiter and Neptune   Earth and Jupiter   Jupiter and Saturn

Figure 10.3

According to geometers Critchlow and Martineau, the relative mean orbits of planets are defined by sacred geometry.

---

[79]"As Above, So Below" is mentioned in the Gnostic Gospel of Thomas: "When you have made the two as one, the internal as the external, the above as below, and the male and female as one, so then will you enter the kingdom of God."

Such obvious benefits did not go unnoticed by other enlightened groups, and permanent expressions of this knowledge were subsequently erected for posterity throughout Europe, in the form of the Parthenon, the Temple of Delphi, Aachen cathedral (whose chapel bears identical ground-plan measurements to Stonehenge), and Chartres Cathedral, one of the most impressive hymns to sacred geometry. The knowledge made its way north to the British Isles, for it is immortalized in Stonehenge. In fact, the "Pythagorean" geometric tradition was already well in use throughout Britain some 3000 years before the Greek mathematician, as evidenced by the formulae adopted for the construction of stone circles (Strachan 1998; Thom 1967).

Obviously the principles of sacred geometry were important enough for scholars and architects to go to enormous lengths to preserve for future generations. Well, that was the idea. These practices were abolished as a form of study by order of Emperor Theodosius in 399 A.D., the net effect being the rise of the Middle Ages. Slowly and corrosively, codes for a life in harmony with the Universe gave way to a predilection for violence, intolerance, terror, and persecution. The last great works based on sacred geometry—namely the Gothic and early Renaissance—were kept alive via Plato, the works of Vitruvius, and whatever Hermetic and Qabbalist writings and philosophies survived suppression by the emerging Catholic Inquisi-

tion. With the move toward an analytical view of the world, connections to holistic and metaphysical practices were severed, and by the time Newton and the scientific secularism of the seventeenth century prevailed, rational logic had gained such dominance that all esoteric knowledge was condemned as occult.[80]

By the twentieth century, this masculine, left-brained worldview had reached its nadir. Man placed Nature over a barrel, harnessing its power, taming its ways, and desecrating its resources to fuel "progress." The dubious high point of this culture has given us the nuclear age and saddled us with a few by-products: global urbanization, depletion of resources, and toxification of the Earth which, social scientists point out, has fueled a meteoric rise in human alienation and criminal behavior. Not surprisingly, worship at our ancient temples is today rarely done for the purpose of enlightenment, but for a snapshot and a souvenir. As these temples become relegated to mere curiosities from an age gone by, so our wonder of the unseen and our connection to the sacred disappears.

And so a pattern emerges: The more disconnected we become from the Universal order, the more dysfunctional we become as a society. And the longer our umbilical connection remains severed, the more we rely on rationalism to explain our reason for being and the further we stray from spirituality. The vicious circle is compounded by Western

---

[80]By definition, *occult* is "that which is concealed from view," just as *esoteric* means "that which is hidden and lies within the individual." The true date of the subduement of esotericism is a subtle matter, for its practice continued in pockets throughout Europe following the Inquisition, a genocide largely concocted between Philip of France and Pope Clement V during the thirteenth and fourteenth centuries. It is fair to say that its effects have contributed to the misunderstanding of esoteric knowledge.

language being a separatist language. As Lawlor explains: "Modern thought has difficult access to the concept of the archetypal because European languages require that verbs or action words be associated with nouns. We therefore have no linguistic forms with which to imagine a process or activity that has no material carrier" (Lawlor 1982). Yet in Eastern languages, subject and object are one. Japanese lovers do not declare to one another "I love you," they declare *aishiteru*, "loving." Subject and object are merged into wholeness, and such a linguistic foundation is probably what enables peoples of the East to accept the mystical side of life more readily than their Western counterparts.

Thankfully, the Universe moves in waves, and the cycle of darkness is inevitably moving once again toward enlightenment. For one thing, science is discovering the geometry within nature. During a demonstration of an electron microscope before the American Association for the Advancement of Science in 1937, it was discovered that the crystalline structure of tungsten is composed of nine atoms geometrically arranged like a cube. Since then, science has further discovered that the physical structure of elements is governed by geometric arrays surrounding a central point. So the general assumption that the nature of matter is fundamentally composed of solid particles has given way to quantum physics, which shows that at a subatomic level, matter is empty, and at its heart lie patterns of energy. The irony here is that by acknowledging geometry as the fundamental basis of matter, science has adopted the stance taken by ancient cultures, elevating these supposed "stone-wielding, loin-cloth primitives" to its highest ranks.

Little wonder, then, that these harmonic laws were so important to the temple builders: they are the laws behind the Universe. And since the Universe was created by God, they reasoned that to embed the harmonic ratios governing the temporal movement of the heavens into these physical structures, the power and the knowledge of the firmament could be bestowed upon the Earth. So, temples became doorways into the mechanics of the physical world and the inner world of consciousness, and the interface would enable anyone to connect with finer levels of awareness.

Today, as alienation from all forms of spiritual and Universal wonder reaches epidemic proportions, expressions of sacred geometry and symbols bearing the hallmarks of an ancient philosophy of harmony are manifesting in our fields. Even skeptics will admit that crop circle designs exhibit a harmony pleasing to the eye much like an ancient temple or classical painting. The proportions are balanced, the shapes rhythmic, the symbols dynamic; even an outlying grapeshot appears to stand like a sentinel at its remote location by premeditated design. By analyzing crop circles in accordance with the laws of sacred geometry and its many expressions, one begins to appreciate the mastermind behind their conception.

Circle: In crop circle designs, then, we see recurring geometrical shapes that are for the most part generated from a central circular form and which develop proportionally by outward expansion, a regenerative principle fundamental to organic life. The circle is representative of the Creator's principle, of cosmic life, from the smallest atom to the largest planet. It has no beginning and no end; all things are divided from within it and, paradoxically, all things are contained within it. It is expressed by all cultures past and present as the symbol of the unknowable, of spirit, and the "breath" of the Universe. It is also the foundation of the entire crop circle enigma; even the "Koch fractal," with its expanding hexagonal mosaics, begins as a large central circle of clockwise-spiraled plants.

Square: If the circle is symbolic of Heaven, the square represents matter and Earth. The

Figure 10.4
"Grid Square."
Etchilhampton,
1996.

Maya, for example, regarded the Earth as a living organism inextricably interconnected with humanity; and in Mayan cosmogony, Hunab Hu is the creator of measurement, movement, and the mathematical structuring of the Universe. This divinity was represented by a square inside a circle, which signified the ether surrounding the four elements of air, water, fire, and earth. A crop version of this appeared at Etchilhampton in 1996.

Squared Circle: When square and circle are given equal areas and superimposed, they represent the fusion between spirit and matter, or harmony on Earth. The proportions of the squared circle were used, for example, as the traditional foundation of the

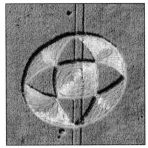

Figure 10.5

The squared circle, traditional plan of the Indian cosmic temple. Wherwell, 1995.

Indian temple and cities based on cosmological principles.

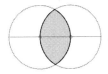

Vesica Piscis: The overlapping of two equal circles births a figure of profound symbolism called the vesica piscis. It is emblematic of the world above and below, of the conjunction of spirit and matter. The figure is associated with Jesus Christ and the Piscean Age; hence the vesica's correspondence to the Christian fish and the shape of the bishop's mitre. The Holy of Holies, it carries the number 2368 in gematria (a number also equated with Jesus Christ) (Michell 1988a). Gothic architecture uses it in the distinctive ogive arch; and in 1996, it appeared as a crop circle near Weyland's Smithy long barrow in Wiltshire.

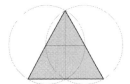

Equilateral Triangle: From within the "womb" of the vesica piscis all the regular polygons of sacred geometry are born. The simplest is the equilateral triangle, the form of completion, since it has a beginning, a middle, and an end, and as such is symbolic of strength and stability. Therefore, it is not by accident that many of the most arresting symbols in religion, science, and commerce are based on the triangle; the Trinity and the three colors that generate the visible light spectrum are examples of two polarities held in balance by a third.

The triangle reigns in Christian iconography, God being the only figure portrayed with a triangular halo. The Creator's "blueprint" appears three-dimensionally as the tetrahedron, whose geometry underlies the molecules of life as well as the best natural conductors of heat, quartz, and diamond. Hardly surprising that one of the most enduring crop circles, Barbury Castle tetrahedron, represents this form.

Spiral: The spiral is the measure of creative forces. The spiral of a galaxy as well as the harmonics of Earth's living organisms are governed by a principle called the Golden Mean

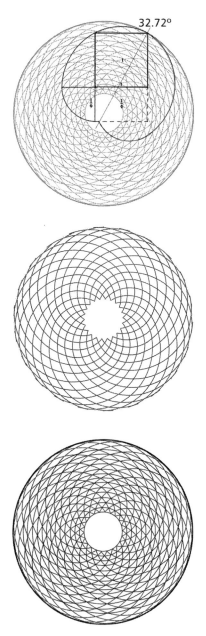

Figure 10.6

Constructing a Golden Mean or phi spiral requires a geometric division in the ratio 1:1.6180339, a tall order on paper alone. The "sunflower" crop circle is composed of 44 such spirals, each one meeting at an angle of 32.72°.

(or phi). Its proportional geometry is seen in the growth patterns of leaves, nautilus shells, the ram's horn, and the bones of the human hand. Its proportions are implicit to Greek and Egyptian temples, as well as Gothic cathedrals, just as its elegant motion was portrayed in the "Triple Julia Set" and the Woodborough Hill "sunflower" of 2000.

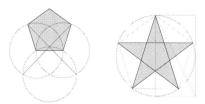

Pentagram: The Golden Mean is extrapolated from the pentagon and the pentagram, the figures most associated with humanity, since the human figure with outstretched limbs is contained within the five-pointed star. Hence it was the symbol of the Pythagorean's humanistic science, and worn as a talisman of good health. The pentagram pervades Native American symbolism, while Christians associate it with Jesus because the pentagram represents the archetypal human (five senses), the

Christed human who has harnessed the occult forces of nature to attain sovereignty over the material world. The angle between two sides of a pentagon is 108 degrees, and as 1080 is the lunar number in gematria, the pentagram's qualities are lunar, feminine, and intuitive (Michell 1988a).

There are many examples of the pentagram as a crop formation symbol. One was the

Figure 10.7
Relationship of pentagonal geometry. "Star," Bourton, 1996.

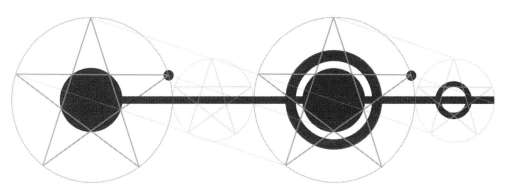

Figure 10.8
Hidden pentagonal geometry of the Alton Priors pictogram, 1991.

Bourton "Star" whose deceptively simple design concealed complex proportional geometry. But just as a crop circle can contain geometry, so can geometry contain a crop circle, and something in this pictogram at Alton Priors provoked studious fascination (see figure 10.8). What looked to many to be nothing more than circles connected by a line was discerned by John Martineau as containing an invisible rhythm. In a visionary moment he observed how its elements could be framed by invisible pentagrams. But was this just a coincidence? After all, anyone can draw a pentagram around a circle. Not so. The clues lay in the strategic position of the two small grapeshot which give the starting reference points. Later, I extended Martineau's work by demonstrating that the geometry could be proportionally extended to encompass all aspects of the design.[81]

So what looked at first to be an ordinary crop circle provided hours of "intellectual and spiritual insight," just as the scholars of old said it would.

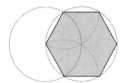

Hexagon: The natural division of the circle into six parts produces the hexagon, which contains the six-pointed star widely referred to as the Seal of Solomon. The hexagon's qualities are rational and solar, as governed by its 6 x 60° triangles, reflective of the solar number 666 in gematria, and not (as fundamentalist Christians

will argue) the devil's license plate. Other characteristics and symbolism behind this figure are vast, so I will touch on only a few significant facets here.

The natural division of a circle allows six circles to fit exactly around the circumference of an equal seventh. Twelve can also be fit around a thirteenth. John Michell has studied these implications and concludes: "It is symbolic of the order of the universe in the fact that twelve equal spheres can be placed around a thirteenth so that each touches the nucleus and four of its neighbors, producing the geometer's image of twelve disciples grouped around the master. Christ, Osiris and Mohammed are among those who are represented as a central sphere with twelve retainers" (Michell 1988a). Michell discovered further veneration for the Seal of Solomon in ancient cultures when he

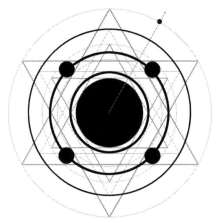

Figure 10.9

Hexagonal geometry defines every element of this simple crop circle. The outer ring represents an imaginary circumference relative to its only grapeshot. This circumference defines the largest six-pointed star. Upton Scudamore, 1990.

---

[81]See John Martineau's *Crop Circle Geometry*. I must point out that my introduction to Martineau's brilliant work came after my own investigations, particularly as his books were (and continue to be) out of print. What is interesting is that some of the early crop circles that I was drawn to analyze had also been chosen by Martineau.

found the figure encoded in the ground plan of Stonehenge.

The Circlemakers have shown a great deal of interest in hexagonal geometry, particularly in 1990 at Upton Scudamore, although the form was not apparent at first (see figure 10.9). Martineau looked at the lonely dot, lying at precisely 30° to the magnetic axis of the formation, and wondered what would happen if he drew a line through the grapeshot at that angle. To his surprise, the line bisected the two inner rings at points where construction lines of a containing hexagon could be drawn.

The points of the two six-pointed stars revealed how the Circlemakers use tangential geometry to marry an invisible matrix to the visible design, revealing why the satellites and the grapeshot are strategically located. As for the grapeshot at Upton Scudamore, it also marked the path of an invisible outer ring containing the entire formation and its hexagonal plan. This is hardly the sort of thing one would achieve by accident.

To show how critical is the ratio between elements in crop circles, I dissected a simple design. The 1987 formation at Whiteparish was one of the first circles to incorporate a ring as well as a ruler-straight spur, as if suggesting "come look at

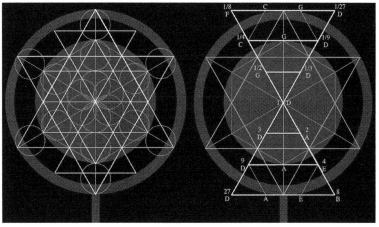

Figure 10.10

The simplicity of the Whiteparish formation, shown in gray, conceals a hexagonal framework (left) and the Drum of Shiva, which contains the proportional frequencies of the pure music scale.

me." As it turns out, both Martineau and I did, independently. The simplicity of the design hides a complex maze of hexagons and hexagrams. But more was to come.

While looking for connections between crop circles and sound, I came upon the Drum of Shiva, a Hindu diagram of the pulsating instrument of creation. Its two equilateral triangles touching point-to-point contain a collection of reciprocal tonal patterns which are found in the pure music scale. To generate these ratios, you need a hexagonal framework to place the points on the "drum" where the proportional ratios occur. By superimposing this figure over the Whiteparish crop circle and its hexagonal framework, it is shown that the elements correspond with an inch-perfect alignment.[82]

Ten years after Whiteparish, the importance of the hexagonal figure was again made clear. After the end of the exhausting 1997 season, I

---

[82]It also validates the hard work undertaken to accurately survey crop formations by Andrews, Delgado, John Langrish, and recently, the dedicated young German Andreas Müller.

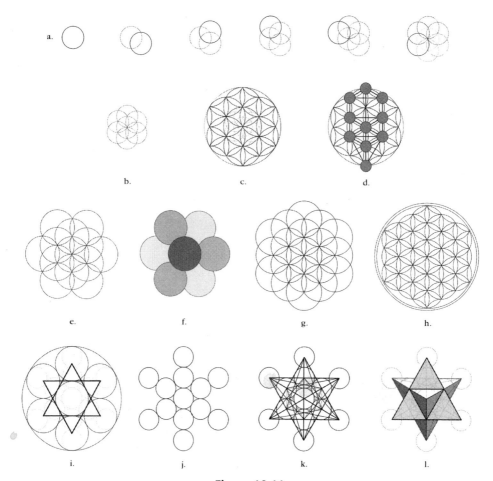

Figure 10.11

The outward expression of the circle in six movements (a) is synonymous with the days of creation. God's "day of rest" is expressed by the complete figure of seven circles (b). The next outward expression creates the Seed of Life (c). Within the Seed lies the Tree of Life (d). The next outward expression (e) creates the Egg of Life, which can be simplified thus (f). The next outward expression (g) creates the Flower of Life (h). Again, this can be simplified as six circles packed around a seventh (i). Within the Flower lie the thirteen circles of the Fruit of Life (j). Connecting the circles generates Metatron's Cube (k) which contains all the geometric energy patterns necessary to create the Platonic solids (l)—the Star Tetrahedron shown here. The Platonic solids are fundamental bonding patterns forming the physical Universe.

was drawing the season's pictograms from surveys and aerial photos. This time- and concentration-intensive labor began to feel more like an initiation into the Mysteries, but the procedure proved to have much merit. Out of forty reported formations in Britain that year, thirteen hexagon-based formations had manifested—thirteen being the number of circles that fit inside a hexagon, and as such, an association with a mysterious Egyptian diagram.

Figure 0.1 *"Julia Set" crop formation appeared in daylight beside Stonehenge. A strong link exists between Neolithic sites of veneration and the siting of crop circles, both in England and throughout the world. Do these ancient and modern temples share a common architect?*

Symbolism in the landscape. The spiderweb is a representation of the Word of God, and is often depicted in the ceilings of temples, as well as on the shaman's staff of the Ashanti people of Ghana. This concept of a Universe formed by vibration or sound is found in a Hopi legend, which speaks of the Spider Woman's song of creation giving life to the forms of the Earth. Avebury, 1994.

Figure 1.17 This 600-foot pictogram sent shockwaves throughout the media and quickly established the concept of crop circles in the minds of millions around the world. Alton Barnes, 1990.

Figure 1.18 Second pictogram to appear on the same night as the one at Alton Barnes; a third would later appear near East Kennett long barrow. Milk Hill, 1990.

Figure 1.15 Crawley Down, 1990.

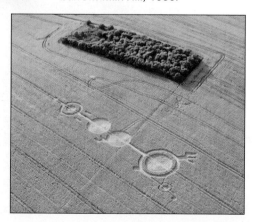

The early morning light brings out the symmetry in the laid wheat. A strong psychic connection exists between crop circles and humans: This crop circle was predicted to appear at this location two days in advance. Roundway, 1999.

Surgical precision of concentric rings. Litchfield, 1996.

Figure 2.8 One of two near-identical pictograms sporting a "key." This one pointed directly at Silbury Hill. Discrepancies between the two designs allowed for the discovery of two hitherto unknown speeds of light (Myers and Percy 1999). East Kennett, 1991.

Figure 3.3 Disorganized floor lay and lack of precision in standing features common to hoaxed crop circles. Overton Hill, 2000.

Figure 4.11 Looking down the spine of this nineteen-circle "fractal" glyph, the elegance of each spiral, complete with central fans, is accentuated in infrared. Liddington hill fort, 1996.

Figure 4.14 *Plant lay resembling rippling water, typical of large, complex glyphs. Note how the crop is elegantly laid in thin bundles as if guided by a beam. Roundway, 1999.*

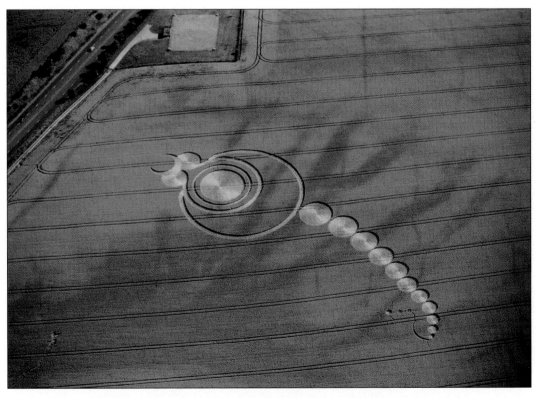

Figure 6.8 *The most dramatic of the "Scorpions." Bishops Cannings, 1994.*

Figure 6.6 "Galaxy." West Stowell, 1994.

Figure 6.3 The floor lay of the West Stowell
"Galaxy" showcases the Circlemakers' precision.

Figure 6.10 *Two temples separated by five thousand years. In myth, the spiderweb is associated with the creative power of the moon. This harmonious crop glyph appears appropriately, then, beside the lunar temple of Avebury. This glyph is also encoded with an invisible pentagram, symbol of the regenerative power of the moon. Avebury, 1994.*

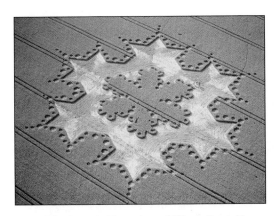

Figure 7.6 *The second "Koch fractal," framed by 204 circles. Milk Hill, 1997.*

Figure 7.30 *"Lotus." Golden Ball Hill, 2000.*

Figure 8.27 Photo taken across the Pewsey Vale showing two vertical beams of light. These are at odds with the angle of natural light for the time of day.

Figure 8.28 "Balls of light" similar to those associated with crop circles are often seen at sacred sites. These were captured at the stone marking the path of the female energy line through the Avebury stone circle. The light phenomena were not visible at the time the image was taken.

Figure 8.29 Green ball of light with faint halo gliding below Adam's Grave.

Figure 8.4 Heat has discolored and stretched the node and created a 90° bend.

Figure 8.6 *Normal heat dispersement in Whitchurch hoax.*

Figure 8.7 *Lichfield formation shows gradation in chlorophyll.*

Figure 8.8 *Oliver's Castle hoax (the red patch is thistle).*

Figure 8.9 *Comparative effect inside Liddington "solar" formation.*

Figure 8.10 *Red streaks show agitation of chlorophyll around the two Liddington formations (1996).*

Infrared images shot under similar conditions, plant types, and maturity.

Figure 9.28 "Coiled Serpent." East Field, Alton Barnes, 1999.

Figure 9.26 This "rose" glyph appeared below Dragon Hill. A significant number of people had a rose color appear across their photographs, this one notwithstanding. Uffington, 2000.

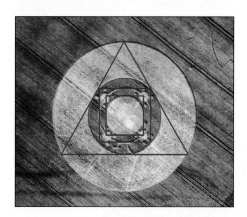

Figure 10.34 The outer circle and inner disc give note C (fifth octave). This is obtained by nesting theorems—the square inside the square inside the triangle. Telegraph Hill, 1995.

Figure 10.35 Each "moon" has a radius equal to the sides of the triangle, and the moons' centers are at the vertices. Littlebury, 1996.

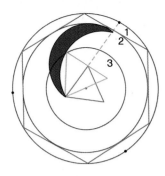

Figure 10.36 *Circles 1 and 2 give note F by the hexagon theorem. Circles 1 and 3 give note A because the side of the red triangle is at the altitude of the yellow triangle. Littlebury.*

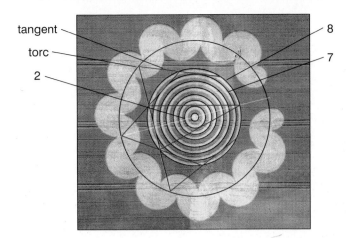

Figure 10.37 *The triangle which fits rings 2, 7, and 8 gives note C (fifth octave). Tangents to ring 7 meet at the torc, confirming this diatonic triangle.*

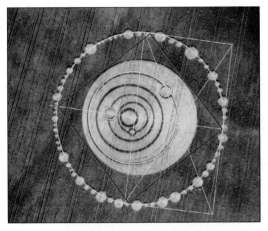

Figure 10.38 *The asteroid circle and the flattened circle in the wheat give note D (second octave).*

Figure 10.39 *Proportional geometry. A pentagram inside a pentagram means that the areas of the outer and inner circles have a ratio of 72, note D (seventh octave). The white outer and inner circles of each web sector give the note C (third octave) of the triangle theorem.*

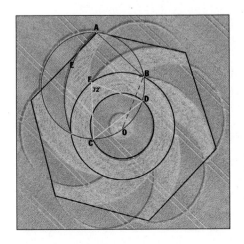

Figure 10.40 *Ptolemy's famous Theorem of Chords applies to circle ABDOC. Radius OA is found from chords AB (the side of the pentagon) plus OB (the side of the hexagon). The hexagon gives note F, while the circles through the cusps of the moons A and B give note A (2nd octave). Barbury Castle, 1997.*

Figure 11.12 *One of Jenny's cymatic images bears a strong resemblance to the Barbury Castle tetrahedron.*

Figure 12.17 *Image of a Shining One, one of the guardians of Silbury Hill, unexpectedly captured on film.*

Figure 12.4 *Dragon hill, below Uffington hill fort, was artificially shaped to receive the first rays of sunlight on the December solstice. This collection point of Earth energy was enhanced by the arrival of the "rose" crop glyph, which lies upon one of its many invisible geodetic energy lines. Uffington, 2000.*

Figure 13.4 *Oldbury hill fort, Cherhill.*

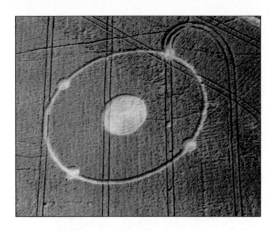

Figure 13.3 *Early "Celtic cross" design. This particular one was dreamed by Colin Andrews the night before it appeared a few fields behind his home. Over the years such coincidences have become an accepted part of the phenomenon. Longstock, 1988.*

Figure 13.18 *Pythagorean symbol of well-being, this pentagram crop glyph became the focus of many reports associated with healing. Bourton, 1997.*

Figure 13.20 *"Wrap yourself in the petals of this flower and the awareness that music becomes light shall be clear to you." Interaction between the Circlemakers and the author. Etchilhampton, 1997.*

Figure 13.15 *Beckhampton, 1998.*

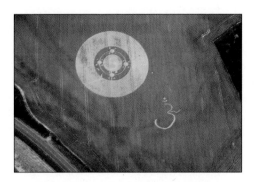

Figure 13.5 *Telegraph Hill, 1995.*

Barton Le Clay, 1996.

Sunflower.

Spiral of life. A vortex of logarithmic curves. Berwick Bassett, 2001.

Flower of Life: To fully appreciate the importance the Egyptians attached to sacred geometry, consider that for them it was a prerequisite for generating mathematics, from which they derived the laws of physics, even the morphogenetic structure behind the physical world. It was the Universal code. This philosophy was attributed to Thoth,[83] founder-god of Egyptian

Figure 10.12
The essential amino acids relative to the Flower of Life.

learning and measure, who "gave to the priests and philosophers of antiquity the secrets which have been preserved to this day in myth and legend. These allegories and emblematic figures conceal the secret formulae for spiritual, mental, moral, and physical regeneration commonly known as the Mystic Chemistry of the Soul. These sublime truths were communicated to the initiates of the Mystery Schools, but were concealed from the profane" (Hall 1928).

The Egyptian Mystery School's main emphasis was on an all-encompassing geometric symbol called the Flower of Life, described in the *Emerald Tablets of Thoth* as the infinite grid of creation. The Flower of Life (also called the Flower of Amenti) is constructed from a circle divided into numerous repetitions of the vesica piscis. The process repeats sevenfold and rotates outward to create a "cell"; with every eighth division, a new outward expression begins and the process repeats ad infinitum, creating a matrix (see figure 10.11).

Although it appears in two dimensions as a series of circles, the diagram actually represents a three dimensional process of spheres within spheres. Consequently, the process resembles the meiotic division of the human cell, making the Flower of Life a geometric metaphor for the unfolding process of nature, a process referenced by the Seven Days of Creation in Genesis and the octave of the music scale (whose significance will be shown in the next chapter). As each of its "cells" contains the pattern of the whole matrix, the Flower also works like a hologram, and as such it is analogous to the Universe: Its branching patterns are said to describe the

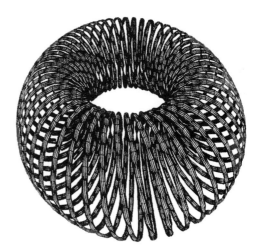

Figure 10.13
Representation of a 3-D tube torus.

---

[83]Pronounced Teh-ho-teh. Also written *Djehuti*, from which *David* is derived. Thoth was known to the Greeks as *Hermes*, from whence comes *hermetic.*

geometry of light interacting as genetic material within the cells of the human body, the arrangement of the genetic code within the DNA, even the branches within the essential amino acids (Braden 1993).

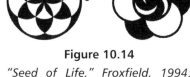

Figure 10.14

"Seed of Life," Froxfield, 1994;
"Egg of Life," Littlebury, 1996.

The Flower's outward rotation is performed by the vortex action of the doughnut-shaped tube torus, a shape fundamental to the generation and regeneration of matter, showing how energy flows into and out of itself—a similar principle to the magnetic field that exists around the Earth and every human being.

In his pioneering body of work on the geometric origins of the Old Testament, Stan Tenen placed a 3-D tube torus within another primal shape, the tetrahedron, and from the combined structure uncovered twenty-seven primary symmetrical positions from which he extracted the Hebrew alphabet exactly in the order the letters originated. Tenen also extrapolated the Greek and Arabic alphabets from similar geometric matrices (Tenen 1992). It is now easy to appreciate why these figures are held to be sacred.

The Flower of Life is the culmination of a number of outward rotations, and each rotation is a form in itself. The first is the Seed of Life, and within it lies a series of circles connected with

pathways, known to disciples of the Qabbalah as the Tree of Life. Hundreds of books have been devoted to explaining this symbol, for in its understanding lies the point of spiritual balance for a human being. The Tree's ten circles (each containing one of the first ten numbers) plus their twenty-two connecting branches are said to constitute the keys to all knowledge, the paths to wisdom. The diagram encodes a secret system such that only by arranging the paths in correct order are the mysteries of creation revealed, a fact concealed in the 32nd Degree of Freemasonry (Hall 1932).[84]

From the outward rotation of the Seed of Life comes the Egg of Life, a pattern that combines the harmonics of music with the electromagnetic spectrum and underlies all structures in biological life. It is from the outward rotation of the Egg that the Flower of Life unfolds. The design has been found "flash-burned" onto the stone wall of the Osirion temple complex in Abydos, Egypt, by a process that nobody can explain; the temple is built with some of the hardest rocks on Earth. The design is referenced in an inscription on Tablet 13 of *The Emerald Tablets of Thoth* as the life force code: "Deep in Earth's heart lies the flower, the source of the

---

[84]Qabbalah is an ancient system of theoretical and practical wisdom, a symbolic map of creation, providing the student with paths or insights towards spiritual growth through the uncovering of hidden knowledge. One of the meanings of Qabbalah is found in the Portuguese word *cavalo* or horse, as maintained by the Knights Templars when they brought the wisdom of the Mysteries to Portugal. It is said that when the student "mounts the horse" he embarks on a quest for knowledge and Universal truth. Interestingly, also derived from *cavalo* is the verb *cavar,* to dig below the surface, and cave (same English meaning, and symbolic of the womb, of going within). In the West, the horse is the symbolic equivalent of the Sphinx, under which the lost Hall of Records is said to be buried, containing all the universal knowledge of Atlantis and other high civilizations. Curiously, major concentrations of crop circles and UFO incidents in England occur near hills marked with figures of horses carved out of the white chalk.

Spirit that binds all in its form. For know ye that the Earth is living in body as thou art alive in thine own form. The Flower of Life is as thine own place of Spirit, and streams forth through the Earth as thine flows through thy form" (Doreal 1925).

The wonder of the Flower of Life's rhythmic proportions is that it is possible to draw the hexagon over the design at any point, thereby validating the importance attached to this symbol by many ancient societies, and still visibly retained within the Jewish religion. In fact, the Flower of Life was considered so important by illuminated societies like the Cathars and Knights Templars that they sacrificed their lives by the thousands to the Roman Catholic Inquisition rather than see its knowledge misused. This is hardly surprising, given that the Flower may contain the mathematical sequences of the code of creation (Braden 1993).

Embedded in the Flower of Life lies the "Fruit of Life." As the name implies, it is the sum and application of this knowledge as it manifests in physical form, and as such, carries within it thirteen systems of information governing the geometric aspects underlying our reality (Melchizedek 1996; Essene and Kenyon 1996).

Five such systems emerge when connecting the centers of the spheres with straight lines.

Figure 10.15

Thirteen formations from 1997 and their relationship within the Flower of Life grid.

This couples the regenerative, feminine nature of the flower (circular) with the masculine principle (straight line). The net product of this marriage is "Metraton's Cube," and from its hexagonal matrix emerge the Platonic Solids, the five crystallizations of the creative thoughts of God, the very bonding patterns of nature (Frissell 1994).[85]

What makes this discussion relevant to crop circles is the fact that a 350-foot image of the Seed of Life appeared in 1994, followed two years later by an enormous Egg of Life, executed with godly precision. It was as if someone were priming us for something.

---

[85]Interestingly, although named after Plato, another Greek sage, Pythagoras, had used these same figures 200 years prior. Yet Pythagoras, along with other Greek scholars of his period, had been initiated in the Egyptian Mystery schools. Knowledge of the Platonic Solids appears to be far older, for stone models of these solids have been unearthed in Neolithic structures over 8000 years old, and as far north as Scotland.

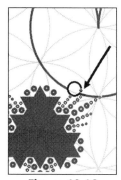

Figure 10.16

"Something" came to light in 1997 with the appearance of the "Tube Torus," followed by the thirteen English formations based on hexagonal geometry. It dawned on me that all these formations could be packed, interlocked, and superimposed over the grid of the Flower of Life. But where to begin?

Energy coming to Earth enters anticlockwise, then upwells clockwise. You can find this instruction carved on the stones of Neolithic chambers throughout the world, although science had to wait some 8000 years before Russian physicists discovered that natural anticlockwise rotating systems add energy, and clockwise rotations release it (Kozyrev 1968). It follows that if the crop patterns are generated in a two-stage process (first programmed from above, then fired from below), that the overlaying of each formation upon the Flower of Life grid should be sequentially performed in a clockwise direction. With all designs placed within this grid, all but one element appears out of alignment: one of the 96 grapeshot in the spiky fractal design in the center. In the diagram (see figure 10.16), this anomalous grapeshot is referenced within the offset ring of an earlier formation. If this is a coincidence, someone took a lot of trouble to make it so.

The Tetractys: That spiky triangle is itself based on another symbol of sacred geometry, the tetractys. Although attributed to Pythagoras, the tetractys can be traced to the Hindus, and prior to them is a matter of conjecture. Like the Flower of Life, what is certain is the association of this figure with the creative process.

Theon of Smyrna, a renowned scholar in antiquity, declared that the ten dots of the tetractys represented the Ten Words of God. To Christians these "words" signified the Ten Commandments; to the Hebrews, the ten spheres of the Tree of Life. However, the numeric symbolism of the tetractys also corresponds to the Hindu model of nine cobras around Brahma, the Egyptian Grand Ennead around Atum, and the Qabbalistic nine legions of angels around the Hidden God.

In the esoteric tradition, if one is inclined to follow the path of illumination, the tetractys reveals the mysteries of Universal nature. This is what Pythagoras did, and he was duly rewarded by discovering that the figure contains the music ratios 4:1 (double octave), 4:3 (the fourth), 3:2 (the fifth), and 2:1 (the octave)—the harmonics that govern creation. Thus enlightened as to these Universal forces and processes, Pythagoras extracted theories concerning music and color from the

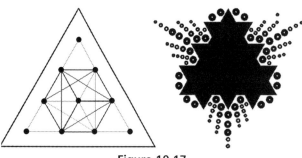

Figure 10.17

Left: The tetractys with the Ten Words of God connected to form a cube and a hexagon; Right: As a crop glyph. Hakpen Hill, 1997.

tetractys: The top three dots he saw as the three elements of Supreme white light,[86] or the Godhead; the remaining seven dots to him represented the colors of the visible spectrum as well as the intervals of the diatonic music scale.

Some interesting things happen when you connect the dots of the tetractys. Apart from creating nine equilateral triangles, you also create a hexagon incorporating the six-pointed star, and a 2-D view of a cube; and by further bisecting the angles, you also produce the lattice grid necessary for the construction of the two "Koch Fractal" crop circles.

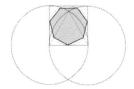

The Heptagon: Unlike other geometrical figures, the seven-sided heptagon has been elusive throughout the crop circle phenomenon. As of 2000, there were exactly seven examples. But given that it is the only geometric shape whose angles cannot be bisected to a whole number, it is hardly surprising. Each angle measures 51.428571. . . .° Why it should be the only polygon which cannot be drawn mathematically perfect remains as mysterious as the philosophical associations surrounding the number seven itself.

This number evokes the seven ages of man, the colors of the rainbow, the day God rested, the number of orifices in the human head, the pillars of wisdom, the number of days that—multiplied by four—regulates both the female and the average of the lunar cycles, the number of abominations, candles, cities, cleansings, continents, covenants, curses, degrees of wisdom, eunuchs, gables, generations, heavens, loaves, mysteries, sins, steps, temples, veils, virtues, wonders, and so on. Seven trumpeters circled the walls of Jericho seven times, just as pilgrims to Mecca walk around the Ka'aba in seven spirals. Seven is balance, hence why Libra, the seventh sign of the zodiac, is the union of the spiritual three with the elemental four, immaculately demonstrated by the square base and triangular elevation of the Great Pyramid of Gizeh, whose base angle, incidentally, measures approximately 51°51'.[87]

Most importantly, particularly in light of our investigation, the heptagon is analogous to the seven notes comprising the diatonic music scale, which we'll discuss later in this chapter.

The Barbury Castle tetrahedron makes for an unusual example of seven-sided geometry, primarily because it is triangular. As coincidences go, the heptagonal connection took me exactly seven years from the date of its appearance to uncover. A numerical clue lay in the seven segments that makes up the odd-looking ratchet sitting on the bottom right of the glyph. But somehow the heptagonal geometry just wouldn't fit over the glyph. What I needed was a starting point.

One thing that always stood out from the otherwise meticulous design of this glyph was

---

[86]The three elements of cyan, magenta, and green, from which all colors are generated, including white. This system is today used in television sets.

[87]Gizeh (simplified as Giza in the West) derives from *Djiseh* or *Jeesah,* which gives rise to the name Jesus (Elkington 2001).

Figure 10.18

Hidden geometry of the Barbury Castle tetra-hedron—pentagonal, hexagonal, and hep-tagonal. Note the kink at point C.

the way in which one of the arms of the triangle was kinked. I recalled an obscure fact from the weavers of Persian carpets, who leave one element imperfect when they create their masterpieces because "only God is perfect." Were the Circlemakers demonstrating their humility? Perhaps. But why does the kink lie opposite the ratchet? I decided to use the kink to project a diameter toward the ratchet, and use its seventh segment as the edge of a circumference. With this, a heptagon could be made to fit the crop glyph (see figure 10.18).

What is unusual about the Barbury Castle tetrahedron—and, as we shall see, a few other "special" crop glyphs—is the way in which it encodes two additional forms of sacred geometry, namely the pentagram and the hexagon. The key to the concealed pentagram lies in the glyph's lower left ball whose thin avenue penetrates exactly five twelfths of the way. From the diagram, you can see how a pentagonal star aligned on this ball frames the glyph's central circle and outer ring with great precision. As for the hexagon, this is numerically referenced by the top ball and its six segments. Here, a series of three nested hexagons each reference the glyph's central circle and rings.

Such a 5:6:7 relationship is significant in that five represents the geometry of organic life, and six the geometry of non-organic things. Together, 5:6 represents the ratio of the retrograde procession cycle of Earth relative to the circumference of its equator in nautical miles, and by this harmonic, life is able to exist here. Seven represents the geometry of the soul, a key with which consciousness imprints the physical body (Myers and Percy 1999). This process of creative manifestation will have great implications in later chapters.

In June 1995, a formation bearing a different type of ratchet design appeared at Cow Down. Here we see how the zigzag pattern is clearly defined by an invisible heptagonal geometry that defines the outer ring (see figure 10.19). However, the central points of the heptagon appear not to reference the middle ring of the formation, normally not a good indication. Yet the two small, inner heptagons clearly define the rest of the design with ease. Like its predecessor at Barbury Castle, this design puzzled me, and again I initially looked for one element that appeared deliberately offset, but with no luck.

A couple of years later I came across a photograph of the same formation taken from a different angle. The group of three grapeshot were shown to be clearly aligned to something else. But what? The middle grapeshot, visibly smaller than its two sisters, suggested the focus of interest lay in the middle ring of the formation itself.

The geometric relationship between outer and middle rings was a perfect equilateral triangle. The significance of this is that the ratio between these two areas produces the mathematical ratio of 4:1, a double octave. If a straight line is drawn through the axis of the grapeshot, a contact point is made between the triangle and the outer heptagon, suggesting that a connection exists between *musical ratios* (the heptagon) and *light* (the triangle) in the circle-making process.

In all, there were seven elements in the Cow Down crop circle, just as the zigzag occupied a seventh portion of the surface area. Seven days after its appearance a 90° deviation from magnetic north was observed on a compass placed at the center of the formation. Such are the coincidences involved in this phenomenon.

But 1998 was the year in which the heptagons showed up *en masse,* the most understated of

which appeared at the base of the hill fort of Danebury Ring. For me this pattern remains one of the most perfect examples of the Circlemakers' art, not only for its elegant demonstration of a complex geometry, but the eloquence and simplicity with

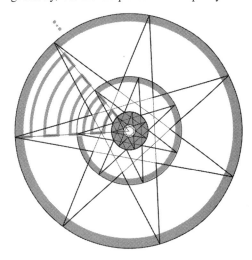

Figure 10.19
Heptagonal geometry. Cow Down, 1995.

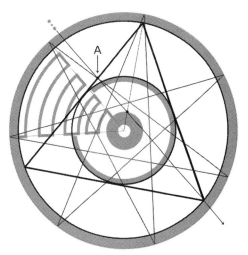

Figure 10.20
An area defined by an equilateral triangle gives a ratio of 4:1, a double octave in music. Its contact point with the heptagon is at point A.

Figure 10.21

Heptagonal crop circle shows a second relationship governed by a perfect square. This creates a ratio of 2:1, an octave in music. Danebury, 1998.

one is essentially looking at the completion and rejuvenation of the Universal cycle, as exemplified by the horizontal figure 8, the infinity symbol. "I am One that transforms into Two, I am Two that transforms into Four, I am Four that transforms into Eight. After this I am One again," states the Egyptian creation myth. I have already dealt with the Buddhist representation of this cosmic cycle, the Wheel of Dharma and its eightfold path of enlightenment, and its related crop glyph. Another manifestation of eightfold geometry came during the 2000 season. In this crop glyph which appeared beside Silbury Hill we see the octagon, and with it a suggestive relationship to Islam (see figure 10.22).

In Islam, the highest pronounceable name of Allah is "The Compassionate," and through His breath the Universe is periodically created, maintained, dissolved, and renewed. With the eight corners of the octagon unfolded, the exhalation or expansion of the Breath of Creation is represented, and through the interplay of the polarities of breath, that form is manifested. This is why octagonal geometry dominates Islamic culture.

Similarly, the periodic table of elements is formed of groups repeating in patterns of eight. Even the doubling of the human cell proceeds in eight stages, so not surprisingly the octagon is also an ancient symbol for the Earth Mother, who sometimes is depicted as an eight-legged spider manifesting the world while spinning the threads of fate for humanity. Within this fate lies the choice for spiritual transformation. Was humanity at a point of periodic renewal when this crop

which it was achieved. The ratio of the area of the circumference running through the semi-circles relative to the circumference marking the outer edge of the formation is precisely 2:1, an octave.

To carry the musical coincidence further, an electromagnetic energy line runs through this area, connecting the Danebury crop circle and hill fort with a church two miles away at Middle Wallop, former home of the London Philharmonic Orchestra's prominent composer/conductor, the late Leopold Stokowski.

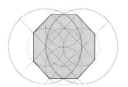

The Octagon: When one comes face-to-face with the eightfold figure that is the octagon,

circle appeared? Were we being invited to choose between repeating the same patterns of behavior or treating Mother with more care and attention?

Time will tell how we chose to respond to this pivotal moment, but traditionally the leap to an eighth step brings spiritual elevation. For example, the letters of the name Jesus add up to 888 in Greek gematria; eight represents the battle between the polarities of shadow and light, wisdom and ignorance. And eightfold geometry forms the foundation of the mystical temple of Shiva, the transformer. The octagon's 135° corner angles add up to 1080, the radius of the Moon, whose eight major phases influence all the water on Earth, a point not lost on the Christian church whose octagonal baptismal fonts are used in the "purification of the unconscious."

Figure 10.22

The octagonal design in the foreground is visually misleading: it is actually two overlapping octagons, giving the edges a slight bowing effect. The formation in the background appeared the same night. Silbury, 2000.

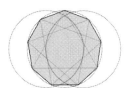

The Nonagon: In January 1999, I predicted that ninefold geometry would appear in crop circles for the first time. I lodged this information with three trusted people and the details were kept in complete confidence until the season was over. And appear they did.

Technically, the nonagon or ennead lies outside the eight geometric expressions of the Universe, but it is nevertheless an important figure since it identifies the limit reached by the regenerative principles of number, as shown by the triangle and the tetractys. Composed of three trinities, it is the ultimate expression of the triad and represents the highest achievement of any endeavor. Possibly this is why Thoth was regarded by the Greeks as Hermes Tresmigestus, "the thrice sacred," and why to early Christians the nonagon was the Star of the Holy Spirit.

Our latter-day cultural expressions still attest to the power of nine: happiness is being on cloud nine; a cat's lives are nine; amen, the end of prayer, is numerically reduced to nine in Greek gematria. The gods, too, enjoy the nine association: Odin hid for nine days in the Yggdrasil tree before gaining wisdom; Demeter,

Figure 10.23
Ninefold formation with six-moon vortex below Oldbury hill fort. Cherhill, 1999.

goddess of fertility, is depicted with nine ears of wheat; the Egyptian Gods of creation, the *Neteru*, were nine. No doubt they were aware that the tail of the human sperm half-cell consists of nine parallel tubes, and the embryo's gestation time is nine months.

When the ninefold crop circles began to appear, they did so in a variety of guises. Three geometric examples are priceless in their harmonic hypnotism: the vortex of nine crescents at Hakpen Hill (see figure 7.22 on page 104), the star and vortex at Cherhill, and a star formation below Sugar Hill (shown here). This last design is unique in that it conceals virtually all sacred geometric forms which are not evident until deciphered on computer.

The Geometry of the Hoaxes: Having applied the rules of sacred geometry to genuine crop circles, it is only fair to test them on the hoaxes. Since the majority are of a kindergarten level of art, it is easy to pick out a few "gems." Taking the hexagonal example at Oliver's Castle

Figure 10.24
With the flattened immature barley now risen, this 460-foot crop formation looks as if embossed. Sugar Hill, 1999.

(the one surreptitiously trampled for that video scam), I applied a hexagonal framework based on the center circle and the six avenues. I already knew from ground observation that some of these were wildly off in their alignment. Seen from the air they fared no better, nor did the other elements of the design, few of which fit the basic geometrical framework with any accuracy.

The ninety-foot flower, made for Arthur C. Clarke, shows the discrepancies between design

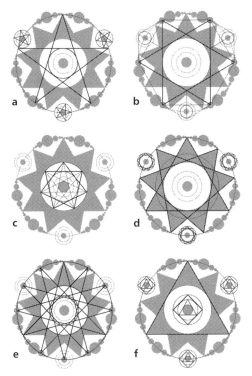

Figure 10.25

*Although outwardly a ninefold crop forma-
tion, the design encodes a range of hidden
geometric relationships: (a) pentagonal;
(b) hexagonal; (c) heptagonal; (d) ninefold;
(e) twelvefold; (f) diatonic.*

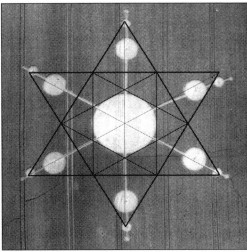

Figure 10.26

*Oliver's Castle hoax and its botched hexagonal
geometry. 1996.*

and desired result, demonstrating how a crop
circle can be mimicked and how hard it is to
achieve the high degree of symmetry of the
genuine ones (see figure 10.27). Team Satan/
circlemakers were proud of their achievement
at Milk Hill in 1998, so I did them the courtesy
of analyzing their ninefold pattern. For a group
that insinuates they made the "Triple Julia Set,"
the discrepancies in this comparatively simple,
and three-times smaller, design are extensive.
No wonder hoaxers regard the discovery of
sacred geometry in crop circles to be "coinci-
dental" and "insignificant."

In June 1995, I found myself flying above the
Hampshire countryside strapped into the seat of a
tiny Cessna. Being 6'5" tall, I was having a tough
time fitting my frame comfortably into the
plane's. Inches beyond my kneecaps spun a well-
traveled propeller, and 500 feet below lay the
Litchfield "Torc" crop circle with its bewitching
bull's eye. But somehow, that wasn't what I was
seeing. What I was looking at was music.

Shortly after landing I drove to the crop formation with Colin Andrews. As we trod the
labyrinthine design I appreciated the rhythmic
flow my feet felt at ease to follow. Later when
we retired to the pub to check the week's notes,
I shared my intuition that a musical thread
seemed to run through the phenomenon. "Oh,
you must get in touch with a good friend of
mine when you return to the States," Andrews
suggested. This good friend was professor
Gerald Hawkins.

I first met Professor Hawkins at the Cosmos
Club in Washington, D.C. The epitome of good

Figure 10.27

Commissioned by Arthur C. Clarke: The geometry on the ground (white) clearly misses the harmonics required for the pentagonal format (black). Hakpen Hill, 1994.

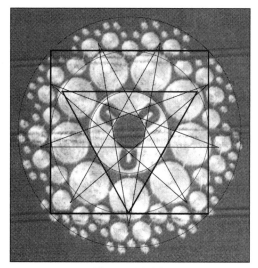

Figure 10.28

Overlay shows the near-miss geometry in this hoax. Milk Hill, 1998.

manners and life-long scholarly dedication, Hawkins impressed me over lunch, and ever since, with his revolutionary discovery that certain crop circles contained diatonic ratios. These are the mathematical laws that govern the Western music scale.

An astronomer by profession (he is the former chairman of the astronomy department at Boston University), Hawkins earned a degree in pure mathematics from London University and wrote the groundbreaking books *Stonehenge Decoded* and *Beyond Stonehenge* which opened up a new field in archaeoastronomy. He possesses an inquiring mind and a precise eye for detail: He once noted that the star Rho Geminorum was missing when the galaxy was projected onto the Boston planetarium's

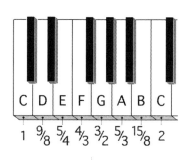

Figure 10.29

The octave and its corresponding mathematical ratios.

ceiling. One would therefore be hard put to argue with his observations.

Hawkins' probe of crop circles was done with an open mind and analytical disposition, initially to see if there were similarities between their geometries and those of Stonehenge. Despite no immediate connections, the whole thing had an air of mystery which tugged at his curiosity.

In 1990, he sat down at his farm to read *Circular Evidence* and its meticulous record of ground observations and uncontaminated data. As he studied the measurements, Hawkins recalls: "I discovered that the first formation in the book was a ratio of 1:1, the next was a ratio of 3:2, the next 5:3 and 4:3. I said to my wife, Julia, 'It looks like I'm tuning your harp. I'm getting a series of diatonic ratios here.'"

Diatonic ratios are what musicologists refer to as the "perfect" intervals of the music scale—they are the white keys on a piano. Hawkins comments:

A ratio in the diatonic scale is the step up in pitch from one note to the other. If you take the note C on the piano, for instance, then go up to the note G, you've increased the frequency of the note (the number of vibrations per second—its pitch) by 1-1/2 times. One and a half is 3/2. Each of the notes in the perfect system has an exact ratio, that is, one single number divided by another, finishing with 2, which would be C octave. The ratios were given by two rules—linear and square: For satellites, the ratio came from diameters, and for ringed circles by areas or diameters squared [figure 10.31]. The creators seemed to know of these fractions, taking care to encode them in the shapes so that they could be retrieved by someone studying aerial photographs.

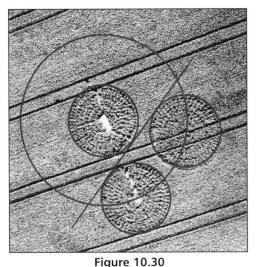

Figure 10.30

The tangent theorem. Corhampton, 1988.

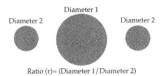

Ratio (r) = (Diameter 1 / Diameter 2)

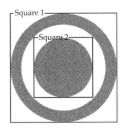

Ratio (r) = (Area Square 1) / (Area Square 2)

Figure 10.31

Hawkins' Rule 1 (top), for spaced circles; and Rule 2, for concentric circles.

And sixteen out of twenty-five crop circles in Andrews and Delgado's book had these fractions. The chances of this happening by accident according to Hawkins' calculations are 1:400,000. Hawkins' discovery slammed the door on a list of proposed causes since diatonic ratios are a human-invented response to sound. "The only place I can find diatonic ratios in nature," he said, passing me a bread roll, "are bird calls and the song of a whale. I don't think the birds made the circles, nor did the whales."

This spelled bad news for Doug and Dave, and for anyone else who had admitted to making all circles "for a laugh." "If they did it for a laugh," Hawkins remarked, "then it doesn't fit with putting in such an esoteric piece of information. I did write to them to ask why they put in the diatonic ratios."

"And what was the reply from these 'men of average intelligence,' as newspapers once described them?" I asked.

"Ha! they didn't reply." He answered. "I think we can eliminate them. It's so difficult to make a diatonic ratio, even more so in the dark.

It has to be laid out accurately, to within a few inches with a fifty-foot circle, for example."

And by 1995, crop circles measuring up to 300 feet were containing diatonic ratios to within a few inches of accuracy.

Ironically, Lord Zuckerman, the former science advisor to the British Government, had suggested to Hawkins that in order to get scientists interested in the crop circle phenomenon he should try to prove that crop circles were the product of the most palatable solution: human hoaxers. This proved to be a wise move. By discovering that crop circles contain all manner of math, Hawkins has inevitably raised the intellectual profile of those responsible, narrowing the field of likely candidates to individuals who knew the math behind the musical scale. That was until these observations prompted him to look for *geometrical* relationships between the circles. Enter Euclid.

Theorem I

Theorem II

Theorem III

Euclid was a Greek mathematician of the third century B.C. whose thirteen-book treatise on mathematics established the basic rules and techniques of the geometry that now bears his name. It is also *pure* geometry. Conver-

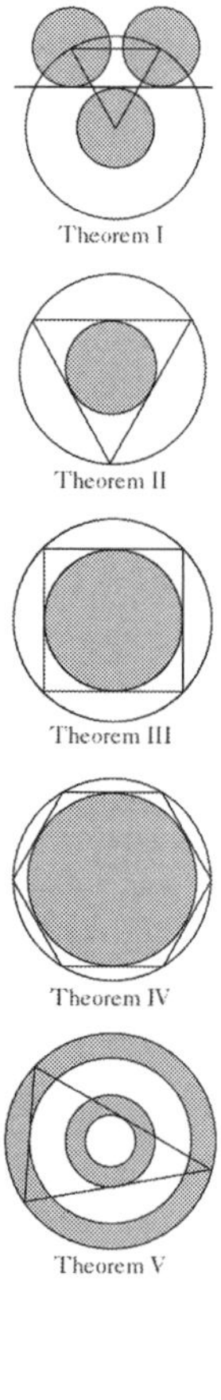

Figure 10.32

Hawkins' crop circle theorems are based on his studies of Euclidean geometry: (I) tangent theorem; (II) triangle theorem; (III) square theorem; (IV) hexagon theorem; (V) general theorem, where expanding and contracting concentric circles give all the diatonic ratios.

Theorem IV

Theorem V

sant with Euclid's theorems, Hawkins looked closely at the early crop circle patterns again. The three triangularly-aligned circles at Corhampton, where the plants had risen to forty-eight spokes, became his prime focus. Hawkins found that all the circles could be touched by three tangents, creating an equilateral triangle, and that by adding a large circle centered on one and passing through the other two, the ratio of the area of large-to-small was exactly 16:3.

Hawkins had found the first crop circle theorem, and it was all based on firm Euclidean geometry. Encouraged, he applied the same rules to other designs that had stood out and discovered three more theorems. The intellectual profile of the Circlemakers was rising by the day.

"These are Euclidean theorems," Hawkins remarked, "but they are not in Euclid's books. I think he missed them, and I can show you a point in his long treatise where they should be— in Book 13, after proposition 12. There he had a complicated triangle-circle theorem, and these would naturally follow. One reason he missed them was he didn't know the value of pi, and probably was not comfortable with the area of circles. Another reason why he missed them was that we are pretty sure that he didn't know the full set of perfect diatonic ratios in 300 B.C."

This was significant because the crop circle theorems also contained diatonic ratios as a natural byproduct of their geometry. The implication now was that whoever made the circles was intellectually on a par with, or superior to, Euclid.

The reaction by the ever-skeptical scientific community to Hawkins' findings was that these theorems could easily be proved by bright, young high school students. "Proving a theorem is one thing, especially after you've been told, but *creating* one is altogether a much harder proposition," Hawkins counters. Then almost by accident he discovered a fifth, more general theorem from which all the others were derived.

To demonstrate how hard it is to conceive of a mathematical theorem, in 1992 Hawkins dangled this brain-numbing puzzle in front of the 267,000 worldwide readers of *Science News*. The idea was to challenge scientists and mathematicians to create, given the other four, this fifth theorem. None figured it out. A further challenge to readers of *Mathematics Teacher* proved equally fruitless. Then in 1995, a version of the theorem appeared, encoded into the Litchfield "Torc" crop circle.

My fork looked lonely, having made few forays between plate and palate.

Up to this point, Hawkins and I had been focusing on the accuracy of the Circlemakers and how their work was constructed with a tolerance of plus or minus one percent. But what about the error margin? Could the rules be reversed and still hit the same ratios? As a test, Hawkins had applied the linear rule to concentric circles and the square rule to satellites; the diatonic ratios simply disappeared statistically. This simple check shows that regardless of the assumptions, musical ratios do not easily occur in patterns.

"There is a slight tendency for the measured diameters to cluster at unit values of meters," Hawkins remarked. "This raises the question: Could the hoaxers strike off the ratios 9:8, 5:4, 4:3, etc. at random by using a bar of fixed length? The answer is no. Taking all the fractions made from the numbers between 1 and 16, the nondiatonic ratio 7:4 should occur often by chance, but it is avoided in the data. Yet the 15:8

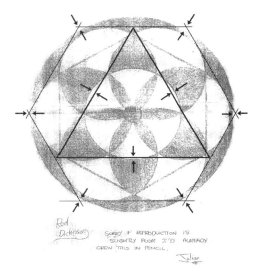

Figure 10.33

Copy of a drawing supposedly used by hoaxers to make the Froxfield "Seed of Life" glyph. Yet when given the Euclidean workout by Hawkins, this simple compass exercise misses the ratios which were found in the 360-foot crop circle.

is found in the circles, even though it should occur less often than 7:4 by chance. Then again we could expect black note ratios like 16:9, but none of these black notes were hit."

One case in point concerns the elegant Froxfield "Seed of Life" crop circle, rumored to be man-made. The sketch sent anonymously to the office of *The Cereologist*, allegedly signed by the leaders, Rod Dickinson (of Team Satan/circlemakers) and a certain "Julian," as the blueprint for the formation, is the standard elementary school compass exercise of placing six circles around the edge of a seventh circle of equal size—but does not give a diatonic ratio (see figure 10.33).

But at Froxfield a critical discrepancy was found: the central circle was smaller, having been reduced by a wide swath to generate, by

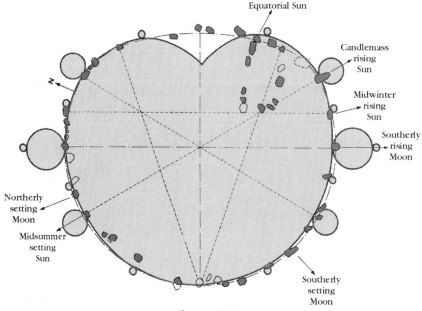

Figure 10.41

The remarkable coincidence between the shape of the "Mandelbrot Set" crop glyph and cardioid stone circles of the British Isles (Castlerigg shown here).

geometry, the exact diatonic ratio of 16/3. So were the hoaxers controlled by an unknown force that night, or was the sketch a hoax in itself? After all, the calculation would have been far easier to make on paper than in wheat.

Since Hawkins' work covered the early phase of this phenomenon, it was reassuring to discover—over the course of our food-free lunch—that the latter-day designs, now much more elaborate in nature and size, still yield diatonic ratios and demonstrate Euclidean theorems.

Up to this point, Hawkins had been working from accurate ground surveys, overlaying the geometries on aerial photographs shot at various angles. This method left some room for skeptics to carp, so as I am versed in computerized photo correction, I offered to eliminate this problem. As if by luck, I had already shot "bull's eyes" of the most important formations before I realized

how crucial a role they were to play. But then such are the coincidences . . . the examples in figures 10.34–10.40 (see pages A10 and A11 in the color section) offer a selection of Hawkins' discoveries as they correspond to the corrected crop circle photographs.

Now at the end of each season I have become accustomed to receiving a telephone call from my good friend, albeit with some trepidation: If he sounds excited, it means he has found new ratios, which for me means days looking at pixels on a computer screen. But this task has borne much good fruit. Hawkins' technique is to take a diameter from a photo and apply the unalterable rules of the theorems. In turn, I receive a set of precise measurements; they will either fit, or they won't. I have yet to see one calculation of his that doesn't. This process of photogrammetry is useful in combing crop circles of later years for further advanced mathematical evidence. As the designs become ever more stylized, it is not immediately clear on the ground if any geometric information is present; only through the observation of aerial photos does the evidence reveal itself, much like the Nazca lines of Peru.

One such example was the opening salvo of 1997. In this case, Hawkins found a perfect fit with his fourth theorem, as well as two diatonic ratios to an accuracy of 0.1 percent. He also found evidence of Ptolemy's theorem of chords (from 150 A.D.), an historic landmark because it was the foundation of trigonometry. Artistic as the Barbury Castle crop circle was, the pattern contains math, and to Hawkins' knowledge, no previous "artist" has used mathematics as a theme. The closest example lies in prehistoric monuments such as Stonehenge, which Hawkins has proved to be a complex astronomical calendar (Hawkins 1965).

Although Hawkins didn't find the connection he'd set out to look for

between crop circles and Stonehenge, it is the "Mandelbrot Set" crop circle[88] that may yet provide the link between crop circles and megalithic structures. The cardioid shape, discovered in 1691 by Jacques Ozanam, is a remarkably good fit with the groundplans of important Neolithic sites such as Castlerigg stone circle in Cumbria and Ireland's Newgrange mound. Its crop circle twin was given the Euclidean workout by Hawkins and found to contain the diatonic ratios 5:2, 2:1, 3:1, and 4:1.

However, the 5:2 ratio is not found in the computerized version of the Mandelbrot Set. Whoever made the cipher in the field deliberately placed the information inside a recognizable

Figure 10.42

Hawkins' diatonic ratios as applied to the "Mandelbrot Set" crop circle. The buds fit in equally spaced circles of Theorem V, from Euclidean geometry. The crop swirl begins at N.

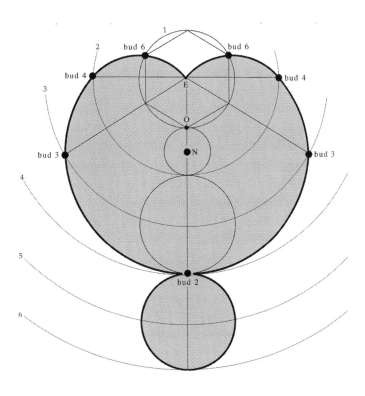

---

[88]Another level of understanding concerning the "Mandelbrot Set" crop circle is given by Myers and Percy.

symbol, but artificially clipped the design by moving the computer iteration origin (and indicated by the crop swirl), enabling the 5:2 to be encoded. As it turns out, the Circlemakers also left out the fifth bud—perhaps because it was not diatonic!

Sometimes I wonder if Gerald was ever aware of seventeenth century plant physiologist Nehemiah Grew's quote: "From the contemplation of plants, men might be invited to Mathematical Enquirys."

Next time you're sitting by a lake, take a straight stick and dip it in the water. Notice the stick appears to curve, yet you know for sure it is straight. You are experiencing the bending of light as it moves from a thin medium (air) into a denser medium (water); this is a simple analogy of how energy behaves as it moves from a rarefied state to a denser one.

In the year 2000, a selection of crop glyphs pointed to a movement away from Euclid's linear geometry, and seemed to introduce the concept of four-dimensional space, although several hints in this direction had already been dropped the year before. While it is beyond the scope of this book to discuss 4-D physics in depth, I feel that by committing my understanding of the subject to paper, other minds may feel drawn to take up the investigation further.

In 4-D there exists no perspective, as we understand it. Objects are seen from *all sides* at once. Obviously, the brain's capacity to comprehend such a concept is limited, so to visualize 4-D space, the brain requires a kind of retraining.

In the 1890s, C. H. Hinton wrote a number of books in which he set out several exercises. One of these requires memorizing sets of colored cubes drawn in different positions, then visualizing them in different combinations.

Hinton's idea was to accustom the mind to perceive the Universe from a "whole-istic" point of view, rather than from a view based on "self." The intended effect is similar to the intent of mandalas: conditioning the mind to view things as they are, and not as they're perceived. In so doing, physical limitations and preconceptions such as up, down, right, left, front, and behind are dissolved. This technique also reinforces the Buddhist view that the physical world is *maya*, an illusion, a projection onto the physical plane.

Then, in 1915, Einstein's theory of relativity was extended to include gravity. This theory abolished the concepts of space and time as absolutes and proposed that gravity is capable of distorting matter and energy: in essence, that space around large masses such as planets is actually curved. In such curved space, Euclidean geometry no longer applies, and a new type of geometry is required to represent this curvature. Part of this insight can be found in the visual paradoxes of the early Greek mathematician Zeno, and in the abstract mathematical concepts of the nineteenth-century mathematician Georg Riemann (Feynman, et al. 1966; Capra 1986; Rucker 1985).

Visual paradoxes, in which dimensional planes are both linear and circular, horizontal and vertical, are useful in training the visual cortex and the brain to more readily accept information in terms of the round and the spiral, the way of nature; in other words, to process spatial information away from the perpetual rut in which it has become stuck: a world compressed into straight lines, flat planes, and right angles.

This evolution in our dimensional perception is evident in art and the way humans have attempted to portray the world around them. You can see it in the linear drawings of animals by

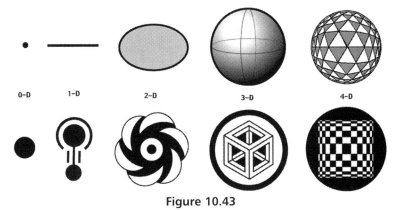

Figure 10.43

Top: How a sphere is perceived on different dimensional planes. Bottom: Possible crop circle equivalents.

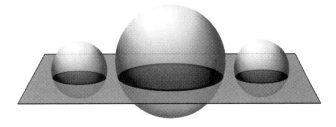

Figure 10.44

4-D spheres penetrating our 3-D plane, such as a field of wheat, would be perceived by us as circles (dark areas).

cave dwellers, to the development of two-dimensional painting and false perspectives common to the Middle Ages, to the more "realistic" portrayal of space following the Renaissance. Today we have the capacity to construct credible 3-D images using holograms. Such a development is not just representative of our cultural progress, but symptomatic of our changing awareness of the world around us, and the way the brain has developed the capacity to process information.

Still, any attempt at describing 4-D space is at best an approximation. We are creatures inhabiting a 3-D world, and lack the necessary translation device, even though elements of either dimension are inherent in each other: in other words, 4-D space is relative to 3-D just as 3-D is to 2-D is to 1-D (see figure 10.43).

In 3-D we can judge the curvature of a sphere because we are capable of perceiving its depth; however, if you try to represent this sphere on a 2-D plane (a sheet of paper), you are essentially removing its depth, and the sphere now becomes a representation of a 3-D object on a 2-D plane. By further removing its illusion of depth, it becomes a plain 2-D circle; remove yet another dimension and this circle becomes a 1-D line. You can then take the analogy further by compressing the perspective of the line until it becomes a 0-D dot.

Using the same analogy, if someone were to place a 4-D sphere on Earth, we would only see a representation of such—a circle (see figure 10.44). To convey the idea of depth, this circle would perhaps contain some visual device, like the shading used to make a circle look like a sphere on a piece of paper. In Edwin Abbott's *Flatland*, the allegorical tale describing different dimensional planes, he wrote: "Your country of Two Dimensions is not spacious enough to represent me [a sphere], a being of Three, but can only exhibit a slice or section of me, which is what you call a Circle" (Abbott 1983).

Figure 10.45

Zeno's paradoxes: infinite plane represented on a square and on a sphere, where the curving perspective is an illusion created by straight lines.

By the same token, if a 4-D sphere were to penetrate our 3-D world, it would only be perceived by us 3-Ders as a circle, and we would no doubt argue that it was nothing more than that. If we handed a sphere to 2-D beings, they, too, would find the concept inexplicable; either they would deny the existence of the sphere or, at best, label it as "mysterious."

This is not a far cry from the way we have up to this point perceived crop circles.

A sphere in 4-D is called a *hypersphere*. Its *hypersurface* is a curved 3-D space located in 4-D space. One method of visualizing such a sphere is to draw an infinite plane made with straight lines. By successively halving each area, the illusion of a diminishing perspective is achieved, slowly giving way to the realization that what we are looking at is now a sphere.

I believe the "net" crop circle at Windmill Hill is trying to illustrate this concept.

Over the course of his illustrious life, the Russian philosopher P. D. Ouspensky discussed the fourth dimension. He wrote:

Either we possess a fourth dimension, i.e., we are beings of four dimensions, or we possess only three dimensions and in that case do not exist at all. If the fourth dimension exists while we possess only three, it means that we have no real existence, that we exist only in somebody's imagination and that all our thoughts, feelings and experiences take place in the mind of some other higher being, who visualizes us. . . . If we do not want to agree with this we must recognize ourselves as beings of four dimensions. Do we not in sleep live in a fantastic fairy kingdom where everything is capable of transformation, where there is no stability belonging to the physical world . . . where the most improbable things look simple and natural . . . where we talk with the dead, fly in the air, pass through walls, are drowned or burnt, die and remain alive (Ouspensky 1931)!

Ouspensky also wrote extensively of the difficulties associated with representing four-dimensional space in three dimensions. He said our perception of it, even if geometrical, is at best only a representation, and that this level of vibration is "inaccessible in a purely physical state." In essence, Ouspensky considered that 4-D is a type of consciousness, and that the greater part of a human lives in 4-D but is only conscious of the physical 3-D part, a concept not dissimilar to the teachings of Buddha: "All compounded things are impermanent," he said, and our suffering arises from our tenacity to cling to people, ideas, and material goods, instead of accepting the transitional nature of reality. Therefore to be enlightened is to flow with, not resist, life. "The past, future, physical space . . . and individuals are nothing but names, forms of thought, words of common usage, merely superficial realities" (Murti 1955).

These perceptions of the fourth dimensional plane offer us a new understanding of crop circles. First, the idea of a crop circle as merely a flat object changes considerably, for if it is a projection of a 4-D object into our 3-D world, what we see in a field is the flat, circular portion of an otherwise invisible but penetrating sphere. And as I demonstrated in chapter 8, this concept is more than idle conjecture. What's more, according to relativity theory, the distortions caused by a change in four dimensional spatial relationships affect the flow of time, and as we already know, time behaves erratically in and around crop circles (see chapter 8 again).

Second, for mystics such as Buddha, Jesus, Mohammed, and Zoroaster, space and time, if not the entire world, were accepted as an illusion, a construct of the mind. By overcoming the bonds of the physical world (primarily gravity) the spirit is free to ascend to other planes of con-

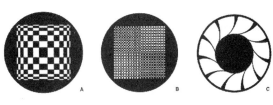

Figure 10.46

Examples of 4-D crop circles? (a) Windmill Hill, 2000; (b) East Kennett, 2000; (c) North Down, 2000.

sciousness to achieve omniscience. These states are very similar to the descriptions in relativistic physics of the space-time characteristics governing the four-dimensional plane.

It would appear that not only are the Circlemakers asking us to question our concept of reality, they are preparing us to accept and develop a 4-D level of being. If so, it is probably the next development in our evolution; after all, as a race we once believed we were inhabitants of a flat, two-dimensional plane called Earth. Now we stand poised to observe our reality from another point of view.

Looking back at the unfolding of the crop circle phenomenon, it appears we have been following a program that progressively teaches us to see *differently*, circle to dumbbell to pictogram to 3-D glyphs to 4-D space. Such non-Euclidean geometrical expressions allow us freedom away from linearity and enable us to understand crop circles as teachings that expand our awareness, removing the boundaries we have imposed on reality, leading ultimately, I believe, to greater consciousness.

No wonder considerable efforts are being undertaken to prevent people from believing in crop circles.

11. Acoustical Alchemy

> In the beginning there was the Brahman, with whom
> was the Word. And the word is Brahman.
>
> —The Rig Veda

> In the beginning there was the Word, and the Word
> was with God, and the Word was God.
>
> —John 1:1

If there is one point upon which both Eastern and Western religious traditions can find common ground it is that sound was present at the beginning of Creation. From the Popol Vuh to the Qur'an and the Bible, accounts of God creating matter through the utterance of a word form the cornerstones of every faith and cosmology.

A word is essentially a vibration, and a vibration creates sound. From audible sound emerges tone, a vibration of constant pitch. Since tones are part and parcel of the harmonic laws of sound frequency, is it possible that crop circles, with their diatonic ratios and harmonic geometries, are expressions of these laws?

As with sacred geometry, the laws of sound were paramount to the purposeful conduct of life throughout ancient civilizations. An appreciation of the importance of sound in antiquity reveals how and why it is a prime ingredient in the manifestation of crop circles today.

When the Egyptians chose to depict the name of God and the creative Word, they did so by encapsulating both in the hieroglyph of the mouth—in essence a vesica piscis—a symbol similar to the shape a vibrating string makes. Just as the forms of sacred geometry emanate from the womb of the vesica piscis, so it is said

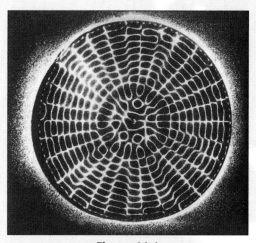

Figure 11.1

Audible sound takes on geometric order as it vibrates lycopodium powder on a steel plate. The forked figures at the center looks remarkably like the OM symbol, as well as the tridents of Neptune and Shiva.

that emerging from the one tone of creation were seven gods, such as the Biblical Elohim, each of whom was associated with a specific

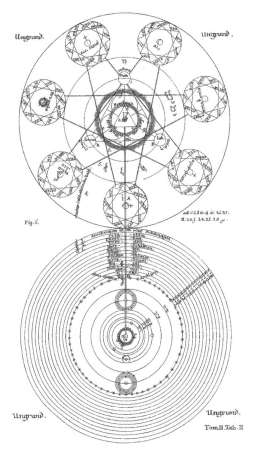

Figure 11.2

Von Welling's seventeenth century alchemical drawing shows the seven rays emerging from the primal tetrahedron or Holy Trinity. The heptagon represents the intervals of the pure music scale; the triangle, the threefold nature of light. It is said that matter "descends" from these vibrations.

task in the creation of the Universe.[89] These gods were often depicted as rays emanating from a triangle of white light, a principle echoed in diagrams such as the tetractys, where the threefold nature of white light gives birth to the seven colors of the visible spectrum and the notes of the diatonic music scale.

Figure 11.3

Egyptian "mouth" hieroglyph.

By 4000 B.C., geometry and sound were inextricably linked, at which time it was already established that the laws of geometry governed the mathematical intervals that made up the music scale. This inseparable bond was certainly taught in the Egyptian Mystery schools, since many of the temples associated with knowledge and transformation structurally encode the same harmonic ratios found in music (Schwaller de Lubicz 1977; West 1993). In fact, the relationship of form and substance to tone was understood to such a degree that structures such as the colossal statues of Memnon used to emit an audible tone when struck by the rays of the rising Sun.

The concepts of divine vibration were certainly understood in the East. Mention the term OM to many people today and they will sarcastically tell you that it's the sound bald incense-heads mutter when sitting cross-legged on Oriental rugs. But it is an altogether more serious matter to Hindus and Buddhists. For them,

---

[89]El is a general Phoenician term for a god; Elohim are best described as "light gods." There are many Els, each associated with a particular creative principle. For instance, the four guardian angels of Earth are: Uri-el (earth/humanity), Mika-el (fire/strength/protection), Rafa-el (air/healing), Gabri-el (water/communication). Both sound and Elohim are attributed the same gematrian value of 86.

OM is *the* cosmic sound, the cause of all Universal matter, because it is, itself, the very source of matter.[90] Hence the Hindu god Krishna was described by his mother as containing the entire Universe in his mouth. Consequently, Hindu science and philosophy are based on this science of vibration, as expressed by the phrase *Nada Brahma* (Sound God).

Like all chants, OM generates geometric forms, and from these forms spring those elaborate geometric patterns called mandalas, which in turn are used as visual aids for meditators to access the mind's remote memory mechanism. Recent experiments demonstrate how form arises from vibration: The five notes of the final chords of Handel's "Hallelujah Chorus," when graphically charted as wave forms and superimposed over each other, create a pentagram.[91]

Like the Hindus, the Chinese believed audible sound on Earth to be a manifestation of a super-physical vibration, an undertone prevailing in every celestial object, what the Greeks would later call "the Harmony of the Spheres." So it is not by accident that the Greek gods were referred to as *akousmata*, the "resonant ones."

Sound is considered to be a vibration of the air, but in the vacuum of space, sound is *thought*. As thought travels into Earth's material plane it is influenced by gravity and the denser layers of the atmosphere where it gains mass—in other words, it physicalizes, taking on the acoustical characteristics of sound as it does so. By this process the Word is said to "descend" from heaven, to be "made flesh."[92]

Yet this is far more than an apt description of the creation of matter, for it also describes the descent of consciousness. When sound encounters physical substances, such as sand, it manifests in geometric forms which, if you recall from the previous chapter, are an expression of consciousness. Sufi tradition has a beautiful story of God imparting the relationship between sound and consciousness to an attentive Moses on the wind-scarred crags of Mount Sinai:

"Musa ke!" ("Moses hear!"), said God. Moses heard God say how He made Man out of clay and then invited the soul to enter. A free spirit by nature, the soul feared being tied down to such a dense and limiting vessel, and so refused to enter the physical body. So God asked the angels to sing, and with their intoxicating melody the soul was guided to enter the body. Needless to say, Moses had a revelation of a Universe constructed by sound which he named *musake*, which today we take for granted as music.

According to Ethiopian cosmology the first humans communicated only through sound and song but gradually forgot the tune and resorted to words. Similarly, the Navajo mention times

---

[90]OM is reflected in the Egyptian *amun*, later adapted by the Christian faith as amen. The frequency of OM originates from the center or solar plexus chakra. Because Western faith has displaced its center too far upward, into the chest and the head, the vibration of amen fails to vibrate with the same effect. Consequently, this is seen as the core of weakness in Western religions (Berendt 1991).

[91]The research was conducted at Delawarr Laboratories, Oxfordshire, UK.

[92]Language is an imitation of sounds heard in nature, each word holding the pattern of energy of that which is imitated. Resonance is the transfer of that energy. For example, the samurai's fighting cry *kiai* induces in the opponent a catatonic fear, creating partial paralysis which reduces blood pressure. This demonstrates the importance of words and names, and why the power of charms and spells should not be taken lightly (Andrews 1966).

of old when shamans could speak onto sand and create pictures. Since this concept of sound or vibration was understood to be the primary catalyst behind the Universe, ancient Mystery schools from the Mediterranean to Tibet considered knowledge of sound to be a refined science, such that many of its teachers (Pythagoras being one) were often musicians as well as priests.

As in Tibet, legends from the Mayans and the Aztecs describe these ancient peoples as scientists of sound, able to split massive stone slabs, dress some of the hardest rocks in geology with dexterity, and move them through the air with the grace of a ballerina to position them with hairline precision. As Laurence Blair writes: "Thus the vast and precisely laid temples of Uxmal and Machu Pichu were raised and patterned—according to this legend—in symphonies of sound. Their religion recognized each individual as having a particular note or pitch" (Blair 1975).

That so many disparate cultures shared the same belief is in itself self-substantiating evidence. Yet this ancient understanding of vibration is also the view taking hold in the enlightened physics community today, which now sees the invisible world of frequencies, rhythms, and magnetic fields as the fundamental principles behind reality. Twentieth-century data show that our solar system is a harmonically

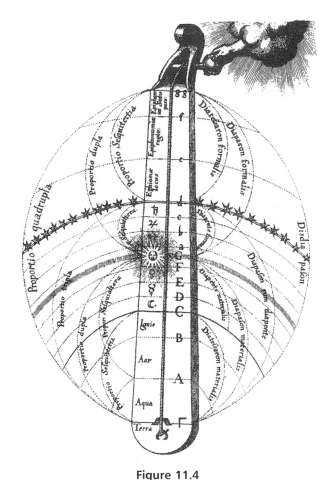

Figure 11.4

The Celestial Monochord, a sixteenth-century illustration describing the relationship between planetary harmonics and the musical scale.

interrelated musical instrument composed of more than forty octaves—the frequency gap between audible sound and visible light.

Similarly, the Earth is modeled as a giant chord, each of its geological layers corresponding to the primary major chord of the overtone scale, the natural tone scale of all music (Keyser 1970). In chemistry, oxygen, with its atomic number of eight, represents the octave, while the nucleus of the oxygen atom is composed of

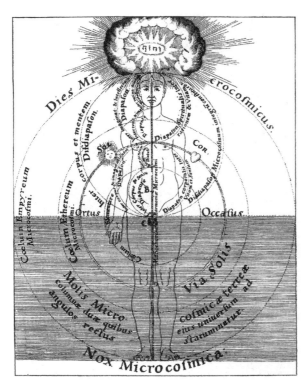

Figure 11.5

The relationship of planetary and musical harmonics relative to the human body. This princi-ple of rhythmic alternation, or ebb and flow, is inherent in the dance of Earth and Moon around the Sun, and was expressed in the Liddington crop glyph.

twelve intervals, seven filled and five empty—exactly the configuration of white and black keys on a piano.

In recent decades, German scientist Hans Keyser discovered how the relationships expressed in the periodic table of elements (our understanding of the formation of matter) resemble the overtone structure in music (Blair 1975). Wilfried Krüger linked the tetractys to the structure of the atom by discovering an asso-ciation between its musical intervals and the fundamental physical ingredients of organic life—nucleic acids (Krüger 1974). Finally, sci-entist and Jesuit priest Andrew Gladzewski, after much painstaking research into the under-

lying thread linking sound harmonics, atoms, plants, and crystals, concluded that "atoms are harmonic resonators" (Gladzewski 1951).

While the basis of these relationships and correspondences may seem esoteric, it is expressed in the law of the octave, a mutual rela-tionship between sound and color in which the notes of the octave correspond to the colors of the visible spectrum. For example, the note "C" is matched with the color red at the bottom of the visible spectrum, because both require 24 Hz to be sensed by the human body. Extreme violet (the note "B"), at the highest end of the scale, requires about 800 trillion Hz (Babbitt 1878; Hall 1928). Each octave is composed of a set of notes, and when one octave is completed another commences. The only difference is that every note now vibrates twice as fast as those in the previous octave, and the process spirals into infinity. The law of dimensions works in the same way, each perceiving reality relative to its own narrow bandwidth. These planes of existence are interconnected by degrees of vibration, the most dense being matter (a common analogy is the way steam cools into water that freezes to ice). Since the human body is itself a set of atoms vibrating at a given frequency, our ability to consciously distinguish notes, colors, and other dimensions is limited, and like a radio station along the dial it only detects those vibrations which fall across its narrow bandwidth. One such occasion happened in 1985 inside the crop circle at Kimpton. . . .

Figure 11.6

One of the "Dolphinograms." Froxfield, 1990.

"God, if only You would give me a clue as to how these are created," Colin Andrews beseeched the heavens that afternoon. The trilling sound the inquiring engineer received by way of a reply would later play havoc with some very expensive camera equipment, yet this hint by the Circlemakers fell on deaf ears, since no further progress was made at the time linking question with reply. Six years later, a new clue was dropped, this time in the form of a group of crop formations labeled by some as "Dolphinograms"—a vesica piscis with a radiating ring at each corner—a representation of the Egyptian hieroglyph "Divine Word" (see figure 11.6).

In his extensive database Andrews had by now amassed several dozen accounts of this sound being heard prior to crop circles forming. One incidence occurred during a nightwatch at the Wandsdyke earthworks near Silbury, when the trilling noise was again caught on tape. Although the high-pitched sound had a beautiful chime-like quality, according to one of the people present, John Haddington, "This doesn't translate onto tape in true fashion, coming out covered by a harsh crackling, static-like noise which is presumably caused by the discharge of high energy" (CPRI and CCCS databases, T. Wilson 1998).

Other witness reports corroborate the sudden absence of the usual dawn chorus of birds and insects, replaced by a sonic emptiness before the trill rises in volume, stopping immediately after the crop is laid down. The sound can play aural hide-and-seek with those present; it can move in nonlinear fashion and abruptly reposition itself a hundred yards away at the slightest intrusion from, say, a person entering a field or a car rounding a hill. This trilling tone therefore, to quote Andrews, "exhibits qualities of behavior, has a possible component of psychic interaction, can emit at extremely high decibels, and has the ability to transmit on radio frequencies, interfering with electronic equipment. None of this is consistent with the abilities of birds" (Andrews and Delgado 1991).

Or insects. To complicate matters, the Australian Aborigines have a sound similar to this unusual trill. During their ceremonies to contact their "sky spirits," a *bora* (a specially shaped piece of wood) is attached to the end of a long string and whirled, creating a noise practically identical to the crop circle hum. A coincidence, surely? However, crop circles have been reported in Australia as early as the early 1960s (T. Wilson 1998); their arrival was often linked with the sighting of unusual flying objects, and many were placed near sacred sites whose rocks were covered in petroglyphs which resembled early crop circle designs.

In cereologist folklore, the Circlemakers have shown an uncanny ability to respond to well-intended requests from those working close to them. No sooner had I entertained the idea of sound as a possible causal factor of crop circles than clues started to appear in the fields. At St. Neots in 1996, not far from the site of the "Mandelbrot Set," a crop circle was being harvested. The design was simple, a large circle with a smaller one resting on its circumference.

At first I didn't give it much thought, only noting that it looked harmonious. Then quite by chance I came across a diagram based upon mathematician A. E. Huntley's formula for combining two important figures: the "3-4-5" triangle and the Golden Mean. The mathematical relationship between the two creates a diagram that generates whole number ratios fundamental to the diatonic musical scale (see figure 11.7).

Within a month, two other glyphs appeared and also suggested a sound theme. The first, at Stockbridge Down, contained a central ratchet feature similar to the lower right spiral of the Barbury Castle tetrahedron. It led me into two years of book-browsing

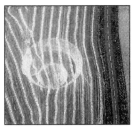 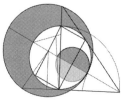

Figure 11.7

Harvested crop circle is governed by the relationship between the 3-4-5 triangle and the Golden Mean, a formula that produces musical ratios.

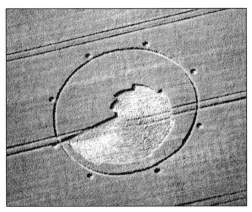

Figure 11.8

"Ratchet" crop glyph. Stockbridge Down, 1995.

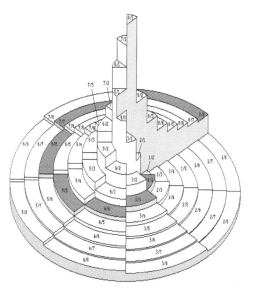

Figure 11.9

Pythagoras' circular lambdoma.

and telephoning before a fascinating American researcher named Barbara Hero met me after one of my lectures.

Hero has worked with a diagram named the lambdoma for more than twenty-five years. While possibly dating back to the Egyptian Mystery schools, the lambdoma is also known as the "Pythagorean Table." It is a diagram defining the exact relationships between musical harmonics and mathematical ratios. By translating sound frequencies in hertz relative to each musical interval into feet, a circular matrix containing all relative harmonic proportions can be constructed. Hero's simple formula is v = fw, which means velocity of sound in air at room temperature (v, approximately 1130 ft/sec.) = frequency (f, expressed in Hz) x wavelength (w, in feet, based on dimensions from the Grand Gallery of the Great Pyramid at Gizeh). As an example, a frequency of 34 Hz gives a wavelength of 33.24 feet.[93]

On the lambdoma diagram, the darkened segments indicating each octave match the ratchet of the Stockbridge crop circle, the latter providing further validation by its eight exterior circles suggestive of the octave.

The potential of this explanation dangled enticingly before me like a present waiting to be unwrapped, when news reached me of a new formation at Goodworth Clatford which had no identifying swirl (nor were its plants characteristically bent). Instead, they were dipped just below the first node, some twelve inches from the top (see figure 11.11 on page 213). I recalled how the Circlemakers had created similar unhoaxable patterns in the past as a means of getting people to pay particular attention, such as the three circles at Corhampton which had led Gerald Hawkins to formulate his first theorem.

---

[93]Personal communication with Barbara Hero. For further information see her book *Lambdoma Unveiled.*

Figure 11.10

Some of the figures generated by the voice of Margaret Watts-Hughes.

Now here were 5,000 square feet of sturdy, immature barley embossed with a type of rose emblem similar to a pattern familiar to the field of sonic patterns called cymatics.

In the 1770s, the Hungarian physicist Ernst Chladni earned the credit of being the first person in the modern era to show vibration in physical form, when he scattered sand on metal disks and watched the particles vibrate as a bow was drawn across the plates, much like on a violin. He called his experiments cymatics—the capturing of sound waves as they travel through physical substances. Although Chladni made many careful drawings from his experiments, showing how the sand consistently realigned itself into geometric expressions, at the time not much fuss was made of these curiosities.[94]

A century later in England, Margaret Watts-Hughes published the first of a series of photos showing the same connection between sound and form. Her images were created by similarly placing a powder or liquid on a disk then letting it vibrate to the sound of a sustained musical note. Having experimented with a succession of musical instruments, Hughes had the most successful results using her voice. Again the particles arranged themselves into geometric shapes, gradually changing into flower patterns such as

pansies, primroses, geraniums, and roses; in some cases the inimitable shape of a fern was created as well as that of a tree. The patterns appeared to increase in complexity relative to the rise in pitch, to the point where a powerful sustained note produced an imprint of a head of wheat. When the receiving medium was changed to liquids of greater viscosity, a perfect daisy flowered on the disc.

In the preface of Hughes' first book, Walter Besant prophetically wrote: "Let us hope that her work may be thought worthy of being taken up and conducted by some man of leading in the scientific world" (Watts-Hughes 1891).

Half a century elapsed before Besant's "man of leading" materialized as Swiss scientist Hans Jenny. In 1967, he published the first of his painstaking studies of the vibrational effects on physical mediums such as water, powder, oil, and sand. He transmitted sound as frequencies through these media and photographed geometrical and harmonic shapes forming as the wave patterns moved through each substance.

Jenny observed how changes in the vibrations (sound frequency) altered the shapes and geometry in the receiving medium. A low frequency produced a simple central circle encompassed by rings; a higher frequency increased the number of concentric rings. As the frequencies rose, so did the complexity of shapes, to the point where tetrahedrons, mandalas, and

---

[94]Chladni's work has since been used to demonstrate wave functions in physics. In a latter-day re-creation of his experiments, a 30 Hz sound frequency emanating from the Crab Nebula, recorded by the Jodrell Bank radio telescope in England, was played onto a metal plate covered with fine sand. The vibrating sand recreated the pattern of the galaxy that had generated the near-infrasonic signal.

images of the five Platonic Solids appeared. Jenny succeeded in physicalizing sound, not only enabling us to observe frozen music, but upholding the teachings of several dozen ancient civilizations in the process. For my research, Jenny's experiments provided the visual connection between crop circles and sound I had been searching for, since many of the vibrational patterns found in his photos appear in crop circle designs (see figure 11.12 on page A12 in the color section).

Figure 11.11

Cymatic pattern in barley. The plants are bent six inches from the top. Goodworth Clatford, 1996.

Some correspondences seem blatant, such as the circles and concentric rings typical of the early 1980s, the tetrahedron at Barbury Castle, even the recent highly structured hexagonal star fractals. Other images reveal the geometry encoded within crop circles that is visible only upon analysis of overhead shots by computer. They also highlight the importance attached in antiquity to square, pentagonal, and hexagonal geometry.

As a further demonstration, Jenny built a tonoscope to translate the human voice into visual patterns on a screen. As a test he had OM chanted into the device, whereupon it produced a circle which then changed into a triangle, six-pointed star, then various pyramidal shapes as found in the Sri Yantra as the last strains of the sacred syllable faded. The letter "O" when intoned alone produced a figure in the shape of an "O."

Such relationships between the geometrical forms of cymatics and the symbols of sacred geometry demonstrate that the underlying order of both the physical Universe and the nature of consciousness are not abstractions of the human mind but a real and structured matrix that binds everything together like God's glue. But there is one more important connection with crop circles: the relationship between the rising complexity in Jenny's cymatic geometries in direct proportion to the rise of dispensed frequency also matches the historical sequential development of crop circle designs, which grew exponentially from simple circles into today's complex pictograms. Therefore if frequency is determining (or is at least part of) the spiraling intricacy of crop circles, that frequency must be rising.

In recent years Paul Vigay has undertaken experiments to gauge frequency discrepancies in and around crop circles. He walks up and

Figure 11.13

Cymatic image relative to the Silbury "Koch fractal."

Figure 11.14

The first "Koch fractal." Note how the central swirl abruptly adopts a hexagonal pattern.

down a field, taking stock of the level of background readings that his meters register and he notices how they abruptly change the moment he crosses a crop circle's perimeter. Outside the Silbury "Koch fractal," for example, background readings hovered in the mid-hundred MHz range, but once he was inside the perimeter, the readings shot up to 260 MHz, reaching 320 MHz as he paced towards the center.[95] This was in 1997. When crop circles made a quantum leap in design complexity two years later, readings jumped to 540 MHz (compared to a general background range of around 150 MHz); in the "Nine Crescents" at Hakpen, Vigay detected a whopping 650 MHz.

By 2000, crop circle design complexity

surged once more, and so did the readings. With the farmer restricting general access to the "Lotus" formation below Golden Ball Hill, this crop circle seemed like a good place for us to carry out a detailed analysis. Vigay's equipment registered a steady 180 MHz background count on our approach, but this quickly climbed to 320 MHz as we reached the perimeter, suddenly shooting to 650 MHz as we stepped onto the formation's unusually agitated floor. When Vigay stopped and turned 90°, the readings dropped to 170 MHz. At this point all alkaline batteries in our equipment died; the lithium ones, however, remained unaffected. The games had begun.

We also noticed electromagnetic signal interference at an extraordinarily high range of

---

[95]Personal communication with Paul Vigay. Details in *Enigma* magazine, issue 15, Portsmouth U.K., 1998, p.8. www.cropcircleresearch.com

1.5 GHz, the highest Vigay has ever picked up,[96] yet minute 1Hz frequency increments either side of 1.5 GHz produced a clear signal. The interference also manifested in a banding effect every six inches or so, as if Vigay were walking into ripples in an agitated pond. While this was going on, I was walking beside him holding two dowsing rods, registering an identical ripple effect on the copper tools.

The anomalies continued. All LCD displays, including a watch, began to darken, but when we rotated them 90° they lightened to normal. Clearly a polarizing effect was taking place with the liquid crystal (silicon), perhaps because the frequency was interfering with the limit of the material itself. One possible confirmation of this came when my camera's silicon-based circuit board got "fried." So, just as Jenny found, the level of frequency appears to correlate with the increase in design intricacy. Crop circles as residual imprints of vibration now becomes a feasible proposition. But how would this work?

Lying like a beached whale amid an evaporated bay, the massive chalk outcrop at Etchilhampton is conveniently ringed by two reservoirs and a well, so not surprisingly it has been a breeding ground for all manner of crop circles. It has offered such delights as a "Solar Logos" and the "Grid Square." However in 1996, a strange glyph there evoked for me a Hindu connection. On one level, the glyph represented the root chakra; a second symbol representing the solar plexus chakra had appeared

two days earlier, two miles to the north at Roundway.

Sanskrit (like ancient Egyptian, Aramaic, Tibetan, Chinese, High Javanese, and Hebrew) is a language held to be sacred because it was faithful to the Word of God, the "language of Light." Hence its characters were considered "sounds of Light." Its syllables were believed to hold geometric vibrations that harness the powers of Light and the octaves of sound to create matter. Not surprisingly, altering the characteristics of this alphabet was a punishable offense. Indian classical music, or raga, is claimed to be similarly endowed, and it uses this quality to raise vibrations and lead one into heightened spiritual awareness. So it is with experiments featuring such music that yield further clues about the way crop circles are formed.

In 1969, her children having left the nest to go to college, Dorothy Retallack was faced with the prospect of becoming a bored housewife, to which she responded by enrolling for a degree in music at Temple Buell College in Colorado. Since the degree required an experiment in biology, Retallack went about proving the effect of music on plants. Of all her experiments, one involving Led Zeppelin, Bach, and the celebrated Indian sitarist, Ravi Shankar, showed how plants leaned away from Led Zeppelin but moved toward the speakers during Bach's preludes. But it was Shankar's sitar that had the greatest effect: the plants bent from the vertical toward the sound in excess of 60° (Tompkins

---

[96] 1.5 GHz is the radio frequency emitted by hydrogen gas, the most abundant element in the Universe. In the late 1950s, SETI (Search for Extraterrestrial Intelligence, the agency featured in the late Carl Sagan's movie *Contact*) postulated that if an extraterrestrial source communicated with Earth, it would do so on this bandwidth. Astronomers and scientists involved with SETI have since listened on this frequency for artificial signals from space.

and Bird 1973), perhaps the closest any human has come at coaxing plants to lie close to a right angle without damage.

No doubt hoaxers will be taking to the fields with sitars now they've been exposed to this.

Similar results have been obtained for at least a century by Indian, American, and Russian agriculturists exposing plants to sound and its vibratory actions. Since the 1930s, the U.S. Department of Agriculture has experimented with sound frequencies to stimulate growth and health in crops. When agricultural researcher George Smith exposed corn to sound in the farming community of Normal, Illinois, the result was a higher heat content in the soil as well as a slight burnt appearance in the plants. Interestingly, Retallack had found that such frequencies also markedly affected the evaporation rate of water. These are conditions synonymous with crop circles. Thirty years before Levengood's experiments with microwaves, Smith speculated that sound energy also increased molecular activity in plants (ibid.).

Experiments on wheat by T. C. Singh and the Indian Department of Agriculture in 1958 used bursts of harmonious music for brief periods through loudspeakers installed in fields. This sprouted the seeds in one-third the normal time, and boosted crop yield by 61 percent, and, unbelievably, increased the plants' chromosome count.[97] When Singh exposed his plants to Indian devotional songs, the number of stomata (surface pores) in the experimental plants was 66 percent higher, the epidermal walls were thicker, and the palisade cells were longer and broader than in control plants, sometimes by as much as 50 percent (Singh 1962–63).

A decade later in Canada, Pearl Weinberger found that exposing seeds to ten minutes of ultrasound during germination also stimulated increased growth (Tompkins and Bird 1973). Similar results were achieved using short bursts of light (ibid.). This invites comparisons to the biophysical and microscopic alterations that were observed many times by Dr. Levengood as described in chapter 8.

We can now see that specifically directed energy in the form of sound is capable of affecting plants in the manner we observe in crop circles. But what type of sound? After all, it is obvious that whatever medium is being used to bend the stalks not only applies firm and gentle pressure, but does so with a fine degree of control.

Ultrasound is capable of interacting with physical elements to an incredible degree. Ultrasound is basically any frequency which lies above the limited human auditory threshold of twenty kHz. It can be aimed, focused and reflected almost like a light beam, and specific frequencies can be focused to cause certain kinds of molecules to vibrate while others nearby are left unmoved. In February 1988, a report in the science section of the *New York Times* described how an ultrasonic beam can make,

---

[97]Trilling and droning sounds, some bordering on the ultrasonic, pervaded Cley Hill and the Warminster area in the summers of 1965 and 1973, creating phenomena where local plant life grew to extraordinary heights, some up to ten times the rate of normal growth. These sounds were accompanied by reports of strange lights in the sky, and debilitation of motor vehicles and other electrical equipment. The Cley Hill area also has a rich history of crop circles. Further references to accelerated plant growth as a result of sound or electromagnetic frequencies can be found in the work of L. George Lawrence, Pearl Weinberger, and T. C. Singh, to name a few.

break, or rearrange molecules and levitate objects.

The higher the frequency of ultrasound, the greater its ability to be directed like a laser beam. This requires readings in the high MHz range, the very ones detected by Vigay. These extremely high frequencies are also of crucial significance because they ally with the human mind's own band of frequencies and are known to affect states of awareness (Hunt 1989). They are used in hospitals to heal muscular ailments and bone fractures. Such healing effects are traditionally associated with sacred sites of standing stone, particularly those in the British Isles where ultrasound signals have been detected (Robins 1982).

By contrast, the lower end of the human hearing range lies around thirty Hz. Below thirty Hz sound is not heard but felt, and at this end of the scale we are dealing with *infrasound*. Infrasonic frequencies interact directly with biological processes, and when combined with high pressure—the acoustic power created at low frequencies can be in the order of kilowatts—they can produce permanent changes in any substances that happen to be in the way, straining them to the point of deformation, including disrupting of chromosomes (Brown and Gordon 1967). Such effects are seen in plants connected with the circle-making process. When people are involved, long-term exposure to infrasound causes harmful and unpleasant conditions such as fatigue and nausea, which are short-term crop circle effects (see the next chapter).

Infrasound is also capable of atomizing water molecules, creating a fine mist above affected surfaces. In 1996, a farmer harvesting his field at Etchilhampton saw what he described as "a series of columns of mist rising like cannon shot from the field next door." It was midafternoon on a dry, summer's day, and in these conditions mist looks very out of place. A few hours later something equally out of place appeared: a series of thirteen crop circles connected by a winding, three-quarter-mile-long avenue. Lying nearby was the "root chakra" Sanskrit glyph and its attendant teardrop. A decade earlier in 1985, a farmer and his gamekeeper, out at 6 A.M. checking their fields at Findon, West Sussex, saw a cloud of steam "rising like a series of fountains" from within a new crop circle.

Vaporization of water is crucial to the way crop circles are formed. In the case of plants and their water-filled stems, sound waves are capable of traveling through the liquid like ripples, compressing and expanding it. Because of the accompanying increase in pressure, the velocity of sound in liquid rises, and in the case of water it is extremely rapid (specifically, 1,480 meters/second to the power of minus one). This creates heat, tearing apart the water molecules, forming vapor, and creating a void inside the plants that collapses the area instantaneously as the energy is released (Blitz 1971).

This action, called vapor cavitation, creates local temperature increases of 5000° K for a fraction of a second.[98] This is enough to bend stems, particularly around the base, where the

---

[98](See Levi 1991 and Putterman 1995) For this information I am indebted to Christopher Baer, of Coral Gables, FL, who lives a few miles from Coral Castle, an extraordinary structure created by the mysterious Latvian, Edward Leedskilin, who cut, dressed, and levitated into place massive blocks of coral using sound.

greatest concentration of water exists. Such extreme heating may explain the burn marks found on crop circle plants, as well as the missing water and usually dry soil. Recall how farmer Rennick in Saskatchewan found such a situation in his crop circle along with a flattened porcupine? It turns out that infrasonic vapor cavitation also creates extremely high pressures equal to 500 atmospheres (Flint and Suslick 1991; Golubnichii, et al. 1979). Perhaps our flattened prickly friend gave up his life both to demonstrate and prove this process.

The high heat potentially generated by infrasound is also evidenced by the lumps of solid carbon sometimes found atop the soil, although it could be argued that these are simply the remnants of burnt stubble from a previous harvest. However, this would not explain rare cases where flies have been found flash-burned and stuck to crop circle plant stalks; nor a type of iron powder (some called it meteoric dust) found glazed to the stems of a formation below Oldbury hill fort in 1993.

Once again, no sooner had I begun to ponder the mechanism responsible for such occurrences when a stranger mailed me an article from an American physics journal, and again the finger pointed to infrasound. Laboratory experiments exploiting the rapid heating and cooling of infrasonic cavitation to synthesize amorphous iron show that the iron does not crystallize as it cools; instead, it forms an amorphous iron powder like a very soft ferromagnet (Suslick, et al. 1991). When Levengood analyzed the curious substance from the crop circle it turned out to be amorphous

iron whose magnetization had been sufficient for a small horseshoe magnet to pick up the wheat heads and stems (Levengood and Burke 1995).

There's one more feature of these sonic frequencies that may help us understand the nature of that other anomaly of crop circles, the tubes of light. Light and sound may seem incompatible at first; after all, unlike the transverse electromagnetic waves that make up light, sound is an acoustic wave comprised of nodes and antinodes (peaks and troughs) which travel longitudinally. Light is both wave and particle, and since every particle is in a state of vibration, its very movement creates a sound.

Conversely, sonic frequencies are known to create light. Laboratory experiments show that the high-intensity sound fields responsible for vapor cavitation are capable of emitting visible light (Barber and Putterman 1991; Berthelot 1988). This sound-to-light process is called *sonoluminescence*, and it is thought to be caused by the production of electrical discharges as water vapor is ionized. And the lower the operating frequency, the greater the effect (Barber and Putterman 1991).

However, this may not be the only way to get light out of sound. Jonathan Goldman, sound therapist and pioneer in the field of harmonics, was visiting at the Palenque complex in Mexico when he was given access to a temple normally off limits to the public. Inside a pitch-dark chamber deep inside the temple, he was instructed by his guide to tone the chamber with his voice.[99] As he did so, the chamber became noticeably lighter, to the point where the

---

[99]*Toning* is a technique performed with intent in sacred sites, where one person or a group of people sing tones which resonate with the local environment. The idea is to purify or activate the site. Chanting the OM inside a long barrow is an example of toning in a chamber.

outlines of the other members of Goldman's group could be seen (Goldman 1992).

Certainly there exists a symbiotic relationship between sound and light. As noted earlier, the process of creation as represented by the tetractys requires the presence of both sound and light. In Egyptian cosmology, Atum Ra, the Sun god, is said to have created the Universe with a "cry of light." In Greek philosophy, *logos*, which means "word" and "sound," constitutes the controlling principle of the Universe as manifested by speech.[100] According to paleolinguist Richard Fester, the words *logos, loud, light,* and *beginning* are all derived from the primal root *leg,* and its mirror, *regh.* Therefore "light," "sound," and "beginning" fundamentally occur at the same moment (Fester 1981).

Sound travels 40 octaves slower than visible light, and it travels fastest through copper, the prime material carrier of electricity. The "slowing down" of light frequencies generates the colors of the visible spectrum, which in turn correspond to notes in the music scale.[101] Therefore, sound can be construed to be the material carrier of light. This process is modeled by the "DNA" crop glyph. It features the two transverse waves or particles (electromagnetism, light) spinning around a longitudinal wave of sound (see figure 11.15); seen three-dimensionally, the sound wave appears to travel within a spiraling tube. Essentially, the "DNA" crop glyph describes much of its own formative process, and perhaps that of the phenomenon of crop circles itself.

The irony here is that the "DNA" crop glyph

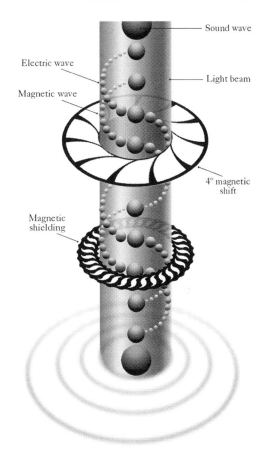

Figure 11.15

Suggested representation of the tube of light that creates crop circles. The wall of the tube is created by the transverse electromagnetic wave, as suggested by the "DNA" crop circle; within the tube flows a longitudinal wave of sound. The magnetic shielding is shown by the "Beltane Wheel" crop glyph (see chapter 8). The "ring torus" crop glyph depicts the 4° shift in the magnetic field, which gives the whole process a type of critical rotation point.

---

[100]The Greek *logos* stems from the Arabic *lauh,* meaning "tablet" (see Richard Fester's *Urworter der Menschheit*). It is interesting how the logos, the "word of God," should have been written on "tablets" and handed to Moses (musa ke).

[101]A law used by the ancient Chinese and introduced into Europe by Pythagoras.

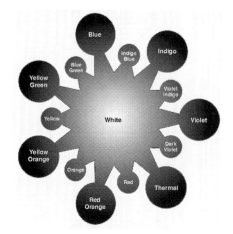

Figure 11.16

The Roundway crop glyph's relationship to Edwin Babbitt's chromatic color (light) spectrum. The glyph's design references the geometries of sound and light, containing as it does two heptagrams, Hawkins' Theorem II, and a concealed triple trinity at the center.

was witnessed being programmed into the field by a tube of intense white light. This "tube" is probably closer in nature to a set of tightly packed spirals, which give the impression of a beam. "As the electron is transformed into quanta, it becomes a ray of light. The point is transformed into a line, into a spiral, into a hollow cylinder" (Ouspensky 1931).

That this specific crop circle is a suggestive representation of the DNA spiral is no coincidence either. DNA depends on outside information for its development; in other words, it needs information sent to Earth in electromagnetic waves of light and acoustic waves of sound. According to biologist Lyall Watson: "Light waves carry both energy and information. It is no accident that the amount of energy contained in visible light is perfectly matched to the energy needed to carry out most chemical reactions" (Watson 1973).

Because light is easier to focus into a tight beam, a higher percentage of its photons reach their intended target. As such, the higher frequencies of, say, a laser beam make it an excellent carrier of information. SETI astronomer Dan Werthimer observes: "You can convey so much information in a laser signal—you can send a whole encyclopedia in a second" (Savage 2001). And there is little doubt that each crop circle conveys a library of information.

If we now take the "DNA" crop formation and link it with others from that season we find a beautiful thread (see figure 11.17). Spiral motions of life (the "Julia Sets"); the relationship between sound frequency and the electromagnetic spectrum (Littlebury "Egg of Life"); a vortex in a liquid medium (Girton); sound frequency in physical form (Goodworth Clatford "cymatic")—all are part of the ebb and flow of Universal energy as epitomized by the season finale at Liddington.

It is interesting to note that the ground attracts infrasound and that males of the animal kingdom rumble low-frequency calls along the ground to warn other animals across long distances. On the other hand, ultrasound is aerial in nature and is used by the female species for communication (Vassilatos 1998; Payne 1998). As such, both infrasound and ultrasound have the ability to carry information over long distances.

However, since sound and light scatter as they pass through the Earth's atmosphere (dispersed by suspended particles and droplets of water), to protect the integrity of an incoming beam filled with information, a shielding device is required. As hundreds of electronic devices have demonstrated when they cross a crop circle's perimeter, this shielding is definitely present. Further evidence of a *contained* energy field is revealed in the lay of the plants, which show evidence of the same geometrically regular patterns of flow found inside an oscillating container (Parlenko 1933).

This is where both the "Beltane Wheel" and the "Ring Torus" crop glyphs become relevant. If you recall from chapter 8, the former suggests a magnetization process and the latter an out-of-phase magnetic shift. Such a manipulation of the local magnetic field could theoretically be used to either repel or contain energy—in other words, to create a shielding device.

So it seems that the combined effects of sound, light, and magnetism explain many aspects of the circle-making process and a large number of its peculiarities.

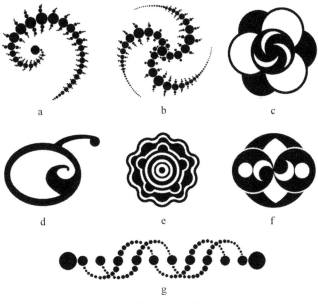

Figure 11.17

Pivotal crop glyphs of 1996 conveying part of the process involved in their manifestation: (a) Stonehenge; (b) Windmill Hill; (c) Littlebury; (d) Girton; (e) Goodworth Clatford; (f) Liddington; (g) Alton Barnes.

Laboratory and field studies in the twentieth century established that exposure to sound and electromagnetic frequencies creates beneficial and unusual effects on plants, while ongoing research into crop circle biophysics reveals unusual alterations and accelerated growth patterns. Through Jenny's groundbreaking work in cymatics, we have confirmation of the links between vibration, creation, and the natural order of life, and their correlation to crop circle patterns. Such patterns collect along nodal lines, just as crop circles manifest upon the Earth's own nodal points.[102]

So it is in the flattened crop that we are shown the pattern of frequency that created it. Just as an oscilloscope transforms invisible vibrations into wave patterns on a screen, each tone creating its characteristic image, so a field of wheat is like Earth's oscilloscope, the crop circle being the sound pattern made visible—the "Word made flesh."

---

[102]The Earth is criss-crossed with lines of electromagnetic energy. The point where two such lines cross is called a node (see next chapter). The theory that crop circles are visible prints of a light beam penetrating the Earth energy grid at its node points was, to the best of my knowledge, considered in 1988 by the late George de Trafford, and only revealed to me in 2001. George's vision was extraordinary, considering that the ideas proposed here were unpublished during his time. He also postulated that each circle corresponded to residual consciousness, hence the designs have differentiating characteristics. This concept is given further credence in chapter 13.

Figure 11.18

Water in vibrating containers flows into regular geometric patterns in accordance to the shape of the container. A similar effect appears in the lay of crop circles.

Already conversant with discoveries by Russian, American, and Canadian scientists that ultrasonic frequencies noticeably affected the growth of plants and seeds, Mary Measures and Pearl Weinberger experimented with audible sound at the University of Ottawa in Canada. After four years of experiments on wheat, their team found accelerated growth. They postulated that the sound frequency produced a resonant effect in the plants' cells, thereby affecting their metabolism (Weinberger and Measures n.d.). Which brings us full circle to Colin Andrews and his trilling sound at Kimpton. At 5.0 kHz, the frequency Measures and Weinberger applied was virtually indistinguishable from the Kimpton trill at 5.2 kHz.

Given their association with harmonics and biological processes, it may turn out that crop circles are carriers of "codes" that can be put to practical, even spiritual use. For a start, there already exists a rich legacy of sound in the healing arts, particularly in the healing rituals and shamanic experiences of ancient cultures which were performed with sound or rhythm. Forty-six hundred years ago the Egyptians were already using incantations to cure all manner of ailments, from infertility to insect bites (Dewhurst-Maddox 1993). In the classical Greek era, the frequencies of flute music were used to ease the pain of sciatica and gout; in fact, Apollo was considered the god of medicine and music. This practice continues with the Aborigines, who play the didjeridu over infected areas of the body, healing wounds and broken bones with its characteristic tones. Modern medicine does the same today by applying ultrasound.

Frequencies and rhythms form the foundation of nature, and because the Universe is in a state of vibration, by implication, so is the human body, whose proportions and DNA are constructed according to the same laws of harmonics found in music. No wonder, then, that in his "Exhortation to the Greeks," Clement of Alexandria likened the human body to a musical instrument. The body's harmonic qualities are similarly acknowledged in a statement by Montanus of Phrygia, a spiritual reformer of the second century A.D., through whom the Holy Spirit was said to have stated: "Behold, man is like a lyre, and I fly over it like a plectrum" (George 1995).

Our predecessors clearly knew what they were doing when they used sound, and modern science upholds their belief. Recent research in bioacoustics shows that a close relationship exists between the diatonic musical scale, the distance between the mean orbits of the planets, and the atomic weights of elements in the human body. Consequently, the atomic scale, when converted into hertz, can be administered as sound into an ailing body. People with eye problems, for example, generally have high levels of iron in their system. Since iron has an atomic weight of 55, by subjecting the patient to a sound frequency of 55 Hz (also the note "A"), their iron level is balanced and their vision is cured (Beaumont 1999).

Barbara Hero similarly considers sound to be an effective formula for healing, so much so that she has built a special keyboard whose notes are tuned to the harmonically related range of frequencies of Pythagoras' lambdoma. When the notes are played, the body and its chakra system responds to the range of intervals to a greater (and noticeable) degree than from a regularly tuned instrument.[103]

In England, Dr. Peter Guy Manners at Bretforton Hall Clinic pioneered cymatic therapy, adapting Jenny's principles and applying them to medical treatments that work in harmony with the human body. Dr. Manners accepts that the body is a complex array of harmonic frequencies, that cells in living tissue function as minute resonators susceptible to the effects of harmonic vibrations. Therefore, just as every organism requires harmonic frequencies to maintain its existence, harmonic frequencies are used to bring unhealthy systems back into equilibrium. This form of treatment has proved so successful since its inception in 1975 that cymatic therapy clinics now operate around the world.

Cymatics, the lambdoma, diatonic ratios, ultrasound—all the things found in crop circles now found in healing? The inference alone is profound, and I expand on this in the next chapter. Meanwhile, there is one final aspect of sound which relates to our understanding of crop circles: its *impact* on people and society.

Human messages of faith, hope, and love are celebrated and carried from generation to generation through song, so as a carrier of information, music makes a perfect vessel. A. E. Huntley observed: "Primordial racial memories are brought to the surface more readily by music than by natural scenery or any other art" (Huntley 1970). It is probable that this is the reason the shape of the human ear, and specifically the cochlea, is a spiral constructed according to the harmonic laws of tone, the same spiral ratio from which thousands of crop circles have sprung.

The importance of sound, in all its forms, is summed up by David Tame in his profound work *The Secret Power of Music*: "Music was not conceived by any [of the advanced civilizations of antiquity] as it is conceived today, as being merely an intangible art form of little practical significance. Rather, they affirmed music to be a tangible force which could be applied in order to create change . . . within the character of man." Tame further observed: "Children all over the world, when they first begin to speak or sing, do so in melodies based firmly upon tonal intervals. These harmonic and melodic principles . . . seem to be by no means arbitrary or theoretical, but are naturally meaningful to the human psyche" (Tame 1984).

---

[103]The keyboard uses a software program written by Barbara Hero's colleague Robert Miller Foulkrod. It is worth noting that the Western music scale has been altered during the past 300 years. A slight change in the frequency of a note by as little as 10 Hz has a fundamental effect on the body. For instance, during World War II the American military raised the frequency of songs played to the armed forces to increase heartbeat and productivity, and sharpen concentration (Hero 1992).

Figure 11.19

A series of overlapping heptagons create the Tawsmead crop glyph.

Infants actually recognize sound before they do color or form. When infants spontaneously sing, the note intervals of their melodies correspond to the diatonic scale. This is an archetypal pattern around the world, indicating that some type of genetic element may exist in humans which allows them to identify these laws of harmony—the same ones Hawkins has identified in crop circle designs.

Perhaps the encoding of these harmonics may be partly responsible for the triggering of childlike behavior in people who spend a substantial amount of time inside crop circles. Feelings of elatedness, exuberance, joy, and innocent wonder are all typical for visitors at these sites. It is as if crop circles unlock a code in the human nervous system. Perhaps the answer is even simpler: music bypasses the brain's logical and analytical filters, and so connects more directly with the passions. The Egyptians knew this, as the hieroglyphs for music, joy, and well-being are one and the same.

This sudden triggering of emotional behavior is further amplified when studying the exposure to harmonic overtones. Robert Lewis, a student of the Rosicrucian Fellowship, writes: "The overtones of all musical sounds progress from the physical world into the spiritual world. This is why music is practically always part of religious services. Whether it be a Hindu mantra, the chant of a Jewish cantor, the call to prayer of a Moslem muezzin, a simple Christian hymn or a Bach Cantata, the purpose of music in religious service is to raise the vibratory rate of a congregation upward through a series of overtones, to a spiritual level" (Lewis 1986).

One serene August morning in 1998, I experienced this for myself when two colleagues and I visited the hours-old heptagonal crop circle at Tawsmead Copse, not far from Alton Barnes. Against the stillness of the air, three high-frequency tones sounded in a continuous loop, audible enough for us to hum along with: F-G-F-G-C. We scanned the empty countryside for an errant ice cream van to no avail. Puzzled, we recorded the tones on tape then thought nothing more of this curiosity.

Back at my New Hampshire house, I came across a diagram known as the "Web of Athena," which demonstrates the heptagon's array of interconnecting lines and how they are constructed from just three line lengths. My guitar, having sat lonely and jilted in the corner all summer, was deputized into

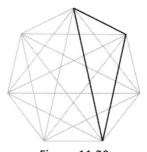

Figure 11.20

The three line lengths of the Web of Athena.

crop circles research. I transposed the line lengths from the Web of Athena onto the ebony fretboard and reproduced, note for note, the tones recorded in the crop circle.

And to think I learned to play guitar just to impress women! I might not have succeeded in that endeavor, but now I began to see a connection between crop circles and those other temples of the soul, sacred buildings. Celebrations to sacred geometry such as the magnificent Gothic cathedral of Chartres in France incorporate specific harmonic proportions in their design that enable the structure to be used as a *sonic* temple; for example, to amplify the frequencies in Gregorian plainchant (Charpentier 1975).

Gregorian chants are rich in high frequency harmonics and produce effects on the body since they charge the central nervous system and the cortex of the brain, as otolaryngologist Alfred Tomatis discovered during his forty-five years of research. (Interestingly, the electron shell of the carbon atom produces the same tone scale as the hexachord of Gregorian chant.) The role of music at these places of veneration was to "release into the earth a form of cosmic energy which could keep civilization in harmony with the heavens. Without such activities, it was thought, all could lose its alignment with the harmony of the universe, with catastrophic consequences" (Tame 1984).

This effect applies to structures scattered across the Earth, from the Anasazi *kivas* in Arizona, and the colossal Neolithic complex of Hagar Qim in Malta, to the long barrows of Wiltshire and Dorset (many of which have folklore associating them with sound and increased states of awareness). Ultimately, the effect of altering brainwave frequencies inside kiva or

crop circle is that the person and the sacred space become one and the same.

Jonathan Goldman studied this intriguing interaction between sound frequency and sacred sites and suggested that the pineal gland in the skull can be stimulated by vocal harmonics (Goldman 1992). The association between the pineal gland and clairvoyance can be traced back to the Egyptian Book of Coming Forth by Light (erroneously translated as "Book of the Dead"); throughout philosophical texts, the pineal gland is referred to as the "Eye of the Gods" or the "Eye of Shiva." So when Egyptian kings chose to place a coiled serpent on their foreheads—at the symbolic point of the "third eye"—it had much to do with their knowledge of, and initiation into, the mysteries of consciousness.

The pineal is described as a cone around which a cord is wound to make it spin, and by so doing, it creates a humming noise (Hall 1932), such as the kind of noise reported to be heard in the head by people who've spent a considerable amount of time inside crop circles, myself included. The pineal is sensitive to sound and long-wavelength light (Wiener 1968). Due to the presence of a tiny quantity of magnetite within the ethmoid bone in the skull, the pineal is one of the parts of the human body that is most stimulated by ultrasound and by fluctuations in the electromagnetic field. And it is already scientifically established that energies in crop circles do stimulate the pineal (Pringle 1999).

Activation of the pineal is accomplished when high frequencies cause the fingerlike gland to vibrate at a rapid speed, like the flickering tongue of a serpent. When kundalini rises up the spine from the root chakra, it too stimulates this "finger" to stand poised like a cobra. This unblocks the passage between the ventricles of the brain and unites the chemical flow of energy between left and right hemispheres, linking the subjective and objective states of consciousness—the visible with the invisible (Hall 1932; Goldman 1992).

As the pineal vibrates faster, it creates a kind of temporary shielding from the pull of gravity, offering consciousness a window through which to connect with the fourth dimensional state. We often experience this liberating effect when we travel to extraordinary and faraway places during sleep. This is why the pineal gland is referred to as the "all-seeing eye" and the "eye of Horus," and why anyone in a receptive state coming into contact with a sympathetic frequency inside a crop circle will most likely experience altered states of awareness.

The correct use of resonant harmonics as a means of elevating awareness is common to many cultures. Aboriginal shamans use it like a key to open a gate to different planes of existence. To create these harmonics the Aborigines rely on the didjeridu, a traditional musical instrument made from a termite-hollowed limb of a tree. In Aboriginal folklore, this instrument was as a gift from the Wandjina, a race of supernatural beings from the Dreamtime who were responsible for the creation of Earth.

The sonic field produced by the didjeridu creates an interdimensional window enabling contact between these beings and the Aborigines.[104]

This may sound like "primitive nonsense" to many in the West, and yet research into psycho-acoustics shows sound is capable of "affecting the resonant fields within intercellular processes down into the genetic levels, even down into the atomic and subatomic levels" (Essene and Kenyon 1996).

Such insights provide an understanding of how the frequencies in crop circles affect humans consciously and subconsciously, particularly as the opening of a window for the soul via the pineal gland can just as easily work the other way, allow it to *receive* information. Suggestive and rhythmic commands aimed at people while they listen to music is already an efficient method of absorbing information and knowledge. Coupled to ultrasonic frequencies, this technique can alter brain-wave patterns, inducing the mind into a meditative and receptive state (Tashev and Natan 1966).

Sound penetrates and overcomes physical barriers. It makes every cell in the body aware that a communication is taking place. Shaped into music, sound becomes a messenger, a carrier for social change. Therefore, crop circles can be looked upon as tones from an unseen reality, self-referencing, their information imparted to the listener through sound, audible or inaudible. Consequently, as a form of communication they are virtually infallible. As Victor Zuckerkandl wrote: "Tones must themselves create what they mean. Hence it is possible to translate from one language into another,

---

[104]The art of multiphonic singing by Tibetan monks produces frequencies similar to Gregorian chants and the didjeridu. The One Voice chord, in particular, rich in harmonic overtones, is said to embody the spirit of masculine and feminine elements of the divine creative spirit, and its sound unites those chanting it with Universal consciousness.

but not from one music to another" (Zuckerkandl 1956). If this is indeed the case, it is feasible the Circlemakers are sending messages that facilitate changes not just on an individual basis, but in our collective consciousness.

"The end of all good music is to affect the soul," remarked Monteverdi. Precisely the impression crop circles are leaving on all those whose antennae are extended and receptive to their transmissions.

12. THE DRAGON AWAKES

Without exception, every megalithic monument is in a certain relationship with subterranean currents which pass, cross, or surround them.

—Louis Merle and Charles Diot, archeologists, 1935

Figure 12.1

Avebury stone circle, Europe's largest repository of Earth energies. Most of the hundreds of stones that originally made up its three rings and two snaking avenues were destroyed by Puritans and fundamentalist religious fanatics in the eighteenth century.

The year 1969 saw the publication of *The Pattern of the Past,* an influential book by Guy Underwood investigating the presence of electromagnetic energy patterns at sacred sites. He wrote:

[The energy's] main characteristics are that it appears to be generated within the Earth, and to cause wave motion perpendicular to Earth's surface; that it has great penetrative power; that it affects the nerve cells of animals; that it forms spiral patterns; and is controlled by mathematical laws involving principally the numbers three and seven. Until it can be otherwise identified, I shall refer to it as the "earth-force." It could be an unknown principle, but it seems more likely that it is an unrecognized effect of some already-established force, such as magnetism or gravity. The earth-force manifests itself in lines of discontinuity, which I call "geodetic lines," and which form a network on the surface of the Earth. The lower animals instinctively perceive and use the lines, and their behavior is considerably affected by them. Man is similarly affected but less strongly, and cannot usually perceive lines without artificial assistance (Underwood 1973).

Not surprisingly, Underwood's book created a resurgence of interest in the ancient landscape. Underwood's geodetic lines[105] are what the Chinese refer to as dragon paths or *lung mei,* the Aborigines as song-lines, and the Irish as fairy paths. Thorough investigations into Earth energies concludes that Britain, if not the entire globe, is crisscrossed with a network of "male" and "female" lines of energy (also termed positive and negative in terms of polarity) (Broadhurst and Miller 1992, 2000; Tersur 1993; Devereux 1992).

The most important discovery at that time was that the thousands of stone circles, obelisks, tumuli, henges, hill forts, long barrows, pagan worship sites, and churches were deliberately sited upon the intersection points of these lines, called *nodes.*

I learned from a British Army tank regiment sergeant that on occasion during maneuvers on Salisbury Plain, their compasses would deviate noticeably at particular locations. These turned out to be on geodetic lines that connected nearby tumuli with local church mounds. And yet the general archaeological stance is that these earthen mounds

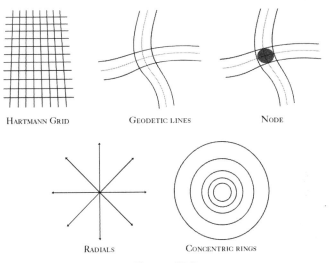

HARTMANN GRID   GEODETIC LINES   NODE

RADIALS   CONCENTRIC RINGS

Figure 12.2

Earth energy organizes itself in various modes. The Hartmann Grid encircles the Earth like a net; geodetic lines vary in width and meander along the countryside linking sacred sites. The crossroads of these lines are called nodes. Energy organized as radials and concentric rings typically radiates from nodes at sacred sites, churches, or crop circles.

---

[105]Much confusion exists in the naming of these energy currents. They are often and incorrectly referred to as *ley lines,* a term coined for straight geometric alignments linking sacred sites; another term used to describe these winding Earth energies is *telluric current.* For the sake of clarity I will use Underwood's geodetic lines; ley lines mentioned in this text also refers to geodetic lines.

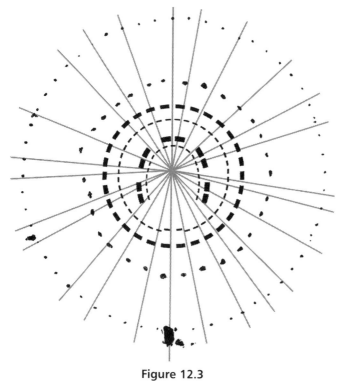

Figure 12.3

Radial energy pattern of Stonehenge, as of 1999.

Great Pyramid at Gizeh was a strategically sited power plant (Dunn 1998).[106]

There is also the unsettling question of why people who supposedly lacked technological means sought to shape by hand some of the hardest stones known to humanity, then to move these stones (weighing as much as fifty tons) across relatively vast distances to bury dead relatives, sacrifice a goat, or prevent their neighbors from stealing their wives.

There is no doubt that throughout their lives—a span of time covering 12,000 years—these sites were adopted for all manner of uses, depending on the need and dictum of the day. In my travels I have come across colossal dolmens used to house rabbits and sheep, but I doubt the original intention was to provide safe shelter for livestock. The monuments of men are not exempt from the ebb and flow of life, and such rhythm brings change: a Roman amphitheatre that once provided the gruesome gladiatorial entertainment of lions and Christians fighting today hosts a pop band; what is today a grandiose London hotel was

are graves, sacrificial sites, or ancient military fortifications. Considering that only 5 percent of excavated sites have actually yielded skeletal remains, this view seems myopic. Like the British tumuli, many Egyptian pyramids have been labeled "tombs" even though no evidence supports this. Only during the Saite period (663–525 B.C.) did it become fashionable to build tombs in the shape of pyramids; in fact, recent evidence strongly suggests that the

---

[106]*Pyramid* is a Greek term from the Hebrew *urrim-middin,* "the measure of light." The Egyptian term is *khuti,* "the lights." *Ur,* the Phrygian and Greek word for light, thus became *pur* and *pyr* (fire). The Great Pyramid of Gizeh is a structure whose measurements are based on the harmonic frequency of light, and its chambers are acoustically tuned to light, mass, and gravitational frequencies.

once a hospital caring for soldiers injured in the First World War.

Similarly, buildings on sacred sites were originally erected for other reasons. The etymology of "temple" signifies a division between sacred and profane space, suggesting that temples facilitated access from one plane to another. In the Gizeh Pyramid, for example, the passageways are often deliberately set low, requiring the initiate to stoop in humility. In many Neolithic long barrows, the passageway takes one westwards to "die" in the profane world, to be reborn in the east, hence the original meaning of orientation.

At Notre Dame Cathedral in Paris, initiates would walk through St. Ann's door in the west, indicating the setting of the Light and immersion in the dark forces of chaos, then proceed towards the east and rebirth in the rising Light. The majority of sacred sites (not to mention most Christian churches built upon them) work in this manner, suggesting their original function was to be points of entry for the fertilizing power of the Heavens.

Obviously, there's much more to ancient sites of veneration than meets the eye. By establishing a link between these doorways of energy (sometimes called dragon energy) and the forces of transformation we can begin to answer the remaining riddles behind the crop circles, namely their deliberate placement near ancient sites, their energy anomalies, and their association with heightened states of awareness. However, looking at what lies behind sacred sites—particularly their misuse during the past 1000 years—reveals why crop circles are causing such consternation among the authorities, religious orders notwithstanding.

One of the earliest references to dragon energy appears in the first century A.D. in *Decline of the Oracles* by Plutarch, who refers to the streams of terrestrial energy, influenced by the Sun and the celestial bodies, that activate oracles and places of invocation (Michell 1983). This energy was recognized by early Chinese geomancers as *chi,* its Christian equivalent being the Holy Spirit. Stone circles and barrows were erected at sites where this energy was concentrated, and consequently they were seen as places where healing or heightened states of awareness could be promoted in accordance with particular phases of the lunar cycle and the equinoxes, when the energy is at its peak.

In *Timaeus,* Plato shows that the geodetic force (particularly when manifested in spiral forms) is a catalyst in the construction of matter, and part of the generative power of Nature through which life comes into being and its equilibrium is maintained. Consequently, animals in enclosed spaces when they are about to give birth try to break out, to seek spots where energy up-wells from the Earth.

That such health-giving properties are instinctively recognized by animals is one reason why the spiral symbol has been held in sanctity, sometimes in the guise of a serpent or dragon, and why Aesculapius and Eileithyia (the gods of medicine and childbirth, respectively) were always associated with snakes (Underwood 1973). This concept is depicted in the Egyptian emblem of the *caduceus,* its twin serpents entwined around a staff. This allegorical concept of megalithic man harnessing the beneficial powers of the Earth with a shaft of stone is mimicked at Christianized sacred sites today in the image

Figure 12.5

The two snakes entwined around the spike, their male and female polarities harmonized beneath a winged Sun. Symbol of the fertilizing power of the Earth, the caduceus has since been borrowed by the conventional medical profession.

Figure 12.6

The crossroads of Earth energies are marked by menhirs, dolmens, tumuli, barrows, or the Greek omphalos, demonstrating the importance of sound and its fertilizing influence upon the Earth. Since electromagnetic energy also congregates at these sites, the strategic positioning of these stones is likened to acupuncture, an ancient method of tapping into the Life Force at 700 points throughout the human body, using needles inserted at these points to correct imbalances of energy flow and hence cure disease. Outeiro, Portugal.

of St. George skewering a luckless dragon.[107]

Singular and erect, the phallic standing stone is the umbilical connection between the energy of Heaven and Earth. This type of pillar in Portugal is called a *betilo,* stemming from the Semitic *Beith-el* meaning "house of God" (hence *Beith-el-hem,* the birthplace of Jesus). These stones, carefully chosen for their high level of quartz (with its electrical and information storage properties), were located at nodes where they could be magnetically charged. With these stones arranged geometrically, they created chambers with resonant acoustical properties, such as long barrows.[108] Acoustical experiments in the

Cairn Euny stone chamber in Cornwall show concentric rings of resonance whose positions are governed by Hawkins' square ratio for crop circles (Jahn, Devereux, and Ibitson 1996).

Tests performed at Neolithic sites show that electromagnetic readings are unmistakably different within these sites, and that psychic ability is greatly enhanced (just as it is in crop circles). The surrounding earthen embankments of hill forts and stone circles provide shielding that reduces outside electromagnetic interference, allowing the individual "to tune in to

---

[107]St. George also symbolizes the harnessing of Earth energy in the service of humanity. This patron saint is often interchanged with the Archangel Michael.

[108]The capstones appear to have acoustical properties of their own. The capstone of the Chun Quoit in Cornwall, for example, reverberates with an assortment of modes based on a major fifth chord interval.

Figure 12.7

Spirals etched at sacred sites throughout the world denote contact points between the physical world and finer levels of reality. Such sites are used to elevate awareness. The direction of the spiral indicates the centrifugal movement of energy: anticlockwise descends; clockwise up-wells from the Earth. The two are often seen in the contra-rotating swirls of crop circle floors.

stations we normally tune out," to quote Colin Wilson.[109] Thus, information is received with greater clarity and efficiency by the radio that is the human being and its resonant antennae, the spine and DNA coil. The resonance found at sacred points such as Delphi, Stonehenge, and the Pyramids is 7.8 Hz, and corresponds to the brainwave frequency of mystics and healers (30 Hz being the typical wakeful state) (Becker and Selden 1985), proving that one of the grand purposes behind these sites was to facilitate the mind into a state of receptivity. Hence why many sites associated with transformation have the trident of *el ayin* inscribed on their stone walls, the same symbol that graces the head of that other sign of transformation, the 1990 Alton Priors pictogram.

That organized religion knew and feared this ability of individuals to receive spiritual guidance at "pagan" sites is seen by the way it supplanted its own structures upon them, some-times with little subtlety (see figure 12.8). During its laborious struggle to maintain control of Europe, a dying Roman Empire created the Catholic Church, and through its offices issued many edicts which sought to eradicate pagan faith at megalithic sites and other oracles. As early as 640 A.D., the Bishop of Noyon warned: "Let no Christian place lights at the temples, or the stones, or at fountains, or at trees, or [stone] enclosures . . . let no one presume to make lustrations, or to enchant herbs, or to make flocks pass through a hollow of a tree or an aperture of the Earth; for by doing so he seems to consecrate them to the devil."

The work of the devil of course being any knowledge pursued outside the strict confines of orthodox belief. Obviously the pagans did not share the Roman Catholic syndicate's opinion that use of sacred sites in any way connected them with the forces of Hell, for 300 years later the clergy were still being instructed to "forbid

---

[109]The walls around Egyptian temples served a similar purpose in defining the calmness of sacred space from the "waters of chaos" that lay beyond.

Figure 12.8

The subtle imposition of Roman Catholicism on an eight-thousand-year-old pagan site of worship in Portugal. The adaptation of pagan sites became a goal of the early Church as it sought to take power away from pagans (meaning "country dwellers"). In England, churches were even built in the middle of hill forts despite these being awkwardly located miles from their congregations.

well-worshipping and divinations with various trees and stones" (Thomas 1971).

By the eleventh century, it seems the needle got stuck in the groove: "No one," Pope Gregory reaffirmed, "shall go to trees, or wells, or stones, or enclosures or anywhere else . . ." and so forth. In their desperation, the Church forced women who cured their children at sacred sites to fast for three years; at one point it even became a criminal offense not to attend mass. And yet, as the sites of stone were proving so beneficial, orders for their destruction met with limited success, so in a change of strategy the Church assimilated them, as a letter from Pope Gregory to St. Augustine shows: "By no means destroy the temples of the idols belonging to the English, but only the idols which are found in them; let alters [sic] be constructed, and relics placed in them" (Thomas 1971).

These orders covered the length and breadth of Europe. But things became more sinister, for in its zeal the Church began to play down the connection of sites with the unseen, as cited in the fatherly advice of the Bishop of Lamego, Portugal: "Be damned all who believe that the souls and bodies of men are subject to the influence of the stars" (de Vasconcelos 1982). All this came from the same people who subsequently adopted the use of amulets and rosaries and then claimed as their own the pagan rites of praise they condemned (de Vasconcelos 1981). So much for the virtues of charity and tolerance extolled by the early Roman Catholic church.[110]

---

[110]As the Roman Empire declined around the fourth century A.D., the Roman Catholic Church filled the structural organization and vacuum of power left by a crumbling Empire. By Emperor Constantine's reign, much of Christ's esoteric texts had been reworded or removed from the scriptures, thanks to dubious interpretations, and Catholicism became a quasi-political religion. In 533 A.D. the Council of Constantinople even deemed the Resurrection a heresy: "Anyone who defends the mystical notion of a soul and the stupendous notion of its return, shall be excommunicated." In other words, persecuted. Consequently, the expansion of Islam into Europe was a blessing for Christians who up to that point had been persecuted by the Catholic Church. My intention is to differentiate between Christianity and Catholicism, and how the compassionate and virtuous faith of Jesus—whose foundation is not dissimilar to both pagan and Eastern mysticism—was later manipulated and used as a tool by the Roman popes to control the public.

Inevitably, churches were built over existing "pagan" sites, in some cases assimilating the stones which had stood there undisturbed for thousands of years. The names of deities were corrupted: the god of purification and fire, Santan, became St. Anne; Morgana became Mary, and so forth. Yet the Church cunningly maintained the connections with the old names since they were well aware of the powers of invocation.[111]

There is no doubt the Church knew of the inherent energy in the sacred sites and how this energy enabled people to connect with higher levels of awareness, or God. Its own seat of power, the Vatican, was itself built on a sacred site marked by a standing stone (Elkington 2001). And so, by introducing itself as an intermediary, organized religion removed direct contact between people and God. Which brings us up to crop circles in our present time.

Given the ability of crop circles to connect people with the unseen and the way in which the circle phenomenon is discredited, are we seeing history repeat itself, not to mention a possible motive behind the Vatican's alleged involvement in debunking crop circles (see chapter 5)?

Over two decades of research in England reveals that crop circles consistently appear on geodetic lines or their tributaries, influencing, charging, even reconnecting the energy of local ancient sites as if reactivating a network of "sleeping" power points. In England the two principal "male" and "female" geodetic energy lines are called the Michael and Mary—so-called because of the predominance of those two names in the churches along their paths. These lines extend from Hopton on the east coast in Norfolk, to St. Michael's Mount on the southwest coast of Cornwall, placing them in direct geographic alignment with the path of the rising Sun on Beltane, or May 1.[112] On their winding, cross-country trek, the lines pass through Avebury and Silbury Hill, the heart of crop circle country. When Paul Broadhurst and Hamish Miller were working on the Michael and Mary thesis in 1988, they inadvertently stumbled upon the first rash of crop circles around Silbury and discovered through dowsing that they all lay exactly on the course of female energy flow (Broadhurst and Miller 1992, 2000).

Dowsing is one of the earliest human arts, a 7,000-year-old profession prevalent in ancient cultures from the Mediterranean to China. In addition to finding underground deposits of water, it has been used to locate minerals, people, even missing submarines. Before its use declined in Britain around the 1930s, dowsing was a profession as common as carpentry, and dowsers would often be called upon to locate sites for wells or veins of minerals. Rosemary Grundy, a dowser employed by the British Admiralty during World War II, map-dowsed enemy harbors for ships worth bombing. According to the pilots who subsequently found

---

[111]The pagans viewed fire as a critical element of life—in cleansing, rebirth, and fertility. To separate pagans from this union, Santan also became the discredited Satan, a destructive, corrupting god that opposed the energy of the one mighty God. Ironically, Satan's other name, Lucifer, means "light bearer."

[112]Bel is derived from the Phoenician Sun god, baal. From this root emerges "bell," showing the creative relationship between sound and light. Many sacred rituals use bells to invoke the gods, one reason behind their use later in churches. Incidentally, English church bells used to be forged in diatonic tones.

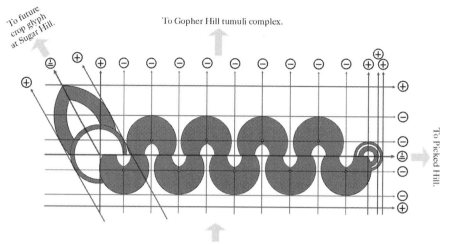

To future crop glyph at Sugar Hill.

To Gopher Hill tumuli complex.

To Picked Hill.

From Milk Hill crop formation.

Figure 12.9

A dowsing map of the "Coiled Serpent" shows how a crop circle's physical pattern manifests relative to an invisible energy grid. As with electricity, such energies are composed of positive, negative, and ground polarities. Here, the crop glyph has appeared along a geodetic line connecting an earlier glyph with tumuli, and another linking Silbury Hill with Picked Hill. A third line leads to a tumulus twenty miles away which later fired another crop circle. This suggests that crop circles and sacred sites are "communicating" with each other.

these targets, her success rate was better than 75 percent. Later, in Vietnam, marine divisions used dowsing rods to locate enemy tunnels, booby traps, and sunken mortar shells (Ostrander and Schroeder 1976). Today it is used in the diagnosis of disease under the name *radiesthesia*, or sensitivity to radiations.

The most celebrated American dowser was Henry Gross, who from the comfort of his kitchen table would dowse maps of Bermuda and locate sources of fresh water on an island where no such sources had previously been found. Subsequent drilling proved him right (Tompkins and Bird 1973). Scientific tests by Russian geologists and hydrology engineers have also proved the human body's ability to locate the unseen, the results published in the Russian peer-reviewed *Journal of Electricity* in

1944. Up to the mid-1970s every major water and pipeline company in America had a dowser on its payroll (Watson 1973), and although the oil industry today still employs dowsers in an unofficial capacity to locate underground deposits, like most modern commerce, it is embarrassed to admit it.

Dowsing is a remote sensing ability. In principle, it works like this: the molecules of the human body, being electromagnetic in nature and composed of alternating magnetic currents (Becker and Selden 1985), interact with external waves of electromagnetic energy. Such sensitivity to the Earth's electromagnetic field is verifiable with highly sensitive proton magnetometers (Tromp 1968). Using the conductivity of the water in the body and the iron in the blood, these waves trigger a muscle response in the nervous system that is transferred to a device held in the hand, normally L-shaped copper rods, Y-shaped hazel twigs, or pendulums. The reaction causes a circular or linear motion in the device, the movement reflecting the answer to a specific question posed by the dowser. In essence, the dowser is accessing information from the local morphogenic field—like typing a word search into a computer to retrieve stored information from an astral reference library.

During the summer of 2000, dowsing was still very much in evidence, employed to establish the provenance of two crop circles. The formations at East Kennett gave me the

Figure 12.10

Crop circle on the node of two crossing geodetic lines at the Neolithic complex of Windmill Hill. The polarities of the east-west line running through the crop circle are the same as the polarities generated by the tumuli.

opportunity to do a comparative test: the first, the "4-D Cubes" formation, revealed several complex dowsing patterns; the second circle, bearing the cliché heart-shape and circumscribed with a "string of pearls," gave no dowsing response. Standing inside it and holding my copper rods I asked for the origin of this crop circle. The answer was "flesh-and-bone humans." Having run through the various names of known hoaxers, one name generated a response from the rods.

Several days later I received a phone call from a colleague who is a friend of the local farmer. "I've been speaking to the farmer at East

Kennett, and he told me the heart formation was man-made with his permission. Apparently it was for a wedding ceremony. You'll never guess who was behind the design."

"I have a fair idea," I replied.

"Rob Irving!"

Precisely the name my rods had revealed.

When I first began to dowse crop circles in 1995, I was walking in the footsteps of a few very experienced dowsers, giving me the benefit of their discipline early in my development. One of these teachers was the late David Tilt, a man who spent the best part of two decades dowsing ancient sites around Sussex; he was cognizant of

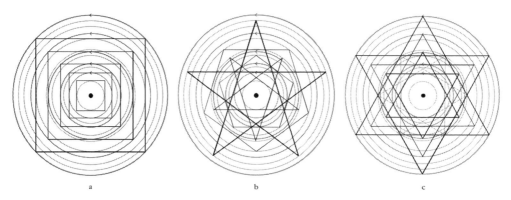

a   b   c

Figure 12.11

Dowsing plan showing twelve concentric rings of energy dowsed around the menhir at Outeiro, Portugal, and how their positions are governed by geometry. (a) Hawkins' square Theorem III; (b) pentagonal; (c) hexagonal.

the geodetic energies at these locales and how they radiated linear patterns or concentric rings.

In 1983, Tilt discovered nineteen lines of energy emanating from the churchyard mound at Berwick, connecting it to nearby tumuli, long barrows, and other church mounds. Four of the lines perfectly aligned with an adjacent stone circle, specifically on points where stones had previously been located. Since crop circles were now turning up beside mounds in his part of the country, Tilt found their appearance coincided with a release of energy from nearby mounds. He commented: "The energy-charge becomes so great that it overflows and discharges itself. When this happens, air which is normally non-conducting becomes a conductor in the vicinity of the strong electrical field and carries the charge away from a number of places on the [radial] energy pattern" (Tilt 1992).

Tilt's observation is consistent with data showing that the strongest ultrasonic readings at stone circles occur between February and March (Robins 1982, 1985)—appropriately just prior to a season's first explosion of crop circles; this signal dissipates to nil as the crop circle season gains momentum. Could the energy-rich sites be facilitating the crop circles? Or could the crop circles be tapping into the geodetic grid?

Tilt also noticed how crop circles had a tendency to appear at the geodetic nodes. This was still the case sixteen years later when my dowsing rods swung violently inside the "Triple Julia Set" in reaction to the crossing of the Michael and Mary lines, as they met at this point on the Neolithic complex of Windmill Hill.

Coming across identical patterns is the lavishly-bearded dowser, Hamish Miller, who has developed his intuitive skills to such a fine degree that he is able to dowse complex and close-knit patterns of discharged energy. The first time this Scottish engineer saw a crop circle he had such a deep recognition of the simple circle-and-ring that it raised the hair on his back. On this auspicious occasion, he dowsed a series of ten invisible concentric rings, some as little as half an inch apart, that defined the outer perimeter of the main circle; inside the ring, he found five more. Miller found the rings traveling upwards in layers, detecting one 500 feet above the ground during an aerial reconnaissance.

On occasion these thin rings are visible as dark concentric bands upon the dew-laden seed heads at the break of dawn, particularly when backlit. This is possibly the result of their heightened electromagnetic charge interacting with the moisture, creating frozen ripples of music, as it were.

With these ripples in mind, I traveled to an area abundant in undisturbed Neolithic sites in a remote part of eastern Portugal. One of the last places in Europe where people maintain a strong connection to the telluric grid, Portugal (the ancient *Lusitania,* the "land that holds the light") has long been a safe haven for all peoples and races, offering tolerance for the persecuted and the unorthodox. With Avebury and Abu Simbel in Egypt, it forms a triangle of energy.

Initially looking for similarities between Lusitanian monuments and their British counterparts, I was surprised to still find them rich in dowsable concentric energy rings, particularly the menhir at Outeiro, one of Europe's tallest. But there was something familiar about the relative areas of these twelve rings, a sense of prevailing harmony, just as Martineau had once seen the ghost image of sacred geometry

Figure 12.12

The four concentric rings of energy dowsed outside the Beckhampton crop circle are generated by extending the pentagonal geometry of the physical design.

embedded within crop circles (see chapter 9).

When I applied the rules of sacred geometry I found that the rings' relationships were governed by the pentagram and the hexagram. The biggest surprise was that the rings containing the only anticlockwise motions of energy were governed by Gerald Hawkins' Theorem III (see figure 12.11). Encouraged, I applied the same analysis to other menhirs and dolmens, and again found the rings were governed by Hawkins' theorems, sacred geometry, or both. I recalled Hamish Miller's early work and how he had found energy fields in the centers of crop circles arranged as Teutonic crosses or as nine-, ten-, and twelve-pointed figures, and how he had regarded these as "similar to the energy contour at points along the St. Michael line where

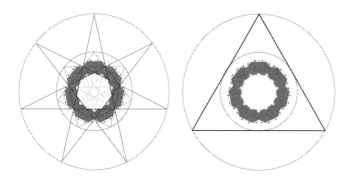

Figure 12.13

The overlapping heptagons of the Tawsmead crop circle define the location of its two exterior energy rings (left). The area of the rings is itself defined by the equilateral triangle of Hawkins' Theorem II, the equivalent of a double octave (right).

the male and female energies crossed each other at particularly sacred places" (Miller 1992).

On my return to England I retrieved my dowsing surveys of crop circles. One was the double pentagram at Beckhampton, where I had found four rings of energy encircling the formation. Could the same geometric correlation exist in a crop circle? This indeed appears to be so. When the pentagrams of the visible crop formation are extended, their points clearly hit the circumference of every dowsed ring, showing that the rings of energy are harmonics of the visible crop design (see figure 12.12).

Was this a coincidence? To find out, I applied the same technique to another survey, the Tawsmead Copse "Heptagon," and found an identical relationship (see figure 12.13). These geometric relationships show that the dowsing response is no accident. By the same token, the energy rings' geometric alignment suggests an effect similar to the overtones and undertones of music, in which the ripples of harmonics are proportionally generated from a source note, and in this case that source note is the physical crop circle pattern itself. This led me to further revelations.

In the opening crop formation of 1999 below Milk Hill (see figure 12.14), the ratios

between concentric energy rings and the crop formation again demonstrated Hawkins' theorems, as well as six-, seven-, nine-, and twelve-fold geometry—quite a demonstration for such an inconspicuous pattern. Of these, the appearance of ninefold geometry was of importance to me since, as I mentioned earlier, I had predicted that type to prevail for the first time. When a complex ninefold star formation next appeared below Sugar Hill, it seemed as if my intuition had served me well. Further validation was provided as the season progressed.

Another surprise came when the physical elements of the crop glyph at Sugar Hill encoded the *dowsed* geometry of the earlier Milk Hill crop formation (see chapter 10, figure 10.25). Given how I'd made the same discovery in 1997, I concluded that the first crop circle of the season embodies the code for the prevailing physical patterns.

The concentric rings dowsed *outside* the Sugar Hill glyph revealed another geometric connection. The farther I paced away from the formation, the more the concentric energy rings bunched up, each now barely an inch apart, before I reached a wall of energy, as if the entire structure was housed in a dome. Plotting these rings on computer, the ratio of the energy field relative to the edge of the formation generated Hawkins' Theorem II, a double octave. I was standing within a dome of sound (see figure 12.15).

As each crop circle season reaches a crescendo, the concentric rings multiply around the circles, as if the Earth were oscillating wildly like a bell struck by a frenzied Quasimodo. More than 150 rings surrounded the "nine crescents" at Hakpen Hill, while Roundway's "double heptagram" generated so many hundreds that I gave up counting while still 100 feet away from its perimeter; in fact, within seven minutes inside this formation I became disoriented and physically sick.

Helping me to validate the discovery of these concentric rings of energy is Paul Vigay, who often walks alongside me with his devices as we pace the tram lines, I with my dowsing rods. Whenever a ring triggers the rods to move, a discrepancy in hundreds of MHz appears on his gauge; these differences are either above or below the local readings.

Such dowsable patterns in the crop circles can be influenced by harmonic vibrations, such as those generated by the sound of a harp played inside the Milk Hill pictogram (1990), that caused all the energy lines to expand (Bloy 1992). I have measured identical effects following toning ceremonies at long barrows and other sacred sites, in which the human voice is combined with intention to awaken the local "dragon."

The late Richard Andrews was a Wessex farmer who had worked with crop circles since their early appearances in the late 1970s. He was a natural dowser. His approach varied slightly to

Figure 12.14

Each of the five simple figures of this crop formation generate one or two concentric rings of energy. In turn, the relationship between physical design and energy yield an array of geometric shapes. Hawkins' Theorem III is evident in the thickness of the bottom ring. Milk Hill, 1999.

Figure 12.15

Dowsing plan of the concentric rings of energy generated by the Sugar Hill glyph. The relationship of energy to physical crop circle is governed by Hawkins' Theorem II, a double octave. Seen in 3-D (bottom), this energy is shaped like a dome, and extends above as well as below the ground.

copter blades over the central vortex within the circle.

Andrews discovered that the physical design of early crop circles was generated within bands made up of three "straight" geodetic lines, and that crop circle features such as boxes or rings manifested at the intersections of positively charged lines. He noticed how crossing lines of "whirlies" (lines of exceptionally strong energy that can rotate dowsing rods) met near the center of a formation and demarcated the cut-off points of the physical design.

Andrews' ability to dowse a "master print" of energy encapsulating the physical formation also showed that, despite the multiple energy patterns onsite, only a portion of this shows up as the crop circle. Even after all visible traces of the crop circle are gone, the dowsable and invisible fingerprint can linger for up to five years.

Since formative forces of energy and matter tend to be spherical, at this point it is worth reminding ourselves of the concept of 4-D space I mentioned in chapter 10. The physical shape of a crop circle may be part of a larger picture, just as people with a finer degree of sensitivity claim. The designs extend dimensionally above and below the ground and the physical crop circle merely represents the flat

others' in that he dowsed the layer of energy three feet above the ground and found that the energy flow at this layer is the reverse of that on the ground itself. Tilt and I independently validated this point, and we believe the layers of energy in crop circles flow in alternating polarities (positive/negative). This may explain why the plants in crop circle floors are often found in layers of contraflow (see chapter 4).

Andrews often took a witness with him to see the effects the energy was having on his dowsing equipment. He handed the tools of his trade to his parish priest one day. The respected man of the cloth was amazed at the rods reacting to the energy polarities, rotating like heli-

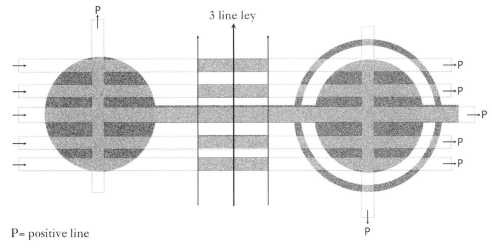

P= positive line

Figure 12.16

Detailed dowsing plan by Richard Andrews of the Chilcomb pictogram. The features of the crop circle are defined by positively charged geodetic lines. The four "boxes" are defined by a three-line ley consisting of positive/ground/positive polarities.

plane of, by way of analogy, an orange that's been sliced in half.

They may have a point. Dowsers find that the crop circles' boundaries conform to strictly delineated energy lines. Paul Vigay's electromagnetic frequency readings drop abruptly the moment he crosses the formation's wall. "The electromagnetic interference frequency inside the unusual 'claw' crop formation at Hakpen Hill (1994) went off the scale, but quickly dropped off six feet outside the circle's perimeter," he commented. No such discrepancies were found in the nearby "crop circle" commissioned by Arthur C. Clarke. The case for the "shielding mechanism" of crop circles, described earlier, continues to build, in which a vertical tube defines the perimeter of the crop circle, or a dome as in the case of the energy field around Sugar Hill glyph.

In April 2000, a series of happenings lent further credence to this theory. Equipped with a perfectly functional camera, I flew in a small airplane over a set of new crop formations. One of these was the four-ringed, octagonal formation beside Silbury Hill. The Sun shone, the camera clicked, nothing unusual to report.

When the negatives were developed, all images were exposed as normal, except for a row of nine frames in the middle which were blank. Either side of these, the images show my approach to and departure from the Silbury Hill "octagon," yet every frame exposed directly above and within its airspace was blank.

My camera technician looked blank, too. After several possible explanations, the most plausible was that the camera had crossed some type of barrier whose electromagnetic frequency had a temporary debilitating effect on the camera's circuit board. News later reached me that another photographer had had an identical experience, this time while flying over the airspace of the "Stretched Net" formation at Windmill Hill.

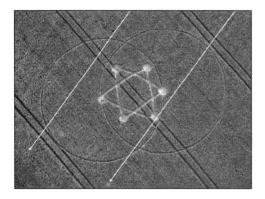

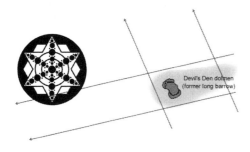

Figure 12.18

When crop circles miss geodetic lines. Top: Man-made design at Whitchurch. Middle: crop circle placed beside Devil's Den only clips one of the dolmen's geodetic lines. Bottom: Examples of hoaxed crop circles that fail to hit nearby geodetic lines (Williams' hoax, center).

Was the design itself trying to convey something? On closer inspection, I noticed that one of the blank frames had actually captured a faint image; it was so slight the photo lab hadn't bothered to print it. I returned to the camera shop and asked for a print. The developed "rainbow" image is all the more curious because it's supposed to be

an overhead view of a crop circle. (See figure 12.17 on page A12 in the color section.)

When subsequent analysis of the negative by camera technicians and Kodak provided no enlightenment, I took the image with me to a channeling session, during which it was revealed that the camera had captured the moment of opening of the energy field at Silbury Hill (I had not shown, or divulged any details concerning the image or its location). The image, I was told, is essentially the energy pattern—a life form—of the "guardian" of Silbury (described as an El, as in Elohim). "Unfortunately the process tends to fry little black boxes!" explained the channeled source.

Since the human mind is capable of emitting pulses of electromagnetic energy, a focused group of people, even an individual, can add an energy pattern to a man-made crop circle—a technique I performed and measured inside a poorly executed heptagram at Overton (for which the perpetrator, Matthew Williams, was later prosecuted). It is important to note that unlike genuine crop circles, residual energy patterns of this nature do not conform to the physical design. No dowsing responses or electromagnetic disturbances are evident in man-made formations, principally because they are rarely sited on energy lines, and never on their nodes.

Once the dowsing connection was made public, adventurous circle fakers began attempting to align their creations in the vicinity of previous crop circles, or at locations historically known to be rich in geodetic lines, but in all cases they missed the mark. For example, despite locating a well-constructed hexagonal pattern yards from the Devil's Den, the makers succeeded in only clipping the edge of the geodetic line running through that stone chamber.

One of the better hoaxing efforts came in 1997 at Whitchurch in Hampshire. When you cross the wall of a crop circle, it normally generates a response from dowsing equipment, but on this occasion when I entered the formation, the rods suspiciously overran the perimeter by a foot-and-a-half before reacting. The dowsable pattern running through the formation was linear but made no reference to its perimeter or physical design.[113] When no other patterns manifested, including the node point, my suspicions rose.

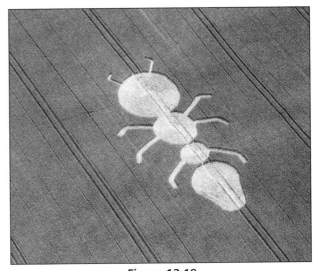

Figure 12.19
"Ant" glyph. East Meon, 1997.

A look around the field revealed two old, isolated oak trees several hundred feet away in the wheat field. This particular type of tree was traditionally planted by druids to mark the paths of geodetic lines; true to form, when I dowsed between the trees I found they were marking a twenty-four-foot-wide line to which the hoaxed circle had been roughly aligned.

A more convincing use of trees-as-markers occurred at the "Ant" formation. During a lull in sample collecting, I stood on the bend of each "leg" and noticed how they precisely referenced a row of six almost-equidistant oaks lining the field; a further two were referenced by the glyph's "antennae." Before I could figure out why, a livid farmer named Will Butler came charging down the tram lines. After a brief, heated exchange, we learned that our team had been given permission to enter the field by a farm worker impersonating his boss. Understanding this, Butler graciously allowed us to continue. Since one of our functions is also to form ambassadorial bonds with farmers, we involved Will in our research and asked him if he knew the history of his patch of land. "Are you aware that this crop circle lies directly on a ley line? You can see it up there," he said, pointing to the gaps between the oaks.

The main geodetic line did in fact amble in from the east and ran through the crop glyph. Since no other ancient markers could be seen from the valley floor, I marked the angles created by the "Ant's" limbs and later superimposed them over a geological survey map. To my surprise, the crop circle referenced twenty surviving tumuli, long barrows, and churches, even two

---

[113]It was later discovered that the hoax had been made as a blind test for CPRI field operatives.

Figure 12.20

The legs and body of the "Ant" reference no less than twenty-four existing barrows, tumuli, Neolithic sites, and chapels, plus two nearby crop circles.

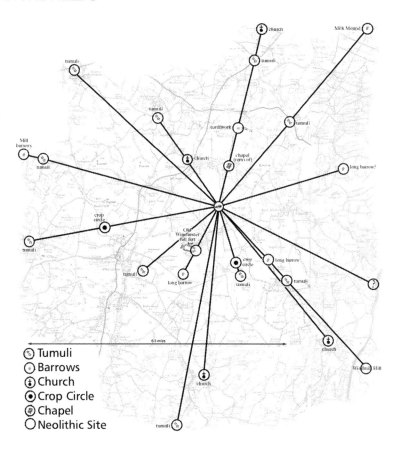

previous crop circles, all within a five-mile radius. It was focusing the energy from local sites, and this possibly explained the incredibly high readings we had been getting. Butler added that his normally placid pets had been agitated the night the formation appeared, and that a military helicopter had reconnoitered the formation shortly after he discovered it at dawn.[114]

When I correlated my findings from the "Ant" with Richard Andrews, he had this to say: "The whole piece showed a very strong dowsable pattern, the most interesting part being the fact that the lines which started in the center stopped at the end of each leg configuration and didn't go beyond that point. The other most interesting part was the pear-shaped component: across the base of the two flat sides were two dowsable lines, cutting the configuration into three sections, but not going beyond the outside edges." Andrews also found that the energy grid across the field had modified its alignments to symmetrically encompass the design; the crop formation acted as a vector of energy, drawing energy into its body and releasing it in concentrated form through its tail.

One key aspect of crop circle energy is that the geometric center and the energy center are seldom the same. The latter lies off-center, usu-

---

[114]Spectrum analysis technology used by the military is capable of detecting local disturbances in the Earth's magnetic field. According to research by Dr. Jonathan Sherwood, this technology can pinpoint crop circles twenty-four hours *before* the physical pattern manifests, and possibly explains why military helicopters are often the first to appear on site.

ally marked by the spiral of the plant lay, above which one finds the active energy point. The polarity is predominantly neutral, and a dowsing instrument will demonstrate this. My experience shows three exceptions to this rule: the "Ant" produced four energy vortices arranged as an invisible square, four feet around the central spiral, the vortices so agitated that pendulums had to be physically restrained from becoming airborne; the Torus formation (1997) produced a still-point of energy 28 feet northeast of the physical center, over which swinging pendulums rapidly became listless, as if sucked by the ground; lastly, the centers of man-made formations produce no dowsing response unless suggested by the mind of an inexperienced dowser.

Thus it is established that crop circles are energetically linked to ancient sites, the Earth, and its magnetic grid.[115] Despite the overwhelming evidence in support of dowsing and its concordant results in crop circles, particularly as a method of detecting their authenticity, it is not infallible. It must be stressed that dowsing is a discipline which requires a high degree of concentration, objective thinking, and, most important of all, *practice*. Many crop circle enthusiasts dowse "genuine" results in formations which are then exposed to be fake, exposing them to the ridicule of the media.

It took Richard Andrews, for example, three years before he figured out how to dowse crop circles. In his opinion, 90 percent of people dowsing crop circles do not know what they are dowsing or why they are getting the informa-

Figure 12.21

Four vortices in the crop mark the crossing paths of geodetic lines. The east/west vortices are misaligned by approximately 10° and match the alignment of its respective energy line. Silbury Hill, 1999.

tion; most troublesome is the problem of auto-suggestion or letting their emotions or beliefs get the better of them. "If you go into a crop circle *believing* it to be real," Andrews cautioned, "you will get all the answers you want, because they'll come from your own mind."[116]

That is good advice, to which I add: Begin your dowsing of a crop circle at the entrance to

---

[115]Further work on Hartmann and Curry grids relative to crop circles has been carried out by Jim Lyons, the CCCS' former science advisor. Discussion of energy related to sacred sites is found in John Davidson's *Subtle Energy,* Blanche Merz's *Points of Cosmic Energy,* and the work of Paul Broadhurst, Hamish Miller, et al.
[116]In conversation with Richard Andrews.

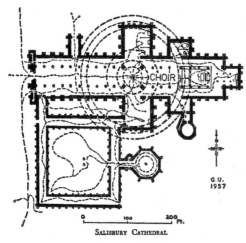

Figure 12.22

Buildings such as Salisbury Cathedral were built according to the underlying paths of geodetic energy thereby concealing the true purpose of the original site. That the energy was of great importance is seen in the way these massive structures would often be erected on ground unsuitable for their weight. Salisbury Cathedral was built on a marsh.

the field before your eyes can fool you. Or come to my lectures, where attendees report their dowsing rods react positively to pictures of crop circles, yet when I show them hoaxes their rods do not move from their normal, at-rest position.

Since all living organisms—including the Earth—are electromagnetic by nature, and the presence of such energy in crop circles affects the environment, by implication this energy must influence people who come into contact with crop circles. Let's examine this idea.

As we saw in chapter 10, geometric shapes are essentially eddies of energy. By constructing an appropriate geometric shape upon a strategic location of the Earth's magnetic grid, one can influence not only the local magnetic field but the entire grid. One practitioner of this art was John Dee, sixteenth-century philosopher, alchemist, astrologer, geographer, and appointee to the court of Elizabeth I of England. He reportedly dissipated the energy of an invading Spanish armada by building a structure comprising two overlaid octagons on an energy node on the Isles of Scilly.

The correspondence of a crop circle's physical pattern to the underlying geodetic current is reminiscent of the way early church sites were selected, particularly when a building was to be erected at an existing pagan site. After marking the position of the geodetic lines, the architect designed the structure according to the flow of energy. Although the building displayed otherwise functional uses, it often concealed unusual deviations of standard building practice which had been necessary to accommodate the underlying patterns of energy (Underwood 1973).

Not surprisingly, three-line bands of energy are referenced at church entrances, particularly those with three doors: each of the two smaller side doors typically carries the positive or negative charge, while the main central door references the neutral/grounding charge.[117] Similarly, a mound, standing stone, or yew tree may mark the spot where the energy coils like an underground spring to "feed" the church. The grapeshot perform the same function for the crop circle.[118]

---

[117]Based on the author's dowsing research of churches in England and Portugal.
[118]The grapeshot appear to function as batteries, supplying a spiral of energy to the crop circle. An identical relationship exists between sites such as Stonehenge and its attendant tumulus. My inspiration for this research came from studying Underwood's meticulous charts of spiral flow at sacred sites.

Shapes also influence the functions taking place within. The pyramid shape, for one, is scientifically proven to affect brainwave patterns and crystalline structures, to the point that it mummifies dead tissue, sharpens blunt razor blades, and enhances the micro-organisms in milk and yogurt. Spherical shapes heal wounds rapidly; and trapezoidal hospital wards improve the conditions of schizophrenics.

Through their use of geometry, acoustic properties, and siting over energy-rich nodes, Gothic cathedrals, in particular, can affect electromagnetic frequencies.[119] When a devotee stands inside these spaces, energy is transferred up the spine to the magnetic deposits in the skull (close to the pineal gland), causing changes in awareness. According to Russian experiments, the ability for telepathy in Gothic cathedrals and stone circles rises by as much as 4000 percent. So like the ancient sites they stand upon, houses of worship affect brainwave patterns, and by adding the beneficial resonances of chant, sonic frequencies impregnate and rejuvenate the Earth's geodetic grid. Isn't it rather ironic that as the use of churches for prayer and psalm reaches its lowest ebb, crop circles appear, reigniting the energy of a grid whose power has lain stagnating?

Crop circles and sacred sites share another common denominator in that both are located above or close to a water source. Water is fundamental to life, and the surface-to-water ratio of the Earth matches that of the human body, making both subject to the gravitational influences of the lunar cycle. Since water is a conductor of electrical energy, the type of rock prevalent at megalithic sites contains a high degree of quartz, a mineral with a natural ability to store a substantial electrical charge. Stonehenge's trilithions, for example, contain a quartz similar to the type used in early radio sets (Cathie 1990). This may explain why at key points in the lunar cycle, energy at stone circles interferes with compasses, and fluctuates background radiation readings and ultrasonic frequencies—situations similar, if not identical, to crop circles.

It is also known that a vortex in water creates an electromagnetic field, and as this energy is built up, it produces antigravitational effects.[120] Since water is found in blood, and blood requires a vortex action to propel it through the veins, it is feasible that the electromagnetic field created by the crop circle's vortex action is capable of affecting the human body, creating conditions that affect it biologically or mentally by inducing altered states.

Curious as to how this life force interacts with dowsers, I investigated the work of retired physicist Dr. Zaboj Harvalik who, as chief of the research committee of the American Society of Dowsers and advisor to the U.S. Army Advanced Material Concepts Agency, had asked himself the very same question.

Motivated by anecdotal evidence that the human body's prime sensor is located at the solar plexus, Harvalik performed a series of controlled experiments in which he covered various sensitive parts of his body with a specially

---

[119]"Gothic" derives from the Scandinavian *guth,* meaning "word."

[120]The antigravitational effects were noted in the studies of water vortices by Viktor Schauberger (Becker and Selden 1985).

shielded cylinder, then walked across an area known to induce strong dowsing responses. The only part of his body that failed to react when blocked from the magnetic waves was the solar plexus.[121] Although unaware of this at the time, it is the location Richard Andrews and I used for accessing the most intriguing dowsing information in crop circles. And we aren't alone—Paul Vigay's most startling electromagnetic frequency discrepancies occur three feet above the ground, the general area of the solar plexus.[122]

Figure 12.23

Examples of crop circles associated with extremely high frequencies and numerous reports of disorientation: Beckhampton, 1998 (left); Roundway, 2000 (middle, right).

The beneficial and detrimental effects of electromagnetism upon the human body are already scientifically established. Less publicized are its effects when delivered *inside* crop circles, where the exertion on the brain's right hemisphere is tremendous; stories abound of people experiencing an inability to perform logical tasks, especially from strangers who have no access to such obscure information.

During his dowsing of crop circles, Hamish Miller noted the effects on people performing left-brain activities while inside the circles. "I found at first some problems in concentrating long enough to do an accurate count of the radials from the centre, and on a number of occasions during the process, I forgot where I put the start marker, or forgot what I had used as a marker, lost the simple count, or was distracted by some triviality. Three times, after lots of practice maintaining the concentration, I experienced what I can only describe as a time slip. The radials count would go from 5-6-7-10 and I would find myself at a considerably different part of the circle on the count of ten from where I had been on the count of seven" (Miller 1992).

Many are the times that my colleagues and I had to perform recounts and remeasurements before finally getting basic calculations, even addition, correct. Since one of my tasks at each site involves a photographic protocol, I have even taken to writing down the list of tasks to be accomplished, yet not a summer goes by where all of the protocols are fully met. The same applies to aerial photography. I often return without half the shots required, even though these are some of the easiest assignments I've ever covered. Once away from the general area of the crop circle, normal cerebral function resumes.[123]

Preliminary tests to monitor brain rhythms via EEG (electroencephalogram) show heightened right-hemisphere activity in people inside crop circles. Some might argue that most of this is the result of people's imagination, yet none of

---

[121]In Hindu philosophy, the solar plexus is the chakra through which the life force flows.

[122]With a few notable exceptions, Vigay's readings cluster around 260–320 MHz. These readings are found in church grounds, albeit at lower frequencies: The sound of a running stream, a bonfire, and the wind combing through trees are 256, 320, and 320 kHz respectively, the very same frequencies attributed to plainsong and church music.

[123]The Rollright stone circle in Oxfordshire has this same effect on people. Its stones are said to be uncountable; in fact, eleven other sites in the British Isles are said to produce this same effect.

these symptoms appear to exist to the same degree outside the formations (Pringle 1994).

The degree to which the energy of crop circles interacts with the human body is evident in its reported effects on its nervous system. Any illness or imbalance in the body tends to become trapped in the muscle tissue in the form of blockages of energy. In applied kinesiology, doctors—specifically chiropractors—locate these blockages by performing muscle tests, in which a patient's muscles demonstrate varying degrees of resistibility when they are subjected to external stimuli, traditionally vitamins and herbs. But in 1995, an experienced and intuitive Boston chiropractor began substituting them for images of crop circles.

Dr. Randall Ferrell is not your average chiropractor, having traveled much of the world with an open mind in an effort to learn a diverse range of healing techniques. In short, he'll apply whatever method works best for his patient regardless of how unorthodox the treatment sounds to conventional Western medicine.

After locating the blocked portion of the body through muscle-testing, Dr. Ferrell runs a number of pictograms over the patient's affected organ (incidentally, the patient is not consciously aware of the image), testing the muscle reaction as he does. Eventually one image locks the muscle, indicating that the affected organ is stimulated by a "chemistry" inherent in the pictogram. Different designs affect different imbalances.

Psychotherapist Geoff Brooks has also experienced first-hand the healing possibilities of crop circles. Conducting a lecture, he distributed images of the 1997 Barbury Castle "six moons" glyph to several members of his audience to gauge whether the crop circle had any

significant effect on them. One participant, a long-time sufferer from acute arthritis, said the pain in her joints suddenly disappeared when she looked at the image.

Another crop circle researcher, Lucy Pringle, has compiled extensive reports of physical and behavioral patterns associated with crop circles. Her data-gathering started in 1990 after she damaged her shoulder so badly in a tennis game that lifting her arm to brush her teeth caused her serious pain. Still experiencing discomfort, she walked into a crop formation, and a few minutes later, "I felt a tingle run through my shoulders, and yes, my shoulder was completely cured. Margaret Randall, who with my sister made up the party, also experienced remarkable healing in the formation and was able to lie flat for the first time in fifteen years" (Pringle 1990).

Dorothy Colles, an eighty-two-year-old artist also suffering from arthritis, visited her first crop circle in 1999, accompanied by Lucy. Dorothy walked slowly around the formation before lying down, asking Lucy to remain nearby to help her get up later. But that help would not be required as Dorothy later vigorously and painlessly got up unsupported—"without the usual arthritic creaks and effort" (Pringle 2000). Likewise, an osteoporosis sufferer was not only relieved of pain after her visit to a crop circle, but has had no recurrence in three years. A person with a tremor condition similar to Parkinson's stopped shaking while sitting in the torus formation, and remained that way for twenty-four hours. A hay fever sufferer walked into a formation made in a canola field, to which she was allergic, yet was cured of her condition (Pringle 1998).

Healing in crop circles is reminiscent of the folklore of healing associated with stone circles.

In Cornwall, passing a sick child through the quartz-rich, doughnut-shaped Men-an-Tol stone is said to cure any ailment; this custom was recently reenacted by villagers in a crop circle in Hungary.[124] The practice might be arrogantly dismissed as the shenanigans of ignorant peasants except that modern medicine now accepts that low levels of electromagnetic energy heals certain ailments, particularly bone disorders. Bones are crystalline structures with similar piezoelectric properties to quartz crystal, and when quartz is subjected to electromagnetic frequencies, its crystalline structure stores information and is even capable of changing shape.[125] So when electromagnetic (or ultrasonic) frequencies are administered to broken bones, they show a remarkable rate of healing. Crop circles and stone circles, possessing electromagnetic and ultrasonic properties and positioned on sites rich in Earth energy and water, can create similar effects.

Entering a crop circle is like stepping inside a weak induction field (in which a variable electromagnetic current is applied or taken away). Such a field is capable of acting on the body at all levels because the body is nothing more than molecules in a permanent state of vibration. Crop circles have the added advantage of geometry, and as I mentioned earlier, the angles in geometric forms contain energy. Consequently, the harmonic properties of a geometric structure create an additional effect on the body, since the body is a pentagonal form in itself. Sound plays its part since it, too, affects the shape, even the color, of blood cells. For example, the note C makes them longer and spherical, and the note A changes their color from red to pink. Cancer cells disintegrate when subjected to 400–480 Hz, which are the notes A-B above middle C (Dewhurst-Maddox 1993).

Many people experience a sharpened awareness, euphoria, calmness, and joy inside crop circles, with a marked increase in vigor hours after leaving them. Lucy Pringle collected two reports of healing from the same formation. "I felt pleasantly lightheaded the whole time, my sinuses cleared. I mentioned this to my companion, and a young man overheard me and said his sinuses had dried up too" (Pringle 1993b).

Sometimes these conditions are accompanied by a gentle tingling on the surface of the skin, particularly the palm, one of the body's most electromagnetically sensitive parts. The effect is similar to that experienced by patients treated with orgone accumulators, an oversized example being Silbury Hill itself.[126] As a dowser

---

[124]Similar effects occurred during appearances of the Virgin Mary at Fatima, Portugal, 1916, and Zeitoun, Egypt, 1968. Both events were witnessed by thousands. Doctors at the time documented hundreds of cases of people healed of cancer, arthritis, even gangrene, and yet none of these people had gone to see the apparitions with the intent of being cured. To appease the skeptics, the Virgin Mary gave predictions of future events as validation of her apparitions, two notable examples being the dates of the Russian Revolution and the Second World War.

[125]The cellular memory stored in bone is the prime reason why Neolithic peoples stored the bones of shamans in stone chambers and long barrows, particularly the skull, the tibia, and the forefinger.

[126]Orgone accumulators were built in the modern era by Wilhelm Reich, whom we now credit with the discovery of this "life force" energy that permeates all space. His accumulators are composed of alternating layers of organic and inorganic material which serve to trap this energy. Pyramid structures around the globe serve a similar purpose by using alternating types of stone to generate alternating positive/negative energy flow. Reich's research was confiscated by the U.S. government and orgone accumulators remain illegal in the United States.

and regular visitor to crop circles, I note this sensation readily, as does Pat Delgado, but the effect is particularly sensed by Reiki practitioners, who report an energizing effect felt through their fingertips, as do their patients, in the form of abnormal heat, even though they're unaware of the practitioners' involvement with crop circles. Excess heat is also associated with orgone treatment.

Overall, the health effects of human interaction with crop circles include elation, a heightened awareness, mental clarity, and physical well-being. A visitor to more than a hundred formations, Lucy Pringle feels a sense of well-being on the majority of occasions, yet at some she has gone pea-green, requiring her to leave post-haste. An acquaintance of mine who lives near Alton Barnes and walks her dogs there daily—and incidentally, has little interest in this phenomenon—entered the "DNA" formation out of curiosity barely four hours after it appeared; both she and the dogs felt nauseous until they left.

A woman who visited the "Triple Julia Set" told me she'd experienced three menstrual periods within the first month after her visit. Her gynecologist initially diagnosed her as suffering from abnormal stress, to which she replied that, as an advertising professional, she is *permanently* stressed and yet this abnormal condition had never manifested before. Another unusual case of bleeding occurred in the Beckhampton "Knot" (1999): three people from a small group of Japanese tourists suffered nosebleeds simultaneously. Interestingly, this was one of a small series of crop circles which I dowsed as having a microwave frequency.

Nausea, headaches, dizziness, disorientation, abnormal menopausal bleeding, lack of mental clarity, excessive fatigue—these symptoms represent the unpleasant side of crop circles. I usually experience a sense of well-being in crop circles, but like Lucy Pringle, there have been times when I have experienced nausea and disorientation within minutes. Dehydration is particularly common. Following my brief stay inside the Beckhampton "Double Pentagram" (1998), I drank six pints of water in half an hour, and continued to feel out-of-sorts for the next twenty-four hours; my colleague that morning fared as poorly.

There appears to be little rhyme or reason for these inconsistencies. From my experience, it seems the negative effects coincide with formations which dowse for extraordinarily high energy, when there is prolonged exposure, or if one enters a crop circle within hours of its appearance. To confuse matters, these symptoms usually reverse as the crop formation ages.

There are two possible causes of such symptoms: microwave radiation and ultrasound/infrasound. The latter can heal or injure depending on its intensity, frequency, and an individual's length of exposure to it. Ultrasound is used in hospitals to treat arthritis and muscular rheumatism; it can also affect the central nervous system, including the lower brain. Both microwave and sonic frequencies affect the pituitary gland and produce auditory signals such as clicking and trilling. Excessive exposure to either causes headaches and dehydration, because inside a resonant cavity such as the human body the dipolar molecules of water are stimulated by extremely high MHz frequencies which create heat and accelerate the dehydration process (Schul and Pettit 1985).

Like quartz, the cell membrane of human connective tissue is piezoelectric, so it has the capacity to carry electrical charges. Similarly, skin is positively charged, while the auric field of the body is negative. Therefore, the human energy field carries alternating charges which react to any electromagnetic field present. In crop circles, this field changes in polarity over time, so its physical effect on a person depends on the type of charge present at the time of the person's exposure.

Studies at the University of California at Los Angeles show how the movement and coordination of the body is relative to the level of its interaction with an electromagnetic field, a change in which creates effects in sensory and motor skills: A saturated field improves motor performance, heightens emotional well-being, and generates excitement and advanced states of consciousness. In a deficit field the results reverse and include diminished intellectual capacity and increased anxiety. Prolonged interaction with a manipulated electromagnetic field also creates fatigue (Hunt 1989). Tingling sensations, mild nausea, and giddiness can be attributed to exposure to frequencies of 100 Hz. Anxiety, extreme fatigue, and headaches occur between sixty-three and seventy-three Hz, while levels between forty-three and seventy-three Hz are responsible for problems with orientation and impairment of intellectual activity.

To put it in a nutshell, when the collection of frequencies that make up the body interact with another frequency, there is either harmony or discord. It all depends on what you are stepping into. We've all walked into a room where certain people, for no apparent reason, make us uncomfortable, just as others make us feel like we've known them for generations. It comes down to sympathetic resonance. Therefore, a crop circle may be your healing temple or it may be your sick building.

While the hundreds of reports in Lucy Pringle's database tend slightly towards the unpleasant—although it has to be said that people generally don't call the doctor to say they feel fine—the emotional effects are largely beneficial. Skeptics point out this is a natural psychological reaction to contact with the unknown. This seems illogical, since it is human nature to fear and protect itself against the unknown. With a phenomenon like crop circles, therefore, one would expect trepidation, not exuberance.

Some people claim they do not "feel" the energy of crop circles at all and dismiss them as bogus, adding that anyone who senses such "cosmic energies" must possess a fertile imagination. You would think that since every physical body is electromagnetic in nature and crop circles exhibit this energy, that surely people would detect this energy at some level. Yet as the biologist Lyall Watson explains: "A very weak electrical or magnetic field becomes noticeable because it resonates on the same frequency as the life field of the organism reacting to it" (Watson 1973). Therefore, if an individual's energy field is not in resonance with the crop circle's, then we have a case of two "tuning forks" not sharing the same tune.

Animals possess sharper senses than ours and cannot be deceived by a "fertile imagination." They are, in effect, the first eyewitnesses to crop circles since they can sense them coming; sheep will attempt to move as far away as possible from a particular field before a formation appears, as in England it is not unusual for grazing land to border crop fields. Birds have been known to break formation above a crop circle's airspace; birds are scared away by ultrasound which is why devices emitting such frequencies are used at airports. Horses refuse to cross the perimeter of crop circles, or they become nervous in their vicinity; if the land on which a crop circle appears later reverts from cereal crop to grazing land, sheep or cows may avoid the particular spot for as long as a year.

Dogs are particularly sensitive to ultrasound, as evidenced by their reaction to pre- earthquake conditions, which are known to emit ultrasonic frequencies. Similarly, normally placid or obedient canines have shown unconventional patterns of behavior hours *before* the arrival of a crop circle. They have been known to bark incessantly from 2 to 4 A.M., to try to bite holes through doors, and to refuse to obey commands. This is a particularly unnatural trait for border collies, the breed of choice on working British farms. Dogs may even refuse to enter new crop circles.

While conducting dowsing surveys in three formations during 1999, I was accompanied by Sue and her dog, Sheba. Sue has owned Sheba for a number of years and is well aware of her normal behavioral patterns, indoors and out. At the Devil's Den hexagonal formation, Sheba sat upright, an air of boredom about her as if saying "Nothing special here. Can we go now?" The formation had no dowsable energy pattern. This was in sharp contrast to the dog's behavior the same afternoon inside formations at Hakpen Hill and Cherhill. Here Sheba immediately marked her territory at each perimeter wall and ran around in a jestful manner, even raising herself up on her hind legs as she meandered the loops and crescents. Sue was astounded at Sheba's uncharacteristic animation.

Sheba resumed normal behavior a considerable distance away from these crop circles, both of which registered some of the strongest dowsing responses I have ever measured. In addition to the complex geodetic lines present there, both designs were surrounded by hundreds of concentric energy rings, each barely six inches apart.

Dogs mark their territory if they feel particularly anxious, and they generally find the energy centers of crop circles and treat them as they would a fire hydrant. In fact, there exists an unusual number of incidences in which these points (not always restricted to the geometric center of the formations) are marked with animal droppings.

Cats react strangely, too. During my third visit to the Liddington crop glyph (1996), I met a couple who couldn't understand why their normally placid cat suddenly became agitated the moment he crossed its threshold. Although used to the outdoors, this cat protested and looked around frantically for a way out of the circle. Once beyond the confines of the formation he regained his habitual composure.

Since these lasting crop circle energies produce measurable effects on humans and animals, I began to wonder if they are carrying a vibratory code which can be used for healing. Being a practical person, I also considered how they would be applied. As we saw in previous chapters, the vibrations of sounds, words, even geometries have the capacity to resonate with people and environment in a way which promotes a harmonious way of being.

Studies at Stanford University in the early 1900s into resonance and the nature of living organisms by the distinguished physician Dr. Albert Abrams, led to the understanding that disease is, in essence, vibratory. Although

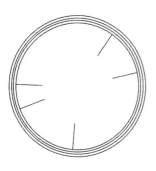 

Figure 12.24

Left: type of diagram used in radionic healing. Right: crop circles generate similar radial energy patterns. Could crop circles ultimately be used for healing?

imprints and transferred to water when required.

Of prime interest here are the radials on Rae's cards, because these patterns are dowsable in stone circles as well as crop circles; one crop circle alone generated twenty-two radials from its center, and many such crop circles are accompanied by reports of healings.

harassed and systematically discredited by corporate medicine and its friends in government, a committee under Lord Holder of the British Parliament investigated Abrams' claims in 1924 and reluctantly admitted, after exhaustive tests, that Abrams' methods were proven to work. In fact, despite being made illegal, radionics was later employed by British and American engineers to improve the quality of crops and boost crop yield during World War II. Scrutiny of Abrams' work by Russian scientists further proved the science to be legitimate (Constable 1977; Wachsmuth 1932; Tomkinson 1975).

The cumulative work of pioneers such as Abrams and his illustrious pupil, Dr. Ruth Drown, gave rise to radionics, an effective method of treating people and other biological systems at a distance simply by tapping a subtle energy source. One type of radionic system used today is that of Dr. Malcolm Rae, in which remedies are stored in their perfect state on simulator cards. Each card contains the geometric representation of a substance in the form of concentric rings and radii. The energy of each remedy is therefore stored in "geometric"

At this point I came across the work of the Institute for Resonance Therapy in Germany, which specializes in the revitalization of ecosystems in distress, such as polluted rivers in the former Eastern Bloc and European forests dying from the effects of acid rain. Resonance therapy, a development of Abrams' radionics, works on the principle that every living organism is surrounded by a morphogenetic field containing a code that enables the organism to survive. When disease or pollution attacks the organism, the code begins to break down and the morphogenetic field contracts.

Treatment is made possible by taking a photograph or a map of the area in question, placing it on a special appliance, and supplying information to the ecosystem that enables it to heal. The "informators" used are symbols or images, usually derived from fractal geometry. When a sympathetic resonance is established between symbol and ecosystem, clear and quantifiable improvements occur to the ecosystem.

Evidence that a healing code is carried in crop circles was discovered when the Institute began using aerial photos of crop circles as "informators."[127]

In strictly controlled experiments, the Institute discovered that crop circles can interact with the morphogenetic fields of systems in distress by supplying a missing code that allows these systems to heal themselves (not a far cry from Dr. Manners' cymatic therapy on human cells, and Dr. Ferrell's muscle testing). So encouraging are the Institute's results that at one point it was hired by the Austrian government to "cure" a park in Vienna where the life force of the trees was diminished—in other words, they were dying.

After three years of treatment the mean leaf density improved 20.7 percent, and vitality in lime trees jumped 37.9 percent, in oaks 34.4 percent, and in horse chestnuts 15.4 percent. The expert who monitored the project stated that this improvement was not explainable "by natural means." The results are even more impressive in light of the data for the vitality in identical tree species in the rest of the region which showed a declining trend in health during the same period.[128] Whether in resonance with or simply by matter of coincidence, when the IRT undertook similar projects in the Czech Republic, the country reported its first major outbreak of crop circles.

When vibrations are encoded into organic substances they give the receiving material vibrational properties whose effect may be passed on to other substances or people (Rothstein 1958). Studies in Japan show how ordinary tap water in a bottle can have its crystalline structure radically altered simply by a person writing, with strong intent, "I hate you" or "I love you" on the label. In a similar way, crystallization patterns in water samples taken from crop circles show how the crystals adopt their underlying geometry[129] (Emoto 1999).

In the early 1980s French allergist Jacques Benveniste conducted experiments whose results had an effect throughout the orthodox scientific community akin to a volcano decimating entire villages. Benveniste proved that a chemical code can be memorized by water even when the original solution has been diluted thousands of times, as is the case with homeopathic medicine which frequently uses "solutions so highly diluted that no molecules of the original active substance should be left to act chemically or biologically."[130] Despite French authorities raiding and closing down his operations (but confiscating his notes anyway), the successful replication of his results by scientists in four countries has vindicated this modern-day

---

[127]The positioning of the images on IRT's apparatus requires a "critical rotation point," where the image suddenly "clicks" with the environment. Is this perhaps the purpose behind the crop circles' 4° phase shift, as discovered by Andrews? See chapter 8.

[128]From personal communication with Franz Lutz, Head of Theory and Research at IRT, and from The Institute for Resonance Therapy Manual, Capellburg, 1994.

[129]Blessing of the water is an ancient ritual whereby water is given healing properties by the focused intent of a shaman. Vestiges of this rite still exist in religious services, although their meaning and effectiveness have, by and large, been lost.

[130]The principles of homeopathy can be traced back to ancient Egypt and the writings of Thoth: "This is the property of our medicine into which the previous body of the spirits are reduced: that, at first, one part thereof shall tinge ten parts of this perfect body: then one hundred, then a thousand and so on infinitely on . . . and by how much more often the medicine is dissolved, by so much the more it is increased in virtue."

heretic[131] (Schiff 1994). It seems that assassination by the Establishment, regardless of method, has become a means of proving someone is on the correct path of inquiry.

Testing Benveniste's theories that water has memory, Lucy Pringle began burying small, water-filled glass bottles in crop circles to see if the water could be potentized by their energy. In one case, blind laboratory analysis by Benveniste found that samples taken inside the center circle of the "Triple Julia Set" showed they had indeed been potentized 51.3 percent and 136 percent above control samples (Pringle 1997).

But it's not just the water that's been imprinted; the seeds appear to have been energetically coated too. This is not surprising considering how seeds from a crop circle sealed in a test tube for a year appear to be in a state of suspended animation compared to control samples in an adjacent tube which developed mold.[132] A hint of the therapeutic potential of crop circle energy is exemplified by an incident in the East Field glyph of 1994 whose geometric elements gave it the appearance of an eye. When Jane Ross entered the formation, she sensed the need to bring some of its seeds home, something she'd never done before. Three months later, Ethan, her twenty-two-year-old son, developed a sudden bleeding of the eye. He was rushed to the hospital where he was diagnosed with a "99 percent malignant" tumor of the retina. Before an operation could be attempted, a three-month observation had to be undertaken to establish the growth pattern of the tumor.

The possibility of saving the young man's vision looked bleak, but despite the pessimistic outlook, Jane placed her son on a self-prescribed routine of positive visualization, meditation, and daily ingestion of seeds from the "eye" crop circle. Over the period of observation, the only part of this program practiced with measurable consistency was the daily seed ingestion.

When Ethan returned to the doctor, his tumor was no longer malignant. In fact, it had shriveled away, leaving no trace, and there was no recurrence. Jane later shared the experience with Isabelle Kingston, who was not surprised. This noted psychic had been "told" that the center of the crop circle was "the center of all possibilities," and that healing would be available from it. As it turned out, it was the only spot in the crop circle where Jane had felt the urge to gather seeds.[133]

Barbara Berge also felt compelled to eat crop circle seeds, despite being allergic to wheat. "The first effects were like having ingested speed—high energy, sleeplessness, nervousness and loss of appetite. I felt I was flying." At first she did not attribute the effects to the

---

[131]Benveniste's work has been further upheld after tests conducted by Professor Madeleine Ennis of Queen's University Belfast, in Milgraum, 2001.

[132]From a test by Isabelle and Edward Kingston.

[133]As far back as 1988, the antiquarian George de Trafford had written from his home in Malta to Colin Andrews, warning him of the energies in crop circles: "Be aware of your own physical self. You are dealing with very high energies which can manifest in various aches and pains. These are not problems. Just recognize them for what they are. It must surely be that your psychic structures are being stepped up through the focus you have in the work you are doing." This observation's implications are pursued in the next chapter.

seeds—until she ate a few more several weeks later: "Within fifteen minutes the same symptoms had reappeared," she said, and they reappeared just before the electrical equipment in her workshop short-circuited.

When her colleagues ate the same grain they experienced similar symptoms: deep body vibrations, the sensation of energy pouring out of their hands and head, sleeplessness, loss of appetite, disorientation.

Interestingly, they also noticed a heating effect around the solar plexus.

When Lucy Pringle later sent Berge another batch of seeds, Berge reported no effects. Little did she know that this test batch consisted solely of ordinary seeds (Pringle 1993b).

All biological systems on Earth are plugged into the Earth's vibratory field, so anything of a vibratory nature interacting with that field—solar flares, radio transmissions, sound, crop circles—will affect all life forms there. The ability of crop circles to resonate with people at a distance via subtle energy falls within the proven ability of remote healing practices which can heal patients at a distance using a mere sample of their hair. Russian scientists know that by decoding the electromagnetic code of an organism, a remedy in the form of a wave pulse can be transmitted via radio antennas to cure a population of that organism. Of course, the reverse also applies. In 1962, the CIA discovered that

Figure 12.25

Left: Crop circle at Alton Priors whose seeds helped cure a retinal tumor. The illusion of an "eye" is the product of a vesica piscis and Hawkins' crop circle theorems. These nesting theorems—the hexagon inside the square inside the triangle—also produce the note F (fourth octave).

the Soviet military had been bombarding the U.S. embassy in Moscow with ultra-low level microwave frequency, to the degree that many of its staff developed cancer (Davidson 1987).[134]

Given the inherent harmony of crop circles, there is reason to believe their purpose is benign, and besides, dragon energy has always been associated with life-enhancing properties, just as Guy Underwood recognized: "A catalyst in the construction of matter and the generative powers of nature . . . part of the mechanism by which we call Life comes into being . . . that balancing principle which keeps all nature in equilibrium" (Underwood 1973). Thus it is plausible that positive, healing energy is implicit in crop circles.

Since this source is unlimited and free, it would not be surprising if pharmaceutical companies were to look upon crop circles as a financial

---

[134]Associated Press reported in May 22, 1995, that psychotronic influencing was also developed by the Russians in response to technology used in America during the 1970s, in which hypnosis and high-frequency radio waves are combined to program behavioral patterns in people. One aim was to make people incapable of feeling. According to the project leader, Valery Kaniuka, the net effect is "the destruction of the human intellect." After the system was made public (ironically through Mikhail Gorbachev's Glasnost Foundation) hundreds of former Soviet soldiers, police, and KGB operatives sued for damages.

Figure 12.26

"Mother is crying" the Hopi called the pictogram at Fawley Down (left), which appeared on August 4, 1990, the day oil wells were blown up in Kuwait. On the right lies an older pictogram showing a wilted Earth, which appeared shortly before that country's invasion by Iraq.

threat. To quote the eminent physician Dr. John Mason Good: "The effects of our medicines on the human system are in the highest degree uncertain, except that they have already destroyed more lives than war, famine, and pestilence combined" (Babbitt 1878). Western healthcare is now the third leading cause of death in the U.S.; in Britain iatrogenic death ranks fourth; and while one in five Australians is killed by conventional medical care, natural remedies with a proven record in efficacy are being banned because they undermine the colossal profits of the pharmaceutical industry (perhaps that should be harmaceutical). Lifesaving cures censored in favor of deadly toxins marketed as leading-edge medicines (Day 2001). Or as David Tansley, an expert on radionics, describes them: "Unorthodox therapies which give results but more often than not appear to have no scientific *raison*

d'etre and thus are not acceptable to orthodox medicine and yet, especially in chronic disease, yield cures not obtained by orthodox means" (Tansley 1976).

Consider, too, that in the transfer of energy from plants to water—a method established by the English pathologist Edward Bach—the healing power of plants is retained in the water's memory capacity. Although Bach's flower remedies are administered to cure all manner of ailments, their primary effect is on the patient's predominant psychological state (Chancellor 1971). If crop circles have the capacity to affect change at this level, the idea of people in charge of their own minds would be cause for sleepless nights for anyone presently engaged in trying to control the public mind.

The imprinting of water at ground level by crop circles has far-reaching implications. This "coded" water is seeping into aquifers that feed rivers and eventually becomes the water we drink.[135] Since the homeopathic process has been proved to act at the cellular level, as potentized crop circle water reaches every ocean, so it inevitably touches every living organism on Earth. And just as in homeopathy, the higher the dilution the greater the resonance, and as it resonates so it generates electromagnetic frequency (Hunt 1989). As Paul Vigay discovered, not only is the electromagnetic frequency rising measurably in crop circles each year, the predominant range detected matches a range in the human body across which no frequencies exist at all (ibid.). Add this to the earlier suggestion that crop circles may be triggering dormant parts in human DNA, and the idea of an "awakening" gains plausibility.

What is certain is that by permeating the Earth and its energy grid, the crop circles are establishing a sympathetic resonance with its living systems. Based on the principles of light and sound, they are unlocking a library of memories stored in the human body, and enabling an interchange of information to be accepted more readily.

As we enter these new temples, they in turn awaken us to the greater reality. For the crop circles are accelerating a change in awareness at a time when we are at greater odds with our natural habitat and with one another. Whoever the Circlemakers are, it is not by chance that the sudden worldwide proliferation of crop circles coincides with a phase in the Earth's history when its natural systems are threatened with ecocide. The Circlemakers appear to be aware of this.

The Hopi were aware of this too when they reacted to a picture of one particular crop formation (see figure 12.26). "Mother is crying," they lamented, "the Earth's blood is being taken and her lungs choked."[136] The very day the formation appeared, Iraqi soldiers were blowing up the oil wells of Kuwait, setting fire to Mother Earth's blood, and choking her lungs with smoke. A second pictogram appeared beside, symbolizing the Native American shield with the four beaver's tails—the four quarters of the Earth connected as one Spirit—all bent and brooding, reminding us like a hieroglyph sent through time how another advanced civilization, the Egyptian, was consumed by the sand when it too lost touch with the elemental world.

[135]A similar conclusion was independently reached by Page and Broughton in *The Circular,* issue 33, CCCS, 1998. Their research on the aquifer connection was mentioned in chapter 8.
[136]From a communication with Colin Andrews.

13. The Other Side of the Veil

Just because fish cannot walk onto dry land doesn't mean life there does not exist.

—Camille Flammarion

During the turning point of the Second World War in 1944, a channeler in England named Helen Duncan received a message from a sailor aboard one of His Majesty's destroyers in the Mediterranean. Unfortunately, the ship and its occupants were not on the Mediterranean at the time, but *under* it, having just been sunk by an enemy battleship.

With the best intention of helping the British war effort, Duncan reported the matter to the Admiralty, giving the specific location of the sunken vessel. The problem for the Admiralty was that the news had reached Duncan before the Admiralty were aware of the loss of their destroyer. Sir Dudley Pound, then first sea lord and chief of naval staff, reportedly took this psychic material as a serious breach of intelligence: "Suppose there is something to what this woman and others are? Our whole intelligence operation could be defeated. Somehow this woman must be silenced." An urgent recommendation, for it turned out that she had told the truth: the destroyer had been

lost with all hands at the precise coordinates she had given.

As a token of their gratitude, the British military arrested Duncan and placed her in front of a judge at the Old Bailey, who expediently put her in jail. And not, as would seem logical, for divulging military secrets and creating a threat to national security. The trial became a double-edged sword—charging her for that would demonstrate that anyone with psychic ability could undermine military secrecy, leaving a target country vulnerable to psychic espionage; exonerating her would confirm there was something to psychic power. So the court charged her under the archaic British Witchcraft Act of 1735 (Barbanell 1945; Roberts 1945).

The ironic twist to Duncan's story is that the military and other government bodies began experimenting with psychic power for themselves. The American government invested much time and money into developing psychic espionage protocols to obtain political and military secrets, to identify military and terrorist targets, and to attempt to influence the thoughts of world leaders to bend to the whims of American foreign policy—essentially training psychics to become deadly weapons (Morehouse 1996; Puthoff 1996).

Across the former Iron Curtain, the atheist Stalinist government publicly denounced psychic ability, telepathy, even faith, as bogus, and systematically destroyed Russian churches as an insurance policy against any possible "invasion of the soul." Yet one of the greatest psychics of all time, Wolf Messing, was employed by Stalin to predict future events and, wait for it, influence the minds of the heads of government in the Eastern Block.

Different folks, same strokes.

So effective was Messing's ability that a fearful Hitler put a bounty of 200,000 deutschmarks on his psychic head. To Messing, working with the subconscious was nothing more than a matter of harnessing natural laws: "Perhaps telepathy works on electromagnetic fields or some field we haven't yet discovered," he opined, but he also emphasized: "Science must take telepathy away from mysticism and find out how it works. Because it does work. Some years ago nothing was done about radio waves. Why can't telepathy bring us similar miracles? It surprises me that scientists don't realize, or don't want to realize, that telepathy happens all the time in their own lives. Isn't this like the savants of the middle ages . . . refusing to admit that electricity exists although they saw lightning all the time" (Ostrander and Schroeder 1976)? Candid advice from a man who once demonstrated his mental abilities by handing a blank sheet of paper to a bank cashier who

promptly stuffed a few million roubles into Messing's briefcase.

The practical and cash-strapped Soviets did not waste time experimenting with hocus-pocus unless they knew that practical applications would come of the research. By 1967 they were investing $21 million on scientific experiments into the paranormal, to the point that telepathic techniques were incorporated into their space programs (ibid.).

During the First World War, the Czech Army used telepathy to locate and capture a unit of Hungarian soldiers, proving that ESP can indeed be a valuable weapon. In 1925 the same army published a handbook titled *Clairvoyance, Hypnotism, and Magnetism.* In fact, Czech trials gave telepathic communication a reliability of 98 percent, making it more reliable than their field telephones or radio transmitters at that time (Campbell 1966).

The field of clairvoyance—or whatever you feel comfortable calling psychic ability—once held a central position throughout the ancient world. Free from the dictates of modern or "civilized" society, our ancestors were perfectly comfortable accessing higher states of awareness, meditating at locations such as a stone circle or a tumulus, where the Earth spirit induced these states of mind. The "hill forts" and "castles" mentioned throughout this book, situated along prominent and often artificially shaped hills were, and continue to be, rich in electromagnetism which stimulates the brain's circuitry, facilitating telepathic communication between "worshippers" from one site to the next,[137] making these sites an early form of cell

---

[137]Personal communication from Isabelle Kingston. Also mentioned in Hitching 1976.

Figure 13.1

How spinning vortices combine to give the illusion of solid matter.

phone. Such long-distance telepathic communication was still practiced in recent times by the Bushmen of the Kalahari (Van Der Post 1952).

The idea that only a limited number of gifted individuals are capable of contacting other levels of reality is a fallacy borne of organized religion, which promotes contact with God as a special privilege reserved for a chosen few, and those of us wishing to do so must contact their local intermediary, the priest or bishop. And yet the prophet Jesus Christ made a clear reference to our precious gift in the Bible (1 Corinthians 3:16): "Do you not know that you are God's temple, and that God's spirit dwells within you? For God's temple is holy, and that temple you are." So there is no such thing as a person without psychic ability, merely one who chooses not to use it.

The most natural expression of the subconscious at work is demonstrated by the anxiety expressed by mothers the moment their newborn babies begin crying at the opposite end of a hospital while having blood samples taken. It seems we're all born with this ability but gradually it gets conditioned out of many. Some retain their psychic ability in the form of *inner tuition*, while others develop their potential by disregarding artificial or preconceived limitations, or

through the study and application of mantras, mandalas, sacred geometry, and now, crop circles.

Like most other intuitive arts, Western society, in particular, has condemned this universal ability as irrational. Yet as Keith Thomas points out in his weighty tome *Religion and the Decline of Magic*, "astrology, witchcraft, magical healing, divination, ancient prophecies, ghosts and fairies, are now all rightly disdained by intelligent persons. But they were taken seriously by equally intelligent persons in the past." Indeed, the psychic sense was only forgotten or suppressed as we came to depend more and more on language and the printed word to get our messages across. Then by the 1700s the new science of the day required that all "magic" be demonstrated and rationalized; those practices that were not quantifiable were cast aside.[138] And yet, Hermetic knowledge, numerology, sacred geometry, even astrology—all these mystical practices were paramount in the development of science, mathematics, the precise observation of the planets and the measurement of time—knowledge we today incorrectly attribute to the fruits of Newtonian and Einsteinean labor.

Psychic ability is, undoubtedly, the hardest practice to prove because of the social barriers placed in front of the quest for its understanding, the biggest of all being ridicule. The results are hard to verify since they are, to a large degree, dependent on personal experience or level of trust in the individuals involved. But on the other side of the former Iron Curtain the

---

[138]Likewise Michael Gauquelin, a French statistician of the 1960s, was hell-bent on discrediting astrology by proving how a person's profession is in no way governed by their rising sign. However, his own statistics, repeated in four separate countries, proved him wrong and established astrology as an art above mere superstition.

story is very different. Since the 1950s Soviet parapsychologists have systematically established telepathy as a valid means of communication. In Bulgaria, psychic abilities have proved so useful that they have been applied throughout education and medicine (Ostrander and Schroeder 1976). What gives eastern scientists the edge is their deep-rooted understanding that nature is composed of both the seen and the unseen, and that many of its phenomena—like infrasound and the greater portion of the light spectrum—lie beyond our five limited senses of perception.

Just as multi-national institutions do not publicly discuss the use of dowsers, so they shy from acknowledging the use of psychics, yet the employment of individuals with a heightened level of sensitivity is becoming more commonplace than one might think. Psychics are employed in locating geological faults, discovering buried archaeological sites, solving computer malfunctions, diagnosing illness, even predicting earthquakes, so something obviously works.

Telepathy has been used in crime-solving in Czechoslovakia since the early twentieth century, just as police forces throughout Britain and America today employ psychics to great effect in solving murder cases. The power of thought is even used to reduce crime: In June and July 1993, a transcendental meditation experiment aimed at reducing the spiraling crime wave in Washington, D.C., produced an 18 percent drop in violent crime during what has historically been the most violent months of the year.[139]

Even so, latterday psychics are susceptible to a backlash of the type of paranoia prevalent in mediaeval times should their methods put at risk the livelihoods of those whose job it is to solve the problem using conventional logic or technology. Sometimes, like Helen Duncan, they are even imprisoned for their efforts.

But the spiral of evolution moves on, and today we are but a breath away from realizing the Universe is not so much composed of matter but of consciousness. Physicists now postulate that behind every atom lies a "ghost" electron which supplies its energy (Irion 2000). Helen Blavatsky's nineteenth-century assertion that "atoms are called vibrations in occultism" is vindicated today by the electron-microscope which reveals that everything that exists does so thanks to vibration. The nucleus of an atom spins at 1,022 Hz per second, the atom at 1,015 Hz, and living cells at 103 Hz. Even the human body is now known to be an "illusion," for if all the empty spaces are removed from it, and all that is left is gathered up, its total mass is no larger than a drop of water. The forces of light, gravity, and sound shape this teaspoon of chemicals into the wondrous vessels that are man and woman. So even inside our very own bodies exist whole levels of existence beyond our conscious perception.

The idea of different worlds at various levels of vibration is now gaining acceptance in quantum physics. As the nineteenth-century physicist Lord Kelvin discovered, all particles are the

---

[139]The experiment was monitored by the University of Maryland, the University of Denver School of Law, and other research institutions. Data and information on these and other experiments throughout the U.S. are available from the Institute of Science, Technology and Public Policy at Maharishi International University, Fairfield, Iowa, 52557. See Roth 1994.

result of vortices spinning at incredible speeds around a single point which creates a swirling ball of energy giving the illusion of solid material (see figure 13.1 on page 264). However, Kelvin was merely rediscovering what the Buddha and yogic philosophers had described centuries before, that "forms of matter are whirlpools in a busy stream," and that the world is *maya*, an illusion. Should the spin of an object exceed that which is detectable by the eye, it becomes both intangible and invisible. Alternatively, if its spin rate slows down, the object appears to "physicalize." In fact, substitute the words "spin," "vibration," or "frequency" for "spirit" and we come ever closer to understanding the nature of the Universe.

As such, crop circles begin to look like thoughts from a creative Universe, places on our plane where the laws of light, sound, and gravity are altered sufficiently for these "wheels of vibration" to spin down and physicalize. And they do so primarily when the Earth's electromagnetic field is at its lowest ebb, between 2 and 3 A.M., the time window when an estimated 95 percent of souls of the deceased leave this world,[140] and the majority of crop circles enter. Therefore, crop circles mark the spot where the veil between worlds is thinnest, allowing us to interact with subtler dimensions.

And for them to make contact with us.

It is easier for our sixth sense (the psychic and intuitive) to connect with dimensions with faster rates of spin because such abilities, including thought, occur at the speeds of light (Hunt 1989; Myers and Percy 1999). A growing number of first-hand experiences shows how this interaction works with crop circles and Circlemakers. On the night of July 21, 1992, Dr. Steven Greer, the founder and director of the Center for the Study of Extraterrestrial Intelligence (CSETI), set up camp with his group near Woodborough Hill in Wiltshire. One night they were met inside an existing crop circle by Gary Keel, Paul Anderson, Colin Andrews, and clairvoyant Maria Ward, among others, to conduct a remote viewing project whereby a predetermined design was projected to the Circlemakers; the pattern consisted of three circles arranged in triangular fashion, each linked by three straight lines. The following morning a report came in of a new formation below Oliver's Castle which bore an exact likeness to the *projected* image. As a bonus, Gerald Hawkins later found its geometry to be diatonic.

A similar project took place in 1993 on farmland below Furze Knoll, a sacred site rich in female energy and marked by an array of tumuli. This time, Paul Anderson went a step further, believing that "the circles are a message of some sort and that they are intended for humans to see and act upon." He proved his intent by renting a portion of the field and constructing a design in the crop.

The dimensions and placements were configured beforehand by mathematician Collete Dowell, who designed it to conform to diatonic principles; the site itself was identified from coordinates provided by archeocryptographer Carl Munck, whose research has demonstrated (beyond reasonable doubt) that the plans of many ancient monuments have been purposely encoded with their latitudinal and longitudinal grid refer-

---

[140]From research by Dr. A. J. Scott-Morley, as personally communicated by David Elkington.

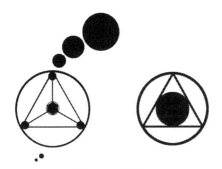

Figure 13.2

Left: Design created below Furze Knoll to contact Circlemakers. Right: Possible reply.

ences (Munck n.d.). To project the design mentally, Anderson was joined inside the completed formation by sensitives Lyn Gladwin and Isabelle Kingston, along with CPRI field researchers.

Days went by without apparent results. Then a month later during a routine surveillance flight, a crop circle bearing the features of Anderson's design appeared, with all the external elements collapsed into the center of the triangle (see figure 13.2). Its measurements yielded further surprises: Anderson had used the unit of measure common to Neolithic architects, the megalithic yard of 2.72 feet;[141] the Surrey formation measured 271.9 feet, one hundred times the size of the original (with a discrepancy of 0.1 percent).

Another experiment, this time using sound to communicate with the Circlemakers, was performed by Pete Glastonbury and a friend, who took up residence inside a crop circle at Berry Pomeroy one evening to play free-style music on stringed instruments tuned to a heptatonic scale. "After fifteen minutes we heard a sound just outside the circle," Glastonbury recalls. "It sounded very like the crackling you hear round your head when taking off a heavy woolen jumper. We both stopped playing. The sound stopped with the music, dying away to the north. The next day we discovered a small formation exactly where we had heard the sound the night before."

Three formations appeared in the neighboring fields, followed a week later by a large dumbbell in a field of oats across the road from the circle Glastonbury had played music in. "All around the edge of the field was a series of small lays (looking rather like runic characters), some so delicate that they terminated in a single stem lying flat to the ground."[142] One wonders: Do the Circlemakers create the glyphs to offer validation for well-intended thoughts?

Or perhaps our thought patterns are creating the crop circles? It has been proven that the mind can affect physical matter directly, particularly when allied with strong intent.[143] Or perhaps the individuals themselves are so in tune with the surrounding energy field that they pick up what may already be encoded. For example, when Colin Andrews lay in bed asking for a pattern to appear as close to his home as possible,

---

[141]The number of transformation is 2.72, and presumably this is why it was the unit of measure for stone circles and other megalithic structures, as discovered by the archeologist Alexander Thom. According to Myers and Percy, the exact figure—2.720699046—is a transdimensional constant, and is equivalent to the ratio between the surface of a sphere and the surface of the tetrahedron it circumscribes. That it should have been used in the manifested crop circle following the meditators connecting between dimensions is therefore above mere coincidence.
[142]Although the formations were soon harvested, three dowsers were taken on three different days to locate the residual energy at the sites, which they did despite wearing blindfolds. My thanks to Mr. Glastonbury for this information.
[143]The conclusion of twenty-five years of tests by the psychologist J. B. Rhine.

he fell asleep and dreamed of a Celtic cross design. He was wakened hours later by farmer Geoff Smith who had just discovered this pattern on land behind Andrews' home. (See figure 13.3 on page A14 in the color section.)

I have noticed that as my involvement with crop circles deepens each year (and with it the accumulation of its energetic effect on my body), I have felt a growing attunement to the Earth's energy, such that I have accurately predicted the glyphs up to seven months prior to their manifestation. This intuition has been refined to the point that during the summer of 2000, driving past West Kennett Long Barrow, I felt as if a situation was about to occur in the field beside it; eighteen hours later a new crop glyph appeared there.

Jim Lyons, former science officer for the CCCS, concluded that "conceiving the general shape of a formation can lead to its manifestation." After recognizing the underlying physics behind the spiral vortex creating crop circles, Lyons wrote to several people suggesting "that the appearance of a torus knot would help our understanding." His wish came true that summer, after which he further reasoned: "If the suggestion is resonant with Nature's underlying rulebook, then manifestation follows naturally" (Lyons 1998).

One July afternoon in 1999, Lyons and eleven other members of the Earth Energy Group of the British Society of Dowsers took a walk along the ridge of the Oldbury hill fort at Cherhill. After surveying its famous chalk horse figure, they held a ceremony in honor of the *genius loci,* letting the spirits know it would be a good place to have a crop glyph. The next day, within fifty yards of their wished-for site, a nine-petaled flower glyph appeared (displaying the geometry both Jim Lyons and I independently predicted for that season). In its center stood a vortex consisting of six crescents—a handy validation of Jim Lyons' vortex theory (see figure 13.4 on page A13 in the color section).

Such interactions have a habit of following the people closely associated with the phenomenon, as if the Circlemakers are offering reassurance. There are also many accounts from strangers who have "received" a crop circle near their homes after asking for specific designs. This implies we are not dealing just with an interactive energy field, but with an energy that is conscious: "I was obsessed with trying to draw seven-pointed stars just prior to leaving for England in 1998," said Dr. Patricia Hill, shortly before those same glyphs sprouted across southern England for the first time (Pringle 2000).

Something tells me she did not cross the Atlantic to create hoaxes, particularly as I had the same premonition at my New Hampshire home. Could all of this be coincidence? After all, some of these crop circles were archetypal symbols. Since the "coincidences" also apply to non-archetypal symbols, the answer appears to be no.

When she began writing *Signet of Atlantis* on July 15, 1991, the American author Barbara Hand Clow spontaneously drew an unusual triangular shape incorporating circles and rings as a guide for her book. Thousands of miles away in England, the Barbury Castle "Tetrahedron" appeared the next evening, bearing such a similarity to Clow's drawing that her German publisher was prompted to fax over a photo of the crop circle.[144] That such experiences occur

---

[144]Personal communication with Barbara Hand Clow.

regardless of distance was supported by Aztec elder Tlakaelel when he drew the sign of the "last ceremonial dance" in Connecticut, and his unusual "scorpion" pattern appeared the same morning beside West Kennett Long Barrow. A psychic in America similarly predicted the "Julia Set" at Stonehenge the very day of its appearance. None of these glyphs are exactly archetypal.

Clow's channeled material from a group consciousness became the focus of her next book, *The Pleiadian Agenda,* which she finished writing in early June 1995. Again she was "given" a symbol for the book, this time a curious zigzag design, said to represent the creation of matter via electromagnetism. A few days later, in an apparent validation of her work, a crop circle bearing this symbol appeared at Cow Down, Hampshire. The story now gets more interesting. Five days prior to the Cow Down crop circle, unbeknownst to Kerry Blower, another crop glyph had appeared twelve miles away on Telegraph Hill (see figure 13.5 on page A15 in the color section). It was the replica of a pattern she had already committed to paper, a pattern that she had received in a dream in Wiltshire (Vigay 1995).

Paul Vigay surveyed the Telegraph Hill crop glyph and picked up considerable radio interference that produced a hum. Paul followed the path of the audible noise and sketched it in his notebook (see figure 13.6). Shortly before leaving, the new batteries in his equipment that should have lasted a year suddenly died; on a return trip to the glyph the same thing happened to the batteries in his camera. Exactly seven days later the Cow Down glyph appeared bearing as its design the exact zigzag pattern of signal interference Vigay had found at Telegraph Hill.

Since Vigay had not mentioned his discovery or shown his diagram to anyone, including Clow and Blower, it is unlikely that a deception took place. Most

a

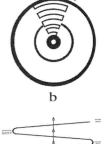

b

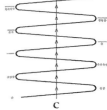

c

Figure 13.6

(a) Vigay's detected interference pattern superimposed over Telegraph Hill crop glyph; (b) Cow Down glyph; (c) diagram channeled by Clow.

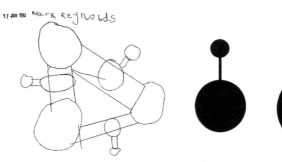

Figure 13.7

Drawing by two-year-old Mark Reynolds (left) predicting two formations that later appeared near his home.

significantly, Vigay's findings appear to validate the information channeled by Clow.

The ability to predict crop circles appears in young children, too. In the June 1992 edition of *Sussex Circular* magazine, readers were asked to submit predictions for the next crop formations to appear in the area. Barry Reynolds' two-year-old son drew his on a piece of paper, dated it June 17, and mailed it. On June 23 and 28, two formations appeared at Patcham, seven miles from their home, incorporating the elements of the boy's drawing (A. Thomas 1992).

One of the most extraordinary cases connecting the power of thought and the manifestation of crop circles concerns the "Lotus" at Golden Ball Hill (2000), a formation that gave me an unsettling feeling of *déjà vu*. It was later revealed to me, through a respected chaneller, that the pattern was a manifestation from a focused group meditation in India—several centuries ago.

At first this may seem far-fetched. However, consider a few things: First, time is a human invention, and outside our dimension time does not exist as such. Possibly due to gravitational and magnetic anomalies, time is even known to behave in unusual ways on our own dimension, as army units stationed on Salisbury Plain know too well, as they often receive radio messages broadcast up to ten years earlier (Rogers 1994). Second, if you recall, this formation gave a frequency of 1.5 GHz, the frequency of hydrogen, and as per CSETI's protocol, the frequency most likely to be used in interstellar or "extraterrestrial" communication.

Naturally, my curiosity deepened, and before long I came across a mantra attributed to a form of Buddhism called Nichiren Shoshu. This mantra is *Nam Myoho Renge Kyo* ("ado-

ration of the Lotus Sutra") and its words break down thus: *nam* is the willpower of the meditating individual; *myoho* is the law of the hereafter (or life after physical death); *renge* is the name of a particular lotus flower and the karmic law of cause and effect; and *kyo* is both word and sound vibration (Berendt 1991). The Lotus Sutra is as important to Nichiren practitioners as the Bible is to Christians, and its meaning appears to support the channeled information of this crop circle as a thought form sent through time and space to appear in Wiltshire.

Sometimes this interaction demonstrates the Circlemakers have a mischievous sense of humor, such as the time I took my former wife for a break away from all the research. We were driving just to the south of Coventry, an area not known for crop circles, when I casually remarked, "Wouldn't it be funny if we had a crop circle follow us on holiday to Scotland? Ha, ha, ha!" Five minutes passed when, along a prominent incline beside the busy stretch of road, a 150-foot glyph grinned back at us. I was forbidden to mention the cc-words for the rest of the trip.

After the incident at Morgan's Hill in 1991, when the monitored field was breached by a crop glyph, one of the men watching the site drove back home to Nottingham to find the identical pattern behind his office. It was sited to the same size and at the same distance away from the building as the original had been with respect to the observation post in Wiltshire.

On occasion the interaction can provide guidance. One August morning in 1996 I arranged to collect two members of our team. After picking up my first passenger I started on the road towards Marlborough, but at a critical point along the route I was compelled to travel the opposite way, towards Avebury. Driving past the stone avenue into Avebury, I suddenly pulled over and exclaimed, "What on earth am I doing? Why am I driving in this direction?"

I know the area perfectly and my passenger, an excellent map reader, was equally perplexed. Undaunted, but not wishing to backtrack, we looked for a way across the Marlborough Downs between us and our intended goal. What happened next is a mystery: in front of us, after a few turns, appeared the M4 motorway—and in a few seconds, eight miles of road were unaccounted for, as if the car had been picked up and dropped off at another location.

Since we were now quite out of our way, the only way back was through Chiseldon. As we left the town, we noticed something. "There's a new crop circle on that hill," shouted my passenger. We had encountered the last circle of the 1996 season.

These are just a few examples of the myriad experiences demonstrating a subconscious communication link between human beings and the Circlemakers. Since the subconscious is essentially a series of electromagnetic vibrations operating in a dimension outside the limitations of time and space, it is clear that the Circlemakers inhabit this world of refined vibration. So who are they?

"We knew that the circles were going to appear in this field and we set up watch for most of the month," George Wingfield remarked while sitting inside the first Alton Barnes pictogram scribbling notes. "A local medium named Isabelle Kingston told us."

Isabelle Kingston is not your run-of-the-mill clairvoyant. Self-effacing and down-to-earth, she projects no sense of self-importance, nor does she indulge in vulgar displays of supernatural parlor trickery. This doctor's daughter originally worked as a liaison officer in a finance house—left-brain credentials for someone now working on right-brain material. When she became a mother her career took a back seat, allowing her the opportunity to develop an interest in dowsing. "I dowsed people for vitamin deficiency. Then I'd ask them to write down a typical week's diet and the results would correlate, proving to me that the dowsing system worked."

The development of her clairvoyant ability began through a chance encounter in a shop with Roger St. John Webster, a well-regarded psychic teacher, who, without introduction, inquired of Isabelle, "When are you going to come to my classes?" Since then she has been a channel through which the main group of Circlemakers often communicate. Or to put it her way, "Why me?"

In 1982, during a meditation with her group on the origins of Silbury Hill, Isabelle received a message from a Universal consciousness called the Watchers, whose purpose, they told her, is to guide humanity through its difficult periods. These enlightened beings also revealed that this "Hill of Light" (*Sil* means light) was an "insurance policy" for this particular period.

Isabelle was instructed to move to Wiltshire, to work on Silbury and the sacred sites around Avebury, and to be part of a phenomenon that "would be raising the consciousness of the Earth." Six years of opening these strategic energy points ensued. At that time in the early 1980s, crop circles were a rare phenomenon, an "aberration of nature," as some said, that received scant coverage even in local papers. Then in July 1988, the Watchers said they would manifest signs of their purpose within seven days. Right on cue, the first sets of quintuplets appeared at the foot of Silbury.[145] In the succeeding three years, Isabelle would be provided with further instructions ahead of time as to the location and the physical attributes of the circles.

"In 1990, I was in a field out at West Kennett, but I got the location of the Alton Barnes one right and even drew it. It was referencing an energy point." In fact, save for a superfluous triangle, her precognitive diagram is identical to the actual glyph; she has since predicted dozens of crop circles.

Her trance readings with the Watchers offer us insights into the purpose behind the crop circles.[146] If the Watchers' statements match the facts and events that unfold in the fields (facts that form the evidence presented throughout this book), they are all the more astonishing considering the information was given in 1989, long before much had been made public about crop circles, let alone even investigated. Here are some excerpts from Isabelle Kingston's channelings of the Watchers:

> You ask the meaning of your circles in the fields. You have been made aware of the presence of the Watchers. Watchers is a name of a collective intelligence which guides you mortal humans. It is an intelligence from outside the planet, linked to angelic beings, part of cosmic consciousness.

We have been coming for years and years, and this has happened many times before. We have been linked with humanity to bring the power necessary to build the New Jerusalem. Your country [Britain] lies in the centre of the great pyramid of light which encircles your world, and the energies of the Watchers bring love through magnetic channels.

The pyramid of power which surrounds [Britain] is the key, in your words, a button to press to activate. You are the immune system of your planet, the healing system which will create the changes, but also there are other keys which will need to be activated. This country is a testing ground, it has to be right before the whole can be lined up with other dimensions. Things changing at Stonehenge, a field of energy is above the stones. [Some crop] circles are the exact dimension of Stonehenge. Circles have appeared as a blueprint for humankind to mark that place as a place of power—it is as though those places are being unlocked. Centres are being awakened, it is part of the Plan.

Your Silbury Hill lies in a field of energy which is an area which draws cosmic power. There are ley lines running through the Earth, and at various points, lines of power are energized. It

---

[145]The quintuplet, sometimes referred to as the "Celtic Cross," is the symbol of Merlin and "the Shining Ones." The latter are synonymous with the *Neteru* (or *Netur*), the Egyptian creator gods who brought knowledge to humanity. They are referenced in the *Emerald Tablets of Thoth,* and their hieroglyph—an "F" attached to an "O"—resembles a guitar. From their name is derived the word "nature," whose Latin meaning is "origin."

[146]My thanks to Isabelle Kingston for permission to publish her channelings. Some of this material was previously published in Alick Bartholomew's *Harbingers of World Change.*

has happened mostly in this part of the country. Similar circles have appeared in other countries. There have also been energy healings to Peru, the Himalayas and the West Coast of America—all places set down many Earth years before. We have come many times but humanity's awareness did not recognize the signs.

Figure 13.8

Silbury Hill, axis mundi *of the Watchers.*

This ancient land holds the balance, it is the key to the world. Many of these [sacred sites] are being cleansed, as if made bright, so that they are channels of the new energy. Many lights have been placed there, but it is as if it needs a cosmic force to actually turn the switch. It is right for many groups to tend the lamp and get ready for the input of power.

In all things you are linked—an invisible web joining all to all and us to you. Therefore work is done for those who may be weaker links in the chain. Spiritual power, power from other dimensions, is drawn down to the Hill of Silbury—the word *sil* derives from the word which means Shining Being. It is the hill of the Shining Beings which showed themselves to the ancient seers and started the work in earnest. The tem-

ples that remain were in fact meant to last until this cataclysmic time in Earth's history. Therefore the foundations were laid to help humanity at a later date. The building of the Hill of Silbury was directed by the Watchers.

The circles at Silbury [1990]—the Watchers helped with this, but this time there are also elemental aspects involved, because this is what is important at the moment. We have in fact to a degree stabilized the planet, but now the natural elements need help.

The energy has been put through [crop circles] through thought-processes, with light beams, rather like your national grid system, so we input power into the Earth's grid. This is to stabilize the energies in the Earth, to stop the Earth destroying you. You have been told of the purpose of the Hill of Silbury: if we placed the circles elsewhere you would not have recognized the connection between the energy of ancient sites and that of crop circles.

It is an intelligence of elemental energy which is linked to other solar systems. You cannot conceive of the energy relayed at this time, but you have experienced sound waves transmitted at high frequency. Change the tempo of the sounds and in this will emerge the code. We will be giving different sounds at this time. It is affirmation of facts which is necessary. You have physical form: matter has form in its being. Matter is not just energy and light, but also molecular formations. There is a printout being shown in the circles, therefore you are being given the body of a form. Each entity shows itself in the formation, therefore you can communicate with these.

There are some formations which link to your natural elements. There are some working within the bowels of the Earth. There are some formations linked with the higher consciousness of the universe. With others there is also a link with the knowledge of the Old Ones. Therefore each formation is different. Some say that you have the inner understanding to feel the difference.

Sometimes [crop circles appear at] the same point, but as a tune of music, sometimes it is not easy to hit the same note. There is a music of the Earth and of the Universe, and a note will be revealed. Gradually the music will be completed and you will recognize the tune. The crop circles are like a score of the music

between the Earth and the cosmos. You do not at this time need to learn to read the score. The best is to feel it.

We give indications of energy [in the circles] and yet even if the secrets were never divulged, they will have changed many, many souls. You can facilitate the circles happening by sitting in a circle, sending out light and opening your hearts. If you wish to truly enter the spirit of the formations, then stand a little away, project your thoughts to that place, connect your mind with the Universal mind of understanding, then you will know whether these circles are of light beings or of man. Understanding has to grow before acceptability becomes possible, so think of the symbols given, and you will know that we are with you.

We give signals in the corn and we give sound in the ear. Changes in eyes, different aches and pains around the body—as though being realigned. Sounds in ears, like Morse code. Information being programmed in for a later date. Always the right ear. Also a two-way exchange at an unconscious level.

How we would like you to understand the mysteries in true clarity, but the minds of many have yet to open fully, and thus the work is painstaking and slow. . . . Seek not to accept the barrier [of rationality]. Seek not in the physical, but seek in the spiritual, for this is where the imbalance lies. You must also understand that the energies being transmitted at this time are a combination of all elements and all elemental beings, as well as interplanetary information. There is a coming-together, therefore one source is not the whole picture, and many varying types of information might well be given.

It is a time for all to work together, thus all must pool their information and find that a vein of pure gold will run through. There is a new code of understanding being transmitted. It is a blueprint of a new energy-coding coming on to the planet. We have communicated before many times: it is usually through thought processes, but now it needs to be seen. Changes are occurring in all people; this sometimes stirs up anxiety and strife before the operation is complete.

An atom of intelligence touches your world and gives you a message for you to unlock. You have been given the task to unlock ancient doorways. The information given to early man has been stored, and we again come to pass the messages on. Part of you still holds the ancient civilizations, and through your genes you have received this information. Within you, you have the blueprint to raise consciousness, to see the unseen, to link telepathically. Each one has, through the choice of your birth, incarnated with these abilities, and that small gene vibrates and grows within and is passed on. You have all walked on this Earth many times but you know you came from other civilizations, other planets. You must protect your world for many will follow. Therefore we give you the help, therefore we give you the key to heal. But it is the task of others on your planet to reconstruct the information that we are giving.

Secrets will be passed and transmitted and it is your task to help and transcribe those messages.

The Aboriginal people understood the dimensions of the Dreamtime, and although the information is lost, the understanding still remains. There was a time when many walked upon the Earth and could link into many dimensions. This facility was lost, but can return at the point of the change-over [consciousness-shift].

[The grapeshot] contain the code that will be understood. Although the great shapes show signs of power, as always, the smaller gems contain the greatest light. These formations came before your planet was as it is now. The formations are like molecular structures and blueprints—like a form of Morse code—and someone will be used to unravel this information, and scientists will be able to use it and put it into practice. It will be possible to use this new form of energy within your lifetimes [by 2007]. The unraveling will start before then.

This new source of energy is now being created and certain beings are being prepared to understand the messages being projected at this time. Power is being created through the intellect of the scientist, knowledge is being awakened; some scientists are very close to the answer—an energy machine. This energy is only partially linked to magnetism. It is linked to the illusion of time. Rather like thought-transference, man will be able to change the molecular structure of things, including himself.

Within the energy-pattern of the circles we give you this information. You humans do not believe your dreams and inspirations, so other methods have to be used. This will happen by the right people being drawn into the understanding. Some of you will be necessary to sit at the sidelines injecting love and light, and only a few will be involved totally.

Amidst all its struggles, humanity does not seem to want to accept that love great and powerful is encircling the world and being transmitted. It is most essential to create the right atmosphere for enlightenment into the grid system of the planet. Those who bring knowledge are here again. We are known as the Watchers, because we can only aid and help. Your Earth cries with tears, and we feel the pain and sorrow of humanity's misunderstandings. We have not the will to change the world—this, my friends, is your work. Do not always look upward, for there is much to love below.

Let's examine some of the points made by the Watchers. They said: "We give signals in the corn and we give sound in the ear. . . . Sounds in ears, like Morse code. Information being programmed in for a later date. . . . Always the right ear. Also a two-way exchange at an unconscious level."

After years of involvement with the circles, an unusual ringing has manifested in *my* right ear; it is high-pitched and yet refined, a waterfall of Morse code. Having suffered from the harsh garble of tinnitus in my left ear for fifteen years, I can rule that out as an explanation since the sound in my right ear is completely different.

Such a ringing noise is often reported by people standing at the summit of the Great Pyramid, itself a highly complex geometric structure which collects and amplifies all manner of electromagnetic and acoustical frequencies. This "noise" could be the sensation of super-high frequency vibrations as they tap upon the drum of the inner ear. This ringing is all sound, and it is said to be present when the entire chakra system is open.

My colleague and a long-time ground researcher, Sheely Keel, has had similar experiences with the right ear noise, particularly during a visit to the Hakpen "Nine Spirals" crop circle. She said: "The noise in my right ear got very loud the closer I got to the center. I was trying to write down how I was feeling but I could not get my mind to work with my hand, so there was a lot of scribbling out, along with unprintable language. When the noise in my right ear was so loud, I was shouting to Colin Andrews, who was with me at the time, telling him what was happening. He was having similar problems. By moving towards the edge of the formation, it seemed to get quieter the closer I got to the edge."

Is it possible that ringing in the ear is a form of communication, part of the Watchers' "two-way exchange at an unconscious level"? In the past, such experiences have been associated with communication between the unseen realms and people; in fact, as mentioned earlier, God is said to have lulled the soul to enter the physical body through sound, and you can find such a description of the descent of consciousness into the physical in an ancient liturgy of the Christian church, in which Jesus describes his origin thus: "When my Father thought to send me into the world, He sent His angel before me, by name Mary, to receive me. And when I came down I entered in by the ear and came forth by the ear."[147]

The Watchers referred to the crop circle trilling noise as "sound waves transmitted at high frequency. Change the tempo of the sounds and in this will emerge the code." This brings me to the work of David Hindley, a Cambridgeshire musician, who found that by slowing down a highly compressed sequence of notes, forty-eight seconds of song from a skylark created nearly thirteen minutes of sheet music. Moreover, the structure of birdsong relates precisely to the principles governing human musical composition, including those underlying the work of Beethoven (Devereux 1992). So, the possibility of a recognizable code transmitted at high frequency is perfectly feasible, and if true, it is a code that interacts with grain and humans.

Such ringing and trilling sounds are often accompanied by a deep, oscillating hum that seems to stick to your head. Many were the occasions during my early contact with crop circles when I walked around the house searching for a defective appliance or a malfunctioning electrical transformer out in the street to account for this hum. Typically, such pulsations are caused by two out-of-phase frequencies: for example, by two tuning forks ringing side-by-side, one at 440 Hz, the other at 460 Hz. The effect of two tones slightly out of harmony with each other generates a pulse that oscillates from ear to ear. The use of certain Tibetan bells and crystal bowls in meditation creates a similar effect (particularly when tuned to F-sharp), the idea being to drive brainwaves into a state of greater receptivity.[148]

We know that crop circle frequencies create heightened states of awareness. As monks working with Gregorian chants have found, by combining these chant frequencies with an electromagnetic field, the stimulation to the brain and physical body is pronounced. As the vibratory level of the body's magnetic field is raised, the brain generates an electrical charge forty-six times greater than average, and at this point, one becomes psychically active.[149] For this reason, the electromagnetic field around a psychic at work needs to be considerably strengthened, and such an increase in electromagnetic energy both precedes and facilitates a change in consciousness (Hunt 1989).

A report by the American Parapsychology Foundation suggests that these conditions already occur in industry. Electronics engineers working with high-frequency machines on occasion suddenly find themselves telepathic, to the point of carrying out tasks before commands are issued (Ostrander and Schroeder 1976). How reassuring this is for supporters of clairvoyance, who have always maintained that it is the stepping-up of the frequency in the electromagnetic field that enables energy from another dimension to slip through as information.

Has the transmission of information to humans by the Watchers taken the form of using humans to make crop circles? Some

[147]According to Walter Birks and R. A. Gilbert in *The Treasure of Montsegur,* the quote is found in the Gospel of St. John, as preserved in Catharist scripture, and found in ancient Christian liturgies.
[148]The profiles of Tibetan bells are shaped like saucer barrows (a type of tumulus with a circular moat), which in turn bear a striking resemblance to the classic "flying saucer."
[149]Tests performed by Dr. Genady Sergeyev of the A. A. Utomski Physiological Institute in Leningrad in the early 1970s.

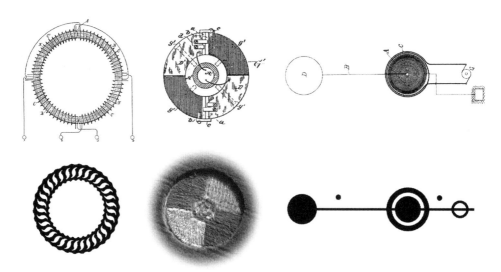

Figure 13.9

Some of the electrical and magnetic transmission devices designed by the genius Nikola Tesla (top) bear a close resemblance to crop circles nearly a century later. What types of technology await deciphering in the crop glyphs?

hoaxers have claimed this. Doug Bower once stated: "Why we did it I cannot explain," to which his partner in crime, the late Dave Chorley added: "It may sound crazy . . . we were being told to go out and do them" (McNish 1991). Bower even admitted this to the press in 1998. Bower may indeed not be able to explain why, and Chorley probably meant what he said about being *told* to go and do it. Of course there could be an Earthly source to their instructions; indeed, the ambiguity of their wording sounds like carefully prepared phrases ripe for interpretation according to the inclinations of the listener.

Other hoaxers, who prefer to remain anonymous, allegedly had similar experiences in that when attempting to execute a predesigned plan they felt mysteriously *compelled* to create a different design once they were in the field. Additionally, the hoaxers' presence at a site already activated as a crop circle may leave them open to subconscious interaction with the Circlemakers.

I was open to this possibility while investigating "Metraton's Cube" below Cley Hill (1997). The glyph appeared at a location that had hosted many circles, and was atop sixteen geodetic lines tied in to the Cley Hill complex, yet the pattern's straight lines did not all dowse in accordance with the underlying geodetic grid, which would be the case in genuine crop circles. However, according to eyewitnesses, the design appears to have "grown" from a simple large circle found the day before. Given that the pattern was clearly tied to the hexagonal "Flower of Life" jigsaw (see chapter 10), this may have been a case where hoaxers vectored information *already present* in the energy field.

Let us move on to another important issue referred to by the Watchers, namely the new forms of technology to be decoded from the glyphs appearing in the first decade of the twenty-first century. Two people who have embarked on the road to new technological wonders are authors David Myers and David Percy. In their book, *Two-Thirds—A History of Our Galaxy*, they provide stunning evidence of a number of crop glyphs encoding technology far beyond the present accepted boundaries of physics.

This technology, they say, includes energy transdimensioning, energy conducting, energy conversion, and components of a gravitron drive and a computer. The two "Key" pictograms at West Kennett and Alton Priors were found to contain information relating to three different speeds of light; other glyphs relate to consciousness-driven, spinning disk technology. (A few paragraphs on this ground-breaking book cannot do it justice, and I reference this work for the sake of those who wish to see another aspect of the "bigger picture.")

Naturally, the consequences of such discoveries in crop circles will have far-reaching consequences for twenty-first century society and how we view our relationship with the world beyond the physical. Such a prediction is grounded in an unusual experiment by the psychopharmacologist Dennis McKenna who, together with his philosopher brother Terence, categorized and chronologically plotted the greatest discoveries and technological developments since 5000 B.C., then fed the information into a computer. After digesting the data, the computer provided a graphic printout showing how these discoveries created a hyperbolic curve that peaked and leveled around 1975.

Intrigued, the brothers programmed the computer to project and predict future discoveries based on this pattern; this time the line took a dramatic upswing as it reached 2011, where-

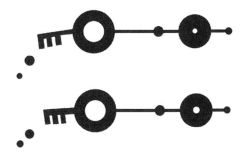

Figure 13.10

Two apparently identical glyphs reveal subtle differences in measurements when superimposed. Myers and Percy discovered these differences to encode three speeds of light. Alton Priors and West Kennett, 1991.

upon the predictions ended. During the last two hours of this time-scale, eighteen barriers will be crossed, some rivaling the splitting of the atom (McKenna and McKenna 1975). These accomplishments would be accompanied by transformations in human consciousness, curiously, in the same year marking the end of the Mayan calendar, which predicts this "Age of Intellect" to be superseded by the "Age of Spirituality" in 2012.

The McKennas' theory seems plausible, considering that in the sixty-seven-year cycle that began with the detonation of the atomic bomb at Hiroshima, technological and social breakthroughs have accelerated faster than in the time between Galileo and Hiroshima. The dramatic and exponential rise in the incidence of crop circles from the 1980s onwards could be one aspect of this acceleration. Like the British physicist Bohm, the McKenna brothers present our Universe as a hologram, a creation of two intersecting "hyper-universes."

The McKennas propose that our holographic Universe consists of sixty-four (8x8) frequencies, of which ours is but one. As these two hyper-universes intersect, our DNA will need to evolve rapidly to cope with all sixty-four frequencies. The event is said to reach its crescendo in 2012. This date came about when the McKennas programmed a computer with the sixty-four time systems, each based on the sixty-four hexagrams of the *I Ching,* which itself is said to be a model of the physical structure of a single helical strand of DNA.[150] Recall from previous chapters the evidence suggesting that crop circles may be involved in the process of altering DNA and you see how the subject can get exciting.

During an uncharacteristic lull in my research in the summer of 1998 I visited Isabelle Kingston. Sitting in the shade of her garden—through which the Michael line goes about its business—we talked about her channeled material and its relevance a decade later. The Watchers' specific task, she said, was still to wake humanity up to the reality of what we are doing to the planet and to respond to our responsibility.

"They came before in human form," Isabelle said. "They were the ones who were the ancient teachers and the tall beings that are in every culture. They said that in order for them to communicate with us they needed to set up the right vibration; and the vibration wasn't just people's psyches but also the energy of the planet, because they are interstellar. That's why the Watchers laid down sacred sites as communication points to be available at a time when it was necessary for them to be in contact with us

again. There are now groups around the world reopening these points so that the communication can again take place.

"They asked to open Avebury and the Wessex triangle. They had been here thousands of years before, and they set up the blueprint of much information, both technical and spiritual, and they were able to perceive how we'd evolve as humanity, giving us a chance to get it right later. . . . They talked about Atlantean consciousness having the technical mind but not the heart, and therefore humanity had the technical wisdom taken away to develop the heart and spirit. So we've taken a backward step. They wish us to have that balance which was missing in those days."

As she spoke the big picture stirred in my head in synchronicity with the spoon in my coffee, and it occurred to me that crop circles are also keys that unlock the practical within people. Without any prompting, she continued: "They would give signs of their intervention. These signs would also unlock the potential within humanity, but it would be the potential for whatever they chose that would be released within them. If they chose to go with ego and domination, that would affect them—or compassion. It would amplify whatever was within, positive or negative. The symbols are not just in one word; they are experienced differently by different people, and so you resonate with particular symbols. And always they talked about the *choice* of humanity—you *choose* what you want to do. You have a choice to muck your world up; you have a choice to make it a better place. They are there to give us help if we need it. But it's up to us."

---

[150] Alain Aspects' work into subatomic particles also implies that not only does objective reality not exist but this apparently solid universe is nothing more than an incredibly detailed hologram. See James Gleick, *Chaos.* My thanks to Anton Milland for bringing this to my attention.

"They said that at some level within us we have the knowledge of the Universe because we come from the Universe. The truths are there but we've become blind to them. They are trying to help us seek into that again. They have been working subtly on people with scientific know-how, helping them see an image which bypasses the brain. As the scriptures said, 'The hand of God will touch the Earth.' The message the Watchers give is that we are not alone. They remind us that we can create our own reality, and that we should acknowledge this potential in every level of society. They are getting us to be responsible, to bring us back to the land, back into sync with the Earth, because we have lost our link with it."

Belief in direct heavenly intervention to cure all our problems certainly finds a lot of support among all sectors of society. Some people might ask, "If these beings belong to the realm of the godly, why all the innuendo? Why not just come down here and fix things?"

Personally, I do not subscribe to the idea of the gods fixing our problems. It is such a ridiculously easy way out. During the last two thousand years, humanity has longed for a savior, yet now it is dawning on us that only *we* can save ourselves from ourselves, or to quote a Hopi elder, "we are the ones we've been waiting for." Salvation is a misunderstood word; it is an expression of the spirit striving to free itself from the bond of the physical body and *religio,* to reunite with its creator. And besides, protecting people from experience rarely leads to true understanding.

The Watchers intervene only if called upon, a point reinforced by Isabelle. "It would take years for us to figure out what the phenomenon was all about. They would just give it to us and we would have to mull it over. We would have to use our computers because there is information there—codes of forms of energy, codes to do with sound and music, and codes to do with healing and spirituality. But only if you choose to see it would it have an effect on you. They can't take our free will away; they are not allowed to do that. It's the Law."

If the Watchers have made cameo appearances throughout our history, it would be of interest to see if those appearances coincided with abrupt cultural leaps, such as our computer age. As the Egyptian *Neteru,* they were associated with the implementation of knowledge and megalithic building practices throughout Egypt, the Near East, and Western Europe. They appeared throughout Ghanian folklore, this time under the guise of the "Shining Ones," just as they did in England. Although no evidence has yet come to light of their presence during the Gothic era—when Europe emerged out of the Dark Ages and into the Renaissance—evidence of crop circles surfaced in Oxford in a seventeenth-century manuscript entitled *The Natural History of Staffordshire.*

In 1686, Robert Plot, then professor of chemistry and keeper of the Ashmolean Museum at Oxford, wrote in the aforementioned book an account of unusual circular designs in fields, "those rings we find in the grass, which they commonly call Fairy circles."[151] The circles

---

[151]There is a potential connection between so-called fairy circles and crop circles in the writings of John Leyland, a chronicler appointed by Henry VIII. In his writings of sixteenth-century English folklore, Leyland describes the origins of the maypole dance patterns traditional to England: "We go out in the early hours and we learn the patterns that appear on grass overnight." My thanks to Sir Lawrence Gardner for this information.

Figure 13.11

The appearance of crop circles in the seventeenth century led Robert Plot to believe the designs were made by "trumpets" of atmospheric energy.

described appear to have been generally 120 feet in diameter, with some as small as six feet, much like our modern-day grapeshot. Plot documented "the rims of these Circles, from the least to the biggest, are seldom narrower than a foot, or much broader than a yard," and he described their circular area as not mathematically perfect circles but slightly ovoid. Plot also noticed color variations in the plants, from a "russet singed colour" to "dark fresh green," and the condition of the soil inside the affected areas which had "differed from the adjoining earth . . . the ground under them much looser and dryer than ordinary," characterized by a "musty rancid smell." So far, this is familiar territory.

Like Terence Meaden three centuries after him, Plot first theorized that these events were the product of weather, particularly lightning of some kind that would arrange itself in a conical manner, breaking through the clouds from some height to strike the ground as a circle (see figure 13.11). The events not only manifested as single

circles but also in patterns of twins and triplets. In Oxfordshire, Plot was shown one circle within another—a ringed circle in today's crop circle language. Others appeared divided into quadrants and sextants, and two had a square within a ring (reminiscent of the "Grid Square"). Like today's circles, they occurred in wide open pastures, ". . . where Trees and Hedges interrupt least" (Plot 1678).

Plot provided sketches of "trumpets" descending from the sky, out of which the energy was believed to have been generated. As odd as it may seem, on April 15, 1991, two eleven-year-old Japanese boys witnessed a glowing orange object descend from the sky at a distance of 300 feet and project a pillar of "transparent white steam." The pillar revolved and grew wider at the base, "giving the impression of a trumpet." As three rings were created in the long grass, a low alternating sound was heard. Minutes later, the "trumpet" retracted and the object bolted into the sky (Wingfield 1994).

Plot's observations also support another little-known, latter-day observation. He wrote: "The earth underneath having been highly improved with a fat sulpherous [sic] matter . . . ever since it was first stricken, though not exerting its fertilizing quality till some time after."

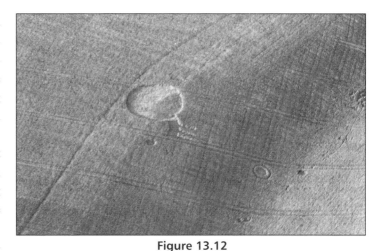

Figure 13.12

"We will give you the key." Humor from the Watchers. Allington, 1990.

Such improved growing conditions have been noted by a number of farmers I have spoken to (all of whom wish to remain anonymous), and as far as I'm aware this information has never been made public. According to the farmers' observations, the affected plants appear "healthier," "more robust," and "with a better sheen." I have seen results from replanted crop circle seeds in which the plants clearly outgrow normal wheat samples by more than six inches; one farmer whose field receives a lot of circles even reports higher crop yields. While this evidence is empirical, it is worth remembering that decades ago laboratory tests on plant growth proved the fertilizing benefits of ultrasound, the same range of frequencies known to exist in crop circles (Tompkins and Bird 1973).

Perhaps this is part of the "new technology" referred to by the Watchers. Perhaps the day is near when this phenomenon will revive an interest in nondestructive methods of farming, so when our children eat an apple they'll once again taste the goodness of the land, not a conglomerate of chemicals.

Assuming Robert Plot ran into the same phenomenon—which by all accounts appears to be the case—this recorded period of crop circle activity in Plot's time neatly coincided with the most recent advance in our civilization, namely, the publishing of Newton's *Theory of Gravity* in 1684. This ushered in the Age of Reason, culminating as it has in the age of industrialization (or degenerating into, depending on your point of view). So have we gone astray since the Watchers' last involvement? Has there been a recent cry for help?

"They particularly came here because they were called upon from England," Isabelle commented. "This was during the original new age movement at Glastonbury in the 1920s and 1930s, led at different times by such luminaries as Arthur Conan Doyle, Tudor Pole, and George Trevelyan. It was a more philosophical movement then. These men had the vision of a new order, a New Jerusalem within this land. Consciousness shifts westwards every two thousand years, so it has moved from Israel to England, just as it will resurface in America around 4000 A.D. But when the consciousness of the planet hits critical mass we get an expression of that consciousness within the fields.

"There's also an interaction with interdimensional entities. This is what the shamans are and were capable of doing—interacting with different dimensions. These entities are still here, just not in the same form as ours. So you get an expression of those other dimensions in the crop circles. You will get different shapes because they are part of the whole strata of interplanetary consciousness."

"So the 'balls of light' are part of that consciousness?" I asked.

"Balls of light are [manifestations of] consciousness that reveal themselves to us in a manner we can recognize. So what we have is a traveling energy or a traveling consciousness that moves around the planet so that we can see it. They travel through time and space. They are just interested and they interact with us through the mind, meditation, consciousness. They are intelligent."[152]

It is said that highly evolved beings are known by their sense of humor, and Isabelle herself has not been immune to the odd prank by the Watchers: "When they said they would give us the key . . . oh boy," she said, rubbing her hands with glee, "we will have the answer to everything." Two days later appeared the first circle bearing an appendage resembling a key.

Guided by the Watchers, the thousands of long barrows, tumuli, and other sacred sites in the landscape were strategically positioned not just to reference the Earth's energy nodes, but also as mirror images of specific constellations.[153] The idea was to draw down the energy associated with star systems so that guidance or knowledge can be received at appropriate times of the month; it also facilitates the "score of music" to be transmitted between the Earth and the cosmos. Isabelle Kingston and her close-knit group have been "opening" these sacred sites so their beneficial energy can again flow onto the land, enriching it and its inhabitants with the Light. And wherever we perform these openings, crop circles invariably manifest, such as the Silbury "Koch fractal."

Another validation of our work appeared in 1994, when a crop circle bearing the infinity symbol appeared outside the tiny village of West Overton. The glyph reflects the spirit of St. Michael, the infinity symbol (and the number 8) being a reflection of the perfect rhythm of ebb and flow of Universal life, with which Mika-el is associated. Behind this crop circle stands the village church dedicated to this saint, and a site the group had just opened. Interestingly, the crop glyph was aligned to the geodetic line that flows not through the present—and relatively modern—church, but through the original one whose ruins are no longer visible.

Each crop circle season brings with it a different theme as the Watchers work on different

---

[152]During his time as professor of physics at the University of Leipzig, Gustav Theodor Fechner came to the understanding that plants are extremely sensitive entities. In his book *Comparative Anatomy* he also developed this understanding of finer realms, and described how angelic beings are spherical in form and communicate through luminous symbols.

[153]Based on the work of Isabelle Kingston and her group; for a similar line of inquiry see Mark Vidler's *The Star Mirror.*

elements. This is reflected in the crop circles' designs each year, a perfect example of form following function. The Watchers started with the simple circles, although these have also been appearing for millennia, for they connect with Earth's primary processes and as such are physical expressions of up-wellings of energy from the living, breathing planet.

Most crop circles lie dormant throughout the land as energy prints, waiting to be triggered at an appropriate time by the natural flow of life force, by premeditated action, and through various means of vibration, such as a beam of light, a sound, or thought. Some of the patterns are laid down when the Watchers visit, connecting with and moving the geodetic energy lines, and calling in on the ancestors as a mark of respect, just as we lay flowers at a grave in remembrance of a loved one.

During the 1998 and 1999 seasons there was a mood swing, as if a new type of energy had lodged itself within the Earth. This energy was reflected in the crop circles: They seemed more agitated, some more disruptive to the body than usual. In others, the veil between the seen and the unseen felt thinner than ever. The mood among people, particularly the competition among crop circle "experts," was abrasive, confrontational, and more polarized than ever. To add to this, a new wave of crop circles appeared whose designs fit neither the recognized hand of humans nor the will of the Watchers. What changed?

"The Watchers appear to have given the message," says Isabelle. "It is time for other consciousness to start taking over. The planet is evolving, raising its vibration, and that makes people very jittery because we are now vibrating at a different pulse. But if you can change your consciousness to be in tune with the planet, life becomes easy."[154]

With the influx of these new frequencies, the Earth's resonant field undergoes changes as it seeks to balance itself. The process inevitably creates biological stress in the human body, manifesting as disease, fatigue, agitation, emotional instability, or physical challenges—the very effects described by the Watchers. "Changes in eyes, different aches and pains around the body—as though being realigned." So we are experiencing the raising of vibration, the shift of Ages, just as our ancestors did before us. And those beings once called the "gods," the Watchers, have returned to guide us through these changes by offering an instruction manual in the form of crop circles.

Jane Ross is another individual who has been accessing the other side of the veil in crop circles. Like Isabelle Kingston, Jane's background in accounting is as remote from channeling as one can get. A sensitive from birth, Jane's direct contact with the phenomenon occurred in 1994, after exposure to a specific design which—like many of us involved in this work—turned a key within her. She is the former U.S. Coordinator for CPRI, and actively takes part in the grueling schedule of information-gathering at crop circle sites every summer.

---

[154]It is important to note that Isabelle is not suggesting the Watchers are no longer involved, merely that other beings are coming to the fore. There are in fact many forms of life and of consciousness involved in making crop circles, of which the Watchers are a core group.

Figure 13.13

Etchilhampton, 1997.

Like Isabelle, Jane receives information about crop circles months prior to their manifestation through trance channeling.[155] The sessions are done in America, and some of the information she receives includes physical descriptions and/or locations of crop circles: "This one will be at Etchilhampton. It has sculpted sides, like crescents. It's a clockwise movement of energy. There seem to be circles or scallops or crescents interlocking on the outside edges of it with a central circle. This is almost like a flower." (See figure 13.13.)

"There will be a rather spectacular design in the Avebury complex. It has spiky-looking edges. It is like a starburst. It is quite beautiful and huge and there will be a lot of interest in it, and it will be quite dramatic. Around the back of Silbury Hill, in that area. That will occur when we are there." And it did, three days after our arrival in England (see figure 13.14). Ross's accuracy continued through 1998, particularly her prediction of a double pentagram looking "like shards of glass" (see figure 13.15 on page A15 in the color section); in 1999, she predicted the locations and times to within forty-eight hours of the crop formations across from Silbury Hill

Figure 13.14

Silbury Hill, 1996.

and behind West Kennett, including the controversial "hoax" at Avebury.

During that season I conducted a joint dowsing/psychic experiment. With Jane working in secret from the psychic angle, I determined the location of future crop circles by following the geodetic lines marked by the first crop circles. The idea was to prove the human ability to connect with the Circlemakers using intuitive channels. I pinpointed nine major formations around Wiltshire to an accuracy of within two fields of where the formations appeared (see figure 13.16). The predictions were lodged with either Colin Andrews or Paul Vigay. As that season reached its climax, I predicted a major design near the steep slopes of Roundway; unknown to me, so had Jane, Isabelle, and Paul. Jane and I decided to scout the area.

My chosen field looked disappointingly quiet. Jane felt the field to the south was more "active," so we watched it from the hilltop, as a movement of anticlockwise energy swirled above the motionless golden crop like liquid air. It was like nothing I had ever seen. Jane predicted that the formation would appear within thirty-six hours, in the early hours of Saturday morning. Rubbing my hands with glee, and without revealing the intended destination, I made a Saturday morning reservation with my pilot.

Given this much advance notice, you would think we could stage a night-watch and film the circle forming. Well, that was the plan. Come Friday night, coffee was poured into thermos, brandy into flask, fleece blankets were rolled

---

[155]Most trance channelers do not remember the communication when revived from trance because the information cannot be processed logically. Once the mind reaches an altered state, the analytical brain is not aware of consciousness because physical body, mind, and soul are operating at different vibratory rates.

up. But as the moment drew closer, our group succumbed to a sudden and inexplicable fatigue, and we were unable to muster any strength to leave the house. Even the prospect of capturing a crop circle forming on film could not motivate us to stay awake. Ironically, we would have a genuine counterpart to the crop circle that, three years earlier, had been filmed barely a mile away at Oliver's Castle for the infamous video hoax (see chapter 7).

But such are the coincidences in this phenomenon.

At first light on Saturday morning, I eagerly made my way to the mist-draped airstrip. My pilot was skeptical. "Save your money. There's no crop circle at Roundway, Freddy. I flew there at 8 P.M. last night. Trust me."

"No, trust *me*, make for that field," I replied. As we flew over Roundway, the curtains of early morning haze fell away as if greeting us with a delicate curtsey.

"Bloody hell!" exclaimed the pilot (see figure 13.17).

During a channeling session a few days later, Jane Ross was told that we had been kept away that night because the energy required to manifest the Roundway glyph would have "fried" anyone in its vicinity. The dowsing response seems to confirm that this had been one of the most powerful formations. With about one hundred feet still between me and the perimeter wall, I counted 300 concentric rings of energy, the most ever. Shortly after, I lost count and concentration. I barely managed to dowse for seven minutes before succumbing to extreme nausea and mental fatigue, as did Jane, who also suffered

dehydration; a third member of our party wouldn't even enter the field. . . .

Another aspect of Jane's contact with the Circlemakers is to take a few minutes to herself inside crop circles and "check her messages," as I teasingly call it. The communication she receives varies in content, sometimes revealing the purpose behind the design, sometimes revealing something about its creators. She received the following at the torus formation (1997): "This circle is given for healing the heart chakra, for cleansing deeply held pain and restoring joy within." I subsequently encountered a dozen people who each described a lifting of weight and a sense of emotional cleansing in this crop circle. Some even cried. Jane's channeled message was not revealed to anyone at the time.

At the "Ant" (1997), Jane received this information: "This was made by insect-types . . . the legs are pointing to areas of overall activation. This circle is directly connected to a wide ley line between two old trees at the head of the

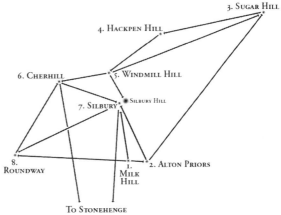

Figure 13.16

Map of crop circles in central Wiltshire during 1999, shown in order of appearance. After the first formation at Milk Hill, each location was subsequently predicted by dowsing.

Figure 13.17

Psychic connection with the Circlemakers. Roundway, 1999.

A short while later she joined me, looking perplexed: "I'm supposed to do a healing session here."

"On what?" I inquired, not looking up as I scribbled some notes.

"On you."

That brought me up short. I was as astonished as she was puzzled. I knew the Pythagoreans associated the pentagonal design with healing power, but little did I know how much. I prepared for meditation, lying on my back, legs slightly apart, arms by my side with palms facing the soil. However, facing the palms downward somewhat compromises their receptivity during meditation—the palms contain points close to the surface of the skin that allow access to the body's electrical matrix. Nevertheless, I do this with my palms so as not to expose my inner elbows, a legacy from my childhood when I received so many injections that, to this day, outstretching my arms with the joints exposed proves torturous. And so I relaxed, closed my eyes and let my mind be still; Jane stood quietly about twelve feet away. Then, unusual things began to happen.

There was a tremendous pressure on my chest, as if an elephant had mistaken it for a footstool. It wasn't painful, just dense. The pressure built for minutes, followed by a sudden

field. It is also aligned to old megalithic sites— Winchester Hill, tumuli, and long barrows. The whole area is being reactivated, and the ley lines are very strong." This would be corroborated by the dowsing performed by Richard Andrews and myself (see chapter 12). Jane's geographical referencing and historical understanding was also correct, quite an achievement for someone who's a stranger to the area.

Two communications by Jane stand out in particular because of the attendant circumstances. The first happened in the Bourton "Star" (1997) below Easton Hill (see figure 13.18 on page A14 in the color section). We walked into this pentagram crop glyph just as the early evening sky bore an unusual platinum-tinged turquoise hue, washing the gently rolling landscape more akin to New Mexico. I wandered away into the formation leaving Jane to check her messages in peace.

slow release of weight down my spine, along my legs and out through my toes, as if a bucket of treacle was literally oozing out through my feet. My body began to feel as light as a feather.

A grip now took hold of my forearms and both my arms began to rotate outwards and lock, my palms exposed to the sky. But for the first time in my life I felt no panic, and accepted the situation with uncharacteristic calm. A tingling sensation ran around the perimeter of my out-stretched body; a singular point of energy mean-dered rapidly in and out of every finger, around my head, my shoulders, down my legs. Every nerve-ending tingled with life. A mental image now appeared: a group of Native American eld-ers, their faces embodying wisdom, skin cracked like dry river mud. Beside them, a young woman dressed in buckskin kept a steady beat on a tribal drum.

Slowly, the image dissipated, superseded by an intense purple light emanating from a distant point and making a beeline into my forehead. This was followed by such intense pressure that my head tilted back-wards as if something was physi-cally trying to drill its way in. My windpipe stretched, my breathing strained. Then it was over.

Forty minutes had elapsed. I got to my feet a little dazed and with obvious discomfort in my forehead. Jane looked amazed: "There is a gathering of Native American tribes here: Red Eagle, Dancing Bear, Spotted Owl, Black Elk, Grandfather Coyote—they're all here."

"There was this woman—"I started to say, but Jane completed the sentence, describing her in detail. "She is the keeper of the rhythm." Jane then documented the incidences that occurred throughout the event, every one of which I could match with a physical experience: The elders had gathered the energy to enter my heart chakra, enabling all negative emotions to be squeezed out through my feet ("like thick, black tar oozing out of your feet"); they reenergized my chakra system ("like an electric field running around your body"); finally, they focused a beam of purple light con-taining information through Jane's hands into my forehead. "I was very nervous about this," she said. "I was afraid you might get hurt because there was a lot of concentrated energy going into this beam."

Throughout the following week we would hear accounts from eight other visitors to this

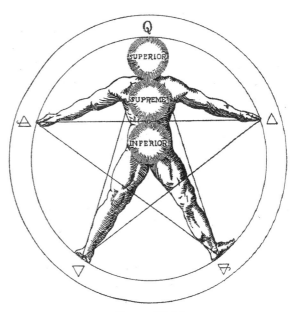

Figure 13.19

The pentagram's relationship to the human body. The five-pointed star is also emblematic of the Christed indi-vidual, one who has achieved spiritual awareness.

site who either reported a sense of well-being or had the feeling of being healed. Two days later, my forehead still aching from the session in the "Star," I met with Colin Andrews for a debriefing, whereupon I announced plans to play a piece of prerecorded music inside a crop circle as a gesture of goodwill, and to ask for guidance as to the connection between sound and crop circles, and how it could be applied in practical terms to benefit others. We looked at photographs of thirty new formations, but none jumped out. "It hasn't arrived yet," I said, rather surprised by my own statement.

Two weeks and several impressive glyphs later I still felt no tug. Then on a sparkling Saturday morning we walked into the field at Etchilhampton, already home to the "Grid Square." A hundred feet away lay a second crop circle. I had a sudden sense of *déjà vu*. "This is it. This is where I need to do my music experiment. This is the Atlantean six-petaled flower," I whispered to my colleague (see figure 13.20 on page A14 in the color section). Neither of us knew what an Atlantean flower was, yet I spoke the words with conviction. Jane had entered ahead of us and was sitting at the opposite end, checking her messages; as we quietly unpacked measuring tapes and pads of paper, she walked over.

"So what did they say?" I asked.

"It's strange. The message is for you. They said: 'The Light flows all around you. Wrap yourself with its healing power. Lyra [the constellation associated with sound] shall reveal the music of

Figure 13.21

5:6:7 geometric relationship encoded in the "Flower."

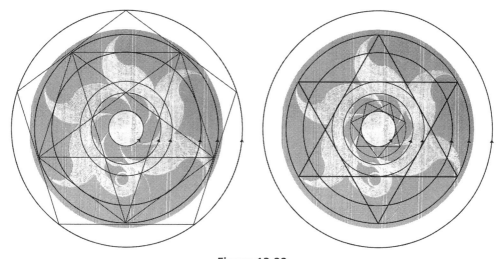

Figure 13.22

5:6:7 geometry relative to the six concentric rings of energy (arrowed circles) discovered in the "Lotus" glyph.

the cosmos should you just ask for it. Wrap yourself in the petals of this flower and the awareness that music becomes light shall be clear to you.'"

With the odd hair still standing on end, I returned to the field alone later that night. The darkness was impenetrable, to the point that I missed the formation and had to walk up and down four different tram lines before I found it. Half an hour later I finally reached the "Flower's" perimeter, and a tingle of energy danced upon my fingertips as I walked through its "door." The wind and the persistent drizzle abruptly stopped.

I sat the tape recorder down and played the music, specially picked as a thank you for the Circlemakers' works of wonder. I couldn't send them a bouquet but I knew for certain they would receive the music, and I expected nothing except illumination. I closed my eyes and let things happen.

Despite the darkness I sensed an intense bright light hovering over me. It included all colors and its intensity was such that my eyelids began to flutter. Admittedly, at this point, the idea of running away was even more intense, so I reminded myself of the benevolence of the source and the sense of guidance that had so far accompanied me on my quest for knowledge. Thus reassured, I continued—with eyes firmly shut. By the time the light dimmed, my shoulders had tensed up. With the back of my head resting against the damp wheat, I experienced a whack to the back of my neck. There was no pain, but my body lost its tension as if a nerve was unpinched, releasing all my trepidation. A sense of distance between body and ground ensued, my arms floating beside me, as if I were suspended horizontally above the ground.

Still conscious, I saw six figures. They were very tall, dressed in long, draping, satin gowns, and they stood on either side of me, watching me, as if transferring knowledge without uttering a word. Behind them, two others directed things with flowing gestures of the hand. I couldn't make out their faces and it didn't matter. I felt perfectly protected, wrapped in a blanket of unconditional love. Again I felt the tingling energy wrap my body, this time running slowly up, down, and across my outstretched left hand, up my arm, eventually inching to the right and across my entire body. The sequence of events must have lasted forty minutes, for when I finally opened my eyes the tape had just stopped.[156]

For a brief moment I had the privilege of penetrating the veil, and in that moment I gained an awareness that music becomes light. This illumination came to me slowly, and would eventually lead me to write this book, something I had never set out to do in my lifetime, at least not consciously.

On one level, the hidden geometry of the "Flower" glyph may have facilitated my interdimensional experience. A shape is an expression of the energies working within it, and in this particular case what lies encoded in the design is the harmonic 5:6:7, the relationship between living things, non-living things, and Spirit (expressed geometrically by the pentagram, the hexagon, and the heptagon). For life to evolve on a planet, things need to be in harmony. On Earth this harmony is 5:6, the relationship between its retrograde precession cycle and its equatorial nautical miles. Completing the formula is seven, the geometry of the Soul, and a key with which the self-aware soul is infused into the physical body (Myers and Percy 1999).

Eventually, my attention began to wander from the "Flower" to the "Grid Square" lying beside it, the pair suggesting a visual analog of right-brain spirituality and left-brain logic. Was there another illuminating piece of evidence waiting there, specifically an explanation to the thump on my neck and the levitation of my body?

Knowledge of antigravity and levitation may have survived in Tibet.[157] An account from the late 1920s describes a ceremony performed by monks standing in a semi-circle around a large boulder. Blowing trumpets and banging drums, they created a tone that levitated the rock up a steep cliff (Illion 1997). Measurements of the arrangement of the instruments relative to the boulder were found to contain specific harmonics which could propel the rock skywards, a process since repeated in laboratory experiments in America using ultrasound, albeit with much smaller objects (Cathie 2001).

Around that time, a five-foot-tall Latvian named Edward Leedskalnin single-handedly erected a castle in Florida made from coral blocks, some weighing as much as thirty tons. He theorized that all matter consists of magnets, and the movement of magnetism in materials

---

[156]It is possible that the light was not above me, but inside me. When the pineal gland is stimulated by ultrasound and by fluctuations in the electromagnetic field, it vibrates at a rapid speed, creating a bio-luminescent effect as well as a humming noise. This would also explain the humming in my right ear which became more pronounced after that night. Furthermore, my experience was not so much of a vision of another world, but the sensation of actually being there, and far more realistic than I could account for in a dream state, as if my being had been momentarily freed from the anchor of gravity and drifted into another level of reality.

[157]Levitation is a feat associated with avatars, who mastered the laws of the Universe and so were capable of transcending the limitations imposed by gravity. Jesus is known to have "walked on the waters," and many images of him show his feet not touching the ground; the same is said of Buddha.

and space gives rise to the electromagnetic Universe. By altering the local electromagnetic field, and consequently gravity, Leedskalnin was able to raise and move colossal blocks of rock effortlessly.

Engineer Christopher Dunn explains: "If we assume, as Leedskalnin did, that all objects consist of individual magnets, we also can assume that an attraction exists between these objects due to the inherent nature of a magnet seeking to align its opposite pole to another. Perhaps Leedskalnin's means of working with the Earth's gravitational pull was nothing more complicated than devising a means by which the alignment of magnetic elements within his coral blocks was adjusted to face the streams of individual magnets he claimed are streaming from the Earth with a like repelling pole" (Dunn 1998).

Had my body in the crop circle also been influenced by magnetic elements? Many of us recall the science experiment in school in which an iron bar is aligned to magnetic north and struck; the blow vibrates the atoms and allows them to be influenced by and align themselves to the Earth's magnetic field. As strange as it may seem, the human body is a type of iron bar because of the large amount of iron in the blood. The night I experienced levitation, I had instinctively lain down inside one of the "Flower's" petals and parallel to a tram line, itself oriented to magnetic north.[158] Essentially, I became the metal bar awaiting a thump. Further, the human body is two-thirds water, and water molecules (a marriage of hydrogen and oxygen), when excited by pressure and given a rapid rate of spin, can be levi-

tated; and ultrasound can supply that needed pressure.

Christopher Dunn's assessment of Leedskalnin's *modus operandi* suggests he had generated a single-frequency, tunable radio signal which, when emitted from the speakers suspended on a wire frame above the rock, achieved the same kind of vibrational effect as a blow with a hammer. This allowed Leedskalnin to vibrate the atoms in the rock and realign their magnetic orientation. Once they were attuned to Earth's magnetic grid he only had to produce a second frequency which enabled the mass of the stones to briefly disengage from the gravitational pull—making them light as a feather.

In this, the Etchilhampton "Flower," like all crop circles, had a distinct advantage in that it already occupied a node on the Earth's geodetic energy stream.

The question now was, where could the two frequencies be coming from? When Jane Ross and I earlier had sat inside the "Grid Square" we recorded an oscillating, high-pitched tone. Its purpose was later made clear during a channeling session: "The frequency of the note that they gave us is important . . . to be used in the opening process. It's a frequency that needs to be used to complete the opening for the individual."

That note—F-sharp—creates an unusual oscillating effect between the two cavities of the brain, especially when generated by the tuned resonant cavity of a quartz crystal bowl. It has a frequency of 5.8 kHz and is traditionally associated with the tone of the Earth; this is a whisker away from that other frequency

---

[158]This brings to mind an unusual instruction in Tablet XIII of *The Emerald Tablets of Thoth, the Atlantean:* "Whilst thy head is placed to the northward, hold thou thy consciousness from the chest to the head."

associated with crop circles—the trilling noise—and its frequency of 5.2 kHz, equivalent to E-flat/E.

F-sharp happens to be the resonant frequency inside the Grand Gallery of the Great Pyramid at Gizeh, and the floor of that corbelled chamber is inclined at an angle of 26.3027°, making its vertical height twenty-eight feet and the height perpendicular to the floor twenty-five feet. Interestingly, all these numbers (as well as other connections to this edifice) are referenced in the "Grid Square."

The two heights of the Grand Gallery are equivalent to the tones F-sharp and E-flat (Hero 1992), which are the "Grid Square" hum and the trilling noise, respectively. So the Circlemakers and the Pyramid designers appear to share the same technology. The Great Pyramid is a harmonically tuned acoustic resonator within whose chambers the magnetic field drops to nearly zero, and in which hydrogen is said to have played a key role. Its acoustics and geometries generate vibrations that interact with its environment, both seen and unseen—its effects on the molecules of steel, meat, and particularly water are already well known. Further, it is more than idle conjecture that the pyramid builders had the technology to neutralize the effects of gravity (Dunn 1998; Tompkins 1988; Toth and Nielsen 1985). The effects of such vibrations on the molecules of the human body alone would be considerable, not to mention the effects on its brainwave patterns. Essentially, the Great Pyramid contains the necessary ingredients that make it a kind of transformational, possibly interdimensional temple.

Due to their strategic positioning on the Earth's energy grid, their encoded geometries, their electromagnetic frequencies (particularly 1.5 GHz, the frequency of hydrogen), and their effects on water and the human body, crop circles can be likened to harmonic resonators which act sympathetically on the planetary and human body as all three operate on the same natural laws.[159]

My levitation experience in the "Flower" would suggest that I was being shown a manipulation of gravity; gravity is linked to the illusion of time, and time is known to be affected inside crop circles. And since crop circles are delivered to us within a tube of spiraling light energy, the vibratory actions contained within this tube at one end provides a mechanism for making plants spiral down into harmonic shapes or, as I experienced, a window for body and soul to connect more freely with other levels of reality.

I was suddenly reminded of the words from the Watchers: "This energy is only partially linked to magnetism. It is linked to the illusion of time. Rather like thought-transference, man will be able to change the molecular structure of things, including himself." How it echoes the sentiments of Thoth in Egypt, thousands of years before, "Man is in the process of changing to forms that are not of this world . . . ye must become formless before ye are one with the light."

Nine months after Etchilhampton I visited Jane at her home in America where she channeled more information concerning my experiences that

---

[159]A resonant cavity is any contained space which allows a prolonged vibration to take place. Resonance is essentially the vibration of a body exposed to another vibration of similar frequency.

night. The Circle-makers involved in the creation of the "Flower" explained they had adjusted my body so that it could receive the information. This was a "scanning"; the beings described their positions relative to my body as well as the two additional figures who had been directing the procedure—exactly as I had experienced it, but had never men-

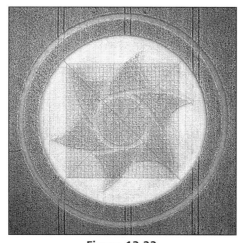

Figure 13.23

The precise referencing of the "Grid Square" glyph inside the "Flower."

tioned to Jane. Then came another revelation, this time concerning the purpose of the "Grid Square" and *its* creators, who turned out to be yet another group of beings; as the Watchers said, there are now many other forms expressing themselves via crop circles.

"This is a highly scientific group . . . they're navigators; they're positioners. . . . They plot the locations in the etheric and the physical of particular types of openings or availabilities of portals through which light and information become available. This 'Grid' was the first crop circle they have ever laid down. They give information to those who can receive it. This particular 'Grid' contains the clues to where the next available opening will be for the information coming through to be received by humans who have their 'antennae' out.

"This information is critical. . . . It is coded,

but individuals are able to understand and decode it through their instinct, or gut level, as you would call it. It's information concerning what is happening as we go through the new energy shift. So it is of a predictive and useful quality in terms of what is coming and how to prepare for it. This 'Grid' was the first reference.

"I see the 'Grid' as four triangles pointing to the center, and there is something to do with the area of each triangle. Open the triangles like petals, pull them outward, take that area and translate it into kilometers, and go out in each direction that many kilometers, and you will find a point. There will be an opening at each one of those four directions. Now they are saying that you can go off on those lines, in any of the four directions, in sequences of royal cubits, and anywhere on those lines you will find an opening point. [The] points [repeat] all around the globe. The date [for the openings] is some combination of the number of squares [in the crop circle]. They will be available on the full moon cycle of 27.2–28 days.[160]

"They did not do the one behind this one [the "Flower"]. [It] was created by a different energy entirely but is related geometrically, but

---

[160]Russian scientists have found that when the Moon is in its full phase, ESP flows more naturally in humans. This occurs every 27.2 days. Could 27.2 be a reference to 2.72, the number of transformation? Also, 27 is the number conspicuous by its absence in the "grid square" crop glyph.

Figure 13.24

Boethian scale of music notation.

Middle Ages in which the Latin alphabet is super-imposed over the diatonic (white) notes of the key-board. In his last fugue, for exam-ple, Johann Sebastian Bach repeats the notes B-A-C-H. On a hunch, Hawkins took the notes found in crop circles geometrics and applied them to the scale using the English alphabet. He ended up with sets of initials that seemed to repeat, but whose initials were they?

not by information. They did it there because they felt they needed to be linked to the other one. If the 'Grid' was by itself it would not be taken seriously, so they linked it with a beauti-fully executed crop circle for validity. It was necessary to decode that crop circle so we could get on with the different kind of openings that will be occurring."

One can now see the relevance of Vitruvius' famous diagram of the outstretched man bisect-ing the square in four directions, as well as the references to measure encoded within the "Grid Square." These bring to mind the earlier associ-ation with the Egyptian town of Saqqara, named after the god of orientation, for the grid was tra-ditionally used for transcribing the order of the heavens upon the physical Earth. This connec-tion between Circlemakers and ancient Egyptian gods was conveyed at the end of Jane's channel-ing: "They keep repeating, 'As above, so below.'"

Jane's readings reaffirm the Watchers' mes-sage of how the crop circles are not attributed to only one agency. Evidence of another type of intelligent group consciousness behind crop cir-cles comes from Gerald Hawkins.

While looking for diatonic ratios, Hawkins recalled that musicians have used the notes of the first octave to encode messages in their music. One of these codes is known as the Boethian, a system of letter notation from the

If a message is being communicated, the logical approach is to consider the initials as belonging to a group. After much referencing to heads of state, popes, and other prominent individuals, no matches were found. Hawkins then noticed how the initials "OL" kept pop-ping up.

Oliver Lodge was a prominent physicist who, among many outstanding achievements, discovered radio (he later sold the patent to Marconi who of course got the credit). In 1910, he devoted his research to psychic phenomena in general, such as the possibility of communi-cation with the departed, and eventually he became one of the presidents of the British Society for Psychic Research. Shortly before he passed away in 1940 (at Lake, ten miles from Stonehenge, and now home to the musician Sting), Lodge wrote down the details of an experiment whereby he would communicate from the other side of the veil.

This experiment, to prove that the spirit and its memory survive after death, was sealed inside seven envelopes and placed inside a safe at the Society. It used a musical code based upon a piano exercise Lodge had learned as a child and which had since become a trivial obsession known only to himself: whenever he was bored, he would rap his fingertips on any surface in that particular sequence.

So was Lodge communicating to us through crop circles? That was certainly the impression formed when the initials "O. L." appeared again in another crop glyph (see figure 13.25). Encoded in that design was Lodge's tapping code—3-3-6-1-2: 3 paws, 3 legs, 6 spokes, 1 central disk, and 2—the ratio of rings containing Hawkins' Theorem III. When Hawkins cross-referenced the remaining sets of initials, they fitted one list only: the first twenty-five presidents of the Society for Psychical Research.

These were by no means your average suburbanites gathering once a month for hocus pocus in the parlor. The group included Charles Richet, Nobel Prize-winner for medicine; John Strutt, Nobel Prize-winner for physics; William Crookes, creator of the cathode ray tube; Henry Sidgwick, ethics philosopher and Society founder; Camille Flammarion, renowned astronomer; and Bishop Boyd Carpenter, chaplain to Queen Victoria, just to name a few. This was a brain trust.

The method employed in the coding is reminiscent of Freemasonic practice in which information is veiled in symbols, often multilayered in meaning. For example, the crop formation at Fordham Place (see figure 13.26) by Euclidean logic gives diatonic ratios 5:2 and 6 (or G sec-

Figure 13.25
Berwick Bassett, 1994.

Figure 13.26
Fordham Place, 1990.

Figure 13.27
Littlebury Green, 1996.

ond octave, and E first octave) which by the keyboard code gives "J. S." for John Strutt, whose estate was ten miles away from the crop circle. Its pattern is based on the vesica piscis and the shape of medieval seals of office, and if the pattern itself is taken as a seal, its impression in wax creates a stylized monogram bearing the initials "JS." The crop circle at Littlebury Green (1996) gives one more name on the list: Frederic Myers, a founder of the Society and a pioneer in telepathy (see figure 13.27).

As with the diatonic ratios, what are the odds of all of this happening by chance?

"With twenty-six letters in the alphabet there are 1/2 x 26 x 27 possible pairs of initials, A. A., A. B., A. C., etc," says Hawkins. "So the probability of any one random pair hitting any one of the twenty-five names on the list is 25/(1/2 x 26 x 27) = 0.071. There are nine geometries with nine hits. By Bernoulli's binomial theorem the probability is a significant 1.7 billion-to-one in favor of our hypothesis."

What are the crop circles telling us about reality? On one level they remind us that the mind is powerful, to the extent that combined with intent, it is capable of producing extraordinary circumstances and influencing events (Rhine 1970). Reality itself is a construct of the mind. This has been the teaching of avatars and mystics since time immemorial, and progressive scientists are now beginning to agree. Our view of reality, therefore, is crucial to the way the Universe develops. As the children's fable says, every time someone says "I don't believe in fairies," somewhere a fairy dies.

The astronomer David Darling expresses this elegantly in his *Equations of Eternity:* "The conscious mind is crucially involved in establishing what is real. That which reaches our senses is, at best, a confusion of phantasmal energies—not sights, not sounds, or any of the coherent qualities that we project outward onto the physical world. The Universe as we know it is built and experienced entirely within our heads, and until that mental construction takes place, reality must wait in the wings."

As such, if our thoughts preclude that no other life forms exist in the Universe except our own, the energy of that thought has serious consequences at some level. This is already established in quantum physics. As the eminent physicist David Bohm discovered, electrons are aware of each other; likewise, the physicist John Bell confirmed that two photons once in contact, though flying apart at the speed of light, remain in contact with each another. By virtue that we too are part of a collective consciousness, our thoughts of fear and denial may be hindering the progress of other forms of life, and so these entities are now making us aware that they exist.[161] Through their crop circles they are nudging us to raise our vibrational rate so that we experience this understanding.

Ancient philosophies maintain that our thoughts generate the physical world, just as God is said to have used the power of thought to generate the light and the sound that manifest as the Universe. If we can acknowledge that an unseen cosmic intelligence is manifesting itself at this critical phase in time, the Circlemakers—be they past prominent humans, entities from diverse star systems, our own group consciousness, or the Watchers, our guiding ancestors—will have succeeded in reminding us that we are part of a greater reality. Just as our thoughts can create actions, so those actions ripple throughout the world, creating consequences undetected by scientific instruments or our normal senses of perception. By taking the view that "reality" is made up of an infinite series of energy bundles, our view of the Universe can open up to all manner of possibilities.

If we can accept the possibility that there is still much information to be extracted from crop circles, as Isabelle Kingston predicts, then we would do well to consider the words of another visionary human, Nicola Tesla: "The day science begins to study nonphysical phenomena it will make more progress in one decade than in all the previous centuries of its existence." With positive progress already reported in the field of resonance therapy, that decade may be nearer than we think. The nudge from our benevolent friends in more refined places may provide us with a lifeline to help reverse the degradation of what nineteenth-century industrialists once arrogantly called "this exploitable, lifeless lump of rock." In the process we may even rediscover something called faith.

Dowser Hamish Miller recalls how during his work on the geodetic lines and crop circles he had the distinct impression of being observed: "I am a practical, well-earthed being, earning my living as a blacksmith, but I had to concede after

---

[161]Phyllis Schlemmer, in Stuart Holroyd's *Prelude to the Landing on Planet Earth.*

some time that the number of the 'Watchers' seemed to increase. Later we even appeared to hear a slight susurrus of discussion round us."

Miller discussed this with Alex Neklessa, a Russian scientist working with the paranormal, particularly with experiments on regression to find out what went wrong with previous civilizations. "An astonishing result seemed to indicate a probability that, in certain cases, two or three parallel realities existed at the same time. If this was the case, and it appears to be more than idle conjecture, is it possible that in our time such a situation could occur? And if so, could a group of highly intelligent and technically advanced beings, living in parallel with us, but in a slightly different time frame, be a little concerned about how we in our wisdom are treating our planetary parent body? And are we receiving a gentle nudge to make us aware that we are not alone, and that we have responsibilities to a wider concept of beings than we have been aware of up 'til now" (Miller 1992)?

Our world consists of hierarchies: in the biological functions of the body, the octaves of music, in a plant community from forest floor to canopy. Just as our hearing and vision are limited in comparison to other species, so must we recognize that different "hierarchies" exist beyond our perception.

Angels describe realms to which our normal senses have no access. Perhaps the Sanskrit writers had this in mind when they created their equivalent of angel—the *deva,* the "shining one."

Gerald Hawkins sums this up with an understatement: "If crop circles are made by hoaxers, then they should stop doing it, because they are breaking the law and damaging the food supply. If they are made by UFO aliens, they shouldn't give us back the dates of our trips to Mars and the names of men from the Titanic era—famous, clever, but now forgotten. If some are transcendental, the power behind it should realize that our culture is not now willing to accept transcendental happenings.

"But if they are indeed transcendental, then society will have to make a big adjustment in the years ahead."

CODA

And (it shall come to pass in the last days), I will show wonders in the heavens above, and signs in the earth beneath.

—The Acts of the Apostles 2:19

In 1901, science discovered that a whole spectrum of color and light exists beyond violet, a spectrum beyond our range of vision. This limitation did not deter the theosophist and clairvoyant C. W. Leadbeater who, around the same period, described in precise detail the finer layers of reality, such as the color and shape of emotions, and the yet-to-be discovered structure of sub-atomic particles (Besant and Leadbeater 1901).

It would be several decades before physicists such as Neils Bohr, aided by the latest technology, made sufficient strides in understanding the map of the atom for the rest of the world to catch up with Leadbeater's "mental" pictures of worlds beyond our physical perception. Forays into the structure of the atom indeed reveal this smallest of particles to consist of other, finer elements—nuclei and shells, which in turn consist of protons, neutrons, and electrons, which are themselves physicalizations of even more refined particles.

The point here is that not only do solid and undeniable scientific facts have a tendency to give way to new perceptions, they also have a stubborn tendency to mirror mysticism. In this case, the hierarchies that sustain the spiritual firmament of woman and man are reflected in the physical world, precisely as Helen Blavatsky stated: "Matter is Spirit at its lowest level, and Spirit is matter at its highest level."

Scientist and shaman, it appears, are aboard separate buses en route to being reunited at the bus station.

While this journey is underway modern culture wrestles with the dilemma posed by the unseen and the "unusual." As Louis Charpentier pointed out, "Science, being the power of the day, has condemned esoteric intellect as occult, dangerous, evil and untrustworthy" (Charpentier 1975). Yet intellect, or *intus lectio,* means "the gift of reading from within," and occult means "that which is hidden from view," which demonstrates how logic and language can obscure our ability to understand. Thus, the overemphasis on rationality is limiting our reality to what can only be seen or touched.

Some will say that crop circles *are* occult, even dangerous, but then the act of consecrating the sacrament at a Christian mass can be deemed just as occult to a Tibetan monk who communicates directly with God through meditation. As the physicist Fritjof Capra puts it: "A page from a journal of modern experimental physics will be as mysterious to the uninitiated as a Tibetan mandala. Both are records of enquiries into the nature of the Universe" (Capra 1986).

Hardly surprising, then, that today's culture struggles to accept the unseen. The new gods of television and marketing are modifying humans from a feeling, hearing race, into a seeing race led by image and fed by statistics. Ironically, this insistence on superficiality as the glue of reality is reducing our ability to "see." To quote Berendt: "No longer do we see the world, we see its images—and unbelievably enough, we are content with that, content with looking at moving pictures. Living almost exclusively through the eyes has led us to almost not living at all" (Berendt 1991).

Cooperation between humanity and the unseen once formed the true foundation of religion, a reminder that faith in the higher faculties has always sought to be of service for and not against humanity. But herded into a cultural amnesia (some would even say brainwashed) by misguided dogma, we have slowly abandoned the spiritual platform, and for centuries this helpful facility has lain fallow. Today we are overrun by triviality and littered with the transient icons of TV culture—a culture so distorted by endless graphic violence that it has even defined two people enthralled in the natural act of making love as irresponsible, even pornographic. Given such a skewed platform it is hardly surprising that when syllables from a cre-ative Universe appear surreptitiously as crop circles, they are not always looked upon with benevolence.

As we've learned from the Watchers, somewhere along the path we have chosen to take the darker road, for just as the Neolithic worldview once favored the receptive, female nature of humanity, so the past few thousand years have reversed in favor of the male, replacing intuition with rationality, cooperation with competition, and compassion with aggression. And now that much of the ancients' original knowledge is lost, all that remains is superstition.

From the moment we open our first textbooks we are still educated within the confines of an outmoded mechanistic worldview. As the brilliant Egyptologist John Anthony West points out, this worldview has preoccupied the education system with quantitative results that fill heads with data at the expense of understanding. Yet the most wondrous elements in the Universe—love and inspiration—continuously fail to be measured, scientifically proved, or quantitatively analyzed, so according to science these states shouldn't exist either (West 1993).

Let us remember that the theories and "laws" of natural phenomena are at best our concepts of reality, rather than reality itself. Such laws are mutable, always destined to be replaced by more accurate laws as experience and understanding is improved. Even Einstein, despite his preoccupation with the stolid acres of physics, believed in a force beyond the quantifiable: "As far as the laws of mathematics refer to reality, they are not certain; and as far as they are certain, they do not refer to reality."

At the start of this book, our rational minds, too, were challenged by this new experience called crop circles, which our vocabulary could not easily define. Now, through the experience of thousands of individuals and validation from the words of the Watchers, we have a greater understanding of their purpose and process. Far from being new, the indications are that this process was known to our Neolithic ancestors and to the ancient Egyptians, cultures that survived for thousands of years because they were founded on an intimate cooperation between physical and spiritual worlds.

Hence the crop circles' relationship with the sacred sites and the interconnected energy grid reminds us that their original purpose was to facilitate a closer connection with other levels of reality, and in so doing, show us how to reawaken the spiritual temples within us and recognize that we need to be more accepting of Spirit.

As Capra said: "Whenever we expand the realm of our experience, the limitations of our rational mind become apparent and we have to modify, or even abandon, some of our concepts." In light of the appearance of crop circles as thoughts from other forms of life, perhaps we need now modify our perception of reality. For years, NASA has sent out radio signals based on unmistakable artificial frequencies to tell other civilizations of our existence. When decoded, these pulses translate into the figure of a human being. Is it really too far-fetched to assume the Circlemakers are applying a similar technique whenever they manifest symbols whose sheer magnetism and euphonious language competes with the best poetry for superlatives?

Perhaps science awaits a suitable medium with which to quantify crop circles; after all, microbes have been around for billions of years yet only with the invention of the microscope was their existence accepted.

Crop circles, like the paradoxes of Zen, are puzzles that cannot be totally solved by logic. To uncover their truth, an awareness based on feeling has to be applied. As symbols, crop circles are comparable to classical Chinese word, which does not represent a well-defined concept but rather a sound symbol of strongly suggestive power that elicits a library of images and emotions, the point being not so much to express an intellectual idea but affect and influence the listener (Capra 1986).

Just as the high civilization that once was Atlantis imploded due to an imbalance of logic over heart, so our unbalanced civilization draws toward its climax. As it does so, the alternating rhythm of the Universe inevitably swings us toward a more harmonious state. These changes are already underway, and ideas that were once seen as improbable and beyond comprehension about the way the Universe works are now seriously entertained.

Amid this ebb of change appear the crop circles, punctuating the timeless landscape, mysterious as the first lightbulb, alien, and yet strangely at home among the Wessex terrain.

Was the choice of location haphazard? The Circlemakers could have chosen China, but would its political control of information allow the message to cross its borders?[162] Or Australia, with its sparse, endless terrain, but would anyone

---

[162]To demonstrate the point, information has only recently reached the West that China is home to a significant number of pyramids, some of which rival those of Egypt.

be there to see the signs? Or America, with its country-sized grain fields, but would its capitalist ideology allow the sharing of information only to the highest bidders?

I am often asked why there seem to be few crop circles reported on U.S. soil despite the bulk of land available. Maybe it's a matter of attitude. Unlike their Canadian counterparts, farmers in Indiana have been more preoccupied with looking for somebody to sue rather than investigating the cause of markings in head-high corn fields, which were cordoned off with police tape as if they were crime scenes. Perhaps for them they were. Likewise in Missouri, crop circles appearing on Amish lands are methodically destroyed before witnesses are able to take photographs. Should you ask them to photograph, the normally placid Amish will threaten to fine you $1500.

With this kind of welcome, few would want to knock on your door.

If contact with nonhuman life continues to follow the U.S. military's example of researching UFOs—shoot them down and analyze them—then it's no wonder contact needs to be made in more subtle ways with people who appear to have every inclination of behaving like barbarians. Yet compare this attitude with that of "pagans" in South Africa in response to crop circles: "Whenever a circle appeared in the fields, the people rushed to erect a fence of poles around the circle. They would dance and perform other sacred rituals honoring the star gods and the Earth Mother.

All the kings and chiefs awaited the arrival of these circles. Their appearance would be cause for celebrations which lasted several days. The celebrations were accompanied by prayers to the gods to watch over the people and talk to them through the sacred sites" (Mutwa 1996).[163]

The choice of Britain as the prime location for crop circles suggests a well-orchestrated plan. They reference sacred sites in a country brimming with ancient markers, where such sites are still honored, where the study of esoteric knowledge survives, and whose language is understood throughout the world, enabling information to be disseminated on a vast scale.

The other question is why have these "encyclopedias in plants" come to our attention *now?*

Several factors mark our time as more favorable for an interaction between our dimension and others. The Mayan calendar is helpful here. Possibly the most celebrated date in this masterpiece is 2012 A.D. The Maya believed that on the winter solstice of that year, an alignment between our solar system and the Milky Way will trigger a time of spiritual acceleration (Jenkins 1998). Likewise, the Aztec calendar shows that we are at the end of a 13,000-year cycle and that significant changes in the Earth and in human consciousness are predestined like clockwork. Native American prophecies, particularly those of the Hopi, describe this time period as the transition from the "Fifth Age" to the "Sixth Age" of humanity. Their prophecies state

---

[163]One is reminded of dancers in stone circles whose movements between the gaps in the stones can generate bioelectricity, creating a condition similar to a dynamo. The electrical charge is stored in the stones and the underlying water, and released with the approach of new groups of people or the rhythm of the Moon. Hence why there exists such a rich folklore of dancing at sacred sites. Such an effect may also explain the festive mood of people who visit the crop circles.

that in previous transitions a disconnect existed between humanity and Earth, along with a polarization of heart and mind. As the gulf between the two became unbridgeable, a collapse of that Age was necessary to establish a new rhythm of harmony.

That planetary alignments can influence the Earth was demonstrated in 1999. On August 11, an alignment of the Sun and Moon with the center of the Earth created a total eclipse of the Sun across northern Europe; later, on December 12, heliocentric astrological charts showed the planets arranged in three grand trines around the Sun, creating a nine-pointed star alignment in the solar system.[164] Either the crop circles were precursors of such events, or the Circlemakers were pointing to their significance, for 1999 saw crop circles referencing ninefold geometry for the first time; two other formations that summer depicted the path of a Moon eclipsing the Sun.

The charts' originators, Marcus Mason and Brett Kellett, echo the growing belief that geometric astrological aspects such as grand trines are grounding new energies in the Earth: "These stellar archetypes of the Sidereal Zodiac are imprinting into our consciousness through the matrix of the Tropical Zodiac, which holds the akashic record of collective human consciousness and evolution. As the new archetypes imprint, the old archetypes, patterns and paradigms are simply falling away."[165]

Preceding these energy shifts and changes are times of confusion and apparent self-destruction, and few will doubt that we are now living in turbulent times. Gregg Braden sees this as one indication of a vibrationary shift:

> Some individuals feel it rippling throughout every cell in their body, perceiving that time, and their lives, are speeding up. Others are experiencing a new kind of confusion, as if nothing in their lives really fits any longer . . . the systems that provide the infrastructure to life and society, inclusive of personal systems such as health, finance and relationships, are in a state of dynamic flux. . . . Whether you believe in the near-term close of a great cycle or not, one fact remains. Within a relatively short period of human history, regardless of your age, you have witnessed events that rocked the very foundations of who and what you believe your world is about (Braden 1993).

As the new codes of energy imprint themselves upon the crystalline structures of the Earth, changes within Her will trigger systems in the body to follow suit because the human energy field seeks to maintain its umbilical connection with Earth Mother.[166] Midwives capable of seeing auras are reporting seeing a new

---

[164]A Grand Trine on the wheel of the zodiac is where an equilateral triangle links the energies of the cardinal, fixed, and mutable sign associated with each of the four elements (earth, air, fire, water). According to A. T. Mann, the geometrically balanced Grand Trines indicate harmonious states of being, and imply a fluid exchange of energy and communication. Interestingly, in particle physics the triangular shape describes the interaction of the basic force-carrying particles, the *quarks*.

[165]My thanks to Marcus Mason and Brett Kellett. For more of their work see www.astrolore.com/article/0006.

[166]Such an effect is also seen in the way the structures of crystals realign when subjected to a new frequency.

Figure 14.1

To the Hopi, the appearance of the crescent on Earth signifies the return of the Star People. Furze Knoll, 1994.

chakra developing in newborn children, between the throat and the heart, suggesting a shift in communication is underway that will move us closer to the heart than the head.[167] In fact, more children of this generation are being born with exceptional abilities—mental, physical, psychic—further indications that, as a species, we are evolving.

As our vibrational rate increases, life appears to be speeding up in our new experience. The more a person's vibratory field is tuned to these global changes, the greater one's receptivity to transcendental ideas, insight, and thought patterns of a penetrating and global scale (Hunt 1989). And through this, consciousness is changed. Disharmonious frequencies in the body, particularly thought patterns, begin to stand out so they can be attended to and healed. Consequently, a person's light or dark aspects are accentuated; life appears to be chaotic, irritating, and frustrating as our cells learn the new tune. Those resisting the process, particularly if they stubbornly cling to old belief systems, are finding the process even more grueling.

According to chaos theory, an evolutionary transition to a higher state is accompanied by the

---

[167]My thanks to Nicola Morgan for this information.

breakdown of the harmonic field system (order). When new energy is introduced, as is the case with crop circles, it reverses the process of disintegration so that matter can be reorganized and enabled to achieve this higher state (Prigogine and Stengers 1984). Order breaks into chaos that builds into order. As science writer James Gleick explains, "The greater the turbulence, the more complex the solution, the greater the jump to a higher state" (Gleick 1987).

One of the positive effects of these changes is that as our vibratory levels rise to match that of Earth's, portions of our sensory systems that have lain dormant for centuries gradually awaken, giving those who so choose the opportunity to access finer levels of reality.

This brings us to another factor explaining the rise in crop circles. The Earth's magnetic field strength, which rises and falls like a wave, has decreased by 38 percent over the past 2,000 years, and it is predicted to keep falling (Braden 1993). Historically, the construction of sacred sites coincides with the peaks and troughs of this wave (Bucha 1967), indicating that our ancestors were aware of these key moments in the Earth's shifting magnetic field, and used such pivotal moments to experience more rapid development of their consciousness. Possibly for this reason they constructed their sites to double-up as astronomical markers, and remind future generations when these cycles are likely to occur. Since we have neglected to maintain this tradition, crop circles are used as reminders.

These reminders—thought waves, geome-tries, frequencies—are housing themselves on the planet to request our reality to move beyond its limitations, to get us to feel rather than think. The pivotal moment of this communication may have occurred on August 17, 1987, the date of Harmonic Convergence. On that day, it is said the Earth reached a position in the galaxy that would facilitate a shift in human consciousness. It, too, was predicted in the Mayan and Aztec calendars, as well as in Native American lore, as the time when "144,000 Sun-Dance enlightened teachers would awaken to become points of Light to help the rest of humanity dance their dream awake." In essence, the shamans of the world received the call to coax the unenlightened from their sleep.

Not having the faintest idea at the time as to why, on that very day I felt compelled to drive one hundred miles to visit Stonehenge for the first time.

When Native American prophecies speak of this change in cycles, they speak of a time "when the Moon will be seen both on Earth and in Heaven." "We had some circles in Indian reservations in the Northwest of the USA, at places where these UFOs, as you call them, visit us each year. It is possible that a connection exists," said the late Chippewa medicine man Sun Bear.[168] Native American tribes maintain they are descended from the Star Nations, races of beings populating different star systems such as Sirius and Orion;[169] the Sioux, for example, trace their origin to the Seven Sisters of the Pleiades.

---

[168]From a speech at the Star Knowledge Conference, South Dakota; further transcripts in *UFO Reality,* issue 5, Dec. 1996.

[169]A number of sacred sites around Silbury Hill are connected with Sirius, the Teacher, as is the Great Pyramid at Gizeh.

In 1994, the Moon did appear on Earth, when crescents were added to the crop circle alphabet. To the Hopi, in particular, this was an emotional occasion, for it was the sign for the return of the Star Nation people, and a fulfillment of prophecy (see figure 14.1 on page 305). In simultaneous visions around the world, indigenous elders were told the time had come to reveal to the rest of the world the spiritual knowledge of the Star Nations, including the influence of Star People on their cultures and spiritual beliefs. So what better place to announce these ancestral truths than at the one location on Earth where all nations are represented: the United Nations. This supposed seat of global unity responded by adopting an unprecedented closed-door policy towards our indigenous brothers and sisters.

Undaunted, Lakota spiritual leader Standing Elk also made an unprecedented move. He convened a gathering of tribes from all over the world in South Dakota, where the Star Knowledge would be shared with Western representatives from diverse backgrounds. During the course of the five-day affair, Standing Elk made a startling announcement: "The Star Nations were the most crucial of all entities, because the thought of other races communicating with the grassroots people would create a major threat to the religious systems, the economy and the educational system of any government.

"The greatest fear in the governmental structures was the knowledge that all forms of 'Star Government' had no monetary systems within their governing structures. Their system was based on the mental, spiritual and universal laws with which they were too mentally and spiritually intelligent to break. The collapse of the monetary system within the United States government and the religious denominations became a national security issue, and so it became an easier task to make the Lakota/Dakota belief system illegal to participate in and practice."[170]

Oglala spiritual leader Floyd Hand emphasized at the gathering that religious figureheads such as Jesus, Mohammed, and Buddha were related to the Star Nations. But, he added, that as their time drew nearer, if warnings were not heeded and appropriate action not taken, so would global catastrophes escalate.

Such tidings are strangely reminiscent of scriptures in which God reveals Itself to humanity in subtle and helpful ways—miracles, healings, divine laws—but when these hints are ignored, cataclysms are used to wake people up, particularly those at the slowest vibratory levels. In light of these revelations, the falsifying and sabotaging of crop circles, regardless of motive or sponsor, begins to resemble the killing of infants by Herod in a desperate attempt to rid himself of the Christ child who would supplant his authority. For it is clear the crop circles are empowering the individual, and in so doing, helping to dismantle an entrenched belief system that has thrived on fear and the conceived powerlessness of people.

Crop circles do this by providing instructions for self-help. They allow us to see the Universe as a series of relationships between a multitude of parts comprising a whole. They

---

[170]From a speech at the Star Knowledge Conference, South Dakota.

show us we have the ability to influence the out-come of our reality through our thoughts and actions. We are already witnessing this in our laboratories: Experiments at Princeton's Engineering Anomalies Research lab show that people's focused intentions affect such mechan-ical constants as the timing of a computerized drumbeat and the motion of pendulums. Thousands of trials reveal machines' obedience to the thoughts of their human operators, and that the human mind is capable of affecting approximately one in every 10,000 random events (Princeton Engineering Anomalies Research 1995; Jahn and Dunne 1987; Nelson et al. 1998). In fact it is predicted that by the explicit inclusion of human consciousness we shall one day come to understand the true nature of matter (Wigner 1970).

As one note in the chorus of creation, the human being is special. Its thoughts become sounds, sounds become words, words generate actions, and coupled with intent, actions manifest all manner of consequences. This makes every one of us responsible and accountable for what we manifest.[171] Fifteen centuries of European his-tory teaches us that if a greater mass of people hold an overly pessimistic image of the future, chances are that image will manifest as reality. Apocalypses are seldom the result of predictions and more the release of pathological behavior in society which creates the situation in the end (Wall and Fergusson 1998). Humanity's war record of the twentieth century alone is reason enough to want change, but to achieve it we must first overcome the cultural illusion that we are somehow separate from the Creative Spirit.

For more than six thousand years, Eastern and pagan mysticism have shown that we can connect with Spirit through our very own antenna, the human body. Through the simple act of pressing the palms together, fingertip to fingertip, we adopt the pose in countless sculptures of figures frozen in the act of praying, a ritual instinctively practiced a billion times every day throughout the world, without many of its participants being aware that it is an action far beyond a call to prayer: By pressing the palms you are activating an electronic system which connects you with the Oneness of creation and allows you, as a part of that Oneness, to intercede upon your own behalf through your thoughts. As the saying goes, "You have the whole world in your hands."

As more people are made aware of this, they are gathering in groups around the world to pray for change. In 1998, a world-wide prayer led by author James Twyman and dedi-cated to averting war between the U.S. and Iraq attracted an estimated twelve million partici-pants. This focused thought for peace resulted in the stepping down of hostilities the following day; in fact, so successful was the effect that Twyman was subsequently invited to Northern Ireland to repeat the exercise. Within three days, arms were finally laid down and peace negotiations commenced.

With their foundations in divine principles, the crop circles' resurgence at this pivotal moment is precipitating a change. At the birth of a new millennium we are already witnessing more ideas based on hope, sustainability, spiri-tuality, and tolerance taking shape than at any

---

[171]"As he thinketh in his heart, so is he" (Proverbs 23:7).

other period in modern history. For this change to manifest we must participate as co-creators. We have asked for help, we have been offered the tools, and we have been shown how they work, but ultimately, we must have the will to implement them.

Just as music plays a mediating role between Heaven and Earth, so crop circles are communication channels between humanity and God, a communication that speaks passively without threatening or shocking, and by this subtle approach, people's views of the world are gently changed. By their appearance in wheat—prime ingredient of bread and the very symbol of the Earth—crop circles provide a nurturing bond between the Earth Mother and her children gathered within the protective bosom of her circle—a circle that lures us irresistibly towards the center by providing games through which we learn. And, just like children, we go away to process what we've learned in time for a new season of lessons.

Like sound, crop circles are a language of feeling, a language beyond the limitation of words. And being a Universal language, it does not align with any one individual, any one religious system, ethnic group, academic curriculum, or political belief. Like flowers responding unquestioningly to the Sun, those who open their hearts to unconditionally embrace the melody of a crop circle become atoned—they become at-one, and like an unplanned meeting with a holy person, the encounter can irreversibly change their view of life.

Charpentier, in his ode to Gothic cathedrals, felt much the same way as I do about crop circles. They are created by specialists who use knowledge and deliver it as a signature in the fields. They use beauty as a bait, arousing the emotions, luring the intellect to embark on creative thinking. They nourish our souls, and as the Prophet Mohammed said: "If I had only two loaves of bread, I would barter one to nourish my soul."

They are the new temples, places of initiation, incantation, and opening.

They are harmonic creations of light, sound, and magnetism, and so they are the mirrors of humanity, guiding us to reflect within, unlocking ancient memories and reminding us that we are not egocentric, but cosmocentric.

Many times have I walked into the Circlemakers' temples and there I found the one element perfectly capable of being reproduced by all human beings.

Love.

BIBLIOGRAPHY

Abbott, Edwin. 1983. *Flatland: A Romance of Many Dimensions.* New York: Barnes & Noble.

Alexandersson, Olof. 1990. *Living Water: Viktor Schauberger and the Secrets of Natural Energy.* Bath: Gateway.

Andrews, Colin. 1994. In CPRI newsletter, Vol.3:1, Branford: CT.

Andrews, Colin, and Pat Delgado. 1990. *Latest Evidence.* London: Bloomsbury.

————. 1991. *Circular Evidence.* London: Bloomsbury.

Andrews, D. H. 1966. *The Symphony of Life.* Springfield, Missouri: Unity Books.

Andrews, Ted. 1996. *Sacred Sounds.* St. Paul: Llewellyn.

Arguelles, Jose. 1985. *The Mayan Factor.* Santa Fe: Bear & Co.

Ash, David, and Peter Hewitt. 1990. *Science of the Gods: Reconciling Mystery and Matter.* Bath: Gateway.

Audus, L. J. 1960. "Magnetotropism: A New Plant Growth Response," *Nature,* Jan. 16.

Babbitt, Edwin. 1878. *The Principles of Light and Colour.* New York: Babbitt & Co.

Bailey, Alice. 1984. *Initiation, Cosmic and Solar.* New York: Lucis Press.

Baines, Paul, Philip Heselton, and Jimmy Goddard (eds). 1985. *Skyways and Landmarks Revisited.* Hull, UK.: Northern Earth Mysteries Group.

Barbanell, Maurice. 1945. *The Case of Helen Duncan.* London: Psychic Press.

Barber, Bradley P., and Seth J. Putterman. 1991. "Observation of Synchronous Picosecond Sonoluminescence," *Nature,* July 25.

Bartholomew, Alick (ed.). 1991. *Harbingers of World Change.* Bath: Gateway.

Beaumont, Richard. 1999. "Breaking the Sound Barrier," *Kindred Spirit,* Vol.3:5, Devon: Totnes.

Becker, Robert, and Gary Selden. 1985. *The Body Electric.* New York: William Morrow.

Bennett, Mary, and David Percy. 1999. *Dark Moon: Apollo and the Whistle-Blowers.* London: Aulis.

Benoist, Luc. 1975. *Signes, Symboles et Mythes.* Paris: Methuen.

Berendt, Joachim-Ernst. 1991. *The World is Sound: Nada Brahma, Music and the Landscape of Consciousness.* Rochester, Vermont: Destiny Books.

Berry, Rod Bearcloud. 1998. "Star Nation Fractal," *Sedona Magazine,* March.

Berthelot, Yves H. 1988. *Journal of the Acoustic Society of America* 84:14, suppl. 1.

Besant, Annie, and C. W. Leadbeater. 1901. *Thought Forms*. Madras, India: Theosophical Publishing House.

Birks, Walter, and R. A. Gilbert. 1987. *The Treasure of Montsegur: A Study of the Cathar Heresy and the Nature of the Cathar Secret*. London: Crucible.

Blair, Lawrence. 1975. *Rhythms of Vision*. St. Albans, UK: Paladin.

Blake, Francine. 1998. Editorial in *The Spiral* magazine, issue 28, March.

Blitz, Jack. 1971. *Ultrasonics: Methods and Applications*. London: Butterworths.

Bloy, Colin. 1992. "Axioms and Experiences," *Dowsing the Crop Circles*. Glastonbury: Gothic Image.

Braden, Gregg. 1993. *Awakening to Point Zero*. Bellevue, Wash.: Radio Bookstore Press.

Bradley, Richard. 1977. *Rock Art and the Prehistory of Atlantic Europe*. London: Routledge.

Broadhurst, Paul, and Hamish Miller. 1992. *The Sun and the Serpent*. Launceston, UK: Pendragon Press.

———. 2000. *The Dance of the Dragon*. Launceston, UK: Pendragon Press.

Brown, B., and D. Gordon. 1967. *Ultrasonic Techniques in Biology and Medicine*. London: Illife.

Brownlee, Nick. 1998. *Sunday People*.

Brunes, Tons. 1967. *The Secrets of Ancient Geometry*. Copenhagen: Rhoudos Publications.

Bucha, V. 1967. *Archaeometry*, Vol. 10.

Burke, John. 1998. "Crop Circle Analysis Shows that Most Are Not Hoaxes," *MUFON Journal*, Sept.

Buttlar, Johannes von. 1980. *The UFO Phenomenon*. London: Book Club Associates.

Campbell, John. 1966. "Sense of Security," *Analog*, Nov.

Capra, Fritjof. 1986. *The Tao of Physics*. London: Fontana.

Cathie, Bruce. 1990. *The Energy Grid: Harmonic 695, The Pulse of the Universe*. Kempton, UK: Adventures Unlimited Press.

———. 1995 *The Bridge to Infinity*. Harmonic 371244, Auckland: Brookfield Press.

———. 2001 "The Harmonics of Coral Castle," *Nexus*, Oct-Nov.

Chancellor, Philip. 1971. *Handbook of the Bach Flower Remedies*. Rochford: C. W. Daniel.

Charpentier, Louis. 1975. *The Mysteries of Chartres Cathedral*. London: Avon Books.

Childress, David Hatcher. 2000. *Technology of the Gods: The Incredible Sciences of the Ancients*. Kempton, IL: Adventures Unlimited Press.

Chorost, Michael. 1992. "The Summer 1991 Crop Circles," Mt. Rainier, MD: Fund for UFO Research.

Chorost, Michael, and Marshall Dudley. 1992a. "What Happened to the Radionuclides Paper?" *The Cereologist*, no.6.

———. 1992b. *MUFON Journal*, Feb.

Clarke, Arthur C. 1994. *Mysterious World*, The Discovery Channel.

Cochrane, Carol. 2001. *The Spiral*, Feb.

Colgrave, Sukie. 1979. *The Spirit of the Valley: Androgyny and Chinese Thought*. London: Virago.

Constable, Trevor James. 1977. *The Cosmic Pulse of Life*. Sudbury, UK: Neville Spearman.

Cooper, J. C. 1978. *An Illustrated Encyclopedia of Traditional Symbols*. London: Thames and Hudson.

Crerar, Tony. 1998. "The Beltane Fiery Wheel," *The Cereologist*, no. 22.

Critchlow, Keith. 1976. *Islamic Patterns*. London: Thames and Hudson.

———. 1979. *Time Stands Still*. London: Gordon Fraser.

Cummings, Claire Hope. 1999. "Entertainment Foods," *The Ecologist*, 29:1, Jan/Feb.

Cutt, John. 1998. "No UFO Over Dunearn," *The Southland Times* (New Zealand), March 8.

Darling, David. 2002. *Equations of Eternity*. New York: MJF Books.

Dauvois, Michel. 1988. "Son et Musique au Paleolithique," *Pour la Science,* no. 253, Nov.

David-Neel, Alexandra. 1936. *Tibetan Journey*. London: The Bodley Head.

Davidson, John. 1987. *Subtle Energy*. Saffron Walden, UK: C. W. Daniel.

———. 1994. *The Secret of the Creative Vacuum: Man and the Energy Dance*. Saffron Walden, UK: C. W. Daniel.

Davies, G. J. 1982. *Temples, Churches and Mosques*. Oxford: Basil Blackwell.

Davies, Paul. 1987. *The Cosmic Blueprint*. London: Heinemann.

Davis, Beth (ed.). 1992. *Cyphers in the Crops*. Bath: Gateway.

Day, Harvey. 1977. *The Hidden Power of Vibrations*. London: Pelham.

Day, Philip. 2001. *Health Wars*. Tonbridge, UK: Credence Publications.

Deardorff, James. 1991. "A Symbol in the Desert," *UFO Magazine,* Sept.

Deetken, Chad. 1993. "Crop Circles in Canada," *The Cereologist,* no. 10.

Delgado, Pat. 1992. *Conclusive Evidence*. London: Bloomsbury.

de Vasconcelos, J. Leite. 1981. *Religiões da Luzitania,* Vol. 3. Lisbon: N.P.

———. 1982. *Tradições Populares de Portugal*. Lisbon: N.P.

Devereux, Paul. 1990. *Places of Power*. Shaftsbury, UK: Blandford.

———. 1992. *Earth Memory*. St. Paul, Minn: Llewellyn.

Devereux, Paul, and D. Thompson. 1979. *The Ley Hunter's Companion*. London: Thames and Hudson.

Dewhurst-Maddox, Olivea. 1993. *The Book of Sound Therapy*. London: Gaia Books.

Diot, Charles. 1935. *Les Sourciers et les Monuments Megalithiques*. Paris: G. Doin.

Dodd, Anthony. 1991. "UFO Update," *The Journal of UFO Investigation,* no. 1.

Doreal, M. 1925. *The Emerald Tablets of Thoth the Atlantean*. Nashville: Source Books.

Duby, Georges. 1966. *Mystical Theology*. Geneva: Corpus Areopagiticum.

Duncan, Tom. 1985. *Success in Physics*. London: John Duncan.

Dunn, Christopher. 1998. *The Giza Power Plant: Technologies of Ancient Egypt*. Santa Fe: Bear and Co.

Dutt, Romesh. 1961. *Ramayana and Mahabharata*. London: Dent.

Elkington, David. 2001. *In the Name of the Gods*. Sherbourne, UK: Green Man Press.

Emoto, Masaru. 1999. *The Message from Water*. Kyoikusha, Japan: Hado.

Ernst, Brune. 1992. *The Eye Beguiled: Optical Illusions*. Koln: Taschen.

Essene, Virginia, and Tom Kenyon. 1996. *The Hathor Material*. Santa Clara: S.E.E. Publishing.

Evans, Kathy. 1993. *Music*. New York: McGraw-Hill Ryerson.

Fester, F. Richard. 1981. *Urworter der Menschbeit: Eine Archaologie der Srachte*. Kosel, Munich: N.p.

Feynman, R. P., R. B. Leighton, and M. Sands. 1966. *The Feynman Lectures on Physics,* Vol. 2. Reading, Mass.: Addison-Wesley.

Findhorn Community. 1975. *The Findhorn Garden*. New York: Harper Perennial.

Flem-Ath, Rand and Rose. 1995. *When The Sky Fell*. New York: St. Martin's Press.

Flint, E. B., and K. S. Suslick. 1991. *Science,* no. 253.

Frissell, Bob. 1994. *Nothing in This Book Is True, but It's Exactly How Things Are*. Berkeley: Frog Limited.

Gardner, Kay. 1997. *Sounding the Inner Landscape*. Shaftsbury, UK: Element.

Gaunt, Bonnie. 1995. *Beginnings: The Sacred Design.* Mich.: Gaunt.

George, Leonard. 1995. *The Encyclopedia of Heresies and Heretics.* London: Robson.

Gerber, Richard. 1996. *Vibrational Medicine.* Santa Fe: Bear and Co.

Gladzewski, Andrew. 1951. "The Music of Crystals, Plants and Human Beings," *Radio-Perception*, Sept.

Gleick, James. 1987. *Chaos.* New York: Viking Penguin.

Goldman, Jonathan. 1992. *Healing Sounds.* Shaftsbury, UK: Element.

Golubnichii, P. I., V. M. Gromenko, and A. D. Filonenko. 1979. *Soviet Physics*, no. 5.

Good, Timothy. 1987. *Above Top Secret: The Worldwide UFO Cover-Up.* London: Sidgwick and Jackson.

Gordon, Cyrus. 1962. *Before the Bible.* London: Collins.

Green, Michael. 1996. "Soil Tests by the Agricultural Development & Advisory Service," *The Cereologist,* no.17.

Grist, Brian. 1991. "The Aquifer Attractor," *The Cereologist,* no 5.

Hall, Manly P. 1928. *Secret Teachings of All Ages.* Los Angeles: Philosophical Research Society.

———. 1932. *Man, the Grand Symbol of the Mysteries.* Los Angeles: Manly P. Hall Publications.

———. 1937. *Freemasonry of the Ancient Egyptians.* Los Angeles: The Philosophers' Press.

———. 1947. *Lectures on Ancient Philosophy.* Los Angeles: Philosophical Research Society.

Hamel, Michael Peter. 1978. *Through Music to the Self.* Shaftsbury, UK: Element.

Hancock, Graham. 1995. *Fingerprints of the Gods.* New York: Crown.

———. 1996. *The Message of the Sphynx.* New York: Crown.

Hawkins, Gerald. 1965. *Stonehenge Decoded.* New York: Doubleday.

———. 1973. *Beyond Stonehenge.* London: Hutchinson.

———. 1983. *Mindsteps to the Cosmos.* New York: Harper and Row.

Haynes, Ofmil. 1997. *The Harmony of the Spheres.* Powys, Wales: Wooden Books.

Hein, Simeon. 2000. "Electromagnetic Anomalies and Scale-Free Networks in British Crop Formations," *The Circular,* no. 38.

Helfman, Elizabeth. 1974. *Signs and Symbols of the Sun.* New York: Seabury Press.

Hero, Barbara. 1992. *Lambdoma Unveiled.* Wells, Maine: Strawberry Hill Farm Studio Press.

Heselton, Philip. 1995. *Earth Mysteries.* Shaftsbury, UK: Element.

Hesemann, Michael (ed.). 1993. *Magazin 2000,* no. 93, April.

Hesemann, Michael. 1995. *The Cosmic Connection.* Bath: Gateway.

Hitching, Francis. 1976. *Earth Magic.* London: Cassell.

Hodson, Geoffrey. 1976. *Music Forms.* Madras, India: Theosophical Publishing House.

Holroyd, Stuart. 1977. *Prelude to the Landing on Planet Earth.* London: W. H. Allen.

Hopkins, Budd. 1987. *Intruders.* New York: Random House.

Huffman, William. 1992. *Robert Fludd, Essential Readings.* London: Antiquarian Press.

Hughes, Martyn. 1990. Editorial in *New Scientist,* August.

Hunt, Valerie. 1989. *Infinite Mind.* Malibu, Calif.: Malibu.

Huntley, A. E. 1970. *The Divine Proportion.* New York: Dover.

Hurtak, J. J. 1977. *The Book of Knowledge: The Keys of Enoch.* Los Gatos, Calif.: Academy for Future Science.

Hynek, J. Allen, and Jacques Vallee. 1975. *The Edge of Reality.* Chicago: Regency.

Illion, T. 1997. *In Secret Tibet.* Kempton, UK: Adventures Unlimited.

Irion, Robert. 2000. "Ghost Atoms," *New Scientist,* July 8.

Jahn, Robert, and Brenda Dunne. 1987. *Margins of Reality: The Role of Consciousness in the Physical World.* Orlando: Harcourt Brace.

Jahn, Robert, Paul Devereux, and Michael Ibitson. 1996. "Acoustical Resonances of Assorted Ancient Structures," *Journal of Acoustical Society of America,* Vol 99:2, February.

Jenkins, John Major. 1998. *Maya Cosmogenesis 2012: The True Meaning of the Maya Calendar End Date.* Santa Fe: Bear and Co.

Jenny, Hans. 1974. *Cymatics II.* Basel, Switzerland: Basilius Press.

John, Kelvin, and Daniel Wolf, translators. 1963. *The Lying Stones of Dr. Berenger.* University of California Press.

Jolly, W. P. 1974. *Sir Oliver Lodge.* Cranbury, New Jersey: Associated University Press.

Jung, Carl Gustav. 1973. *Psychology and Alchemy.* London: Arkana.

Kanzhen, Chiang. 1993. *AURA-Z Journal,* Vols. 1–3.

Keel, John. 1975. *The Mothman Prophesies.* New York: Dutton.

Keen, Montague. 1992. *Scientific Evidence for the Crop Circle Phenomenon.* Norwich: Elvery Flowers Publications.

———. 1994. "The Bythorn Wonder: An Inquiry," *The Cereologist,* no. 12.

Keyser, Hans. 1970. *Akroasis: The Theory of World Harmonics.* Boston: Plowshare.

Khan, Hazrat Inayat. 1991. *The Mysticism of Sound and Music.* Boston: Shambhala.

Khanna, Madhu. 1979. *Yantra: The Yantric Symbol of Cosmic Unity.* London: Thames and Hudson.

Kozyrev, Nikolai. 1968. "Possibility of Experimental Study of the Properties of Time," U.S. Dept. of Commerce. JPRS 45238.

Krönig, Jürgen. 1991. "Authority's Attitude to World Changes," *The Cereologist,* no.5.

Krüger, Wilfried. 1974. *Das Universerum Singt.* Munich: Trier.

Kruth, Patricia, and Henry Stobard, eds. 2000. *Sound.* Cambridge, UK: Cambridge University Press.

Lawlor, Robert. 1982. *Sacred Geometry.* London: Thames and Hudson.

Leadbeater, C. W. 1927. *The Chakras.* Madras, India: Theosophical Publishing House.

Le Mée, Katharine. 1994. *Chant.* London: Rider.

Leonard, George. 1978. *The Silent Pulse.* New York: E. P. Dutton.

Lethbridge, T. C. 1973. *The Legend of the Sons of God.* London: Sidgwick and Jackson.

Levengood, W. C. 1994. "Anatomical Anomalies in Crop Formation Plants," *Physiologia Plantarum* 92.

Levengood, W. C., and J. A. Burke. 1995. "Semi-Molten Meteoric Iron Associated with a Crop Formation," *Journal of Scientific Exploration* 9:2.

Levi, Barbara. 1991. "Light Comes from Ultrasonic Cavitation in Picosecond Pulses," *Physics Today,* November.

Levin, Flora. 1994. *The Manual of Harmonics of Nicomachus the Pythagorean.* Grand Rapids, Mich: Phanes Press.

Lewis, Robert. 1986. *The Sacred Word and Its Creative Overtones.* San Jose, Calif.: Rosicrucian.

Lockyer, J. N. 1894. *The Dawn of Astronomy.* London: Macmillan.

Loução, Paulo Alexandre. 1999. *Os Templarios na Formação de Portugal.* Lisbon: Esquilo.

Lyons, Jim. 1998. "Bubbles and Knots," *The Circular,* issue 31.

McKenna, Terrence and Dennis. 1975. *The Invisible Landscape.* New York: Seabury Press.

McNish, John. 1991. "Crop Circle Communiqué," *Circlevision.*

Mallery, G. 1972. *Picture Writing of the American Indians,* Vol.1. New York: Dover.

Mann, A. T. 1993. *Sacred Architecture.* Shaftsbury, UK: Element.

Manning, Jeane. 1996. *The Coming Energy Revolution.* New York: Avery.

Marciniak, Barbara. 1992. *Bringers of the Dawn.* Santa Fe: Bear and Co.

Martineau, John. 1992. *A Book of Coincidence.* Powys, Wales: Wooden Books.

———. 1996. *Crop Circle Geometry.* Powys, Wales: Wooden Books.

Meaden, Terence. 1985. *Journal of Meteorology,* Vol. 10.

———. 1989. *The Circles Effect and Its Mysteries.* Bradford on Avon: Artetech.

———. 1991. *Crop Circles and the Plasma Vortex: The Crop Circle Enigma.* Bath: Gateway.

Meehan, Aidan. 1993. *Spiral Patterns.* London: Thames and Hudson.

Melchizedek, Drunvalo. 1996. *The Ancient Secret of the Flower of Life.* Prescott, Ariz.: Hummingbird.

Men, Humbatz. 1990. *Secrets of Mayan Science/ Religion.* Santa Fe: Bear and Co.

Merz, Blanche. 1987. *Points of Cosmic Energy.* Saffron Walden, UK: C. W. Daniel.

Michell, John. 1975. *The Earth Spirit.* London: Thames and Hudson.

———. 1977. *A Little History of Astro-Archeology.* London: Thames and Hudson.

———. 1982. *Megalithomania.* London: Thames and Hudson.

———. 1983. *The New View Over Atlantis.* London: Thames and Hudson.

———. 1988a. *The Dimensions of Paradise.* London: Thames and Hudson.

———. 1988b. *City of Revelation.* London: Thames and Hudson.

———. 1990. "Reports and Sketches," *The Cereologist,* no. 2.

———. 1991. "Geometry and Symbolism at Barbury Castle," *The Cereologist,* no. 4.

———. 1992. *Dowsing the Crop Circles.* Glastonbury, UK: Gothic Image.

———. 1997. *Secrets of the Stones.* New York: Penguin.

———. 1998. *Twelve Tribe Nations.* London: Thames and Hudson.

Milgrom, Lionel. 2001. "Thanks for the memory: Experiments have backed what was once a scientific heresy," *The Guardian,* March 15.

Miller, Hamish. 1992. "On the Connection with Ancient Sites," in *Dowsing the Crop Circles.* Glastonbury, UK: Gothic Image.

Morehouse, David. 1996. *Psychic Warrior.* New York: St. Martins Press.

Morgan, Marlo. 1994. *Mutant Message from Down Under.* New York: HarperPerennial.

Mück, Otto. 1958. *Cheops und die Grosse Pyramide.* Berlin: Olter Walter.

Munck, Carl. "The Code of the Ancients," *Atlantis Rising,* nos.12 & 15.

Murti, T. V. R. 1955. *The Central Philosophy of Buddhism.* London: Allen & Unwin.

Mutwa, Credo. 1996. *Isilwane: The Animal.* Cape Town, S. Africa: Struick.

Myers, David, and David Percy. 1999. *Two-Thirds: A History of Our Galaxy.* London: Aulis.

Nasr, Seyyed Hossein. 1964. *An Introduction to Islamic Cosmic Doctrines.* Boston: Harvard University Press.

———. 1976. *Islamic Science.* Westerham, UK: World of Islam Festival Publications.

Nelson, R. D., et al. 1998. "FieldREG II: Consciousness Field Effects: Replications and Explorations," *Journal of Scientific Exploration* 12:3.

Okochi, Ryogi. *Thinking Behind the Japanese Language.* unpublished.

Ostrander, Sheila, and Lynn Schroeder. 1976. *Psychic Discoveries Behind the Iron Curtain.* London: Abacus.

Ouspensky, P. D. 1931. *A New Model of the Universe.* London: Kegan Paul.

Page, Steve, and Glen Broughton. 1999. "The Underground Connection," *The Circular,* no.33.

Palgrave-Moore, Pat. 1992. *Crop Circle Classification.* Norwich: Elvery Flowers Publications.

Parlenko, G. E. 1933. "Oberflachenwellen auf einer in einem bewegten Tank enthaltenen Flussigkeit," *Philosophie Magazine*.

Patterson, Alex. 1992. *A Field Guide to Rock Art Symbols of the Greater Southwest*. Boulder: Johnson Books.

Payne, Katy. 1998. *Silent Thunder: In the Presence of Elephants*. New York: Simon and Schuster.

Pennick, Nigel. 1991. *The Secret Lore of Runes and Other Ancient Alphabets*. London: Rider.

Petraeus, Cornelius. c.1578. *Sylva Philosophorum*. N.p.

Pfeiffer, Ehrenfried. 1936. *Formative Forces in Crystallization*. London: Rudolf Steiner Publishing.

Plot, Robert. 1678. *The Natural History of Staffordshire*. Oxford, UK: Ashmolean.

Pope, Nick. 1996. *Open Skies, Closed Minds*. London: Simon and Schuster.

Prigogine, I., and I. Stengers. 1984. *Order Out of Chaos*. New York: Bantam.

Princeton Engineering Anomalies Research. 1995. PEAR Technical Note 95004, May. Princeton: Princeton University.

Pringle, Lucy. 1990. "Headaches or Healing," *Crop Circle Enigma*, Bath: Gateway.

———. 1993a. "The Bluffer's Bluff is Called," *The Cereologist*, no.10.

———. 1993b. *The Circular*, 4:1.

———. 1994. *The Circular*, issue 16.

———. 1996. "Frolics Amid the Fractals," *The Circular*, issue 27.

———. 1997. "Facts and Figures or Flights of Fancy," *The Circular*, issue 28, CCCS.

———. 1998. *The Circular*, issue 33.

———. 1999.*Crop Circles: The Greatest Mystery of Modern Times*. London: Thorsons.

———. 2000. "Dreams, Disappearances and Magic Carpets," *The Circular*, issue 38.

Puthoff, H. E. 1996. "CIA-Initiated Remote Viewing Program at Stanford Research Institute," *Journal of Scientific Exploration* 10:1.

Putterman, Seth J. 1995. "Sonoluminescence: Sound into Light," *Scientific American*, Vol. 272, Feb.

Randles, Jenny, and Paul Fuller. 1990. *Crop Circles: A Mystery Solved*. London: Hale.

Reuters. 2000. "IBM Sells Air Force New Supercomputer to Identify UFOs," November 22.

Rhine, J. B. 1970. *Mind Over Matter*. London: Macmillan.

Roberts, C. E. (ed.). 1945. "The Trial of Mrs. Duncan," Old Bailey Trial Series no. 3, London: Jarrolds.

Roberts, Paul William. 1995. *In Search of the Birth of Jesus*. New York: Riverhead.

Robins, Don. 1982. "The Dragon Project and the Talking Stones," *New Scientist*, 21 Oct.

———. 1985. *Circles of Silence*. London: Souvenir Press.

Rogers, Ken. 1994. *The Warminster Triangle*. Warminster, UK: Coates and Parker.

Roth, Robert. 1994. *Transcendental Meditation*. Auckland: Donald I. Fine.

Rothstein, J. 1958. *Communication, Organization and Science*. New York: Falcon Wing Press.

Rothwell, Norman. 1988. *Understanding Genetics*. Oxford: Oxford University Press.

Rubtsov, Vladimir. 1991. "Soviet Ice Ring," *MUFON UFO Journal*, no. 282.

Rucker, Rudy. 1985. *The Fourth Dimension and How to Get There*. London: Rider.

Rutherford, Adam. 1945. *A New Revelation in the Great Pyramid*. London: The Institute of Pyramidology.

Savage, Neil. 2001. "Bright Encounter," *New Scientist*, Jan 6.

Schauberger, Viktor. 1998. *The Water Wizard: The Extraordinary Properties of Natural Water*. Bath: Gateway.

Schiff, Michael. 1994. *The Memory of Water*. London: Thorsons.

Schimmel, Annemarie. 1993. *The Mystery of Numbers*. Oxford: Oxford University Press.

Schnabel, Jim. 1993. *Round in Circles*. London: Hamish Hamilton.

Schneider, Michael. 1994. *A Beginner's Guide to Constructing the Universe*. New York: Harper Collins.

Schul, Bill, and Ed Pettit. 1985. *The Secret Power of Pyramids*. New York: Fawcett Publications.

Schwaller de Lubicz, R. A. 1977. *The Temple of Man*. Brookline, Mass.: Autumn Books.

Service, Alastair, and Jean Bradberry. 1993. *The Standing Stones of Europe*. London: Widenfelt and Nicolson.

Shames, Lawrence. 1989. *The Hunger for More*. New York: Times Books.

Sharkey, John. 1975. *Celtic Mysteries*. New York: Thames and Hudson.

Sheldrake, Rupert. 1988. *Presence of the Past*. London: Collins.

Sherwood, Ed and Kris. 1998. "The 1996 Laguna Canyon Crop Circle Formation," *The Cereologist*, no. 22.

Shuttlewood, Arthur. 1973. *The Flying Saucers*. London: Sphere.

Singh, T. C. 1962–63. "On the Effect of Music and Dance on Plants," *Bihar Agricultural College Magazine* 13:1.

Sinnett, A. P. 1893. *Stonehenge and the Pyramids*. London: Theosophical Publishing House.

Sitchin, Zecharia. 1980. *The Stairway to Heaven*. New York: Avon.

———. 1990. *The Lost Realms*. New York: Avon.

Strachan, Gordon. 1998. *Jesus, The Master Builder*. Edinburgh: Floris.

Stringfield, Leonard. 1957. "Inside Saucer Post 3-0 Blue," *CRIFO*, Cincinnati, Nov. 4.

Suslick, K. S. et al. 1991. "Sonochemical Synthesis of Amorphous Iron," *Nature* 353.

Tame, David. 1984. *The Secret Power of Music*. Wellingborough, UK: Turnstone Press.

Tansley, David. 1976. *Radionics Interface with the Ether Fields*. Saffron Walden, UK: C. W. Daniel.

Tashev, T., and T. Natan. 1966. "Suggestology," *Bulgaria Today*, no. 9.

Tenen, Stan. 1992. *Geometric Metaphors of Life*. San Anselmo, Calif.: The MERU Foundation.

Tersur, Francoise. 1993. *The Druids and the Esoteric Tradition*. Lisbon: Maio.

"The Men Who Conned the World," 1991. *Today* newspaper, September 9.

Thom, Alexander. 1967. *Megalithic Sites in Britain*. Oxford: Oxford University Press.

Thomas, Andy. 1992. *Sussex Circular* magazine, issue 6, June.

Thomas, Charles. 1991/92. "Magnetic Anomalies," *The Cereologist*, no.5, Winter.

Thomas, Keith. 1971. *Religion and the Decline of Magic*. London: Weidenfields and Nicolson.

Tilt, David. 1992. "On Crop Circles and an Ancient Energy System," in *Dowsing the Crop Circles*, Glastonbury, UK: Gothic Image.

Tomkinson, Henry. 1975. *The Divination of Disease: A Study in Radiesthesia*. London: Heath Science Press.

Tompkins, Peter. 1988. *Secrets of the Great Pyramid*. London: Penguin.

———. 1997. *The Secret Life of Nature*. San Francisco: HarperSanFrancisco.

Tompkins, Peter, and Christopher Bird. 1973. *The Secret Life of Plants*. New York: Harper and Row.

———. 1992. *Secrets of the Soil*. London: Arkana.

Toth, Max, and Greg Nielsen. 1985. *Pyramid Power*. Rochester, Vermont: Destiny Books.

Tromp, S. 1968. "Review of the Possible Physiological Causes of Dowsing," *International Journal of Parapsychology* 10:4.

Underwood, Guy. 1973. *The Pattern of the Past*. London: Abacus.

Vallée, Jacques. 1975. *The Invisible College*. New York: Dutton.

Van Der Post, Laurens. 1952. *The Lost World of the Kalahari*. London: Hogarth.

Vassilatos, Gerry. 1998. "Lost Science," Eureka, Calif.: Borderland Research Foundation.

Vidler, Mark. 1998. *The Star Mirror.* London: Thorsons.

Vigay, Paul. 1994. "Crop Circle Hoaxing: Is it a Real Threat to the Genuine Phenomenon?" *Enigma,* issue 4.

————. 1995. *Enigma,* issue 8.

von Welling, Georgius. 1735. *Opus Magi: Cabbalisticum et Theosophicum.* Hamburg: N. p.

Wachsmuth, Gunther. 1932. *Etheric Formative Forces in Cosmos, Earth and Man.* New York: Anthroposophic Press.

Wall, Kathleen, and Gary Fergusson. 1998. *Rites of Passage.* Hillsboro, Ore.: Beyond Words.

Watson, Lyall. 1973. *Supernature: The Natural History of the Supernatural.* London: Hodder and Stoughton.

Watts-Hughes, Margaret. 1891. *The Voice Figures.* London: Hazell Watson Viney.

————. 1904. *The Eidophone Voice Figures.* London, Christian Herald.

Weil, Simone. 1987. *Intimations of Christianity Among the Ancient Greeks.* London: Ark.

Weinberger, Pearl, and Mary Measures. "The Effect of Two Sound Frequencies on the Germination and Growth of a Spring and Winter Wheat," *Canadian Journal of Botany.*

West, John Anthony. 1993. *Serpent in the Sky.* Wheaton, Ill.: Quest.

Wheatley, Dennis. 1990. *Dowsing with a Difference.* Swindon, UK: Braden Press.

White, Andrew Dickinson. 1896. *A History of the Warfare of Science with Theology in Christendom.* N. p.

Whitlock, Robin. 1999. "The Trouble with Transmitters," *The Ecologist* 29:5, Aug.

Wiener, Harry. 1968. "External Chemical Messengers," *New York State Journal of Medicine.*

Wigner, E. P. 1970. *Symmetries and Reflections: Scientific Essays.* Cambridge, Mass.: M.I.T Press.

Wilson, Colin. 1998. *Alien Dawn.* London: Virgin.

Wilson, Robert. 1985–2000. *Cosmic Trigger.* Vols.1–3. Tempe, Ariz.: New Falcon.

Wilson, Terry. 1998. *The Secret History of Crop Circles.* Paignton, UK: CCCS.

Wingfield, George. 1990. "The Crop Circles in 1990," *The Cereologist,* no. 2.

————. 1991a. "The Doug and Dave Scam," *The Cereologist,* no. 5.

————. 1991b. *The UFO Report 1992.* London: Sidgwick & Jackson.

————. 1992a. "Towards an Understanding of the Nature of the Circles," *Harbingers of World Change.* Bath: Gateway.

————. 1992b. "Circular Conundrums of '92," *The Cereologist,* no. 7.

————. 1993. "The Works of the Devil," *The Cereologist,* no. 10.

————. 1994. *The Circular,* no. 22.

Yogananda, Paramahansa. 1996. *Autobiography of a Yogi.* London: Rider.

Zuckerkandl, Victor. 1956. *Sound and Symbol: Music and the External World.* London: Routledge and Kegan Paul.

Zuckerman, Lord. 1991. "Creations in the Dark," *New York Review,* November 21.

Other Publications

Proceedings of the First International Conference on the Circles Effect, ed. Terence Meaden and Derek Elsom, TORRO/CERES, Oxford, 1990.

Paísagens Arqueologicas a Oeste de Évora, C.M.E., Évora, 1997.

Resources

Freddy Silva. For photos, diagrams, and information on current crop circles research, please visit his website, the Crop Circular.
www.lovely.clara.net

Hans Jenny's cymatics images: MACROmedia, 219 Grant Road, Newmarket, NH 03857.
www.cymaticssource.com.

Steve Alexander. For details on how to purchase photographs, postcards, calendars, and books, please send a stamped, addressed envelope to 27 St. Francis Road, Gosport, Hants. PO12 2UG, UK. Tel/fax 44 1705 352867, or 02392 352867.

Lucy Pringle. Research in Electromagnetic effects in living matter/photographer. For details of photos and calendars, send a stamped, addressed envelope to 5 Town Lane, Sheet, Petersfield, Hants. GU32 2AF, UK. Tel/fax 44 1730 263454.

Crop Circles Publications

The Cereologist
John Sayer, Editor, 17 Spindle Road, Norwich NR6 6JR, England.

The Circular, magazine of the CCCS.
Subscription inquiries to Dr. Andrew King, Kenberly, Victoria Gardens, Biggin Hill, Kent TN16 3DJ, England.

Websites

The Crop Circular. www.lovely.clara.net

Paul Vigay. www.cropcircleresearch.com

Canadian Crop Circle Research Network. www.geocities.com/cropcirclecanada

Dutch Centre for Crop Circles Studies. www.dcccs.org/

Crop Circle Connector.
www.cropcircleconnector.com/anasazi/whatsnew.html

ARTWORK CREDITS

Figure 0.1:	Steve Alexander
Figure 0.2:	Freddy Silva
Figure 1.1:	Freddy Silva
Figure 1.6:	Busty Taylor
Figure 1.7:	Busty Taylor
Figure 1.9:	Busty Taylor
Figure 1.10:	Paul Vigay
Figure 1.11:	Busty Taylor
Figure 1.12:	Busty Taylor
Figure 1.15:	George Wingfield
Figure 1.17:	Jason Hawkes
Figure 1.18:	Isabelle Kingston
Figures 2.1a and 2.1b:	Colin Andrews
Figure 2.2a:	James Deardorff
Figure 2.7:	Andrew King
Figure 2.8:	George Wingfield
Figure 2.9:	Adapted from David Myers and David Percy
Figure 2.10:	Richard Wintle
Figure 2.11:	George Wingfield
Figure 3.1:	Freddy Silva
Figure 3.2:	Freddy Silva
Figure 3.3:	Freddy Silva
Figure 4.1:	Freddy Silva
Figure 4.2:	Freddy Silva
Figure 4.3:	Freddy Silva
Figure 4.4:	Freddy Silva
Figure 4.5:	Anthony Horn
Figure 4.6:	Mike Hubbard
Figure 4.7:	Freddy Silva
Figure 4.9:	Freddy Silva
Figure 4.10:	George Bishop
Figure 4.11:	Freddy Silva
Figure 4.12:	Freddy Silva
Figure 4.13:	Jane Ross
Figure 4.14:	Freddy Silva
Figure 4.15:	Freddy Silva
Figure 4.16:	Jane Ross
Figure 4.17:	Freddy Silva
Figure 4.18:	Freddy Silva
Figure 4.19:	Freddy Silva
Figure 4.20:	Freddy Silva
Figure 4.21:	Freddy Silva
Figure 4.22:	Freddy Silva
Figure 4.23:	Freddy Silva
Figure 4.24:	Freddy Silva
Figure 4.25:	Freddy Silva
Figure 4.26:	Freddy Silva
Figure 4.27:	Freddy Silva
Figure 5.2:	Andrew King
Figure 5.3:	Colin Andrews
Figure 5.4:	Mike Hubbard
Figure 5.5:	Lucy Pringle
Figure 6.2:	George Wingfield
Figure 6.3:	Chad Deetken
Figure 6.4:	Andrew King
Figure 6.5:	Mike Hubbard
Figure 6.6:	Steve Alexander
Figure 6.8:	Steve Alexander
Figure 6.9:	Lucy Pringle
Figure 6.10:	Andrew King
Figure 6.12:	Freddy Silva
Figure 6.13:	Freddy Silva
Figure 6.14:	Ruben Uriarte
Figure 6.15:	Lucy Pringle
Figure 6.16:	Lucy Pringle
Figure 6.17:	Steve Alexander
Figure 6.19:	Lucy Pringle
Figure 6.20:	Andrew King
Figure 6.21:	Freddy Silva

Figure 6.22:	Russell Stannard
Figure 6.23:	Freddy Silva
Figure 6.26:	Freddy Silva
Figure 6.27:	Isabelle Kingston
Figure 6.28:	Freddy Silva
Figure 7.2:	Lucy Pringle
Figure 7.4:	Mike Hubbard
Figure 7.5:	Steve Alexander
Figure 7.6:	Frank Laumen
Figure 7.11:	Frank Laumen
Figure 7.12:	Lucy Pringle
Figure 7.13:	Frank Laumen
Figure 7.14:	John Sayer
Figure 7.15:	Lucy Pringle
Figure 7.16:	Richard Wintle
Figure 7.18:	Lucy Pringle
Figure 7.19:	Freddy Silva
Figure 7.22:	Freddy Silva
Figure 7.25:	Freddy Silva and Russell Stannard
Figure 7.27:	Freddy Silva
Figure 7.28:	Freddy Silva
Figure 7.29:	Freddy Silva
Figure 7.30:	Freddy Silva
Figure 7.31:	Freddy Silva
Figure 7.32:	Frank Laumen
Figure 7.34:	Freddy Silva
Figure 7.35:	Freddy Silva
Figure 8.1:	Freddy Silva
Figure 8.2:	Freddy Silva
Figure 8.3:	Freddy Silva
Figure 8.4:	Freddy Silva
Figure 8.5:	After Page and Broughton, Brian Grist
Figures 8.6 to 8.10:	Freddy Silva
Figure 8.15:	Mike Hubbard
Figure 8.21:	From a survey by John Langrish, CCCS
Figure 8.23:	Freddy Silva
Figure 8.24:	Ken and Rosemary Spelman
Figure 8.25:	Ken and Rosemary Spelman
Figure 8.26:	Freddy Silva
Figure 8.27:	Freddy Silva
Figure 8.28:	Jane Ross
Figure 8.29:	Freddy Silva
Figure 9.19:	Freddy Silva
Figure 9.24:	Freddy Silva
Figure 9.26:	Freddy Silva
Figure 9.28:	Freddy Silva
Figure 9.32:	Adapted from Norman Rothwell and Gregg Braden
Figure 10.1:	Freddy Silva
Figure 10.3:	Adapted from John Martineau
Figure 10.8:	After John Martineau
Figure 10.9:	After John Martineau
Figure 10.12:	Adapted from Gregg Braden
Figure 10.22:	Freddy Silva
Figure 10.23:	Freddy Silva
Figure 10.24:	Freddy Silva
Figure 10.41:	From a survey by Alexander Thom
Figure 11.1:	Hans Jenny
Figure 11.2:	Georgius Von Welling
Figure 11.4:	Robertus de Fluctibus
Figure 11.6:	Richard Wintle
Figure 11.7:	Diagram adapted from Robert Lawlor
Figure 11.9:	Robert Miller Faulkrod
Figure 11.11:	Steve Alexander
Figure 11.12:	Richard Wintle, Hans Jenny
Figure 11.13:	Freddy Silva, Hans Jenny
Figure 11.14:	Freddy Silva
Figure 11.18:	Top and middle adapted from Parlenko
Figure 12.1:	Freddy Silva
Figure 12.4:	Freddy Silva
Figure 12.6:	Freddy Silva
Figure 12.7:	Freddy Silva
Figure 12.8:	Freddy Silva
Figure 12.10:	Freddy Silva
Figure 12.16:	Adapted from Richard Andrews
Figure 12.17:	Freddy Silva
Figure 12.19:	Freddy Silva
Figure 12.21:	Freddy Silva
Figure 12.22:	Guy Underwood
Figure 12.25:	Gerald Hawkins geometry
Figure 12.26:	Colin Andrews
Figure 13.3:	Colin Andrews
Figure 13.4:	Freddy Silva
Figure 13.5:	Freddy Silva
Figure 13.6:	[A.] Paul Vigay; [C.] Barbara Hand Clow
Figure 13.8:	Freddy Silva
Figure 13.12:	Isabelle Kingston
Figure 13.15:	Frank Laumen
Figure 13.17:	Freddy Silva
Figure 13.18:	Freddy Silva
Figure 13.20:	Frank Laumen
Figure 14.1:	Andrew King
Pg. A1, Avebury	Andrew King
Pg. A3, Roundway	Freddy Silva
Pg. A3, Litchfield	Freddy Silva
Page A15, Barton Le Clay	Russell Stannard
Pg. A16, Sunflower	Freddy Silva
Pg. A16, Berwick Bassett	Freddy Silva

INDEX

About the Author

For much of his professional life, Freddy Silva has been an art director, writer, and photographer, working primarily in graphic design and advertising. A lifelong student of Earth Mysteries, his passion was rekindled in 1990 after seeing an image of a crop circle. He has since become one of the world's leading researchers of the phenomenon, combining his knowledge of ancient systems, problem solving, and image communication to raise awareness of crop circles. A keen dowser and student of the Mysteries, he has written numerous magazine articles, and lectures throughout the U.S. and Europe.

Hampton Roads Publishing Company

. . . for the evolving human spirit

Hampton Roads Publishing Company
publishes books on a variety of subjects,
including metaphysics, health, integrative medicine,
visionary fiction, and other related topics.

For a copy of our latest catalog, call toll-free
(800) 766-8009, or send your name and address to:

Hampton Roads Publishing Company, Inc.
1125 Stoney Ridge Road
Charlottesville, VA 22902

e-mail: hrpc@hrpub.com
www.hrpub.com